The Debate on Classes

ERIK OLIN WRIGHT

Uwe Becker
Johanna Brenner
Michael Burawoy
Val Burris
Guglielmo Carchedi
Gordon Marshall
Peter F. Meiksins
David Rose
Arthur Stinchcombe
Philippe Van Parijs

VERSO
London · New York

First published by Verso 1989
Collection © Verso 1989
All rights reserved

Verso
UK: 6 Meard Street, London W1V 3HR
USA: 29 West 35th Street, New York, NY 10001–2291

Verso is the imprint of New Left Books

British Library Cataloguing in Publication Data

The debate on classes.
    1. Social class. Marxist theories
    I. Wright, Erik Olin
    305.5'01

    ISBN 0-86091-251-5
    ISBN 0-86091-966-8 pbk

US Library of Congress Cataloging-in-Publication Data

Wright, Erik Olin.
    The debate on Classes / Erik Olin Wright and others
        p.   cm.
    ISBN 0.86091-251-5 — ISBN 0-86091-966-8 (pbk.)
    1. Social classes.   2. Marxian school of sociology.   3. Wright,
Erik Olin.   Classes.   I. Title.
HT609.W723   1989
305.5—dc20

Typeset by Leaper & Gard Ltd, Bristol, England
Printed in Finland by Werner Söderström Oy

Contents

Acknowledgments   vii

The Contributors   viii

Preface   ix

Introduction

1   A General Framework for the Analysis of Class Structure
Erik Olin Wright   3

PART I: Methodological Issues

2   Exchange on *Classes*   47

      Reflections on *Classes*
      Erik Olin Wright   49

      The Limits of Wright's Analytical Marxism and an
      Alternative
      Michael Burawoy   78

      Reply to Burawoy
      Erik Olin Wright   100

3   Classes and Class Analysis
Guglielmo Carchedi   105

4   Class Theory: Still the Axis of Critical Social Scientific
Analysis?
Uwe Becker   127

PART II: Theoretical Issues

5   Symposium on *Classes*   157

    New Directions in Class Analysis
    Val Burris   157

    Education, Exploitation, and Class Consciousness
    Arthur Stinchcombe   168

    A Critique of Wright's Theory of Contradictory Class
    Locations
    Peter F. Meiksins   173

    Work Relations and the Formation of Class Consciousness
    Johanna Brenner   184

    Exploitation, Identity, and Class Structure:
    A Reply to My Critics
    Erik Olin Wright   191

6   A Revolution in Class Theory
    Philippe Van Parijs   213

7   Constructing the (W)right Classes
    David Rose and Gordon Marshall   243

PART III: Reconsiderations

8   Rethinking, Once Again, the Concept of Class Structure
    Erik Olin Wright   269

Index   349

Acknowledgments

We are grateful to the following journals for granting permission to reprint articles: "A General Framework for the Analysis of Class Structure," *Politics and Society*, vol. 13 no. 4 (1984); "Exchange on *Classes*," *Berkeley Journal of Sociology*, vol. 32 (1987); "Classes and Class Analysis," *Capital and Class*, vol. 29 (1986); "Class Theory: Still the Axis of Critical Social Scientific Analysis?", *Politics and Society*, vol. 17, no. 1 (1989); "Symposium on *Classes*," *Critical Sociology*, vol. 15, no. 1 (1988); "A Revolution in Class Theory," *Politics and Society*, vol. 15, no. 4 (1986–87); "Constructing the (W)right Classes," *Sociology*, vol. 20, no. 3 (1986).

The Contributors

UWE BECKER is Associate Professor of Political Sociology at the University of Amsterdam, Netherlands.

JOHANNA BRENNER is Associate Professor of Sociology and Women's Studies at Portland State University, USA.

MICHAEL BURAWOY is Professor of Sociology at the University of California at Berkeley, USA.

VAL BURRIS is Professor of Sociology at the University of Oregon, USA.

GUGLIELMO CARCHEDI teaches in the Department of Economics at the University of Amsterdam, Netherlands.

GORDON MARSHALL is Lecturer in Sociology at Essex University, UK.

PETER F. MEIKSINS is Associate Professor of Sociology at the State University of New York at Geneseo, USA.

DAVID ROSE is Lecturer in Sociology at Essex University, UK.

ARTHUR STINCHCOMBE is Professor of Sociology at Northwestern University, USA.

PHILIPPE VAN PARIJS teaches Sociology at the University of Louvain, Belgium.

ERIK OLIN WRIGHT is Professor of Sociology at the University of Wisconsin at Madison, USA.

Preface

In this volume the reader will find the debate provoked by the publication of Erik Olin Wright's already influential *Classes* (Verso, 1985), together with Wright's sustained reconceptualization prompted by this discussion.

Classes was distinguished by its clarity of exposition, its orientation to research and its concern for the wider relevance of sociological theory and findings to politics, philosophy and history. These qualities will also be found in the present collection. Readers who have not read *Classes*, or who would like to refresh their memory of it, will find its principal theses summarized in Chapter 1.

Political parties, trade unions, or campaigning organizations all need a map of the society in which they operate, and few matters are less contestable today than the persistence of social differentiation and inequality. What allies may be sought by those seeking social transformation and what interests are at stake when the prevailing pattern of social relations is challenged? The contributors to *The Debate on Classes* are concerned with these issues as well as with the adequacy of present sociological models.

Wright's original work drew on Marxist and Weberian ideas to link class theory to historical development and to the different interests, outlook and potential of the various major social classes. One of Wright's most original perceptions has been the insistence that individuals do not necessarily fit into only one social class and that there is in fact a series of 'contradictory class locations' in which some find themselves at the intersection of different class positions. This fruitful idea is retained by Wright in the bold reformulation to be found in Chapter 8 of this volume.

The Debate on Classes is an example of a scholarly—and political—controversy in which there is also a willingness to re-examine preconceptions and to submit argument to empirical tests.

Verso
April 1989

Introduction

A General Framework for the Analysis of Class Structure*
Erik Olin Wright

The Point of Departure: Neo-Marxist Analyses of Class Structure

At the heart of the recent resurgence of Marxist theorizing on the problem of class has been what might be termed the "embarrassment" of the middle class. For all of their disagreements, all Marxists share a basic commitment to a polarized abstract concept of class relations. Yet, at least at first glance, the concrete class structures of contemporary advanced capitalist societies look anything but polarized.[1] This empirical evidence of a large middle class has provided critics of Marxism with one of their principal arguments against Marxist class theory. In response, a variety of solutions to the problem of the middle class have been proposed in the recent Marxist debates.

Without going into any detail, it is possible to identify four broadly different strategies that Marxists have adopted to deal with the conceptual problem of nonpolarized class positions within a logic of polarized class relations.[2] First, the class structure of advanced capitalist societies really *is* polarized; the "middle class" is strictly an ideological illusion. This position deals with the problem of the middle class by

---

*This essay appeared in 1984, just before the publication of *Classes*. It represents a basic summary of the core arguments of the book, and does not reflect any of the new thinking of the problems of class which has been stimulated by the subsequent debate.

1. The scope of this paper will be restricted to the problem of class *structure* as such. This is not to suggest that class structure exhausts class analysis: the problems of class formation, class struggle, and class consciousness are also important and will be touched on briefly toward the end of the paper. My assumption is, however, that the decoding of the structural properties of class is a conceptual precondition for elaborating these other aspects of class theory. For a discussion of the interconnection among these aspects of class analysis, see E.O. Wright, *Class, Crisis and the State* (London: Verso, 1978), pp. 97–108.

2. For a more detailed review of these alternatives, see E.O. Wright, "Varieties of Marxist Concepts of Class Structure," *Politics and Society*, vol. 9, no. 3 (1980).

denying the problem itself. Second, the middle class should be viewed as a *segment* of some other class, typically a "new petty bourgeoisie" or "new working class."[3] In this strategy the basic class map of capitalism remains intact, but significant internal differentiations within classes are added to the analysis of class structure. Third, the middle class is really a new class in its own right, completely distinct from either the bourgeoisie, the proletariat, or the petty bourgeoisie. Sometimes this class is given a specific name, such as the Professional Managerial Class,[4] sometimes it is simply called "the New Class."[5] By adding entirely new classes to the class structure, this approach more radically alters the class map of capitalism than the class-segment strategy. Fourth, the positions aggregated under the popular rubric "middle class" are not really in *a* class at all. Rather they should be viewed as locations that are simultaneously in more than one class, positions that I have characterized as "contradictory locations within class relations."[6] Managers, for example, should be viewed as simultaneously in the working class (in so far as they are wage laborers dominated by capitalists) and in the capitalist class (in so far as they control the operation of production and the labor of workers). This strategy departs most from the traditional Marxist vision of class structure since the very meaning of a "location" is altered: there is no longer a one-to-one correspondence between structural locations filled by individuals and classes.

I no longer feel that this fourth solution is satisfactory. Specifically, it suffers from two important problems that it shares with most other neo-Marxist conceptualizations of class structure: it tends to shift the analysis of class relations from exploitation to domination; and it implicitly regards socialism—a society within which the working class is the "ruling class"—as the only possible alternative to capitalism.

Domination versus Exploitation

Throughout the development of the concept of contradictory class locations I have insisted that this was a reformulation of a distinctively

---

3. The leading proponent of the concept of the "new petty bourgeoisie" is N. Poulantzas, *Classes in Contemporary Capitalism* (London: Verso, 1975). For the new-working-class concept, see S. Mallet, *La Nouvelle Classe Ouvrière* (Paris: Seuil, 1963).

4. B. Ehrenreich and J. Ehrenreich, "The Professional and Managerial Class," *Radical America*, vol. 11, no. 2 (1977).

5. A. Gouldner, *The Future of Intellectuals and the Rise of the New Class* (New York: Seabury Press, 1979); and G. Konrad and I. Szelenyi, *Intellectuals on the Road to Class Power* (New York: Harcourt, Brace, Jovanovitch, 1979).

6. E.O. Wright, "Class Boundaries in Advanced Capitalist Societies," *New Left Review*, no. 98 (1976); and *Class, Crisis and the State*. See also G. Carchedi, *The Economic Identification of Social Classes* (London: Routledge and Kegan Paul, 1977).

Marxist class concept. As part of the rhetoric of such an enterprise, I affirmed the relationship between class and exploitation. Nevertheless, in practice the concept of contradictory locations within class relations rested almost exclusively on relations of *domination* rather than exploitation. Reference to exploitation functioned more as a background concept to the discussion of classes than as a constitutive element of the analysis of class structures. Managers, for example, were basically defined as a contradictory location because they were simultaneously dominators and dominated. Domination relations were also decisive in defining the class character of "semiautonomous employees"—locations that, I argued, were simultaneously petty bourgeois and proletarian by virtue of their self-direction within the labor process—since "autonomy" defines a condition with respect to domination. This same tendency of substituting domination for exploitation at the core of the concept of class is found in most other neo-Marxist conceptualizations of class structure.

For some people, of course, marginalizing the concept of exploitation is a virtue, not a sin. My own view, however, is that this is a serious weakness. The marginalization of exploitation both undermines claims that classes have "objective" interests and erodes the centrality Marxists have accorded class in social theory.

The concept of domination does not in and of itself imply any specific interest of actors. Parents dominate small children, but this does not imply that they have intrinsically opposed interests to their children. What would make those interests antagonistic is if the relation of parents to children were exploitative as well. Exploitation, unlike domination, intrinsically implies a set of opposing material interests. If we wish to retain some sense in which the interests of individuals as members of classes are not simply whatever interests those individuals subjectively hold, then the shift to a domination-centered concept renders this more difficult.[7]

Domination-centered concepts of class also tend to slide into what can be termed "the multiple oppressions" approach to understanding

---

7. The concept of "objective interests" is, needless to say, highly contested, and even if we place exploitation at the center of our analysis of class it is still problematic to assert that classes so defined have unequivocal objective interests. The claim rests on the assumption that individuals have objective interests in their material conditions of existence regardless of what they think, but this claim is open to dispute. For useful discussions of the problem of objectivity of interests, see: R. Geuss, *The Idea of Critical Theory: Habermas and the Frankfurt School* (Cambridge: Cambridge University Press, 1981); W. Connolly, "On Interests in Politics," *Politics and Society* 2, no. 4 (1972), pp. 459–77; and I. Balbus, "The Concept of Interest in Pluralist and Marxist Analysis," *Politics and Society*, February 1971.

society. Societies, in this view, are characterized by a plurality of oppressions each rooted in a different form of domination—sexual, racial, national, economic—none of which has any explanatory priority over any other. Class, then, becomes just one of many oppressions, with no particular centrality for social and historical analysis. How important class is in a given society becomes an historically contingent question.[8]

Again, this displacement of class from the center stage may be viewed as an achievement rather than a problem. It may be that class should not occupy a privileged place in social theory. But if one believes, as Marxists traditionally have believed, that only by giving class this central place is it possible to develop a scientific theory of the trajectory of historical development, and in particular, a theory of the real historical alternatives to capitalism, then the domination-centered concept of class risks eroding the theoretical justification for Marxian class analysis itself.[9]

Classes in Postcapitalist Societies

Classical Marxism was absolutely unequivocal about the historical prognosis for capitalism: socialism—and ultimately communism—was the future of capitalist societies. The bearer of that necessary future was the working class. The polarized class structure *within* capitalism between the bourgeoisie and the proletariat thus paralleled the polarized historical alternatives *between* capitalism and socialism.

The actual historical experience of the twentieth century has called into question, although not unambiguously refuted, this historical vision. As I have argued elsewhere, it is necessary to at least entertain the possibility of postcapitalist class structures.[10] The difficulty is that with

---

8. This view is characteristic of what is sometimes called "post-Marxist" radical theory. Some of the leading examples of this work include: M. Albert and R. Hahnel, *Marxism and Socialist Theory* (Boston: South End Press, 1981); J. Cohen, *Class and Civil Society* (Amherst: University of Massachussetts Press, 1982); and S. Aaronowitz, *The Crisis of Historical Materialism* (New York: Praeger, 1981).

9. One might also argue that the importance Marxists accord class is *not* necessary for a theory of historical trajectories. Such a theory could perhaps be based on gender, the state, or other factors. Indeed, the legitimacy of a theory of historical trajectories can itself be rejected. Historical development could be viewed as a strictly contingent outcome of an array of autonomous causal processes rather than having any overall determination. These are serious objections and cannot be dismissed out of hand. For present purposes my claim is simply that if one does want to retain the traditional Marxist commitment to class analysis, then the shift to a domination-centered concept of class poses problems. For a preliminary discussion of some of these arguments, see E.O. Wright, "Gidden's Critique of Marxism," *New Left Review*, no. 139 (1983); and idem, *Classes* (London: Verso, 1985), ch. 2.

10. E.O. Wright, "Capitalism's Futures," *Socialist Review*, no. 68 (1983).

very few exceptions, the conceptual frameworks adopted by Marxists for analyzing capitalist class relations do not contain adequate criteria for understanding postcapitalist classes.[11] In particular, all of the class categories in my analysis of contradictory locations within class relations were either situated firmly within capitalist relations (bourgeoisie, managers, workers) or in contradictory locations involving basically precapitalist relations (semiautonomous employees, the petty bourgeoisie, small employers). There were no elements within this analysis of class relations in capitalist society that could point the direction for the analysis of postcapitalist classes. The result is a tendency for discussions of postcapitalist class structures—the class structures of "actually existing socialism"—to have a very ad hoc character to them.

Given these conceptual problems—the shift from exploitation to domination and the lack of a conceptual basis for analyzing poscapitalist classes—there are really two theoretical alternatives that could be pursued. One possibility is to celebrate the shift to a domination-centered concept and use this new class concept as the basis for analyzing both capitalist and postcapitalist society. This would lead class analysis firmly in the direction of Dahrendorf's analysis of classes as positions within authority relations.[12] A second alternative is to attempt to restore exploitation as the center of class analysis in such a way that it can both accommodate the empirical complexities of the middle class within capitalism and the historical reality of postcapitalist class structures. It is this second course of action that I will pursue in the rest of this paper.

The basis for this reconstruction of an exploitation-centered concept of class comes from the recent work of John Roemer.[13] While Roemer himself has not been particularly concerned with problems of empirical investigation or the elaboration of concrete maps of class structures,

---

11. A partial exception to this can be found in arguments for the existence of a "new class" of intellectuals and/or bureaucrats in capitalist and postcapitalist society. See: A. Gouldner, *The Future of Intellectuals*; and I. Szelenyi and W. Martin, *New Class Theory and Beyond* (unpublished book manuscript, Department of Sociology, University of Wisconsin, 1985).

12. R. Dahrendorf, *Class and Class Conflict in Industrial Society* (Palo Alto: Stanford University Press, 1959).

13. Roemer is a Marxist economist engaged in a long-term project of elaborating what he calls the "microfoundations" of Marxist theory. His most important work is entitled *A General Theory of Exploitation and Class* (Cambridge: Harvard University Press, 1982). A debate over this work in which I participated appears in *Politics and Society*, vol. 11, no. 3: J. Roemer, "Recent Developments in the Marxist Theory of Exploitation and Class", and E.O. Wright, "The Status of the Political in the Concept of Class Structure." Roemer is actively engaged in a circle of scholars who meet periodically to discuss problems of the conceptual foundations of Marxist theory that includes Jon Elster, G.A. Cohen, Adam Przeworski, Philippe von Parijs, Robert Van der Veen, Robert Brenner, and myself.

nevertheless his work does provide a rich foundation for such endeavors. As I will attempt to show, with suitable modification and extension, his strategy of analysis can provide a rigorous basis for resolving the problems in the concept of contradictory class locations.

Roemer's Account of Class and Exploitation

The Concept of Exploitation

We observe inequalities in the distribution of incomes, the real consumption packages available to individuals, families, groups. The concept of exploitation is a particular way of analyzing such inequalities. To describe an inequality as reflecting exploitation is to make the claim that there exists a particular kind of causal relationship between the incomes of different actors. More concretely, we will say that the rich exploit the poor when two things can be established: that the welfare of the rich causally depends on the deprivations of the poor—the rich are rich *because* the poor are poor; and that the welfare of the rich depends upon the *effort* of the poor—the rich, through one mechanism or another, appropriate part of the fruits of labor of the poor. The first of these criteria by itself defines *economic oppression*, but not exploitation. Unemployed workers, in these terms, are economically oppressed but not exploited. Exploitation implies both economic oppression and appropriation of at least part of the social surplus by the oppressor.[14]

The traditional Marxist concept of exploitation is clearly a special case of this general concept.[15] In Marxian exploitation one class appropriates the surplus labor performed by another class through various mechanisms. The income of the exploiting class comes from the labor performed by the exploited class. There is thus a straightforward causal linkage between the poverty and effort of the exploited and the affluence of the exploiter. The latter benefits at the expense of the former.

Roemer has attempted to elaborate this view of exploitation using two strategies. The first of these involves studying through a series of formal mathematical models the flows of "surplus labor" from one category of actors to another in the course of various exchange relations; the

---

14. For a fuller discussion of the distinction between economic oppression and exploitation, see Wright, *Classes*, ch. 3.

15. Roemer has demonstrated, convincingly I think, that there are particular circumstances in which Marxian exploitation does not correspond to this more general definition: there are cases where there are labor transfers from one actor to another that would be technically exploitative in the Marxian sense but that do not satisfy the above conditions. For the present purposes we need not engage these special cases.

second involves adopting a kind of game-theory approach to specifying different forms of exploitation. Let us briefly examine each of these in turn.

The Labor-Transfer Approach

The analysis of labor transfers is an extension of the traditional Marxist view of exploitation, although Roemer self-consciously does not rely on the labor theory of value in order to explore such labor transfers.[16] The main target of his analysis is the view, commonly held by Marxists, that a necessary condition for the exploitation of labor in a market economy is the institution of wage labor. Roemer demonstrates two basic propositions. First, Roemer demonstrates that exploitation can occur in an economy in which all producers own their own means of production and in which there is no market in labor power and no credit market (that is, no borrowing). The only things that are traded are products. In such an economy if different producers own different amounts of productive assets such that different producers have to work different numbers of hours to produce the exchange-equivalent of their own subsistence, then free trade among these producers will lead to exploitation of the asset poor by the asset rich. What Roemer shows in this simple economy is not simply that some producers work less than others for the same subsistence, but that the workers who work less are able to do so *because* the less-endowed producers have to work more. The critical proof in this example is that if the asset-poor person simply stopped producing—died—and the asset-rich person took over the asset-poor's assets, then the asset-rich producer would have to work longer hours than before to maintain the same subsistence.[17] There is thus not merely an inequality among the producers in this economy, but exploitation as well.

---

16. While Roemer's work should not be viewed as an example of the "Sraffian" critique of the labor theory of value, he shares with Sraffian economists like I. Steedman, *Marx after Sraffa* (London: Verso, 1977), the thesis that the labor theory of value should be dismissed entirely. It is, in Roemer's view, simply wrong as the basis for any theoretical understanding of exchange and unnecessary for an understanding of capitalist exploitation.

17. The technical form of the argument involves constructing general equilibrium models based on relatively simple maximizing behaviors of the actors. As in all general equilibrium models, these models depend upon the specific assumptions adopted concerning preference structures and production functions. Recently, in an essay entitled, "Should Marxists Be Interested in Exploitation?" Working Paper no. 221 (University of California, Davis, Department of Economics, 1983), Roemer has shown that it is possible to construct models in which the outcomes violate the logic of the concept of exploitation (for example, if the preference for leisure over labor declines as ownership of assets increases, then it can happen that labor transfers will flow from the rich to the poor under certain institutional arrangements). For the purposes of the present analysis, I will ignore these complications.

Second, Roemer demonstrates that there is complete symmetry in the structure of exploitation in a system in which capital hires wage laborers and in a system in which workers rent capital (that is, systems with credit and labor markets). For this analysis, he compares the class structures and patterns of exploitation on the two imaginary islands, "labor-market island" and "credit-market island." On both islands some people own no means of production and other people own varying amounts of the means of production. The distribution of these assets is identical on the two islands. And on both islands people have the same motivations: they all seek to minimize the amount of labor-time they must expend to achieve a common level of subsistence.[18] The two islands differ in only one respect: on the labor-market island people are allowed to sell their labor power, whereas on the credit-market island people are prohibited from selling their labor power but are allowed to borrow, at some interest rate, the means of production. Roemer shows that on each island there is a strict correspondence between class location (derived from ownership of differing amounts of means of production, including no means of production) and exploitation status (having one's surplus labor appropriated by someone else). This is what he terms the "Class-Exploitation Correspondence Principle." He also shows that the two class structures are completely isomorphic: every individual on one island would be in exactly the same exploitation status on the other island.

The upshot of these two propositions (and others that Roemer explores) is the claim that market-based exploitation is strictly a consequence of inequalities in the distribution of the means of production. However, while this may typically play itself out through a labor market, this is only one concrete institutional form for such exploitation: it is not the necessary condition for the exploitation to occur.

The Game-Theory Approach

While the labor-transfer analyses of exploitation were primarily designed to reveal the underlying logic of exploitation in market exchanges, the game-theory approach is used by Roemer to compare different systems of exploitation. The idea is to compare different systems of exploitation by treating the organization of production as a "game" and asking if a coalition of players would be better off if they withdrew from the game under certain specified procedures. Different

---

18. The results are robust over a range of motivational assumptions, but not over every possible preference structure.

types of exploitation are defined by the withdrawal rules that would make certain agents better off.

More formally, Roemer argues that a coalition of actors S can be said to be exploited, and another coalition S' (the complement of S) can be said to be exploiting, if "there is no alternative, which we may conceive of as hypothetically feasible, in which S would be better off than in its present situation, [and if,] under this alternative, the complement to S . . . would be worse off than at present."[19] The counterfactual in these two conditions is meant to convey the sense in which the welfare of S' is causally dependent upon the deprivation of S.[20]

Roemer uses this strategy to define three kinds of exploitation: feudal exploitation, capitalist exploitation, and what he refers to as socialist exploitation. Let's begin with capitalist exploitation. Workers own no physical assets (means of production) and sell their labor power to capitalists for a wage. Are workers exploited under capitalism? The answer to this question, in the game theoretic formulation, requires posing an alternative game to the game of capitalism within which the two conditions specified above hold. What is the alternative? It is a game within which each worker receives his/her *per capita share of society's total productive assets.* What Roemer demonstrates is that if the coalition of all wage-earners were to leave the game of capitalism with their per capita share of society's assets, then they would be better off than staying in capitalism, and capitalists would be worse off. The "withdrawal rule" in this case—leaving the game with per capita shares of physical assets—then becomes the formal "test" of whether or not a particular social system involves capitalistic exploitation.

In contrast, the withdrawal rule to specify feudal exploitation is leaving the game with one's *personal assets* (rather than one's per capita share of total social assets). This is equivalent to the feudal serf being freed from all obligations based on personal bondage. Peasants would be better off under such circumstances; feudal lords would be worse off.[21]

---

19. Roemer, *A General Theory*, pp. 194–5.

20. Strictly speaking, in terms of the general definition of exploitation presented at the outset of this discussion, these two criteria merely define economic oppression, not exploitation, since the results do not imply anything about the relationship between the effort of the exploited and the welfare of the exploiter. Roemer recognizes this difficulty and has added a number of additional criteria at various points in his analysis to eliminate certain problems (for example, the handicapped exploiting the well-bodied). Nevertheless, these two counterfactual criteria remain the core of Roemer's game theoretic analysis.

21. But note: workers in capitalism are *not* feudalistically exploited; they would be worse off, not better off, if they withdrew from the game of capitalism with only their personal assets. As Roemer argues, the claim by neoclassical theorists that wage earners in capitalism are not exploited is generally equivalent to the claim that they are not feudalistically exploited, that is, that they are not subjected to surplus extraction based on relations of personal bondage. See Roemer, *A General Theory*, p. 206.

The concept of the socialist exploitation is the least systematically worked out in Roemer's analysis. The withdrawal rule in this case is leaving the game with one's *per capita share of inalienable assets* (skills). A coalition will be said to be socialistically exploited if it would improve its position by leaving with its per capita skills while its complement would be worse off under such circumstances. This implies that people with high levels of skills in the game receive high income not simply because they have high skills, but because of the differentials in skill levels across actors. The highly skilled would become worse off if the unskilled obtained skills; they thus have an interest in maintaining skill differentials, and this is what underpins the claim that their income reflects exploitation.[22] If a skilled person's income reflected no more than the amount of time and resources it takes to obtain the skill, then there would be no skill-based exploitation. The higher incomes would simply be reimbursement for real costs incurred. The argument behind skill exploitation is that people with scarce skills receive incomes above the costs of producing those skills, a "rent" component to their income; it is this element that constitutes exploitation.[23]

Class and Exploitation

The central message of both of Roemer's strategies for analyzing exploitation is that the material basis of exploitation is inequalities in distributions of productive assets, or what is usually referred to as property relations. On the one hand, inequalities of assets are sufficient to account for transfers of labor surplus; on the other hand, different forms of asset inequality specify different systems of exploitation. Classes are

---

22. The asset-exploitation nexus thus depends upon the capacity of asset-holders to deprive others of that asset. The social basis of exploitation, understood in this way, is quite similar to Frank Parkin's characterization of Weber's concept of social closure as "the process by which social collectivities seek to maximize rewards by restricting access to resources and opportunities to a limited circle of eligibles." F. Parkin, *Marxism and Class Theory: A Bourgeois Critique* (New York: Columbia University Press, 1979). While Parkin's central concern is with the kinds of attributes that serve as the basis for closure—race, religion, language—Roemer's is with the nature of the resources (productive assets) over which closure is organized.

23. Marx did not refer to the inequalities in income in a socialist society as the result of exploitation, and he did not refer to the relation between the skilled and unskilled as a *class* relation; nevertheless, Roemer's account corresponds well to Marx's analysis of inequality in socialism as laid out in his *Critique of the Gotha Program*. In that document Marx emphasized that skill-based inequalities would persist in socialism and that distribution would be on the basis of "from each according to his ability, to each according to his work." Only in communism would distribution be on the basis of need, which in effect implies that skill differentials would cease to be assets (income-generating wealth).

then defined as positions within the social relations of production derived from these relations of exploitation.[24]

These conclusions have led Roemer to challenge directly the tendency of Marxists (like myself) to define class relations primarily in terms of domination relations within production. Of course, exploiting classes dominate exploited classes in the sense of preventing the exploited classes from taking the exploiting class's productive assets. But domination *within* production, Roemer insists, is not a central part of defining class relations as such.[25]

In previous work I have criticized Roemer's position on this issue.[26] I argued that class relations intrinsically involved domination *at the point of production*, not simply in the repressive protection of the property relations as such. I now think that Roemer is correct on this point. That capitalists boss workers around within production is unquestionably an important feature of most historic forms of capitalist production and may play an important role in explaining the forms of class organization and class conflict within production. However, the basis of the capital–labor relation should be identified with relations of effective control (that is, real economic ownership) over productive assets as such.

One of the reasons why I resisted Roemer's conceptualization of classes in terms of property relations is that it seemed to blur the difference between Marxist definitions of class and Weberian definitions. Weberian definitions, as I construed them, were "market based" definitions of class, whereas Marxist definitions were "production based." The reputed advantage of the latter was that production was more "fundamental" than exchange, and therefore production-based class concepts had more explanatory power than market-based concepts.

What now seems clear to me is that definitions of classes in terms of property relations should not be identified with strictly market-based

---

24. Roemer's conceptualization of the relationship between class and exploitation is similar in certain aspects to Alvin Gouldner's, although Roemer is unaware of Gouldner's work. Gouldner defines the "New Class" as a *cultural* bourgeoisie defined by its control over "cultural capital," where "capital" is defined as "any produced object used to make saleable utilities, thus providing its possessor with *incomes*, or claims to incomes defined as legitimate because of their imputed contribution to economic productivity." (*Future of Intellectuals*, p. 21). While Gouldner does not characterize this income allocation process in terms of exploitation, Roemer's exploitation concept would fit comfortably within Gouldner's general approach.

25. This is not to imply that domination in the labor process is *institutionally* unimportant, or indeed, that such domination does not in practice intensify capitalist exploitation and reinforce the capital–labor class relation. Roemer's point is simply that it is not the actual criterion for class relations; that criterion is strictly based on property relations as such.

26. Wright, "The Status of the Political."

definitions. Property-relations accounts of classes do not define classes by income shares, by the results of market transactions, but by the productive assets that classes control, which lead them to adopt certain strategies within exchange relations and which thereby determine the outcomes of those market transactions.

Toward a General Framework of Class Analysis

Extending Roemer's Analysis

The heart of Roemer's analysis is the linkage between the distribution of productive assets of various sorts and exploitation. Different mechanisms of exploitation are defined by different kinds of assets, and different class systems are defined by which of these assets is most important for shaping the patterns of exploitation in the society.

In Roemer's own explicit formulation, only two kinds of assets are formally considered: physical assets (alienable assets in his terminology) and skill assets (inalienable assets). The distinction between exploitation in feudalism and exploitation in capitalism revolves around the nature of the withdrawal rules with respect to physical assets (withdrawing with one's personal assets to define feudal exploitation versus withdrawing with one's per capita share of assets to define capitalist exploitation). The feudal case, however, can be characterized in a somewhat different way. Labor power is a productive asset.[27] In capitalist societies everyone owns one unit of this asset, namely themselves. In feudalism, on the other hand, ownership rights over labor power are unequally distributed: feudal lords have more than one unit, serfs have less than one unit. To be sure, it is not typical of feudalism for serfs to own no labor power— they are generally not slaves divested of all ownership rights in their own labor power—but they do not have complete effective control over their own persons as productive actors, and this is what it means to "own" one's own labor power assets.[28] The withdrawal rule that defines feudal exploitation can then be specified as leaving the feudal game with one's per capita share of society's assets in labor power, namely one unit. Feudal exploitation is thus exploitation (transfers of labor) that results

---

27. See G.A. Cohen, *Karl Marx's Theory of History: A Defense* (Princeton: Princeton University Press, 1978), pp. 40–41, for a discussion of why labor power should be considered part of the forces of production (that is, a productive asset).

28. In this formulation, slavery should be viewed as a limiting case of feudal exploitation, where the slave has no ownership rights at all in his/her own labor power, while the slave owner has complete ownership rights in slaves.

from inequalities in the distribution of assets in labor power.[29]

Reformulating feudal exploitation in this manner makes the game-theory specification of different exploitations in Roemer's analysis symmetrical: feudal exploitation is based on inequalities generated by ownership of labor-power assets; capitalist exploitation on inequalities generated by ownership of alienable assets; socialist exploitation on inequalities generated by ownership of inalienable assets. And corresponding to each of these exploitation-generating inequalities of assets, there is a specific class relation: lords and serfs in feudalism, bourgeoisie and proletariat in capitalism, experts and workers in socialism.

But how, it might be asked, should "actually existing socialist societies" be theorized within these categories? The anticapitalist revolution in Russia resulted in the virtual elimination of private property in the means of production: individuals cannot own means of production, they cannot inherit them or dispose of them on a market, and so on. And yet it seems unsatisfactory to characterize such societies simply in terms of skill-based exploitation. Experts do not appear to be the "ruling class" in those societies, and the dynamic of the societies does not seem to revolve around skill inequalities as such.

Roemer recognized this problem and introduced what he termed "status exploitation" to deal with it.[30] The exploitation exercised by bureaucrats is the prototypical example. "If these positions," Roemer writes, "required special skills, then one might be justified in calling the differential remuneration to these positions an aspect of socialist [skill-based] exploitation. . . . [However] there is some extra remuneration to holders of those positions which accrues solely by virtue of the position and not by virtue of the skill necessary to carry out the tasks associated with it. These special payments to positions give rise to *status exploitation.*"[31]

Roemer's concept of status exploitation is unsatisfactory for two principal reasons. First, it is outside of the logic of the rest of his analysis of exploitation. In each of the other cases, exploitation is rooted in relations to the forces of production. Each of the other forms of exploitation is "materialist" not only because the concept is meant to explain

---

29. In this formulation it might be possible to regard various forms of discrimination—the use of ascriptive criteria such as race, sex, nationality to bar people from certain occupations, for example—as a form of feudal exploitation. In effect there is not equal ownership of one's own labor power if one lacks the capacity to use it as one pleases equally with other agents. This view of discrimination corresponds to the view that discrimination is antithetical to "bourgeois freedoms."

30. Roemer is an economist, and the use of the word *status* was not meant to evoke the meanings generally attached to this word in sociology.

31. Roemer, *A General Theory*, p. 243.

material distribution, but also because it is based on the relation to the material conditions of production. "Status" exploitation has no necessary relationship to production at all. Second, it is hard to rigorously distinguish status exploitation from feudal exploitation. The "lord" receives remuneration strictly because of an incumbency in a position, not because of skills or ownership of capital.[32] Yet, it hardly seems reasonable to consider the logic of exploitation and class in the contemporary Soviet Union and in fourteenth-century feudal Europe as being essentially the same.

The problems with the concept of status exploitation can be solved by analyzing exploitation based on a fourth element in the inventory of productive assets, an asset that can be referred to as "organization." As both Adam Smith and Marx noted, the technical division of labor among producers is itself a source of productivity. The way the production process is organized is a productive resource independent of the expenditure of labor power, the use of means of production, or the skills of the producer. Of course there is an interrelationship between organization and these other assets, just as there is an interdependence between means of production and skills. But organization—the conditions of coordinated cooperation among producers in a complex division of labor—is a productive resource in its own right.

How is this asset distributed in different kinds of societies? In contemporary capitalism, organization assets are generally controlled by managers and capitalists: managers control the organization assets within specific firms under constraints imposed by the ownership of the capital assets by capitalists. Entrepreneurial capitalists directly control both kinds of assets (and probably skill assets as well); pure rentier capitalists ("coupon clippers") only own capital assets. Because of the anarchy of the capitalist market, no set of actors controls the technical division of labor across firms.

In state bureaucratic socialism, organization assets assume a much greater importance.[33] Controlling the technical division of labor—the coordination of productive activities within and across labor processes—becomes a societal task organized at the center. The control over organization assets is no longer simply the task of firm-level managers but

---

32. Roemer acknowledges the similarity between feudal exploitation and status exploitation but treats this just as an interesting parallel rather than as a problem. Ibid., p. 243.

33. The term *state bureaucratic socialism* is somewhat awkward, but I do not know of a better expression. The term *statism*, although I have used it elsewhere in discussing such societies (E.O. Wright, "Capitalism's Futures," *Socialist Review*, no. 68 [1983]) has the disadvantage of identifying the class relations strictly with the state as such rather than with the material basis of exploitation in such societies (control over organization assets).

extends into the central organs of planning within the state. Exploitation in such societies is thus based on bureaucratic power: the control over organization assets defines the material basis for class relations and exploitation.

This notion of organization assets bears a close relation to the problem of authority and hierarchy. The asset is organization. The activity of using that asset is coordinated decision making over a complex technical division of labor. When that asset is distributed unequally, so some positions have effective control over much more of the asset than others, then the social relation with respect to that asset takes the form of hierarchical authority. Authority, however, is not the asset as such; organization is the asset and is controlled through a hierarchy of authority.

The claim that effective control over organization assets is a basis of exploitation is equivalent to saying that nonmanagers would be better off and managers/bureaucrats worse off if nonmanagers were to withdraw with their per capita share of organization assets (or equivalently, if organizational control were democratized); and that by virtue of effectively controlling organization assets managers/bureaucrats control part or all of the socially produced surplus.[34]

A Typology of Class Structures, Assets, and Exploitation

If we add organization assets to the list in Roemer's analysis, we generate the more complex typology presented in Table 1. Let us briefly look at each row of this table and examine its logic. Feudalism is a class system based on unequal distribution of ownership rights in labor power. What "personal bondage" means is that feudal lords have partial effective economic control over vassals. The empirical manifestation of this unequal distribution of ownership rights over labor power in classical feudalism is the coercive extraction of labor dues from serfs. When corvée labor is commuted to rents in kind and eventually money rents, the feudal character of the exploitation relation is reflected in legal

---

34. This "control of the surplus," it must be noted, is *not* the equivalent of the *actual* personal consumption income of managers and bureaucrats, any more than capitalist profits or feudal rents are the equivalent of the personally consumed income of capitalists and feudal lords. It is historically variable both within and between types of societies what fraction of the surplus effectively controlled by exploiting classes is used for personal consumption and what portion is used for other purposes (feudal military expenditures, capitalist accumulation, organization growth). The claim that managers-bureaucrats would be "worse off" under conditions of a redistribution of organization assets refers to the amount of income they effectively control, which is therefore potentially available for personal appropriation, not simply the amount they personally consume.

prohibitions on the movement of peasants off the land. The "flight" of a peasant to the city is, in effect, a form of theft: the peasant is stealing part of the labor power owned by the lord.[35] Feudal lords may also have more means of production than serfs, more organizational assets, and more productive skills (although this is unlikely), and thus they may be exploiters with respect to these assets as well. What defines the society as "feudal", however, is the primacy of the distinctively feudal mechanisms of exploitation. Accordingly, feudal class relations will be the primary structural basis of class struggle.

The bourgeois revolutions radically redistributed productive assets in people: everyone, at least in principle, owns one unit. This is what is meant by "bourgeois freedoms," and in this sense capitalism can be regarded as an historically progressive force. But capitalism raises the second type of exploitation, exploitation based on property relations in means of production, to an unprecedented level.[36]

The typical institutional form of capitalist class relations is capitalists having full ownership rights in the means of production and workers none. Other possibilities, however, have existed historically. Cottage industries in early capitalism involved workers owning some of their means of production, but not having sufficient assets to actually produce commodities without the assistance of merchant capitalists. Such workers were still being capitalistically exploited even though there was no formal labor market with wages. In all capitalist exploitation, the mediating mechanism is market exchanges. Unlike in feudalism, surplus is not directly appropriated from workers in the form of coerced labor. Rather, it is appropriated through market exchanges: workers are paid a wage that covers the costs of production of their labor power; capitalists receive an income from the sale of the commodities produced by workers. The difference in these quantities constitutes the exploitative surplus appropriated by capitalists.[37]

---

35. In this logic, once peasants are free to move, free to leave the feudal contract, then feudal rents (and thus feudal exploitation) would be in the process of transformation into a form of capitalist exploitation. That transformation would be complete once land itself became "capital," that is, it could be freely bought and sold on a market.

36. It is because capitalism simultaneously largely eliminates one form of exploitation and accentuates another that it is difficult to say whether or not in the transition from feudalism to capitalism overall exploitation increased or decreased.

37. It should be noted that this claim is logically independent of the labor theory of value. There is no assumption that commodities exchange in proportions regulated by the amount of socially necessary labor embodied in them. What is claimed is that the income of capitalists constitutes the monetary value of the surplus produced by workers. That is sufficient for their income to be treated as exploitative. See G.A. Cohen, "The Labor Theory of Value and the Concept of Exploitation," *Philosophy and Public Affairs*, vol. 8 (1979), for a discussion of this treatment of capitalist exploitation and of its relation to the labor theory of value.

Table 1 Assets, Exploitation and Classes

Type of class structure	Principal asset that is unequally distributed	Mechanism of exploitation	Classes	Central task of revolutionary transformation
Feudalism	Labor power	Coercive extraction of surplus labor	Lords and serfs	Individual liberty
Capitalism	Means of production	Market exchanges of labor power and commodities	Capitalists and workers	Socializing means of production
State bureaucratic socialism	Organization	Planned appropriation and distribution of surplus based on hierarchy	Managers/bureaucrats and nonmanagement	Democratization of organizational control
Socialism	Skills	Negotiated redistribution of surplus from workers to experts	Experts and workers	Substantive equality

Anticapitalist revolutions attempt to eliminate the distinctively capitalist form of exploitation, exploitation based on private ownership of the means of production. The nationalization of the principal means of production is, in effect, a radical equalization of ownership of capital: everyone owns one citizen-share. Such revolutions, however, do not eliminate, and indeed may considerably strengthen and deepen, inequalities of effective control over organization assets. Whereas in capitalism the control over organization assets does not extend beyond the firm, in state bureaucratic socialism the coordinated integration of the division of labor extends to the whole society through institutions of central state planning. The mechanism by which this generates exploitative transfers of surplus involves the centrally planned bureaucratic appropriation and distribution of the surplus along hierarchical principles. The corresponding class relation is therefore between managers/bureaucrats—people who control organization assets—and nonmanagers.

The historical task of revolutionary transformation of state bureaucratic socialism revolves around the equalization of effective economic control over organization assets, or, equivalently, the democratization of bureaucratic apparatuses of production.[38] This does not imply total direct democracy, where all decisions of any consequence are directly made in democratic assemblies. There will still inevitably be delegated responsibilities, and there certainly can be representative forms of democratic control. But it does mean that the basic parameters of planning and coordinating social production are made through democratic mechanisms and that incumbency within delegated positions of responsibility does not give incumbents any personal claims on the social surplus.[39] Such equalization, however, would not necessarily affect exploitation based on skills/credentials. Such exploitation would remain a central feature of socialism.

"Skill" in this context is not a trivial concept. The mere possession of enhanced laboring capabilities acquired through training is not sufficient

---

38. This, it should be noted, is precisely what leftist critics within "actually existing socialist societies" say is the core problem on the political agenda of radical change in these countries.

39. Lenin's original vision of "Soviet" democracy, in which officials would be paid no more than average workers and would be immediately revocable at any time and in which the basic contours of social planning would be debated and decided through democratic participation, embodied such principles of equalization of organization assets. Once in power, as we know, the Bolsheviks were either unable or unwilling to seriously attempt the elimination of organization exploitation. For a discussion of these issues in the context of the Russian Revolution and other attempts at workers' democracy, see C. Siriani, *Workers' Control and Socialist Democracy* (London: Verso, 1982).

to generate relations of exploitation, since the income of such trained labor may simply reflect the costs of acquiring the training. In such cases there is neither a transfer of surplus, nor would the untrained be better off under the game-theory specification of exploitation. For a skill to be the basis of exploitation, therefore, it has to be in some sense scarce relative to its demand, and there must be a mechanism through which individual owners of scarce skills are able to translate that scarcity into higher incomes.

There are basically three ways that skills can become scarce: first, they may require special *talents* that are naturally scarce in a population; second, access to the training needed to develop the skill may be restricted through various mechanisms, creating an artificial scarcity of trained people; third, a certification system may be established that prohibits uncertified people from being employed to use the skill even if they have it. In all of these cases, the exploitation comes from the skilled/certified individual receiving an income that is above the costs of production of the skills by virtue of the scarcity of the availability of the skill.

In this conceptualization of socialism, a socialist society is essentially a kind of democratic technocracy. Experts control their own skills and knowledge within production, and by virtue of such control are able to appropriate some of the surplus out of production. However, because of the democratization of organization assets, actual planning decisions will not be made under the direct control of experts but will be made through some kind of democratic procedure (this is in effect what democratization of organization assets means: equalizing control over the planning and coordinating of social production). This means that the actual class power of a socialist technocratic exploiting class will be much weaker than the class power of exploiting classes in other class systems. Their ownership rights extend to only a limited part of the social surplus.

This much more limited basis of *domination* implied by skill-based exploitation is consistent with the spirit, if not the letter, of Marx's claim that socialism is the "lower stage" of "communism," since classes are already in a partial state of dissolution in a society with only skill-based exploitation. Communism itself, then, would be understood as a society within which skill-based exploitation itself had "withered away," that is, in which ownership rights in skills had been equalized. This does not mean, it must be stressed, that all individuals would actually *possess* the same skills in communism, any more than eliminating property rights in means of production implies that all individuals would actively use the same amount of physical capital. What is equalized is effective control over skills as a productive resource and claims to differential incomes resulting from differential use of skills.[40]

Some Unresolved Problems

The general framework laid out in Table 1 offers an abstract conceptual basis for clarifying a variety of empirical and theoretical problems in neo-Marxist class theory while avoiding some of the limitations of earlier class-structure concepts. Nevertheless, there remain a number of unresolved problems and internal inconsistencies, some of which may ultimately prove "fatal" to this attempt at reconceptualization. Two of these are particularly glaring and deserve some comment: the ambiguous status of skills as the basis for a class relation, and the problematic character of organization as an asset.[41]

Skills and Class

While the ownership of skill assets, particularly when institutionalized in the form of credentials, may constitute a basis for exploitation, it is much less clear that it should be treated as the basis for a class relation (except insofar as skills or credentials might enable one to gain access to other kinds of assets). In each of the other types of assets—labor power, physical capital, organization—there is a clear correspondence between the distribution of the asset and a particular form of social relation—lord–serf relations, capitalist–employee relations, manager–worker relations. In the case of skill/credential assets there is no such correspondence: experts and nonexperts do not exist in the same kind of well-defined social relation as lords and serfs or capitalists and employees. Experts may thus have distinct interests from nonexperts, but they are not clearly constituted as a class in relation to nonexperts.

Ultimately, what this relative vagueness in the link between skill exploitation and class relations may imply is that the expert-versus-

---

40. It may be utopian to imagine a society without skill-based exploitation, or even a society without organization-asset exploitation, particularly if we reject the claim that a future society will ever exist in a state of absolute abundance. In the absence of absolute abundance, all societies will face dilemmas and trade-offs around the problem of distribution of consumption, and such dilemmas may pose intractable incentive problems in the absence of exploitation. For a careful exposition of the problem of utopian fantasies in Marxist theory, see A. Nove, *The Economics of Feasible Socialism* (Hemel Hempstead: George Allen and Unwin, 1983).

41. For a much more extended discussion of these and other problems, see Wright, *Classes*, ch. 3.

nonexpert distinction should perhaps be treated as a form of *strati-fication* within classes rather than a class relation itself. This could, for example, define a type of class *fraction* within particular classes.

In spite of these difficulties, throughout the rest of this paper I will treat skill/credential assets as the basis for a dimension of class relations. As we shall see, this will be particularly useful in rethinking the problem of middle classes. I will thus provisionally ignore the ambiguities in class analysis posed by the problem of skills.

Organizational Assets

There is a troubling asymmetry in the treatment of organization assets in the analysis of class and exploitation. In the case of each of the other assets it seems appropriate to say that the exploiting classes "own" the assets in question: feudal lords have ownership rights in their serfs; capitalists own the means of production; experts own their skills (or at least their credentials). But it does not seem appropriate to describe managers or bureaucrats as "owning" organizational assets. While it may still be the case that their effective control over these assets is a basis for exploitation, such control is quite different from the ownership relations of other assets and may call into question the argument that such control is the basis for a dimension of class relations.

As in the case of problem with skills, I will bracket this difficulty throughout the rest of this paper. The attempt to create a symmetrical concept of class across qualitatively distinct class systems may in the end be both unnecessary and unhelpful. Nevertheless, I will provisionally continue to treat organization assets and the corresponding forms of exploitation and class relations in a manner parallel to the treatment of labor power, capital, and skill assets.

Abstract discussions of concepts are continually plagued with loose ends, ambiguities, inconsistencies. At some point it is necessary to set aside these difficulties and explore the implications of the concepts under discussion for concrete empirical and theoretical problems. This will be the task of the rest of this paper. In the next section we will examine a range of theoretical implications of the framework elaborated in Table 1. This will be followed by a brief examination of some empirical research using the proposed concepts.

Implications of the General Framework

In this section we will explore the implications of the framework in Table 1 for three problems in class analysis: the problem of understanding the class character of the "middle class"; the relation of class structure to class formation; and the problem of class alliances. In each case my comments will be suggestive rather than exhaustive, indicating the basic lines of inquiry that can be followed from this starting point.

The Middle Classes and Contradictory Locations

The framework in Table 1 enables us to pose the problem of middle classes in a new way. Two different kinds of nonpolarized class locations can be defined in the logic of this framework:

1. There are class locations that are neither exploiters nor exploited, that is, people who have precisely the per capita level of the relevant asset. A petty bourgeois, self-employed producer with average capital stock, for example, would be neither exploiter nor exploited within capitalist relations.[42] These kinds of positions are what can be called the "traditional" or "old" middle class of a particular kind of class system.

2. Since concrete societies are rarely, if ever, characterized by a single mode of production, the actual class structures of given societies will be characterized by complex patterns of intersecting exploitation relations. There will therefore tend to be some positions that are exploiting along one dimension of exploitation relations and are exploited along another. Highly skilled wage-earners (for example, professionals) in capitalism are a good example: they are capitalistically exploited because they lack assets in capital, and yet they are skill exploiters. Such positions are what are typically referred to as the "new middle class" of a given system.

Table 2 presents a schematic typology of such complex class locations for capitalism. The typology is divided into two segments: one for owners of the means of production and one for nonowners. Within the wage-earner section of the typology, locations are distinguished by the two subordinate relations of exploitation characteristic of capitalist society—organization assets and skill/credential assets. It is thus possible within this framework to distinguish a whole terrain of class locations in capitalist *society* that are distinct from the polarized classes of the capi-

---

42. Note that *some* petty bourgeois, in this formulation, will actually be exploited by capital (through unequal exchange on the market) because they own such minimal means of production, and some will be capitalistic exploiters because they own a great deal of capital even though they may not hire any wage-earners. Exploitation status, therefore, cannot strictly be equated with self-employment or wage-earner status.

Table 2 Basic Typology of Exploitation and Class

Assets in the means of production

Owners (%)	Nonowners (wage laborers) (%)			Organization assets
1 Bourgeoisie US 1.8 Sweden 0.7	**4 Expert manager** US 3.9 Sweden 4.4	**7 Semicredentialed manager** US 6.2 Sweden 4.0	**10 Uncredentialed manager** US 2.3 Sweden 2.5	+
2 Small employer US 6.0 Sweden 4.8	**5 Expert supervisor** US 3.7 Sweden 3.8	**8 Semicredentialed supervisor** US 6.8 Sweden 3.2	**11 Uncredentialed supervisor** US 6.9 Sweden 3.1	> 0
3 Petty bourgeoisie US 6.9 Sweden 5.4	**6 Expert nonmanager** US 3.4 Sweden 6.8	**9 Semicredentialed worker** US 12.2 Sweden 17.8	**12 Proletarian** US 39.9 Sweden 43.5	–
	+	> 0	–	
		Skill assets		

United States: N = 1487
Sweden: N = 1179

Note: Distributions are of people working in the labor force, thus excluding unemployed, housewives, pensioners, etc.

Source: Comparative Project on Class Structure and Class Consciousness.

Table 3 Basic Classes and Contradictory Locations in Successive Modes of Production

Mode of production	Basic classes	Principal contradictory location
Feudalism	Lords and serfs	Bourgeoisie
Capitalism	Bourgeoisie and proletariat	Managers/bureaucrats
State bureaucratic socialism	Bureaucrats and workers	Intelligentsia/experts

talist *mode of production*: expert managers, nonmanagerial experts, nonexpert managers, and so on.[43]

What is the relationship between this heterogeneous exploitation definition of the middle class and my previous conceptualization of such positions as contradictory locations within class relations? There is still a sense in which such positions could be characterized as "contradictory locations," for they will typically hold contradictory interests with respect to the primary forms of class struggle in capitalist society, the struggle between labor and capital. On the one hand, they are like workers, in being excluded from ownership of the means of production.[44] On the other hand, they have interests opposed to workers because of their effective control of organization and skill assets. Within the struggles of capitalism, therefore, these new middle classes do constitute contradictory locations, or more precisely, contradictory locations within exploitation relations.

This conceptualization of the middle classes also suggests that historically the principal forms of contradictory locations will vary depending upon the particular combinations of exploitation relations in a given society. These principal contradictory locations are presented in Table 3. In feudalism, the critical contradictory location is constituted by the bourgeoisie, the rising class of the successor mode of production.[45]

43. The labor-force data in this table come from the comparative project on class structure and class consciousness, University of Wisconsin. Details of the coding of categories and the operationalization of variables can be found in Wright, *Classes*, appendix 2.

44. This is not to deny that many professionals and managers become significant owners of capital assets through savings out of high incomes. To the extent that this happens, however, their class location objectively begins to shift, and they move into an objectively bourgeois location. Here I am talking only about those professional and managerial positions that are not vehicles for entry into the bourgeoisie itself.

45. The old middle class in feudalism, however, is defined by the freed peasant (yeoman farmer), the peasant who, within a system of unequally distributed assets in labor power, owns his/her per capita share of that asset.

Within capitalism, the central contradictory location within exploitation relations is constituted by managers and state bureaucrats. They embody a principle of class organization that is quite distinct from capitalism and that potentially poses an alternative to capitalist relations. This is particularly true for state managers who, unlike corporate managers, are less likely to have their careers tightly integrated with the interests of the capitalist class. Finally, in state bureaucratic socialism, the "intelligentsia" broadly defined constitutes the pivotal contradictory location.[46]

One of the upshots of this reconceptualization of the middle class is that it is no longer axiomatic that the proletariat is the unique, or perhaps even the central, rival to the capitalist class for class power in capitalist society. That classical Marxist assumption depended upon the thesis that there were no other classes within capitalism that could be viewed as the "bearers" of an historical alternative to capitalism. Socialism (as the transition to communism) was the only possible future for capitalism. What Table 3 suggests is that there are other class forces within capitalism that potentially pose an alternative to capitalism.[47] This does not imply that there is any inevitability to the sequence feudalism–capitalism–state bureaucratic socialism–socialism–communism; state bureaucrats are not inevitably destined to be the future ruling class of present-day capitalisms. But it does suggest that the process of class formation and class struggle is considerably more complex and indeterminate than the traditional Marxist story has allowed.[48]

This way of understanding contradictory class locations has several advantages over my previous conceptualization. First, certain of the specific conceptual problems of the earlier analysis of contradictory locations within class relations disappear. In particular, one of the more serious problems with my previous conceptualization of contradictory

---

46. Theorists who have attempted to analyze the class structures of actually existing socialism in terms of a concept of a new class generally tend to amalgamate state bureaucrats and experts into a single dominant class location, rather than seeing them as essentially vying for class power. Some theorists, such as Konrad and Szelenyi and Gouldner, do recognize this division, although they do not theorize the problem in precisely the way posed here. See, for example, G. Konrad and I. Szelenyi, *Intellectuals on the Road to Class Power* (New York: Harcourt, Brace, Jovanovitch, 1979); Gouldner, *The Future of Intellectuals.*

47. Alvin Gouldner and others have argued that historically the beneficiaries of social revolutions have not been the oppressed classes of the prior mode of production, but "third classes." Most notably, it was not the peasantry who became the ruling class with the demise of feudalism, but the bourgeoisie, a class that was located outside of the principal exploitation relation of feudalism. A similar argument could be extended to manager-bureaucrats with respect to capitalism and experts with respect to state bureaucratic socialism: in each case these constitute potential rivals to the existing ruling class.

48. For an extended discussion of the thesis that capitalism has multiple possible futures, see Wright, "Capitalism's Futures."

class locations centered on the category "semiautonomous employees." Autonomy always seemed more of a characteristic of working conditions than a proper dimension of class relations as such, and as a result there was a fair amount of skepticism in my characterization of semiautonomous employees as constituting a distinctive kind of location within the class structure. In my empirical research on class structure, the semiautonomous category also proved particularly troublesome, generating a number of quite counterintuitive results. For example, janitors in schools who also perform a variety of "handiman" tasks ended up being more autonomous than airline pilots. These specific problems disappear in the reconceptualization proposed here.

Second, treating contradictory locations in terms of exploitation generalizes the concept across modes of production. The concept now has a specific theoretical status in all class systems and, indeed, has a much more focused historical thrust, as represented in Table 3.

Third, this way of conceptualizing "middle class" locations also makes the problem of their class interests much clearer than before. Their location within class relations is defined by the nature of their material optimizing strategies given the specific kinds of assets they own or control. Their specific class location helps to specify their interests both within the existing capitalist society and with respect to various kinds of alternative games (societies) to which they might want to withdraw. In the previous conceptualization it was problematic to specify precisely the material interests of certain contradictory locations. In particular, there was no consistent reason for treating the fundamental material interests of semiautonomous employees as necessarily distinct from those of workers, and certainly not as opposed to those of workers.

Finally, this exploitation-based strategy helps to clarify the problems of class alliances in a much more systematic way than the previous approach. In the case of contradictory locations it was always rather vague how the tendencies for contradictory locations to ally themselves with workers or nonworkers should be assessed. I made claims that such alliance tendencies were politically and ideologically determined, but I was not able to put much content to such notions. In contrast, as we shall see below, the exploitation-based concept of contradictory location helps to provide a much clearer material basis for the analyzing problem of alliances.

Class Structure and Class Formation

In classical Marxism, the relationship between class structure and class formation was generally treated as relatively unproblematic. In particular, in the analysis of the working class it was usually assumed that there

was a one-to-one relationship between the proletariat defined structurally and the proletariat engaged as a collective actor in struggle. The
transformation of the working class from a class-in-itself (a class determined structurally) into a class-for-itself (a class engaged in collective
struggle) may not have been a smooth and untroubled process, but it
was an inevitable one.

Most neo-Marxist class theorists have questioned this claim of a
simple relationship between class structure and class formation. Generally it has been argued that there is much less determinacy between the
two levels of class analysis. As Adam Przeworski has argued, class
struggle is in the first instance a struggle *over* class before it is a struggle
between classes.[49] It is always problematic whether workers will be
formed into a class or into some other sort of collectivity based on
religion, ethnicity, region, language, nationality, trade. The class structure may define the terrain of material interests upon which attempts at
class formation occur, but it does not uniquely determine the outcomes
of those attempts.

The conceptual framework proposed in this paper highlights the relative indeterminacy of the class structure–class formation relationship. If
the arguments of the paper are sound, then class structure should be
viewed as a structure of social relations that generates a matrix of
exploitation-based interests. But because many locations within the class
structure have complex bundles of such exploitation interests, these
interests should be viewed as constituting the material basis for a variety
of *potential* class formations. The class structure itself does not generate
a unique pattern of class formation; rather it determines the underlying
probabilities of different kinds of class formations. Which among these
alternatives actually occurs historically will depend on a range of factors
that are structurally contingent to the class structure itself.

Class Alliances

Once class analysis moves away from the simple polarized view of the
class structure, the problem of class alliances looms large in the analysis
of class formations. Rarely, if ever, does organized class struggle take the
form of a conflict between two homogeneously organized forces. The
typical situation is one in which alliances are forged between classes,
segments of classes, and above all, contradictory class locations.

---

49. A. Przeworski, "From Proletariat into Class: The Process of Class Struggle from
Karl Kautsky's *The Class Struggle* to Recent Debates," *Politics and Society*, vol. 7, no. 4
(1977).

Individuals in contradictory locations within class relations face three broad strategies in their relationship to class struggle: they can try to use their position as an exploiter to gain entry as individuals into the dominant exploiting class itself; they can attempt to forge an alliance with the dominant exploiting class; or they can form some kind of alliance with the principal exploited class.

In general, the immediate class aspiration of people in contradictory locations is to enter the dominant exploiting class by "cashing in" the fruits of their exploitation location into the dominant asset. Thus, in feudalism, the rising bourgeoisie frequently used part of the surplus acquired through capitalist exploitation to buy land and feudal titles, that is, to obtain "feudal assets." Part of what a bourgeois revolution consists of, then, is preventing the feudalization of capitalist accumulation. Similarly, in capitalism, the exploitative transfers personally available to managers and professionals are often used to buy capital, property, stocks, and so on, in order to obtain the "unearned" income from capital ownership. Finally, in state bureaucratic socialism, experts try to use their control over knowledge as a vehicle for entering the bureaucratic apparatus and acquiring control over organization assets.

Dominating exploiting classes have generally pursued class alliances with contradictory locations, at least when they were financially capable of doing so. Such strategies attempt to neutralize the potential threat from contradictory locations by tying their interests directly to those of the dominant exploiting class. When these hegemonic strategies are effective, they help to create a stable basis for all exploiting classes to contain struggles by exploited classes. One strategy is to make it easy for people in contradictory locations to enter the dominant class; another is to reduce the exploitation of contradictory locations by the dominant exploiting class to the point that such positions involve "net" exploitation. The extremely high salaries paid to upper-level managers in large corporations almost certainly means that they are net exploiters. This can have the effect of minimizing any possible conflicts of interests between such positions and those of the dominant exploiting class itself.

Such hegemonic strategies, however, are expensive. They require allowing large segments of contradictory locations access to significant portions of the social surplus. It has been argued by some economists that this corporate hegemonic strategy may be one of the central causes for the general tendency toward stagnation in advanced capitalist econ-

---

50. See S. Bowles, D. Gordon, and T. Weiskopf, *Beyond the Wasteland* (New York: Anchor, 1984). The argument is that the growth of managerial costs associated with the growth of the megacorporation is one of the key factors undermining productivity growth in certain capitalist countries.

omies, and that this in turn may be undermining the viability of the strategies themselves.[50] The erosion of the economic foundations of this alliance may generate more anticapitalist tendencies among experts and even among managers. Particularly in the state sector, where the careers of experts and bureaucrats are less directly tied to the welfare of corporate capital, it would be expected that more "statist" views of how the economy should be managed would gain credence.

The potential class alliances of contradictory locations are not simply with the bourgeois. There is, under certain historical situations, the potential for alliances with the "popular" exploited classes—classes that are not also exploiters (that is, they are not in contradictory locations within exploitation relations). Such classes, however, generally face a more difficult task in trying to forge an alliance with contradictory locations, since they generally lack the capacity to offer significant bribes to people in those positions. This does not mean, however, that class alliances between workers and some segments of contradictory locations are impossible. Particularly under conditions where contradictory locations are being subjected to a process of "degradation"—deskilling, proletarianization, routinization of authority—it may be quite possible for people in those contradictory locations that are clearly net exploited to see the balance of their interests being more in line with the working class.

Where class alliances between workers and various categories of managers and experts do occur, the critical political question becomes defining the political and ideological direction of the alliance. If the analysis presented in this paper is correct, these contradictory locations are the "bearers" of certain futures to capitalism, futures within which the working class would remain an exploited and dominated class. Should workers support such alliances? Is it in their interests to struggle for a society within which they remain exploited, albeit in noncapitalist ways? I do not think there are general, universal answers to these questions. There are certainly circumstances in which a revolutionary state bureaucratic socialism may be in the real interests of the working class, even though workers would remain exploited in such a society. This is the case, I believe, in many Third World countries today. In the advanced capitalist countries, however, radical democratic socialism, involving the simultaneous socialization of capital and democratization of organization assets, is a viable, if very long-term, possibility.

Empirical Implications

The concept of exploitation identifies situations in which there are intrinsically opposed material interests between actors. The characterization of a class structure as rooted in a complex pattern of exploitation relations, therefore, is meant to provide insight into the distribution of fundamental material interests across positions in that structure and the corresponding lines of cleavage in class conflicts.

The empirical question then becomes how this complex typology of class locations is related to a variety of "dependent" variables. In the present analysis, I will focus on two of these: income and class attitudes. I will briefly discuss the rationales for analyzing each of these variables, the data sources to be used in the analysis, and the construction of the operational variables. Once these preliminaries are completed we will turn to the empirical results themselves.

Rationales for Variables

While the relationship between the theoretical concept of exploitation and empirical data on personal income is not a simple one, the two should nevertheless be closely related. If, therefore, ownership or control of productive assets is in fact the basis for exploitation, then incomes should vary systematically across the cells of the class typology in Table 2. More specifically, we can make two basic hypotheses: (1) mean incomes should be polarized in the class structure between the bourgeoisie and the proletariat; and (2) mean incomes should increase monotonically in every direction from the proletariat corner of the table to the expert-manager corner, and from the petty bourgeoisie to the bourgeoisie. Examining the relationship between class structure and income, therefore, is a way of adding credibility to the theoretical claims underlying the class typology.

The rationale for examining class attitudes is that such attitudes should at least tend to reflect the real interests of incumbents of class positions and thus will vary systematically across the cells of the class typology. Two objections can be raised against studying attitudes. The first is that class structure is meant to explain class struggle, particularly the organized forms of class actions, not inter-individual variations in mental states. The second is that even if class location shapes individual mental states, responses to an attitude survey are an inappropriate way of tapping those class-determined mental states. Mental states are sufficiently context-dependent that the responses to the artificial context of a survey interview cannot be viewed as indicators of mental states in the real life situations of class relations.

Both of these objections need to be taken seriously. To the first I would say that even if the ultimate object of explanation of class structure is collectively organized class struggles, it is individuals who participate in those struggles, who make the decisions to act in particular ways, and thus individual mental states have to be implicated in the process in one way or another. To the second objection, I would argue that to the extent mental states are context-dependent, then the relationship between class location and class attitudes as measured by a survey should be attenuated, not strengthened. The context of the survey interview should tend to scramble the results, add noise to the real effects of class location. If, therefore, we observe a systematic relationship in spite of this context-distortion, this should add confidence in the meaningfulness of the results.

Data

The data we will examine comes from a large, cross-national project on class structure and class consciousness.[51] In the present analysis we will consider the data from only two countries, the United States and Sweden. Within the family of advanced capitalist countries with roughly similar levels of technological development and average standards of living, these two societies represent almost polar cases: the United States has among the highest levels of real income inequality (that is, after taxes and transfers) of any developed capitalist society, while Sweden has the lowest; Sweden has the highest proportion of its civilian labor force directly employed by the state (over 45 percent), while the United States has the lowest (under 20 percent); Sweden has the highest level of governance by social democratic parties of any capitalist country, while the United States has had the lowest. Because of this basic similarity in the levels of economic development combined with these salient political differences, the comparison between Sweden and the United States on the effects of class on income and attitudes should be particularly interesting.

Variables

The income variable is total personal annual income, before taxes, from all sources. It therefore combines wage income with various sources of nonwage income. The class-attitude variable is a scale constructed by combining the responses to six items, each of which has a fairly transparent class content.[52] For example, respondents who agreed with the

---

51. Details of the study can be found in E.O. Wright, C. Costello, D. Hachen, and J. Sprague, "The American Class Structure," *American Sociological Review*, December 1982; and Wright, *Classes*.

52. Complete details on the measures we will use can be found in Wright, *Classes*, appendix 2.

statement "Employers should be prohibited by law from hiring strike-breakers during a strike" were classified as having taken the pro-working-class position, those who disagreed with this statement were classified as having taken the procapitalist position. The scale goes from −6 (the respondent takes the procapitalist position on all six items) to +6 (the respondent takes the proworker position on all items).

The ownership of productive assets that underlies the class structure typology is operationalized through the use of a wide range of questions on decision making, authority, property ownership, occupational skills, and educational credentials. There are, needless to say, a host of methodological problems with these measures, particularly the measures of skill/credential assets. For this reason I have trichotomized each of the assets. The two poles of each dimension constitute positions with unambiguous relations to the asset in question. The "intermediate" position is a combination of cases with marginal assets and cases for which the measures are ambiguous.

Empirical Results: Income

Table 4 presents the data for mean personal income by class for the United States and Sweden. In general, the data in this table are strongly consistent with the theoretical rationale for the exploitation-based conceptualization of class structure.

In the United States, income is strongly polarized between the proletarian cell in the typology and the bourgeoisie: the former earn, on average, just over $11,000/year, the latter over $52,000. In Sweden, the results are not as clear: the bourgeoisie in the sample has essentially identical income to expert managers. However, there are only eight respondents in the bourgeoisie category in the Swedish sample, and they are certainly relatively small capitalists. Also, because of the very heavy taxation on personal income in Sweden, capitalists take a substantial part of their income in kind rather than in cash. It is impossible to measure such nonmonetary elements in personal income with the data we have available, thus the figure in Table 4 is certainly an under-estimate. Hypothesis 1, that mean incomes should be polarized between the bourgeoisie and the proletariat, is thus strongly supported in the United States and is at least provisionally supported in Sweden.

The results for hypothesis 2, that mean incomes should increase monotonically from proletarian to expert manager and from petty bour-geoisie to bourgeoisie, are less equivocal. In both the United States and Sweden incomes increase in a largely monotonic manner in every dimension of the table as you move from the proletarian corner in the class-structure matrix to the expert-manager corner. The only

Table 4 Mean Annual Individual Incomes by Class Location in Sweden and the United States

Assets in the means of production

Owners	Nonowners (wage laborers)			Organization assets
1 Bourgeoisie US: $52,621 SW: $28,333	4 Expert manager US: $28,665 SW: $29,952	7 Semicredentialed manager US: $20,701 SW: $20,820	10 Uncredentialed manager US: $12,276 SW: $15,475	+
2 Small employer US: $24,828 SW: $17,237	5 Expert supervisor US: $23,057 SW: 18,859	8 Semicredentialed supervisor US: $18,023 SW: $19,711	11 Uncredentialed supervisor US: $13,045 SW: $15,411	> 0
3 Petty bourgeoisie US: $14,496 SW: $13,503	6 Expert nonmanager US: $15,251 SW: $14,890	9 Semicredentialed worker US: $16,034 SW: $14,879	12 Proletarian US: 11,161 SW: $11,876	−
	+	> 0	−	
		Skill assets		

United States: N = 1282
Sweden: N = 1049

Note: Entries in cells are the means for gross annual individual income from all sources before taxes. The Swedish incomes were converted to dollars at the 1980 exchange rate.

Source: Comparative Project on Class Structure and Class Consciousness.

exceptions are that categories 10 and 11 (uncredentialed managers and uncredentialed supervisors) are essentially identical, and categories 6 and 9 (credentialed and semicredentialed nonmanagerial employees) are essentially identical in both the United States and Sweden. Given the conceptual status of the "intermediate" categories of "uncredentialed supervisors" (category 11) and "semicredentialed workers" (category 9), these results are not inconsistent with the theoretical model.

What is particularly striking in the pattern in Table 4 is the interaction between the two dimensions of exploitation relations among wage-earners. The increase in average income is relatively modest as you move along either organization assets or credential assets taken separately (as you move along the bottom of the table and the right-hand column). Where the sharp increase in incomes occurs is when you combine these two exploitation mechanisms (moving along the top of the table and the left-hand column of among wage-earners). Hypothesis 2 is thus strongly supported.[53]

Empirical Results: Attitudes

Table 5 presents the mean values on the class-consciousness scale by class location in the United States and Sweden. Several generalizations can be drawn from these results.

The Overall Pattern of Variations   In Table 5 the overall *pattern* of variations in means (not the actual value of the means, but the patterning of the means) is quite similar in the United States and Sweden. In both countries the table is basically polarized between the capitalist class and the working class (in neither table is there a significant difference between proletarians and semicredentialed workers).[54] In both countries the values on the scale become decreasingly pro-working class and eventually procapitalist class as one moves from the proletarian corner of the table to the expert-manager corner of the table. As in the results

---

53. In a separate analysis, not reported here, in which nonwage income was the dependent variable, the same monotonic pattern was observed, only with a considerably steeper differential between workers and expert managers. See ibid., ch. 6.

54. In the United States, expert managers are slightly more procapitalist than the bourgeoisie itself, but the difference is sufficiently small that they should be treated as essentially equally polarized with respect to the working class. It should be remembered in this context that most respondents in what I am calling the "bourgeoisie" are still fairly modest capitalists. Eighty-three percent of these capitalists employ less than fifty employees. Only 8 percent of expert managers, however, work for businesses with less than fifty employees. It would be expected that if we had data on a sample of large capitalists, the results would be somewhat different.

for income, the means on the attitude scale change in a nearly monotonic manner along every dimension of the table. And in both countries,
the means become increasingly procapitalist as you move from the petty
bourgeoisie to the capitalist class proper among the self-employed.[55]

The Degree of Polarization   While the patterning of differences in
attitudes is similar in the two countries, the degree of polarization within
that common pattern is dramatically different. In the United States the
difference between the capitalist class and the working class is just over
2 points on the scale; in Sweden the difference is 4.6 points. (The difference between these differences is statistically significant at the .01 level.)
The data indicate that there is basically an international consensus
within the capitalist class on class-based attitudes, whereas no such
consensus exists in the working class: Swedish and American workers
differ on this scale by nearly as much as US workers and capitalists.

Class Alliances   The pattern of class alliances—the ways in which the
terrain of class structure becomes transformed into class formations—
suggested by the patterns of consciousness in Table 5 varies considerably
in the two countries. In Sweden the only wage-earner category with an
emphatically procapitalist ideological position is expert managers; in the
United States, procapitalist positions penetrate further into the wage-
earner population. In the United States, only the three cells in the lower
right-hand corner of the table can be considered part of a working-class
coalition; in Sweden the coalition extends to all uncredentialed wage-
earners and all nonmanagement wage-earners, and at least weakly
includes semicredentialed managers and semicredentialed supervisors as
well. Turning these results into proportions of the labor force in Table 2,
in the United States approximately 30 percent of the labor force are in
class categories within the bourgeois coalition whereas in Sweden the
corresponding figure is only 10 percent. Correspondingly, in Sweden
between 73 percent and 80 percent of the labor force (depending upon
whether or not semicredentialed managers and supervisors are included
in the coalition) are in classes within the working-class coalition,
whereas in the United States only 58 percent of the labor force are in the

---

55. It might be objected that these results could be artifacts of other variables that are
not included in the analysis. The sex composition of class categories, for example, could
conceivably explain the observed patterns across the cells in the table. I have analyzed the
results in Table 5 controlling for a range of possible confounding variables—age, sex, class
origin, union membership, income—and while certain details are affected by these "controls," the basic patterns remain intact. For a discussion of this multivariate analysis, see
Wright, *Classes*, ch. 7.

Table 5   Class Consciousness by Location in the Class Structure

I United States

Assets in the means of production

Owners	Nonowners (wage laborers)			Organization assets
				+
				> 0
				−
1 Bourgeoisie −1.31	4 Expert manager −1.46	7 Semicredentialed manager −0.34	10 Uncredentialed manager −0.29	+
2 Small employer −0.87	5 Expert supervisor −0.78	8 Semicredentialed supervisor −0.24	11 Uncredentialed supervisor +0.54	> 0
3 Petty bourgeoisie −0.09	6 Expert nonmanager −0.09	9 Semicredentialed worker +0.78	12 Proletarian +0.78	−
	+	> 0	−	Skill assets

II Sweden

Assets in the means of production

Owners	Nonowners (wage laborers)		
1 Bourgeoisie −2.00	**4 Expert manager** −0.70	**7 Semicredentialed manager** +1.03	**10 Uncredentialed manager** +1.81
2 Small employer −0.98	**5 Expert supervisor** +0.07	**8 Semicredentialed supervisor** +0.74	**11 Uncredentialed supervisor** +1.98
3 Petty bourgeoisie +0.46	**6 Expert nonmanager** +1.29	**9 Semicredentialed worker** +2.81	**12 Proletarian** +2.60

Organization assets: +   >0   −

Skill assets: +   >0   −

Note: Entries in the table are means on the working-class consciousness scale. The values on the scale range from +6 (pro–working class on every item) to −6 (procapitalist class on every item).

Source: Comparative Project on Class Structure and Class Consciousness.

working-class coalition.[56] The working-class coalition in the United
States is thus not only less ideologically polarized with the bourgeoisie
than in Sweden, it is also much smaller.

Interpretations

Several general conclusions can be drawn from these results. First, the
data are systematically consistent with the proposed reconceptualization
of class in terms of relations of exploitation. In both the analysis of
income and attitudes, the basically monotonic relationship between
these variables and location along the exploitation dimensions of the
class typology add credibility to the concept.

Second, the data support the thesis that the underlying structure of
class relations shapes the overall pattern of class consciousness. In spite
of the dramatic political differences between Sweden and the United
States the basic pattern linking class structure to class consciousness is
very similar in the two countries: they are both polarized along the three
dimensions of exploitation, and the values on the consciousness scale
basically vary monotonically as one moves along these dimensions.

Finally, while the overall patterning of consciousness is structurally
determined by class relations, the level of working-class consciousness in
a given society and the nature of the class coalitions that are built upon
those class relations are shaped by the organizational and political practices that characterize the history of class struggle. For all of their
reformism and their efforts at building a stable class compromise in
Swedish society, the Swedish Social Democratic Party and the associated
Swedish labor movement have adopted strategies that reinforce certain
aspects of working-class consciousness. Issues of power and property are
frequently at the center of the political agenda, social democratic state
policies tend to reinforce the material interests of capitalistically
exploited wage-earners, and at least the radical wing of the labor movement and the Social Democratic Party keep alive the vision of alternatives
to the existing structure of society.

In contrast to the Swedish case, political parties and unions in the
United States have engaged in practices that, wittingly or unwittingly,
have undermined working-class consciousness. The Democratic Party
has systematically displaced political discourse away from a language of

---

56. These estimates are based on the following aggregations from Table 5: Swedish
bourgeois coalition = cells 1, 2, 4; US bourgeois coalition = cells 1, 2, 4, 5, 7, 8, 10;
Swedish working-class coalition = cells 6, 9, 10, 11, 12 (low estimate) and also 7, 8 (high
estimate); US working-class coalition = cells 9, 11, 12. Note that in neither country is the
petty bourgeoisie—category 3—part of either coalition.

class. While of course there are exceptions, the general tendency has been to organize social conflicts in nonclass ways and to emphasize the extremely limited range of alternatives for dealing with problems of power and property. State welfare policies have tended to heighten rather than reduce class-based divisions among wage-earners. And the ineffectiveness of the labor movement to unionize even a majority of manual industrial workers, let alone white-collar employees, has meant that the divisions of exploitation-based interests among wage-earners have tended to be large relative to their common interests *vis-à-vis* capital. As a result, as the rhetoric of the 1984 presidential campaign reflected, the labor movement is regarded as a "special interest" group in the United States rather than as a representative of the general economic interests of wage-earners.

The net result of these differences in the political strategies and ideologies of parties and unions in the two countries is that class has considerably greater importance in Sweden than in the United States: class location and class experiences have a bigger impact on class consciousness; classes are more polarized ideologically; and the working-class coalition built upon that more polarized ideological terrain is itself much bigger.

Conclusion

The heart of the proposal advanced in this paper is that the concept of class should be systematically rooted in the problem of forms of exploitation. In my previous work, and in the work of many Marxists, the concept of class had effectively shifted from an exploitation-centered concept to a domination-centered concept. Although exploitation remained part of the background context for the discussion of class, it did not systematically enter into the elaboration of actual class maps. That shift, I now believe, undermines the coherence of the concept of class and should be replaced by a rigorous exploitation-centered conceptualization.

If the arguments in this paper are persuasive, the specific exploitation-centered class concept that I have elaborated has several significant advantages over my own previous approach to class (and by extension, other existing class concepts). First, the exploitation-centered concept provides a much more coherent and compelling way of understanding the class location of the "middle class" than alternative concepts, both in capitalist societies and in various kinds of noncapitalist societies. The middle class ceases to be a residual category or a relatively ad hoc amendment to the class map of polarized classes. Rather, middle classes are defined by the same relations that define the polarized classes themselves; the difference lies in the ways those relations are structurally combined in the concrete institutional forms of a given society.

Second, the exploitation-centered concept provides a much more coherent way of describing the qualitative differences among types of class structures than alternative concepts. The abstract criteria for assessing the class relations of a given society are consistent across qualitatively distinct societies and yet allow for the specificity of any given society's class structures to be investigated. The concept thus avoids the kind of ad hoc quality that plagues most other class concepts as they move across historically distinct types of societies.

Third, the exploitation-centered concept is more systematically *materialist* than domination concepts. Classes are derived from the patterns of effective ownership over aspects of the forces of production. The different kinds of exploitation that define different kinds of classes are all linked to the qualitative properties of these different aspects of forces of production.

Fourth, the exploitation-centered concept provides a more *historical* class concept than do domination-centered concepts. It is the forces of production that impart whatever discretionality exists to epochal social change.[57] Since in the framework discussed in this paper, the class-exploitation nexus is defined with respect to specific forces of production, the development of those forces of production is what gives an historical trajectory to systems of class relations. The order to the forms of society presented in Tables 1 and 3, therefore, is not arbitrary but defines a developmental tendency in class structures.

Fifth, the concept of class elaborated in this paper has a particularly sustained *critical* character. The very definition of exploitation as developed by Roemer contains within itself the notion of alternative forms of society that are immanent within an existing social structure. And the historical character of the analysis of the possible social forms implies that this critical character of the class concept will not have a purely moral or utopian basis. Class, when defined in terms of qualitatively distinct asset-based forms of exploitation, provides a way of describing both the nature of class relations in a given society and the immanent possibilities for transformation posed by those relations.

Finally, the exploitation-centered concept provides a much clearer linkage to the problem of interests than domination-based concepts.

---

57. See E. O. Wright, "Giddens's Critique of Marxism," *New Left Review*, no. 139 (1983), for a discussion of why the forces of production can plausibly be viewed as giving history a directionality.

And this, in turn, provides the basis for a more systematic empirical analysis of the relationship between the objective properties of class structures and the problems of class formation, class alliances, and class struggle.

PART I

Methodological Issues

Exchange on *Classes*

Introduction*

Karl Marx, like Auguste Comte, thought the study of society to be properly a "science." And yet, as increasing numbers of sociologists have repudiated Comte's positivist tradition in the past decades, Scientific Marxism has lost ground to hermeneutic and other traditions. It has become, almost, a term of insult among critical leftists who equate it with some crude and naive structural determinism. Seen in this context, Erik Olin Wright's *Classes* is an ambitious project—not just to deal with the Marxist problem of the continued existence of the middle classes, but also to refurbish the somewhat tarnished reputation of Scientific Marxism in an era in which the very meaning of "science" is debatable and often debated.

In what follows, the editors, in cooperation with other graduate students in the Berkeley Department of Sociology, put a series of methodological questions to Wright, who had temporarily joined the faculty. Michael Burawoy, also a member of the faculty at Berkeley, provides a critique of Wright's methodology and presents an alternative. Wright then presents a short rebuttal. (Methodology is considered here at an almost meta-methodological level: not so much "how to," but instead the *study* of "how to.") The background for much of this discussion is found in the post-positivist methodological inquiries of the last three decades. To attempt a summary of this literature in twenty-five words or less, we might say that authors such as Thomas Kuhn, Imre Lakatos, Paul Feyerabend, and Michel Foucault—plus others too numerous to list—have tried to cast doubt on the once unproblematic relations between theories and facts.

Kuhn, for instance, has argued that scientists work within paradigms

---

*By the editors of the *Berkeley Journal of Sociology*.

which limit the types of evidence they may consider. Though Kuhn himself did not apply his theory of scientific paradigms to the *social* sciences, sociologists have appropriated his ideas to explain, and occasionally to justify, the blinders which every sociological tradition forces them to wear. Lakatos has adopted the notion of research programs, and has added the optimistic argument that science can be assured of eternal progress: the programs which become dominant do so because they have dramatic success at uncovering and explaining facts which the earlier program had not even looked for. Feyerabend has called into question the very idea of an independently existing fact: in his view, facts are created by theories. One cannot use a telescope to discover facts about a star, for instance, until one holds the belief that stars are susceptible to accurate examination by telescopes. And Foucault has called attention to the power dimension involved in the scientific production and analysis of facts. The object of study is often, first, objectified, and second, subjected to analysis for the sake of control. Here, evidence is created, and it is created for the purpose of subjugation.

This thumbnail sketch has touched on several points which will be put to Wright in the following questions. And Wright is particularly qualified to discuss these issues: though survey research is his primary method of analysis, he has displayed in *Classes* a sensitivity to more theoretical issues in methodology. An entire section of his book (Chapter 2) is devoted to explicating the limits of the Marxist paradigm within which he intends to work. Wright recognizes the problems in deriving theories directly from facts (p. 20), and he makes explicit his methodological stance: "that empirical adjudications are always between rival concepts or propositions, not directly between a proposition and the 'real world' as such." (p. 189)

Though *Classes* shows clearly the attention Wright has paid to the relation between facts and theories, some issues remain about the relation of one theory to another. For this reason, we will start with a series of questions on this subject, before moving on to questions about the proper use of scientific evidence and about the extrascientific implications of the scientist's method.

REFLECTIONS ON *CLASSES*
Erik Olin Wright

1 Theory vs Theory

1.1 *In Chapter 2 of* Classes *you list six "conceptual constraints" within whose limits the Marxist must operate. But other Marxists, certainly, would come up with different lists. For instance, one school might emphasize the importance of class struggle in determining class consciousness. Others might take ideology as a separate factor. And so on, as you admit (p. 27). By what criteria do you choose your Marxism?*

To answer this question I need to first very briefly review the context in which I elaborated the list of conceptual constraints on the concept of class structure within Marxist social science. In order to study anything, we need concepts—the categories within which we ask questions, observe the world, organize our possible explanations. A radical empiricist would claim that the only fundamental constraint on the formation of concepts is the way the world is. All anti-empiricist methodologies argue, in various ways, that our concepts are also constrained (and in some versions, exclusively constrained) by the theories within which they function. These theories, in turn, are constructed by linkages of various sorts among the very concepts which the theory constrains.

The central task of *Classes* is to solve a problem of concept formation: how to produce an adequate concept for the "middle classes." If one adopts an anti-empiricist methodological stance towards the process of concept formation, then it is essential to specify the theoretical conditions which any legitimate concept of the middle class must fill (where, by "legitimate," I mean that the concept is capable of functioning in the theory in question). Thus the attempt at elaborating a list of conceptual constraints. My claim in Chapter 2 of *Classes* is that the following six constraints on the concept of class structure are common to most varieties of Marxist theory: 1. Class structure imposes limits on class formation, class consciousness and class struggle. 2. Class structures constitute the essential qualitative lines of social demarcation in the historical trajectories of social change. 3. The concept of class is a relational concept. 4. The social relations which define classes are intrinsically antagonistic rather than symmetrical. 5. The objective basis of these antagonistic interests is exploitation. 6. The fundamental basis of exploitation is to be found in the social relations of production. The first two of these constraints define what *explanatory* tasks "class structure" is meant to accomplish; the last four specify interconnected properties of this concept if it is to accomplish these tasks. If one were to ask, "What makes a Marxist concept of class structure 'Marxist'?", the answer would be: "The concept conforms at least to these six conceptual criteria."

I am not claiming, it should be emphasized, that these six conceptual criteria define what is Marxist about Marxist theory in general, but simply what is Marxist about the concept of class structure. And I am also not saying that all Marxists would *limit* the conceptual constraints on class concepts to these six criteria—additional constraints would undoubtedly be present in certain traditions of Marxism. There may even be some additional constraints which all Marxists share, although I have not been able to figure out what these might be.

In your question you point out that "other Marxists would come up with other lists. For instance, one school might emphasize the importance of class struggle in determining class consciousness. Another might take ideology as a separate factor." This is undoubtedly true, but the issue is not whether other Marxisms would emphasize additional factors, but whether they would reject any of these constraints. Do any Marxists deny that class structures must be defined relationally, that these relations are antagonistic and exploitative, and that exploitation is rooted in the social organization of production? All that is being claimed is that these constraints are in fact common to Marxist conceptualizations of class structure, and therefore any *Marxist* concept of the "middle class" must, at a minimum, conform to these criteria.

Now, three kinds of arguments could be raised against this particular list. First, it could be argued that there are no common criteria that unite the diverse concepts of class structure across all Marxisms. Some Marxisms, indeed, might even reject the concept of class structure itself. This is a reasonable objection, but it really amounts to a rejection of the claim that there is any conceptual unity whatsoever among self-styled "Marxist" theorists, at least around the concept of class. It implies that the word "Marxist" has been appropriated by radically incommensurate theories. This criticism does not, however, undermine the legitimacy of the inventory of conceptual constraints as such, but merely its identification with some historical usages of the label "Marxist".

Second, it could be argued that all varieties of Marxist "theory," like most other existing social theories, are so far from constituting coherent, systematic scientific paradigms, that it is impossible to specify meaningful conceptual constraints on any process of concept formation. Social theories, it could be argued, are more or less chaotic collections of terms, intuitions and specific explanations rather than coherent abstract systems of thought. Even Marxism, which has aspirations to be such an abstract framework, contains so many disjointed and contradictory elements that it is best thought of as a loosely coupled discourse than a coherent scientific system of concepts. If this is correct, then the elaboration of a list of conceptual constraints such as the list which I propose should be viewed primarily as an attempt at *producing* order within the theoretical space of Marxism rather than simply *discovering* the underlying order which already exists.

Finally, one could accept the legitimacy of the enterprise of constructing a list of formal constraints on the concept of class within Marxism, and yet argue that this particular list is not a proper specification of these constraints. This could, of course, be a valid criticism, but the burden in such a criticism is showing what alternative set of constraints are constitutive of the Marxist theory of class. I continue to believe that as a matter of *empirical generalization* about "actually existing Marxisms," these criteria are broadly common to Marxist concepts of class structure and that most of these criteria are shared by Marxist theorists who in other respects would sharply disagree on theoretical issues. Contrary to what you suggest in your question, I believe that *Marxist* theorists who emphasize ideology and class consciousness still believe that class *structures* are constituted by antagonistic exploitative relations rooted in production.

To assert that virtually all theorists who would call themselves "Marxist" as a matter of fact explicitly or implicitly operate under these conceptual constraints does not mean, of course, that specific Marxist theorists would not quibble with some of the details of those six criteria. Some theorists would certainly object to the expression "historical trajectories of social change" in the second constraint on the grounds that this suggests, perhaps, a unilinear, deterministic path of historical development. They would agree that class structures define fundamental qualitative lines of demarcation between types of societies that have occurred in history, but they would reject any strong claims about these types being arrayed in any logically ordered temporal sequence, as suggested by the expression "trajectory." Other theorists would question the claim that class structures impose *limits* on class formation and class struggle in the first criterion. Such limits, many Marxists have argued, are imposed by the totality of social relations, not simply class relations. While all Marxists would agree that class struggles do operate within some kind of social relationally imposed limits (struggles are not just a matter of subjective will on the part of people), and they agree that class relations are *part* of the limit-imposing process, many would not want to simply assert that class structures as such impose these limits.[1] And certainly there would be intense debate over the precise *content* to be put on the terms in any of these criteria: "relational" in constraint number 3, "antagonistic" in number 4, "exploitation" in number 5 and "production" in number 6. The point is not that there would be complete agreement on all of the details of these criteria or on the meanings of all of the concepts contained within them, but that they in practice define the conceptual terrain upon which debates over the theory of class structure are waged within Marxism.

What I have said so far concerns the methodological standing of these six criteria for class structural concepts. The last sentence in your question, however, raises a broader issue: "By what criteria do you choose *your* Marxism?" While I may be correct that most Marxists in fact would accept these six constraints on the concept of class structure, this does not answer the question about the criteria I use to justify my general theoretical posture within Marxism. Much of my discussion of the remaining questions you have posed will, in effect, constitute an answer to this broader question, but I will state in abbreviated form my basic position here.

All theoretical choices derive their meaning from the "contrast space" in which they occur. "Choosing" a variety of Marxist theory is a contrast with alternative Marxisms, and the criteria implicit in the choice depend, in part at least, upon which alternative is being considered.[2] As I see it, my particular brand of Marxism is a result of a sequence of three basic choices within the array of historically available Marxisms. Each choice involves different criteria.

Choice 1: Scientific versus "nonscientific" (perhaps: antiscientific) Marxism. I do not pose this initial choice as scientific versus critical Marxism (as does Gouldner, for example), because I believe that scientific Marxism is a variety of critical theory: it attempts to provide the scientific foundations for a nonarbitrary immanent critique of capitalism. The first choice, therefore, is not between science and critique, but directly a choice over the status of Marxist theory as a scientific project.

---

1. It should be noted in this regard that the statement in constraint no. 1 is not that only class structures impose limits on class struggle, but simply that they do impose such limits. I find it hard to imagine that any Marxist *who uses the concept of class structure* would reject this relatively weak claim.

2. In what follows I am *not* discussing the criteria involved in my choice of Marxism over either non-Marxist social theory in general or "post-Marxist" radical social theory in particular, but rather the criteria involved in choosing among Marxisms. The choice of Marxism as such involves other issues.

What do I mean by this? Fundamentally I mean that the task of Marxist theory is to produce *explanations* of *real* phenomena that exist in the world independently of the theory.[3] Whether or not imperialism is a real cause of deepening underdevelopment in parts of the Third World depends upon how capitalist penetration actually works, not upon the categories of the theory of imperialism. Whether or not the sexual division of labor around childrearing is a real cause of the reproduction of male domination depends upon how mechanisms in psycho-sexual development actually work, not upon the discourses of our theories of psycho-sexual development. Whether or not we have *knowledge* of these mechanisms of underdevelopment and reproduction of male domination, however, depends upon the availability of adequate explanatory theories (I will discuss the problem of "adequacy" in answers to subsequent questions), but the mechanisms themselves have a real existence independent of this knowledge.

The first choice among Marxisms, therefore, is whether or not one wishes to embark on the difficult path of actually producing explanations of the world. The alternative is to restrict one's efforts to producing *descriptions* of the world, *interpretations* of the world, or *philosophical commentaries* about the world. There may be no guarantees of success in this explanatory enterprise, or even of knowing with certainty whether or not one has been successful (that is, there is no absolute way of knowing when one has produced knowledge), but the first criterion for my choice of a type of Marxism is that it attempts to produce explanations.

Choice 2: Analytical versus dogmatic Marxism. This is, undoubtedly, a highly contentious way of posing the second choice. By analytical Marxism I mean this: the heart of all scientific theory is the dual process of elaborating concepts and deploying them in the construction of theories. Analytical Marxism insists on the necessity of laying bare the assumptions that underlie these concepts and spelling out as clearly and systematically as possible the steps involved in linking them together within a theory. "Dogmatic" Marxism, in contrast, defends its use of concepts through a variety of other forms of argumentation: citations from canonical textual authority (typically through Marxiological argu-

---

3. This does not mean that the theories we produce are not *in* the world as well as *about* the world. Marxist theory itself produces effects in the world once it is embodied in ideologies, in political programs, in sociology curricula. This does not, however, pose fundamental problems to social theory, so long as one believes that the effects of theory on social processes can themselves be theorized (explained). That social theory must be reflexive—explaining both its own production and its own effects—does not imply that it cannot also be scientific.

ment); arguments based on ulterior political justifications (a particular concept is rejected *simply* because it is politically "undesirable" without further argument); appeal to vague and imprecise abstractions whose content is never systematically elaborated (such as the common use of "dialectics" to defend Marxist concepts). To be analytical in this sense does not imply a commitment to particular substantive positions, but to the importance of breaking down concepts, making explicit and systematic distinctions, defending the fine points of definitions, etc.[4]

Choice 3: Empirical (but not empiricist) versus theoristicist Marxism. I believe, for reasons which will become clearer in my responses to subsequent questions, that in order to have any confidence that the explanations produced within Marxist theory are in fact explanatory of anything, they must be produced in articulation with empirical research agendas. Analytical precision and coherence alone does not ensure explanatory power. Neither, of course, does empirical research alone. For Marxist explanations to advance, the two must be combined. The word "combined" is fraught with difficulties and ambiguities, but these difficulties are not so severe as to make theoretical advance impossible. In any event, this ambition is embodied in the third dimension of choice.

The list of six constraints on the concept of class structure can't be viewed as somehow methodologically derived from these three choices over the type of Marxism which I pursue. These six constraints all involve substantive claims about class theory, and substantive claims can never be logically derived from methodological principles.[5] Nevertheless, the effort at producing such a list can be seen as motivated by these general methodological commitments. This list is meant to specify in an analytically explicit way what class structure is meant to explain.

---

4. The expression "analytical Marxism" has been identified with what is sometimes called "rational choice Marxism." This identification is unjustified. While it is certainly true that rational choice Marxists are analytical, and equally true that analytical Marxists are often drawn to rational choice theory because of its clarity and precision, there is no necessary relationship between the two, and many analytically oriented Marxists reject rational choice theory as an adequate way of building theories of society. For a discussion of rational choice Marxism, see A. Carling, "Rational Choice Marxism," *New Left Review* no. 160 (1986). For an anthology of recent work by self-styled analytical Marxists, see J. Roemer (ed.), *Analytical Marxism* (Cambridge: Cambridge University Press, 1986). For a critique of the methodological individualist aspirations of certain analytical Marxists, see E. Sober, A. Levine, and E.O. Wright, "Marxism and Methodological Individualism," *New Left Review*, no. 162 (1987).

5. I strongly agree with Barry Hindess and Paul Hirst's arguments in *Marx's Capital and Capitalism Today* (London: Routledge and Kegan Paul, 1977, ch. 4), on this point: substantive theoretical claims about the world cannot be derived from epistemological doctrines. Such doctrines may make it possible to make certain substantive claims, but substantive claims require specific arguments about mechanisms, causes, processes, and these cannot be logically inferred from methodological principles.

1.2 *In Chapter 5 you "adjudicate" between your triaxial, exploitation-centered theory of class and other theories of class. Your theory wins, but the theory belonging to the person setting the terms of debate always seems to win. Isn't this like playing prosecutor and judge at the same time—and is there any way to adjudicate fairly between rival theories?*

First, a point of clarification: the adjudication at issue in chapter five is actually between alternative *concepts* of *class structure* rather than alternative theories of classes. Of course, the presupposition of concept-adjudication is that these concepts fit into some general theory, but in this particular case I made the assumption that the contending concepts all fit into the *same* general theory. This is important, because the task of concept adjudication within a common general theory is much easier (if still often difficult) than the adjudication between contending general theories. When concept adjudication occurs *within* a general theory there is an agreement about what the concept in question is meant to explain (this is what it means to say that they are contending concepts within the same theory); the debate is over the appropriate elaboration of the concept for it to accomplish this explanatory task, not over the object of explanation itself.

A theorist engaged in the task of adjudication may be prosecutor and judge at the same time, but she or he is not also the jury. The jury is the intellectual community engaged in the theoretical debate in question, and the "verdict" of such juries involves examining the cases presented by contending attempts at adjudication. As I point out in my methodological discussion of the problem of adjudication, the results of such adjudication are usually ambiguous: some concepts appear more coherent theoretically, but less consistent with observations than their rivals; some concepts appear consistent with some theoretical constraints, but not others; etc. It is because of these ambiguities that debates over given conceptual definitions can go on and on. But this does not mean that such debates can never be resolved, that certain rivals can never be eliminated.

Within the constraints of a given theory, adjudication can be fair or unfair, honest or dishonest. Dishonest adjudication occurs when the theorist surveys a range of alternative empirical results and only reports those that are consistent with the desired verdict. Dishonest adjudication occurs when concepts are operationalized in ways that privilege the desired outcomes. But such biases are not inherent in the adjudication process. In the case of the conceptual adjudication in *Classes*, there are a number of results which I present which run counter to the conceptual position I am trying to defend. And in a recent paper on the transformation of the American class structure, I show that an earlier adjudication

between Marxist and post-industrial theories of changes in class structures is not supported by evidence from the 1970s.[6] In any case, the real
safeguard to fairness is not the scholarly integrity of the investigator, but
the openness of the challenges from alternative views and the intellectual
capacity of the "jury" to juggle the ambiguities of contending
adjudications.

1.3 *All academics, it is probably fair to say, try to come up with something new. But* Classes, *with its reconceptualization of classes and its
appropriation of statistical procedures, seems to be quite a break from the
Marxist tradition in which you place yourself. Do you feel that you are
founding a new subtradition within Marxist thought—and if so, what are
the implications of such a position?*

My work in *Classes*, and my earlier work in empirical class analysis, are
by no means the first examples of relatively sophisticated use of statistical analyses by Marxists.[7] Nor does my preoccupation with sorting out
the underlying assumptions and logic of key concepts within Marxism, in
this case the concept of class, represent a novel innovation in Marxist
theory. What is probably true, however, is that *Classes* and the earlier
work of which it is an extension are relatively unusual in trying to do
both of these: to aspire to analytical precision in the elaboration of
concepts and statistical rigor in empirical investigation.

The biographical roots of this particular *gestalt* are to be found in the
intellectual and academic context in which I first seriously engaged both
Marxism and sociology. As a radical intellectual in the early 1970s I was
an enthusiastic participant in the renewal of Marxist theory, first in
terms of the problem of the state and subsequently the problem of
classes. But I was also an enthusiastic budding academic and wanted
Marxist ideas to have an impact within sociology as a discipline. As a
missionary proselytizer I wanted to "save sociology" from the sins of
bourgeois thought as well as to "save Marxism" from the sins of dogmatism.[8] The joining of statistical methods with conceptual rigor seemed

---

6. See E.O. Wright and B. Martin, "The Transformation of the American Class Structure: 1960–1970," *American Journal of Sociology*, July, 1987.

7. To cite just a few other examples, see M. Reich, *Racial Inequality* (Princeton:
Princeton University Press, 1981); R. Friedland, "Class Power and Social Control: the War
on Poverty," *Politics and Society*, vol. 6, no. 4 (1976); G. Esping-Anderson, *Politics
Against Markets* (Princeton: Princeton University Press, 1984); A. Przeworski and J.
Sprague, *Paper Stones* (Chicago: University of Chicago Press, 1986).

8. Michael Burawoy, in a personal communication, suggested the tension in my work
between these two missions of salvation.

the most powerful way of accomplishing these two goals.

Does this combination constitute the basis for a new subtradition within Marxism? If it is part of a subtradition, I would not characterize this so much as the joining of *quantitative techniques* and conceptualization, but of systematic empirical research and conceptualization. I do not in any way privilege quantitative analysis over qualitative data as bases for empirical investigation. The kinds of data used to engage empirical problems should be strictly determined by the questions being asked and the evidence needed to discriminate between alternative answers. What is characteristic of the empirical research in this "new subtradition," then, is not so much its reliance on statistical procedures as such, but its stress on the importance of formulating explicit causal models of *variations* in the theoretical objects of the research. The actual research can take forms as diverse as quasi-experimental designs of comparative qualitative case studies, as in Burawoy's work in industrial sociology, or multivariate quantitative data analysis. The critical point is that the causal models (or what I have called in a more Marxian voice "models of determination") are explicit and that they are deployed to explain variations.

2 Theory and Evidence

2.1 *You argue that concepts are constrained by theoretical frameworks (p. 20) and that data are constrained by "real mechanisms in the world" (p. 58). But while you elaborate the conceptual constraints, the empirical constraints on data remain unclear. What are these "real mechanisms" and how do they constrain the data?*

To claim that data are constrained by real mechanisms in the world is to reject the idealist claim that "facts" are *entirely* produced by "discourses." A radical idealist view of data is based on three correct theses:

1. Our theories determine what questions we ask.

2. Our conceptual frameworks determine the categories in terms of which we make our observations and thus determine what we can see.

3. There is therefore no such thing as theory-neutral or concept-neutral facts.

From these correct premises, however, an unjustified conclusion is drawn: facts are wholly constituted by theories. While concepts may determine what we *can* see (the range of *possible* observations), it does not follow from this that they determine what we *do* see (the actual observations within that range). The "transcendental realist" argument against idealism is that within the range of possible facts determined by our concepts, real mechanisms in the world, mechanisms that exist independently of our theories, determine our actual observations.[9] It is in this sense that data is constrained by the world, not just by our theories of the world.

A realist claim of this sort is based on a distinction between three domaines of "reality", which Bhaskar calls the domaine of the *real*, of the *actual* and the *empirical*, to which correspond three ontological categories: *mechanisms, events* and *experiences*.[10] Bhaskar argues that mechanisms should be seen as generating events, and these events, in conjunction with various conditions of perception/observation, in turn generate our experiences (that is, observed "facts"). In a simple way this can be diagramed as follows:

Figure 1   Logic of Production of Facts in a Realist Philosophy of Science

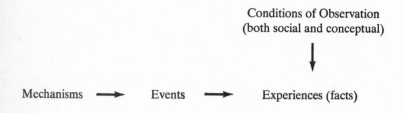

The claim that experiences are not identical to events and mechanisms is the basis for the rejection of empiricism; the claim that experiences are shaped by mechanisms and events (and not entirely explainable by conditions of perception) is the basis for the rejection of radical idealism. One of the pivotal consequences of this position in the philosophy of science is that it helps to explain how factual anomalies are produced within theories. If theories were entirely self-confirming, if they determined the actual experiences of the observer, then anomalies

---

9. I am following R. Bhaskar, *A Realist Theory of Science* (Brighton: Harvester Press, 1978) in adopting the expression "transcendental realism." This position is contrasted both to what Bhaskar calls "transcendental idealism" (the view that facts are wholly constituted by concepts) and what he calls empirical realism, or what is generally called simply empiricism (the view that there is an identity between facts and mechanisms).

10. Bhaskar, ibid., p. 56.

would not occur: theories could produce facts entirely consistent with the theories. Observational anomalies are possible because the real mechanisms in the world that exist independently of our theories shape our actual observations.

Question 2.1 asks "what are these 'real mechanisms' and how do they constrain the data?" The answer to that question, of course, depends entirely upon the substantive problem under consideration. The real mechanisms in the formation of class consciousness are different from the real mechanisms in the production of economic crisis. And the specific ways in which they constrain data also vary with substantive problem. It is the central task of scientific theories—at least if one adopts a realist perspective on theory construction—to try to understand these mechanisms.

Let me give a specific empirical example of these issues to try to add further clarity to the problem of the interaction of real mechanisms and conceptual categories in the production of "data." Let us look at the problem of class formation, specifically at the formation of what might be termed ideological class coalitions. Class *structures* can be viewed as a relational terrain upon which multiple possible class formations can be historically created. One of the tasks of class analysis is to study the process by which these possibilities are actualized. One kind of data that is relevant to observing class formations is the distribution of ideologies across various categories in the class structure. When the people in different class locations share similar ideological configurations, we can say that they are part of a common ideological class coalition. Now, to explore this set of issues several critical conceptual tasks have to be accomplished: we must abstractly specify what we mean by class structure and by ideology; we must operationalize these abstract concepts into observational categories; and we must gather observations using those categories based on those abstractions. For argument, let us suppose that we have adopted the class structural framework advocated in *Classes*. This implies that the class structure can be represented as a multidimensional matrix of locations determined by the distribution of exploitation-generating assets. Figure 2 indicates how I will represent this matrix for present purposes.[11]

Now, on the basis of the logic of this conceptualization of class structure, it is possible to specify a range of possible ideological class formations that could be built on this structural foundation. Several of these are illustrated in Figure 3.

---

11. This is a slight simplification of the elaboration in Chapter 3 of *Classes*, since the distinction between capitalists and small employers has been dropped.

Figure 2   Matrix of Class Locations within the Class Structure of
Contemporary Capitalism

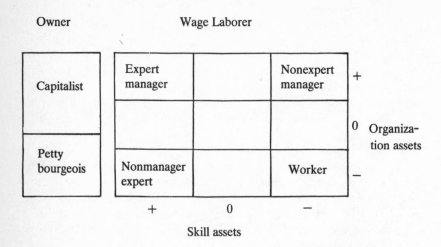

Let us suppose that after we elaborate and operationalize our concepts and conduct our observations, we obtain an empirical map similar to model 1: that is, workers and capitalists are ideologically polarized with an ideological buffer "middle-class" coalition in between. The realist framework for understanding the production of these data implies a particular agenda for someone who is skeptical about the interpretation of these "facts." The burden on such a critic is to propose an alternative explanation for the results, for the "experiences" represented in the empirical map. The critic has a *double* task: first, to elaborate an alternative account of underlying mechanisms, and second, to explain how, with those alternative generative mechanisms, these results are produced by the conceptual framework of the observer. That is, the critic needs to present a model of the *conditions of possibility* for these observations given an alternative theory of generative mechanisms.

For example, let us suppose someone objects to this asset-based exploitation model of the relation between class structure and class formation and argues that ideological formations are not the result of such mechanisms at all, but of the strategies of political parties. Parties, of course, operate under theories, and if party leaders *believe* that something like model 1 in Figure 3 below explains ideological proclivities, then they may adopt strategies which in fact produce these results. Party strategies may generate self-fulfilling prophecies: if the leadership of socialist parties believes that only workers are amenable to socialist

Figure 3 Formable and Unformable Class Formations in Contemporary Capitalism

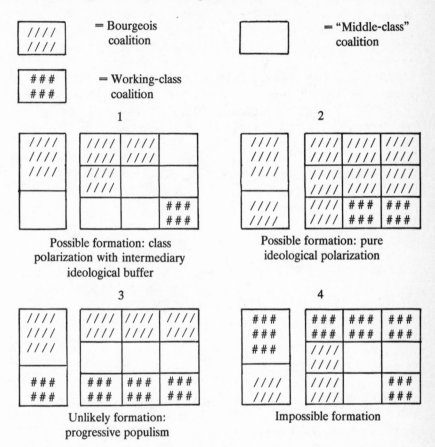

Possible formation: class polarization with intermediary ideological buffer

Possible formation: pure ideological polarization

Unlikely formation: progressive populism

Impossible formation

ideas, and organize their mobilization drives accordingly, then only workers will be prosocialist ideologically. But—it might be argued— workers actually have no greater inherent predisposition to accept such ideas than do people in any other class category. The same argument holds for the strategies of parties supporting pro-capitalist ideologies or any other kind of ideology. The distribution of ideologies in a population, then, would not be the result of any inherent or natural susceptibilities of people in different class locations to particular ideologies but of the intersection of the diverse strategies of various parties (and other ideology-producing institutions).

The implication of this alternative view is that *if* we could find a political environment in which a socialist party tried to mobilize capitalists and managers and workers, whereas procapitalist parties mobilized experts and petty bourgeois, then in fact the pattern represented in model 4 in Figure 3 could occur. The only reason it does not occur empirically is because parties falsely believe that people in different "objective" locations are likely to be more responsive to certain ideologies than to others.

This criticism is framed in terms of the requirements of realist theory of science: it not only poses an alternative mechanism, but explains the conditions of possibility for the empirical observations. Figure 4 illustrates the explanatory shift represented by this criticism.

Figure 4   Competing Models of Consciousness Formation

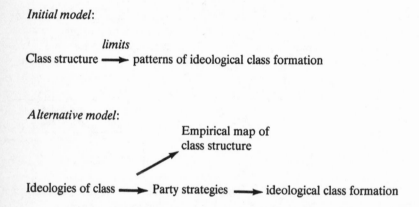

Initial model:

                          limits
Class structure ⟶ patterns of ideological class formation

Alternative model:

                                        Empirical map of
                                        class structure

Ideologies of class ⟶ Party strategies ⟶ ideological class formation

The initial theory posed a simple relationship between class structure and class consciousness: class structure imposes limits of possibility on ideological class formation. The challenging model asserts that the empirical association between class structure and ideological formations is spurious: ideologies of class explain *both* the empirical map of class structure *and* patterns of ideological class formation (via the intervening mechanism of party strategies). Furthermore, this kind of realist critique of the initial model poses a quasi-experimental design for adjudicating the contending claims: what we need to find is a society with the same basic class structure but with parties targeting radically different kinds of people for recruitment. Of course, the fact that it is impossible to conduct the experiment means that it will be very difficult to resolve the debate. Indeed, this is partially why debates in social science are often so protracted. But the criticism still recognizes both the existence of real mechanisms and the mediation of conceptual frameworks in the production of "facts."[12]

2.2 Classes *presents a Mertonian balance between theory and empirical research. In fact, the book seems to be an exemplary model of "logical positivist" scientific inquiry. Is this an accurate description of your methodological views?*

It is often quite unclear to me exactly what methodological prescriptions (virtues or sins) are being subsumed under the rubric "positivism." *If* positivism is simply the view that theory and empirical research need to be "balanced" in some kind of systematic interaction, then indeed I would describe my work as "positivist"—in contrast to both theoreticism and empiricism.

"Positivism," however, is generally taken to mean not just a "balance" between theory and empirical research, but a particular way of understanding the relationship between the two. As discussed by Bhaskar, positivism is generally associated with the view that "empirical invariances are necessary for laws" and that "the conceptual and the empirical jointly exhaust the real."[13] A transcendental realist perspective on theory construction rejects the identification of empirical invariances (constant conjunctions of events) with laws. In its place the more complex understanding reflected in Figure 1 above is adopted: underlying generative mechanisms are seen as producing events which in turn, in conjunction with observational mechanisms, produce experiences (the domaine of the empirical). Empirical regularities are thus always the result of the operation of at least two ontologically distinct mechanisms: the mechanisms of observation and the mechanisms producing the events. This implies that unless the scientist adopts a strong theory of observation, it will be impossible to distinguish between empirical regularities

---

12. The example given above is from debates in class theory. I could equally well have chosen an example from gender theory. Much traditional gender analysis has argued for "natural" differences between the sexes: men are more aggressive, women are more nurturant, etc. A realist feminist critique would argue that some unspecified mechanism (patriarchal culture or male domination, for example) explains the conditions of possibility for the empirical observations of the traditional model. Again, the quasi-experimental design for definitively establishing the realist feminist thesis—the observation of gender differences in the absence of male domination—makes these debates particularly difficult to resolve.

13. Bhaskar, *A Realist Theory of Science*, p. 20.

produced by the observational mechanisms from regularities produced by underlying mechanisms in the phenomenon under study. It is in this sense that theories are a *precondition* for understanding empirical regularities—and thus "laws"—rather than simply a generalization of observational regularities.

This perspective on science is not an esoteric doctrine. It is in fact the implicit stance of most real scientific practice. The search for spurious empirical relations, the insistence on the distinction between simple correlation and causation, the treatment of "laws" as "laws of tendency" (and thus their effects being empirically blockable by countervailing mechanisms) rather than "empirical invariances"—all of these are at the heart of good scientific practice.[14] Positivism may have been the predominant current in the philosophy of science, but it is not the implicit philosophy of the actual practice of science.

2.3 *You use a series of eight questions to determine survey respondent's class consciousness, which you are then able to manipulate statistically as a quantitative variable (pp. 146–7). To do so you must presume that class consciousness is something susceptible to measurement. How do you justify such a presumption?*

Class consciousness is *not* susceptible to measurement. Class consciousness is a concept that specifies a set of mechanisms; what is "measurable" (observable) are the effects of this mechanism. *If* class consciousness is a real mechanism—if this concept actually designates something real in the world—then it must generate events (this is what it means to be a mechanism), and if it generates events, then in conjunction with our observational procedures, these events can generate "facts." That is, consciousness can be placed within the ontological framework of Figure 1 in the following manner:

---

14. The relation between mechanisms, events and experiences in Figure 1 supports the treatment of explanatory laws as laws of tendency. Since the world is an "open system" in which countless mechanisms are operating simultaneously, it is always possible that a given mechanism is present, but its empirical effects are blocked by the operation of some other mechanism. This means that the presence of a given mechanism is not sufficient to produce the empirical consequence; it simply produces tendencies, tendencies whose realization depends upon a range of other conditions. This is precisely why experiments are so important in science: by adding theoretically controlled causes to the natural world—the causes imposed by the experimenter—a law of tendency can be observed as producing empirical invariances. These invariances between mechanism and experience (observation), however, are *consequences of the experiment*: they do not occur in nature.

Figure 5   Class Consciousness, Attitudes and Questionnaire Responses

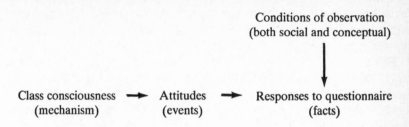

The "facts" gathered in a survey, therefore, are removed from class consciousness in a double sense: first, these facts are removed from consciousness because the attitudes which they reflect are not identical to class consciousness as such; and second, they are removed from consciousness because they are determined by the observational conditions of the survey as much as they are determined by the attitudinal "raw materials" which they attempt to measure.

Two central aspects of these observational conditions affect the nature of the facts embodied in the survey. First, and most obviously, there is the formulation of the questions themselves. The questions in any survey reflect the conceptual frameworks of the observer: not only the topics, but the subtle aspects of wording are shaped by the conceptual presupposition of the designer of the questionnaire. The range of possible "facts" from a survey is thus determined, in part, by the conceptual constraints imposed in the survey design. Second, and less obviously, the administration of a survey to a respondent is a social process, and this process also affects the translation of attitudes (the events produced by consciousness) into data. To just illustrate the point, many respondents experience the survey encounter as a kind of "examination" and are therefore concerned about giving the "correct" answer (in spite of being explicitly told that "there are no right answers; we are interested in your opinions"). The answers, therefore, may have less to do with attitudes rooted in class consciousness than with attitudes towards testing and authority.

It is sometimes argued that the social relational context of survey interviews is so powerful that it destroys any possibility of treating survey responses as measures of the attitudinal events produced by class consciousness.[15] The only observations that are capable of reflecting the

---

15. For a defense of such arguments, see G. Marshall, "Some Remarks on the Study of Working-Class Consciousness," *Politics and Society*, vol. 12, no. 3 (1983).

events produced by consciousness are unobtrusive observations, either from direct participation in the social struggles embodying class consciousness or from the spontaneously produced texts and records of those struggles. While the problem of the conceptual framework of the observer would still be present in such "naturalistic" observations (as they are in all observations), the social interactions of the observer with the people under study would less pervasively influence the "facts."[16]

These are serious objections to using survey data as measures of consciousness-producing events. If one adopts a radically empiricist approach to theory construction in which theories are no more than inductively arrived at generalizations from the data, then the kinds of measurement distortions discussed above would be very damaging. Unless one had reason to believe that the distortions caused by the measurement procedure are random, then any descriptive generalizations built on those observations could not be extended beyond the context of attitudes-in-interviews. Ironically, perhaps, it is within a narrowly positivist philosophy of science that the distortions of survey methods would most seriously undermine the usefulness of surveys as a strategy of empirical research.

If one adopts a realist approach to science, however, the problems of observational distortions in survey research do not necessarily invalidate research using such data. The data from a survey are not used to generate inductively arrived at descriptive generalizations, but to construct quasi-experimental designs for testing various theoretically elaborated causal models. In such a context, a critic of using survey data has to do more than simply demonstrate distortions in the measurements. These distortions have to be such as to produce systematic biases in the results *relative to the theoretical model under investigation.* Distortions can simply scramble results, or they can reduce the strength of the empirical predictions of the model, or they can produce strong empirical corre-

---

16. One could also, of course, reject the basic model in Figure 5 by arguing that the events produced by consciousness are not attitudes—discursively accessible opinions of individuals—but actions (practices). The implicit model would then be that the underlying subjective mechanisms designated by "consciousness" directly shape the practices of actors without affecting their consciously held opinions on anything. Such a model, I would argue, is more appropriately called a model of class *un*consciousness than consciousness. The point of talking about "consciousness" is that we believe that social practices should be viewed as *intentional* actions rather than just "behaviors." And if intentions are important in explaining actions, then it is important to study the various aspects of the discursively accessible subjective states that frame the formation of intentions: the preferences of actors, the views of alternative courses of actions, the theories people hold of the consequences of different choices, etc. These are basically what "attitudes" are meant to designate.

lations completely contradicting a given theoretical model.[17] The distortions generated by the method of observation need not reinforce the theory of the observer—there is no *a priori* reason to assume that the biases have the character of a "self-fulfilling" prophecy (that is, theories need not produce observational biases that are self-validating of the theory). As in any theoretical criticism within a realist framework, therefore, a critic of the measurements in a survey must explain the "conditions of possibility" for the empirical relations generated by the data.

In the specific context of the research reported in *Classes*, there is little reason to believe that the measurement distortions would tend to artefactually produce associations between exploitation-centered concepts of class structure and the empirical measures of class consciousness. So long as the data are being used to adjudicate between theoretically specified models, therefore, the burden is on a critic to show that the results favor one model over another because of the measurement strategy rather than because of the real mechanisms in the theory.

One of the implications of these comments is that survey research in general, and perhaps research on such concepts as class consciousness in particular, is mainly useful for studying well-specified theories rather than for making novel "discoveries" about the world. It is much harder to have confidence in highly counter-intuitive, unexpected results, in results which correspond to no theoretical model, than in results which are strongly supportive of one or another existing explanation. Of course, descriptive anomalies and counter-intuitive results in survey research, like in any other kind of research, can provoke the construction of new theories. But because of the seriousness of the problem of observational distortions, it is always necessary to treat descriptive surprises with particular suspicion in surveys.

3 Role of the Scientist

3.1 *Politics come last in* Classes, *literally: the subject is discussed only in a six-page postscript. Does your scientific method preclude considerations*

---

17. The chronically low explained variances in regression equations predicting attitudes reflects, I think, the pervasiveness of noise in such data. Many respondents literally answer the questions randomly: they do not listen to the interviewer, they are distracted by other concerns, they simply want to get the interview over and say whatever pops into their head without reflecting on the question. The result is that the *explainable* variance in a survey question (that part of the total variance that is systematically generated by any underlying mechanisms) is much lower than the empirical variance.

*of ethical and political issues, or is there some other explanation for the
relative absence of such consideration?*

While it is true that the only place in the book where I explicitly engage
"politics" is in the final few pages, I do not think that this implies that
the rest of the book is unconcerned with political and normative issues.
Indeed, the preoccupation of the book with the problem of exploitation
reflects ethical concerns: to characterize the generative mechanisms of
class relations in terms of exploitation is to bring questions of justice and
oppression into the heart of the concept of class. Similarly, a range of
substantive discussions in the book are centrally preoccupied with political issues: the discussion of the historical trajectory of forms of exploitation and the successive eliminations of forms of exploitation, the
discussion of class alliances and class formation, the discussion of the
relationship between class structure and state structure, and so on. It is
hard for me to see why these discussions are seen as somehow non-
political.

Still, most of the book is concerned with clarifying conceptual issues
and not with politics as such. Whether this signals a "relative absence" of
political discussion or not, it is certainly the emphasis of the book. This
emphasis, I think, is related to my "scientific method": if one adopted a
more empiricist approach to concept formation and theory construction,
there would be little call for such elaborate attention being paid to the
nuances of the concept of class. If the definitions of concepts are treated
simply as heuristic conventions, then there is no need to specify and
justify the theoretical presuppositions of a given definition or to attempt
to adjudicate between rival definitions. The fact that so much of the
book is concerned with concept formation in this sense is a consequence
of the underlying method.

I do not, however, see these methodological concerns as in tension
with normative and political interests. The reason for worrying about
how best to conceptualize the "middle class" is because inadequate
concepts impede the construction of adequate theories, and inadequate
theories impede our explanations of social and political problems. Marx
is famous for saying that the point is not merely to interpret the world,
but to change it. The methodological premise of my work is that in order
to effectively change the world, one must understand it.

3.2 *Survey research and statistical analysis are methods of social
analysis well-entrenched in the American sociological community, which
is not known for its rebelliousness. Is this conformist method at odds with
a revolutionary theory and praxis?*

Any method for generating explanations of real mechanisms is necessarily in a creative tension with revolutionary "praxis," and in that sense could be seen as "at odds" with revolutionary activity. Revolutionary praxis requires deep and absolute commitments, a suspension of skepticism, a willingness to believe in the viability of historical alternatives to the extent that one is willing to risk one's life for their achievement. Scientific debate, on the other hand, requires perpetual skepticism, a constant questioning of certainties, an insistence on the provisional character of all explanations and on the problematic status of all predictions for the future. Revolutionary militancy requires true believers; scientific method rejects the possibility of absolute truth.

The tension is therefore not between something called "conformist method" (whatever that means) on the one hand, and a harmonious couplet "revolutionary theory and praxis" on the other.[18] The tension is fundamentally between revolutionary theory itself (understood as the scientific theory of revolutionary transformation) and revolutionary praxis. The tendency within the Marxist tradition for revolutionary theory to be transformed into revolutionary ideology reflects this tension. Marxism as Ideology provides certainties. It has a ready explanation for everything. Its rhetoric, at least in certain historical situations, is powerful in campaigns of mobilization. When Marxism becomes an Ideology in this sense, it is no longer at odds with revolutionary praxis and commitment, but it also ceases to be a scientific theory capable of producing new explanations and understandings of the world.

The contrast being drawn here between "Ideology" and "scientific theory" is, needless to say, a controversial one. Many radicals want to argue that science is *no more than* a form of ideology. If ideology is defined as any and all systems of ideas embodied in the subjectivities of actors, then of course, by definition, all scientific theory must be "ideology." This is equivalent to simply saying that science is a form of thought, which is hardly a bold insight. If, on the other hand, we use the term "Ideology" to designate a particular structure of thought, a particular mode of cognition in which ideas are ordered authoritatively in terms of some closed system of principles and are not subject to any internal principles of auto-critique and revision in light of "empirical" evidence, then it is no longer trivial to say that science is "just" ideology. This is the sense in which I believe there is a deep tension between revolutionary theory (science) and revolutionary praxis: revolutionary praxis needs revolutionary ideology, but revolutionary theory, to remain scientific,

---

18. The expression "conformist method" is highly tendentious in this question. It is clearly meant to impugn the *motivations* for adopting the method (conformism) rather than to constitute a serious evaluation of the method.

must constantly challenge all ideology.[19] While I believe that it is certainly the case that scientific practices (like all practices), and thus the theories produced by those practices, are influenced by ideology, often pervasively, I do not believe that scientific theories are reducible to ideology.

Question 3.2 above implies that a method of data gathering (surveys) and analysis (statistics) can be used for only certain kinds of theories (anti-rebellious conformist theories). As a matter of historical record, it is worth noting that neither Marx nor Lenin held such views: Marx was involved in survey research (a survey of Belgian workers) and was certainly willing to use the forms of statistical data analysis available in his time, and Lenin did not hesitate to engage in quantitative data analysis where appropriate. This, of course, does not settle the methodological question, for both Marx and Lenin may simply have uncritically used "conformist" methods themselves.

What would have to be true about a theory for survey data and statistical analysis to be intrinsically inappropriate? Survey data is simply data gathered by asking people questions about themselves—about their work, about their biographies, about their ideas. A census, for example, is no more than "survey research" on the whole population. If knowing the distribution of the population into different occupations is relevant for a theory, then survey data are appropriate. There are two bases upon which one could categorically reject survey data. First, on strictly methodological grounds it can be argued, as suggested in the discussion of question 2.3 above, that the interviewing relation so powerfully deforms responses to survey questions, that they cannot be treated as measures of the salient "events" in a theory. Particularly when the attempt is to measure "attitudes," the resulting data, it could be argued, is simply an artifact of the interview and is thus useless in investigating important theoretical problems. Second, apart from the problem of measurement distortions, it could be claimed that the mechanisms postulated in the theory are unconnected with the subjective reports of individuals about their lives, even if those reports could be accurately

19. It is very important in this discussion not to get bogged down in the problem of how best to deploy words. If one insists on using the term "ideology" in the encompassing sense of all subjectively constituted systems of thought, then the tension discussed here can be reframed as a tension between two types or aspects of revolutionary ideology: revolutionary scientific ideology and, perhaps, revolutionary religious ideology. Revolutionary ideologies often become a kind of secular religion, at least in so far as in certain historical settings Marxism involves "sacred" texts, talmudic scholars, anointed priests and rituals which affirm ultimate meaning. As a motivating revolutionary ideology, Marxism shares with traditional religions a preoccupation with telos and ultimate meanings. While god is replaced as the wellspring of that telos by "history" or "class struggle," the cognitive processes in defending the vision of that telos are not so different from theology.

recorded. Data obtained from the reports of subjects would thus not provide access to any of the events generated by the mechanisms of the theory.[20]

The first of these objections has some plausibility, but it has nothing to do with a tension between survey methods and "revolutionary theory"; it would constitute a tension between survey methods and any explanatory theory. The second objection, on the other hand, has no plausibility. While it may be the case, as Marxists have always argued (in good realist fashion) that many of the key mechanisms of social determination operate "behind the backs" of actors, it is certainly not the case that Marxist theory insists that subjects have no knowledge of any of the events produced by those mechanisms. This does not mean, of course, that survey data is necessarily the best kind of data for answering Marxist questions, but simply that it is not inherently proscribed by the explanatory principles of Marxism.

What about quantitative methods of data analysis? For a theory to be logically incompatible with statistical analysis, none of the mechanisms postulated in the theory can produce quantitative variations—either in the sense of variations in *degree* along some dimension or variations in the *probability* associated with some event. While it may certainly be the case that it is difficult to measure such quantitative variations on the conceptual terrain of Marxist theory, there is no inherent reason why quantitative analysis is incompatible with the causal processes postulated in Marxist theory. Again, as with the issue of survey data, this does not mean that quantitative analysis has a privileged standing within Marxist theory. Indeed, a good case can be made that because of the impossibility of adequately measuring the appropriate quantitative variations, statistical research is generally unsuitable for many of the central questions Marxists ask. The point is merely that there is no *inherent* incompatibility between Marxism as a scientific theory of society and such techniques of observation and data analysis.

I think that the suspicion many Marxists have of quantitative methods comes, at least in part, from the common practice among sociologists (and other social scientists) to invert the proper relationship between method and substance. Many sociologists begin with a bag of technical tricks and then ask: "What questions can I address with these methods?" Many dissertations are motivated not by passionate engagement with the substantive theoretical issues in some subfield of sociology, but by a

---

20. Thus, for example, one might reasonably argue that survey research is incompatible with certain types of psychoanalytic theories, at least in so far as none of the salient events in the theory are discursively accessible to the subject.

desire to apply some elegant technique. Students are forced to invest a lot of time and energy into learning these techniques (at least in some academic programs) and thus have an interest in using them in their research. Much quantitative research is thus methods-driven rather than theory-driven.

Methods-driven research tends to produce work of relatively marginal theoretical contribution. This is not logical necessity—one could begin with a method and still ask interesting and important questions. But in practice, methods-driven research usually reflects a general disengagement of the researcher from theory as such. The most profound theoretical problems and debates tend to be quite distant from the practical matters of research and thus considerable theoretical work is necessary to translate those issues into researchable questions. If one begins with methods, then it is unlikely that this theoretical work will be accomplished. The result is that methods-driven research tends to be preoccupied with exceedingly narrow problems, relatively unconnected with enduring theoretical debates.

Marxists—and other theoretically minded social scientists for that matter—thus have good reason to be suspicious of research strategies that put methods at the center stage and ask only those questions which are answerable with a limited set of techniques. But it does not follow from this that they need be suspicious of quantitative methods as such.

In fact, there are many debates within the Marxist tradition that can really only be resolved through quantitative study. For example, in recent years there has been an important debate over the problem of whether or not the technological and organizational changes in advanced capitalism have the effect of "deskilling" the labor force. This has important theoretical and political implications. It is possible through intensive case studies to document clear instances where such deskilling has occurred. And it is possible to elaborate a theoretical argument for why the underlying mechanisms of capitalism tend to generate such deskilling effects. But, as many theorists have also recognized, there are countervailing mechanisms for reskilling, and plenty of empirical examples where this has in fact occurred. The only way to assess the relative causal weights of these tendencies and countertendencies and thus the cogency of the overall deskilling argument is to attempt to measure skills, their transformations over time, and their relationship to various technical and organizational characteristics of work. Such research could involve "surveys" (gathering data from individuals about their work) and would surely involve quantitative analysis (both of the temporal changes in skills and of the correlations between changes in skills and changes in the technical and organizational properties posited in the theory). Again, this does not mean that quantitative methods have any kind of privileged status within Marxism, but simply that there are theoretical questions for which such methods are essential for producing serious empirical answers.

3.3 *Given the respect and prestige which quantitative science commands in the United States, and especially in the academic community, can your method be considered a strategy for winning support for Marxism?*

I first embarked on doing quantitative research deploying Marxist concepts in the early 1970s. From the start, this research had three general objectives. First, and foremost, I hoped that the research would contribute to the reconstruction of Marxist theory itself. Debates within Marxism have always tended to be highly abstract and conceptual, and while historical and qualitative data is often deployed within those debates, rarely had the empirical side of the debates been played out in the form of systematically testing formal causal models. I saw such research as essential if Marxism was to advance as a social science, and quantitative research was one way of doing this.

Secondly, I did hope that by adopting a research strategy that deployed sophisticated design and techniques, Marxism would seem more respectable among non-Marxists, and that this would expand the institutional space for all sorts of Marxist work within the academy. Marxism is often viewed as a purely ideological theory (in the sense discussed in question 3.2 above) incapable of framing its propositions as "testable hypotheses" about the world. In part this characterization is itself ideologically motivated by anti-Marxists, but it has to be acknowledged that dogmatism within the Marxist tradition has also contributed to this intellectual image. "Multivariate Marxism" (as my research strategy has sometimes been dubbed) was one way of combating this image.

Finally, I had some hopes that the research itself would actually convince some people of the theoretical virtues of Marxism. Not only did I have hopes of creating more tolerance for Marxist work among non-Marxists, I had the fantasy that by sheer intellectual energy and empirical power my research would convert some of the opposition.

It has now been ten years since I published my first "Multivariate Marxist" paper with Luca Perrone, "Marxist Class Categories and Income Inequality."[21] What is my assessment of these grand objectives?

In terms of the contribution of the quantitative research I have pursued on Marxism as such, so far the direct results have been relatively

---

21. *American Sociological Review*, 1977, vol. 42, no. 1 (February).

modest. Mostly, the data analysis has served to lend moderate support to particular theoretical arguments about class structure and its effects, but frequently—as chronically occurs in this game—the results are ambiguous, troubled by noise and weak correlations and thus fail to provide compelling adjudications between rival arguments. There have, of course, been some interesting surprises. I had not expected, for example, to find such pervasive and often dramatic interactions between class and gender. My expectation had always been that class mechanisms would more or less have the same empirical effects for women as for men, but this is simply not the case.[22] But overall it remains the case that the direct empirical payoffs of the research have, so far at least, not been spectacular.

Indirectly, however, the research has had significant effects. One of the virtues of quantitative research is the way in which it forces explicit definitions and operationalizations of concepts. It is much more difficult to use vague and unspecified categories when you have to defend a particular strategy of measuring them. Furthermore, in having to formally specify the causal model underlying the analysis, one is forced to engage a range of theoretical issues about the connections among concepts which otherwise might remain unelaborated. In short, being forced to operationalize both concepts and theories can contribute significantly to their abstract reformulation and clarification.

Let me give two examples from my recent work to illustrate this. Perhaps the central practical task in my research has been the operationalization of the concept "class structure." In my earlier work, one of the key elements in this concept was the category "semiautonomous employees," a class location which I described as occupying a contradictory location between the working class and the petty bourgeoisie. As it turned out, it was exceedingly difficult to operationalize this category, to provide explicit criteria which could be used without producing anomalies (for example, an airline pilot being more proletarianized than a janitor). These operational classification anomalies were one of the central spurs to the reconceptualization of class structure represented in *Classes*.

A second example concerns the analysis of class consciousness. In a recent data analysis, I initially wanted to study "class mobility effects" on ideology and constructed a range of models to pursue this task. In the course of operationalizing class consciousness and specifying the causal

---

22. These issues are discussed in "Women in the Class Structure," *Politics and Society*, vol. 17 no. 1, 1989, pp. 35–66; and "Temporality and Class Analysis: A Comparative Study of the Effects of Class Trajectory and Class Structure on Class Consciousness in Sweden and the United States," *Sociological Theory*, vol. 6 no. 1, 1988.

models, it became clear that a unidimensional measure of class consciousness was completely inadequate. Since "mobility" effects tap a temporal dimension of the lives of individuals, it occurred to me that it would be worth trying to rethink the problem of measuring consciousness in terms of what could be called the "temporal" dimension of consciousness—whether the consciousness in question had a forward or backward time horizon. In the end this led to an argument which characterized *class identity* as temporally backward and *subjective class interests* as temporally forward, and this in turn suggested a particular pattern linking these temporal dimensions of consciousness to biographical class trajectories and to current class location. I doubt very much if this reconceptualization would have been provoked in the absence of the operational tasks of quantitative research.

What about the second general objective of my research—creating more institutional space for Marxists in the academy? There is no doubt that there are more radical intellectuals in faculty positions in sociology departments today than fifteen years ago and that more Marxist and other "critical" sociological work is published in major journals. Perhaps ironically, while in recent years Marxism as a theoretical framework has lost considerable support among radical intellectuals, it has gained at least some credibility as a contending and legitimate perspective within sociology in general. I do not, however, believe that this trajectory in the academic fortunes of Marxist theory has been primarily a result of the existence and successes of quantitative "Multivariate Marxism" as such. Qualitative historical and comparative research by Marxists has done at least as much to legitimate academic Marxism in American sociology as quantitative research. Symptomatic of this was the publication in 1982 of the special supplement, *Marxist Inquiries: Studies of Labor, Class and States*, to the *American Journal of Sociology*. Only three of the nine contributions to the volume were quantitative, and neither of the editors of the supplement, Michael Burawoy and Theda Skocpol, uses quantitative techniques in their own research.

While quantitative research has been part of enlarging the influence of Marxism within American sociology, there is little evidence that it has played the decisive role in this expansion. What I think is more important has been the general seriousness with which Marxist and other radical sociologists have pursued systematic research in general, regardless of the technologies deployed in that research.[23] The quality of this

---

23. In this context I couple "Marxist" sociology with other "radical" sociology. Most mainstream sociologists do not make the distinction between self-conscious Marxism and more general radical/critical perspectives. Theda Skocpol, for example, continues to be viewed as a Marxist sociologist by many (perhaps most) American sociologists in spite of her repeated insistence that her work is in dialogue with Marxism but not Marxist.

research both in terms of the conceptual framing of the questions asked and the practical execution of the empirical strategies has often been exceptionally high, and this has impressed many critics of the radical theoretical orientation of this work.

I do not want to suggest that this expansion of the institutional space for Marxist and radical scholarship is simply the result of dispassionate appreciation by mainstream sociologists of the intellectual quality of the work. The acceptance of radical scholarship required the creation of a political climate of relative intellectual pluralism and tolerance, and this depended in many instances on struggle. Nevertheless, in the context of such struggles for recognition, the general quality of research, whether qualitative or quantitative, by Marxist and radical sociologists was important.

Finally, has the quantitative "respectability" of my research actually converted anyone to Marxism? I originally had visions of glorious paradigm battles, with lances drawn and the valiant Marxist knight unseating the bourgeois rival in a dramatic quantitative joust. What is more, the fantasy saw the vanquished admitting defeat and changing horses as a result.

What has been striking over the past decade is how little serious debate by mainstream sociology there has been in response to the outpouring of neo-Marxist research. I have generally been unable to provoke systematic responses to my research among mainstream sociologists, of either a theoretical or empirical kind. A similar silence seems to be the general response to the quantitative research of most other radical scholars. The main effect of my research on the mainstream, as far as I can tell, is that certain "variables" are now more likely to be included in regression equations. What I envisioned as a broad theoretical challenge to "bourgeois sociology" backed up by systematic empirical research has resulted in the pragmatic appropriation of certain isolated elements of the operationalized conceptual framework with little attention to abstract theoretical issues.

It is now clear to me, as perhaps it should have been from the start, that support for Marxism as a social theory is not primarily a question of a belief in its analytical and explanatory power. It is primarily a political question. The production of systematic and rigorous research, therefore, could not in and of itself "convert" anyone to Marxism. For one thing, on the basis of research alone no one would be convinced of the importance of the questions being asked. For another, the distance between the conceptual framework of any general theory and the concrete results of an empirical study is too great for anyone to be convinced of the virtues of the former simply because of the empirical power of the latter. And finally, the results of quantitative analyses in sociology, if presented honestly, are always so messy and filled with ambiguities and inconsistencies, that without any other reasons for adopting a particular set of theoretical commitments, the results by themselves could never convince someone to abandon one general framework for another.

It might be concluded from these observations that quantitative research, and perhaps all empirical research, is *irrelevant* to extending the influence of Marxist theory. This would be, I believe, a false conclusion. While politics may be at the heart of the explanation for why intellectuals adopt particular theoretical perspectives, I do not think that political motivations are a sufficient explanation. The fact that Marxist theory has become an exciting and productive terrain on which to ask questions and pursue research is also important. While the actual results of this research in and of themselves do not convince anyone to become a Marxist, the fact that Marxist research produces results—produces new knowledge—is essential if Marxism is to be a contending theory within social science.

THE LIMITS OF WRIGHT'S ANALYTICAL MARXISM AND AN ALTERNATIVE

Michael Burawoy

1 The Context of Our Disagreement[1]

I had just launched myself into the job market in 1975 when Erik Wright, a Berkeley graduate student but unknown to me at the time, called to tell me that a letter of defamation had arrived from a very prominent Chicago sociologist. It accused me of the worst sins of left sectarianism and, so Wright said, had ruined any chances of my getting a job at Berkeley. I had better put a stop to its circulation to other departments. We met three months later when he and a number of other Berkeley graduate students together with a select group of faculty and even the odd staff member organized an undercover interview to resurrect my candidacy. In the end they were successful. In those days students' sense of political efficacy—a dwindling legacy of the New Left—was enhanced by the dramatic political split in the department. It was a time of Marxist renaissance, particularly in Berkeley around *Socialist Revolution, Kapitalistate* and the *Berkeley Journal of Sociology*. Since then Marxism has become a little more established within sociology and 1950s style red-baiting and black-listing is more of an anachronism. But there is no room for complacency. The long struggle against Wright's appointment here last year might have succeeded had the department been less unified in his defence. The denial of tenure to radical thinkers or even their expulsion from academia are a continual reminder of the seamier side of life in the liberal university. Nevertheless, it is true that the political context, both within and outside the university, has changed over the last twelve years and we must ask what sort of Marxism it calls for.

Twelve years ago Wright was finishing his dissertation where he developed his now celebrated reconceptualization of class structure of advanced capitalist societies. His project was to reformulate Marxist

---

1. In this paper I have followed Wright in not appealing to authorities and texts to defend my arguments and in using examples from my own research to illustrate an alternative methodology. I'd like to thank Carol Hatch for her biting comments on a late draft.

notions of class so as to come up with a class map that took into account the differentiated character of contemporary capitalist class structures without losing the Marxian idea of class polarization. It was, of course, more than a retheorization of class. It used Michigan Survey data to map the contours of the American class structure and to demonstrate that a Marxian notion of class can more powerfully explain income inequality than theories relying on human capital or status attainment. It combined conceptual rigor with empirical adjudication that has become the hall-mark of Wright's work. At that time I too was completing my dis-sertation which by a coincidence neatly complemented his own, in that it examined the microdynamics of class within a single capitalist firm. We were both committed to what was then called "Marxist structuralism" and our intellectual mentors were Louis Althusser, Etienne Balibar, and Nicos Poulantzas.

On reflection my commitment to this Marxist science was thrust upon me by the Chicago sociology department, dominated by a narrow-minded hostility to Marxism. To demonstrate that Marxism, for me sharply distinguished from sociology, could more effectively explain social phenomena became a survival strategy. Wright, on the other hand, from the beginning was a deep-seated believer in the virtues of science. Just as Wright's move to Madison only reinforced his commit-ment to the pursuit of science as universal truth, the atmosphere at Berkeley stimulated my own doubts about Marxist science, at least as I had been practicing it. We have never argued out our differences in print. I am, therefore, delighted that the *Berkeley Journal of Sociology* should have celebrated Wright's return to Berkeley by asking him to elaborate some of the assumptions underlying his Marxism. I'm even more delighted to have this opportunity to respond.

2 Science and Revolution

Let us go to the heart of the matter. Of all Wright's claims I find the one that science and revolution are antithetical the most disturbing. Certainly the unity of science and revolution, has traditionally been seen as the core of Marxism and symbolized by the lives of all the great Marxists: Marx, Engels, Trotsky, Luxemburg, Lukács, Lenin, and Gramsci. Wright comes to a different conclusion. "Revolutionary militancy requires true believers; scientific method rejects the possibility of absolute truth . . . Marxism as Ideology provides certainties. It has a ready explanation for everything. Its rhetoric, at least in certain histori-cal situations, is powerful in campaigns of mobilization. When Marxism becomes an Ideology in this sense, it is no longer at odds with revolutionary praxis and commitment, but it also ceases to be a scientific theory capable of producing new explanations and understandings of the world." These characterizations of revolution and science strike me as odd. Revolutionary activity requires true believers to be sure but it also requires a willingness to change one's views, to adopt new strategies at critical conjunctures. Was not a certain revolutionary skepticism the secret of Lenin's success and that it was sometimes found wanting the secret of Trotsky's ultimate demise? Equally, as I shall be at pains to show, the skepticism of the scientist is ineffective without passionate commitment not just to the scientific enterprise but also to a given theoretical framework. A certain dogmatism is necessary to discipline and channel the readiness to abandon one set of beliefs for another. Without dogmatism there is only chaos.

Given then that the opposition of science and revolution is far from obvious, indeed arbitrary, what are we to make of Wright's insistence on that opposition? It permits a shift of commitment away from revolution toward science. As individuals we have to make a choice, he seems to be saying, either we take the high road of science with its inherent skepticism toward final truth or we take the low road of revolution with a religious commitment to a mobilizing ideology.[2] Society also has to make a choice: at the extremes we have the repression of science—the Stalinist solution—and on the other side we have the repression of revolution—the liberal solution. Wright appears to be more inclined to opt for the latter.

By presenting, what I believe to be a false antithesis, he readjusts the relationship between truth and politics. In his Berkeley days, he had "visions of glorious paradigm battles, with lances drawn and the valiant Marxist knight unseating the bourgeois rival in a dramatic quantitative joust. What is more, the fantasy saw the vanquished admitting defeat and changing horses as a result" (p. 44). There was an unquestioning faith that truth would serve the Marxist cause, adopted on political and moral grounds. Now, the tables are turned and the ultimate grounding of Marxism is its truth. If it is not true then it is not politically defensible. For Wright to call himself a Marxist is to believe that Marxist theories are true or more precisely the closest approximation to the truth. They are the most faithful maps of the world we possess. Should feminism

2. Wright puts to rest any doubt where he stands in the choice. In note 19 he writes, "As a motivating revolutionary ideology, Marxism shares with traditional religions a preoccupation with telos and ultimate meanings. While god is replaced as the wellspring of that telos by 'history' or 'class struggle,' the cognitive processes defending the vision of that telos are not so different from theology."

demonstrate a greater "truth," produce better explanations, then he would transfer his commitment.[3]

It is no longer Marxism per se that is emancipatory but its truth, its correspondence with the "real" world. Wright believes that the pursuit of an autonomous science, what we used to call "theoretical practice" after Althusser, is a necessary weapon of emancipation. Bhaskar supplies the rationale: "the essential movement of scientific theory will be seen to consist in the movement from the manifest phenomenon of social life, as conceptualized in the experience of the social agents concerned, to the essential relations that necessitate them. Of such relations the agents involved may or may not be aware. Now it is through the capacity of social science to illuminate such relations that it may come to be 'emancipatory'. But the emancipatory potential of social science is contingent upon, and entirely a consequence of, its contextual explanatory power."[4] As scientific knowledge approaches a cognitive appropriation of the real mechanisms it will be a more effective instrument of emancipation.

When social science shows that pre-existing ideas are false and at the same time necessarily generated by real mechanisms, then we have a critique of ideology as false consciousness. This is how Bhaskar can claim that scientific Marxism is also critical theory.[5] Establishing the discrepancy between a "scientifically proven" reality and the commonly accepted reality becomes a road to emancipation. It is a form of idealism at odds with the materialist theses that ideas cannot be abstracted from the context of their production and that they have a social force only when they resonate with the interests of actors. It is no accident that a

---

3. As I shall argue below there is no danger of demonstrating the superiority of feminism over Marxism or *vice versa*. Such broad frameworks with their very different problematics are incommensurable. The corollary is that Marxists who abandon Marxism because it is false are rationalizing a rejection based on other, usually political or moral, grounds. So I predict that Wright will always be a Marxist, despite his skepticism.

4. R. Bhaskar, *The Possibility of Naturalism* (New York: Humanities Press, 1979), p. 32.

5. Here Wright departs somewhat from Bhaskar. When Wright says that "scientific Marxism is a variety of critical theory" he means to restrict the standpoint of critique to tendencies immanent in reality. Those tendencies are discovered scientifically by penetrating appearances to real mechanisms. By identifying what could be with what ought to be he avoids arbitrary or utopian moral critique. But what if there are a multiplicity of tendencies? What happens if those tendencies point only to a bleaker future? Can one even decide what those tendencies are? For example, Wright has a fascinating theory of history in which the movement from one epoch to another entails progressive elimination of forms of exploitation. This is indeed a bold conjecture but is there any reason to believe it apart from its aesthetic and optimistic qualities? Could one even justify it on scientific grounds? Is it not a morality wrapped in the guise of science, a morality that is grounded in extra-scientific assumptions? Anyway Wright is just not clear about the relationship between normative and scientific claims.

thorough going realism ends up as a form of idealism. They are natural
bedfellows. Endowing the pursuit of "truth" with an emancipatory function justifies the eclipse of the material forces of revolution.

Nor is it difficult to understand why it might be appealing to bracket
revolution in order to give science undiluted attention. These are not
revolutionary times here. It is just difficult to be a revolutionary in the
United States today without also being isolated as a lunatic. But that is
no reason to make a virtue out of a necessity, to celebrate the surrender
of revolutionary goals in the name of science, to adapt to the exigencies
of the day.

Furthermore, the demise of radical groups and movements has also
forced Marxism to retreat behind academic walls, so that we are
tempted to adopt other academics as one's reference group. Here there
is the danger that Marxism be reduced to an ideology of intellectuals
whose professional interests masquerade as the interests of all. It has
always been difficult to be a Marxist in the United States; it is particularly difficult when conservative politics are ascendent. So there are
no easy responses to the pressures corroding Marxist ideals. We require,
in my view, a grounding to Marxism at odds with an autonomous
science pursuing explanations of real phenomena that exist in the world
independently of theory. This view of science plays into the hands of
those who would wash them of revolution. We have to seek an alternative.

Is Bhaskar's science then the only possible Marxist science? My claim
is that not only is it not the only form of science but it has no privileged
position among the different sciences. In the brief comments that follow
I want to argue that the realist view of science is fundamentally flawed
on its own terms so that we need not be shy about picking an alternative
which holds greater promise for the unity of science and revolution. I
develop such an alternative which comprehends knowledge as produced
and validated through transformative practices. This applies no less to
scientific knowledge which advances through the generation and then
solution of anomalies that emerge through engagement with the world.

3 Is a Realist Social Science Possible?

Bhaskar's book is called *The Possibility of Naturalism*. He asks what
must be true about the social world if we are to study it as we study the
natural world. He passes lightly over the problems of knowing that social
world. Yet these problems appear to turn the possibility of naturalism
into its impossibility. And I think Wright's work demonstrates this
conclusion.

Wright sets up a model in which "facts" are doubly determined, on the one side by real mechanisms acting independently of our knowledge and on the other side by the social and conceptual context of the production of knowledge. That "facts" are shaped by social practices and theoretical frameworks sets up an insuperable barrier to any direct apprehension of those real mechanisms. We can never be sure what in the data is the result of the mechanisms we seek to comprehend and what is due to the "distorting" influence of the scientific process itself. Furthermore, because the mechanisms cannot be directly comprehended, any set of observations which seem to refute a conjectured mechanism can be countered by postulating an additional alternative mechanism. The inescapably provisional character of any claims about the existence of particular mechanisms leads in two directions: the abandonment of a realist approach to science or the willingness to live with an acute and chronic uncertainty. Wright prefers the quicksand in which we must be prepared to relinquish our views at any moment. His commitment to a realist approach to science is the source of his celebration of skepticism.

Since we cannot apprehend real mechanisms directly there is no way of knowing whether a postulated mechanism corresponds to reality. The best we can do is try and show it is nearer "reality" than some other rival postulate. Let us consider Wright's example of the adjudication of his own and Poulantzas's concept of class (*Classes*, Chapter 5). Here he shows that those people who fall into Poulantzas's middle class but into Wright's working class are more like the agreed-upon workers than the agreed upon middle class in terms of their income and their class consciousness (as measured by Wright's variables). The results clearly favor Wright's concept. But he is very cautious in drawing the conclusion that the mechanism corresponding to his concept is nearer "reality" than Poulantzas's.

First, alternative mechanisms might be postulated that explain the apparent superiority of his class concept. Perhaps some other mechanism is at work which would explain why the people in the disputed category should be closer to workers than the middle class. Wright examines two—gender and trade union membership. When, first, men and women, and then trade union members and non-trade union members, are separated out his earlier conclusions are if anything strengthened. But one can always think of further possible mechanisms to take into account, for example, size of employing enterprise. It might be that those of Wright's workers who Poulantzas regards as petty bourgeois (essentially those who are unproductive or mental laborers) are to be found in large firms which promote greater working class consciousness.

A second source of uncertainty lies in the production of the data. Namely, it is possible that the mode of questioning, and the questions asked predispose the people in the disputed category to give answers more like workers than middle class. For example, research shows that survey respondents are sensitive to the order in which questions are asked. Wright's questions concerning the class position of respondents, which come before the attitude questions, highlight issues of autonomy and subordination in the workplace which would lead unproductive and mental laborers to identify with the working class. A survey that emphasized more the productive/unproductive and mental/manual divisions might give results more consonant with Poulantzas's concept.

Finally, there is the uncertainty of barking up the wrong tree. That Wright's concepts do better than Poulantzas's is not incompatible with the view that they are both wide of the mark and that a third very different set of concepts drawn perhaps from a different theory, say Weberian status groups, does much better in explaining the distribution of income and attitudes. The top of the mountain may be enshrouded in clouds so that Poulantzas and Wright don't realize they are scrambling around in the foothills. So the first task must be to try and discover how far they are from the summit by dropping their rivalry and staring around. They should start by comparing theories and not concepts. Of course, Wright did in fact do precisely this in his dissertation turned book, *Class Structure and Income Determination.* There he claimed to show that human capital theory was less successful in explaining income inequality than his own class theory based on contradictory class locations. But, as he himself admits, such an adjudication is fraught with even more uncertainties than the adjudication with Poulantzas. Given the infinite array of alternative mechanisms they could draw upon and the different ways of conceptualizing and thus measuring income inequality, human capital theorists would have no difficulty in countering with a model that did better than Wright's. And it is just as possible that a theory of status groups could be made to do better than both.

All I want to suggest here is that the process of adjudicating among concepts or theories in terms of their capacity to comprehend mechanisms which exist independently of our knowledge but whose existence we can only apprehend through that knowledge is not just a hazardous but a futile task. Wright is only too well aware of its pitfalls but still feels that through skepticism and honesty we can approach the truth.

4 Adjudication versus Puzzle Solving

It is not just that adjudication in the hunt for real mechanisms is futile but it comes at great cost. Let us return to the example of Wright versus Poulantzas. How might Poulantzas have responded? Poulantzas's agenda was to understand how advanced capitalism survived the revolutionary temper of the working class in Western Europe. One answer concerned the character of the state. A second answer concerned the development of a class alliance between the old and the new petty bourgeoisie. This theory is not refuted by demonstrating that it explains less of the variance in attitudes than Wright's concept of class for two reasons. First, he is concerned with countries such as France (not the United States) where there had been intense class struggle and second, he would insist on more activist conceptions of class conflict (including strikes, participation in social movements, etc.). Of course Wright recognizes this problem, that to adjudicate between two concepts they have to have the same explanatory task. That's why he sets up his six strictures on the Marxist concept of class. Yet even if all Marxists abide by those strictures, their agendas in formulating the concept of class may still differ.

In order to adjudicate between two theories the imposition of homogeneity of explanatory task is even more severe. To adjudicate between Marxist class categories and human capital theory one has to assume that the goal of each is to explain income inequality.[6] This is a dubious proposition since human capital theory is concerned with the efficient allocation of resources whereas Marxism is concerned with the transcendence of capitalist inequalities. In a sense different theories are climbing different mountains. The agendas are different and therefore in Wright's terms they are incommensurable. If it is feasible at all, adjudication can only take place between concepts that have been designed to explain the same phenomena. This can only take place within a single paradigm and even then within a very constricted conceptual space.

Two conclusions seem to follow. First, the choice between theories and often between concepts cannot be reduced to a process of "empirical adjudication." Extra-empirical considerations necessarily enter. In other words the antithesis between analytical and dogmatic Marxism is a false one. Contra Wright, it is necessary to defend the "use of concepts through a variety of other forms of argumentation," including

---

6. Wright recognizes that income inequality is only one concern, and a minor one at that, of both human capital theory and Marxism and that he is not in fact adjudicating between the two theories.

"arguments based on ulterior political justifications" (p. 25). To deny the necessity of dogma is in fact to subvert the analytical process of "laying bare the assumptions that underlie these concepts and spelling out as clearly and systematically as possible the steps involved in linking them together within a theory" (p. 25). I challenge him to defend his commitment to Marxism in terms of its capacity to produce more "truthful" explanations of real phenomena than say Weberian theory. I am not seeking to substitute political criteria for empirical ones. The claim is weaker: empirical considerations are a necessary but not a sufficient criterion in theory choice.

My second conclusion concerns the effect of empirical adjudication on the development of theory. Homogenizing the explanatory tasks of concepts in order to make them compete involves suppressing the problems for which they were designed. Analytical Marxism as Wright defines it has little to say about the problems of Marxism. The essential task is to define the concepts clearly so that their explanatory power can be measured. We hear little about the abiding anomalies of Marxism or of Marxist theories of class: the defeat of the working class in the West and the East, the failure of Western working classes to fulfill their revolutionary mission and of the Eastern working classes to inaugurate a classless society.

Rather than define Marxism first and foremost by the strictures it imposes on the concept of class I would define Marxism by a historically evolving sequence of anomalies, misfits between two theoretical constructs: anticipations and facts. Where Wright sees the growth of knowledge as a process of adjudication through which we achieve ever closer representations of reality I view it as solving puzzles and in the process creating further puzzles. Theories or rather the sequence of theories which compose what we call research programs can be compared on the basis of their puzzle solving capacity or the generation of new facts, anticipations some of which are corroborated. This is not to deny the importance of adjudication between rival concepts or theories but rather to say that the adjudication takes place with respect to the prior elucidation of particular puzzles.[7] The task is not to decide how the world "really is" which seems to be Wright's (in my view impos-

7. Progressive research programs are ones in which puzzle solving leads to the prediction of new phenomena, some of which are corroborated. Degenerate research programs tend to patch up anomalies without generating any new knowledge. Thus, where Wright sees adjudication very much as the capacity to explain what we already know and argues that prediction is futile, I would argue the opposite. It is easy to provide *ad hoc* theories to explain what we already know to be the case but it is quite difficult but not impossible to develop theories that successfully predict hitherto unknown and unexpected phenomena. This is the real test of theoretical advance. The great Marxists, including Marx Luxemburg, Lenin, Trotsky, and Gramsci were all endowed with great prophetic powers.

sible) agenda but to decide why the world doesn't conform to Marxist expectations!

5 Positivist Knowledge versus Practical Knowledge

The argument above adds up to the following: the realist view of science is strong in stating its ontological premises but weak in dealing with the epistemological problems it raises.[8] We can never be sure we are approaching those real mechanisms and the attempt entails a necessary separation of science and revolution as well as the repression of the fundamental problems which define Marxism. The realist ontology does not sit comfortably in a contemporary Marxist chair so we should look around for an alternative which permits the unity of science and revolution at the same time as promoting the progressive development of the Marxist research program—a program that keeps up with the puzzles history continually generates while constructing new belts of theory to solve those puzzles and stimulate new ones. The rest of the paper elaborates such an alternative ontology.

Part of the realist world view is to see only one alternative to itself, namely idealism, that the world is an ideological creation. By acknowledging that the facts are socially produced as well as being determined by mechanisms existing independent of us, Wright is already making a concession to idealism. Indeed, this is precisely what makes his process of adjudication so constraining. Instead of such a strained amalgam of realism and idealism I would propose to go beyond both to embrace a different theory of knowledge. In this perspective the world is neither external to us waiting to be mapped nor is it a figment of our imagination but exists in an inseparable relationship to us. The world does not exist outside our relationship to it. We cannot separate ourselves from the world we study. We create and recreate that world and in the process develop our knowledge of it. There is no way we can catapult ourselves out of our self-made prison. Rather, we have to learn to live within it. There is no archimedean standpoint of objectivity. Or as the young Kolakowski once wrote, "in all the universe man cannot find a well so deep that, leaning over it, he does not discover at the bottom his own face."[9]

---

8. By "ontology" I mean theories about the nature of the world, about what exists, and by "epistemology" I mean theories of how we can know about the world.

9. The feminist critique of positivist science as male science—the critique of constituting the world as other in order to "master" it—leads to the same alternative ontology as I outline here. Of course, the convergence of ontologies does not preclude a fundamental divergence of theoretical and political agendas.

These two ontologies give rise to different accounts of the relationship between theory and practice. The one that Wright defends, which we can call a *positivist knowledge*, sees cognition as reflecting the world. Valid knowledge seeks to copy an external world, which is viewed as a pre-existing entity. This view can be found in the philosophical writings of Engels and Lenin. Both regard political practice as a means of *verifying* theories that seek to capture the real mechanisms that govern the world. Here theory and practice are connected but separate. The alternative perspective, that of *practical knowledge* to be found in Marx's early writings and most succinctly in his *Theses on Feuerbach*, regards cognition as an instrument of adaptation. Consciousness is born of practical needs that develop through our relationship to the world—a world that is constructed through interaction with it. Here political practice is the *basis of knowledge*, theory and practice are inseparable.

Knowledge, in this framework, is a function of engagement with the world. The more thoroughgoing, radical that engagement, other things being equal, the more profound our understanding. In seeking to transform the world we learn about the forces resisting transformation. In this sense, science requires revolution. It is no accident that the most profound and prophetic Marxist thought has come from reflections of those most deeply engaged in revolutionary activity. It is not a passive organization of pregiven data designed to maximize the explained variance that leads to understanding the forces operative in the world but engaging the world, challenging it, putting it on trial.

If science thrives on revolution, does revolution profit from science? That's a more difficult question that we can begin to answer only by following a further implication of our theory of knowledge. If knowledge is produced through engagement with the world, different engagements produce different accounts of the world which are equally valid so long as they conform to certain technical requirements, such as agreement with commonly accepted experiences.[10] This necessarily introduces a certain relativism in which theories correspond to constellations of interests. The production of knowledge is therefore an inescapably political process.

Let us take an example from Wright's reflections. "Whether or not imperialism is a real cause of deepening underdevelopment in parts of the Third World depends on how capitalist penetration actually works, not upon the categories of imperialism" (p. 24). This sounds reasonable

---

10. Because human beings share a great deal in the ways they appropriate the world, so our knowledge of the world must conform to certain common experiences, which are then constituted as facts.

but is it? We have already argued how difficult it is to ascertain those "real clauses" precisely because our data are so colored by our "categories" and because any postulated mechanisms can be saved from refutation by the conjecture of another one. But there's more to it.

Within Marxist theory a seemingly endless and fascinating debate has unfolded as to the causes of underdevelopment. On the one hand there are those who stress the transfer of surplus from peripheral to core countries (satellite to metropolis). This is the premise of Frankian "development of underdevelopment," of Cardoso's dependency theory, of Wallerstein's world systems theory, of Amin's unequal development theory. On the other hand there are those who stress the mechanisms through which dominant classes in the Third World countries pump surplus out of the direct producers. This is how Lenin explains the backwardness of Russia. It is the basis of the theory of modes of production. The underlying premise is that the class character of Third World societies inhibits development. The debate seems as irresolvable as it is ferocious. At stake are the interests of two different classes or intellectuals who represent those classes, the interests of the dominant classes in the Third World who seek to blame not their own domination but external forces for economic backwardness and the interests of subordinate groups who point to the class character of the society in which they live.

But it is obviously more complicated. It is not only that perspectives on the Third World are intimately tied to the class interests *there*. They are also tied to constellations of interests in the imperial power. Radicals in the United States, working on their home terrain, aim their blows at the United States administration's involvement in Third World countries and so they are naturally led to embrace some form of dependency or world systems approach. This speaks to the political reality in which they have to operate. The point is this: to adjudicate between these two theories of underdevelopment is not only scientifically futile but ignores the entrenched interests defending each position. By not acknowledging that theory is deeply rooted in interests, adjudication does violence to the very reality it seeks to explain.

I am reminded of the most insane project I have ever undertaken. Twenty years ago I became interested in the role of education in economic development. For a set of largely arbitrary reasons I decided to study "the problem of the medium of instruction in Indian universities." I wanted to know whether from an educational point of view it would be more effective for Indian students to learn in their regional language, in Hindi or in English. There were different arguments arraigned on each side of the debate and I was going to undertake a scientific adjudication! I planned to administer a comprehension test to economics students in different colleges in different parts of India. Half a class would take the test in English and the other half the same test but in the regional language. Believe it or not I actually carried out this research in four states, chosen for their different language policies in education.

However, I was quickly shaken out of my naivety when I discovered there was no way to isolate the educational question from political issues. The struggle over the medium of instruction, involving demonstrations, riots and strikes in many states, was a struggle over regional autonomy and the class and regional distribution of opportunities for upward mobility. Only from the haven of a distant university could one imagine reducing the problem to an adjudication of the educational effectiveness of those different policies! When I wrote up the research I relegated the results of my enormous scientific labors to a two-page appendix. By ignoring the constellation of interests in the struggle, adjudication not only violates reality, not only condemns itself to irrelevance but, as we shall see, can unwittingly become an instrument of domination.

6 From the Standpoint of Politics

We can now pose two questions. First, how should academic Marxists enter the political fray? That is, how should science enter practice? Second, how should the political fray enter the academic terrain? That is, how should practice enter science? This section addresses the first question while the following section addresses the second.

For knowledge to have an effect, that is become a social force it has to resonate with the relevant practices. So that if social scientists want to shape the world they must work very closely with those whose interests they seek to defend. As the following research underlines, this involvement should embrace not simply the production of knowledge but should extend to its dissemination.

Fifteen years ago I completed a study of the localization of the labor force in the Zambian Copper Mines. At the time of independence in 1964 Zambia was a prototype of the enclave economy. Ninety-five percent of the country's export earnings came from copper production, controlled by two multinational corporations—the gigantic South African based Anglo American and the British Company, Roan Selection Trust. Zambia was the fourth biggest copper producer in the world. The mines were run by white managers, engineers, and administrators. A strict color bar prevailed, in which no blacks had any authority over any whites. In the colonial era the mining companies, trying to capitalize on cheap black labor, had tried to "advance" blacks into higher positions by fragmenting tasks hitherto monopolized by whites. "Africanization" had been slow because of resistance from trade union and staff associations representing white employees and where it did take place it never breached the color bar, but rather shifted its position. In the years after independence several reports on Zambian-ization appeared. Figures were presented showing that indeed Zambians were moving into higher level positions and that the number of expatri-ates was declining albeit at a slower rate. What was the story behind these figures?

In 1968 I took up a position as a research officer in the mines' personnel research unit. My hidden agenda was to study the companies' strategy to the new post-colonial regime. Zambianization of mine employees became the focus of the study. I spent one and a half years working for top management in the personnel field, followed by two and a half years of further research while I was a student at the University of Zambia. In opposition to the "neo-colonial" explanations of under-development, stressing the subordination of the Zambian economy to international economic forces, I chose to focus on the perpetuation of class relations from the colonial era. I argued that all the attention given to the Zambianization of the labor force concerned the movement of blacks into higher positions and distracted attention from the unchanging class and racial order of the organization. Zambianization forecasts had been fulfilled but without undermining the color bar. Where Zambians were promoted into white positions, a new higher position would be created into which the displaced white would be moved. Alternatively an entire department might be Zambianized and at the same time stripped of its previous functions which would be handed over to a new body made up of whites. Naturally Zambian workers and expatriate managers blamed the helpless Zambian successors for the inevitable lapses in organizational efficiency.[11]

Why was no one doing anything about this? Did the government know? Of course they did but their interests, I argued, were to ensure that copper mines continue production. They did not want to rock the boat by insisting on more orderly Zambianization which would have scared expatriates. Futhermore, they were quite content to have expatri-ates running the mines because they were politically weak. Had Zambianization proceeded from the top down this might have provided an alternative base of power from which to threaten the government.

---

11. As I have since learnt, these strategies are quite common in US organizations when women or blacks are "advanced" into higher positions in the name of affirmative action.

The trade unions had been largely muzzled and the workers had been pacified with wage increases.

With the manuscript complete I went to the mining companies, who still knew nothing of this research, to seek publication. They were dumbfounded and told me I must be out of my mind to think that they would let me publish an independent assessment of such a sensitive political topic as Zambianization, let alone one with such controversial conclusions. I protested. 'Was I factually incorrect?" How could I be since I defended my case studies with company "facts" collected while I had been an employee. No, the problem was my interpretation. I got annoyed, threatening to publish anyhow so they compromised by sending me to the government.

Two years previously the mines had been nationalized, cementing the apparently cozy relationship between state and corporation. I went to see the officer responsible for Zambianization on the mines. This newly created position was occupied by an expatriate who had left the mines. It was my fortune that he wanted to clean up the Zambianization program. He read my manuscript and quizzed me endlessly and finally said he thought it was terrific. Why? Because it was an "objective" scientific account. Oh, yes? Well, he said, you criticize the mining companies, the government, the expatriates, the black trade unions and even the workers. So? So it must be objective. Because it culled lots of statistics as well as offering in-depth insider analysis, because it took a stance against everyone, because it would be published by the Institute for African Studies, and because I was an academic it had all the trappings of objectivity and therefore could be that much more effectively used against the mining companies. Science is mobilized not in the abstract interest of truth but in the concrete interest of domination.

This is even clearer if we continue the story. Following publication and the commotion the report stirred the mining companies used it as a weapon against the mine managers to trim their bloated organizational structures. A study blatantly hostile to the mining companies was used by them to advance their profits by streamlining the Zambianization process.

It was profoundly naive to think that by casting out an indictment of the most powerful forces in society, they would be forced to compromise their interests. It is not enough to work with oppressed groups in the research process, the collaboration has to continue in the process of dissemination. Because we don't control the balance of political forces our work can always be used in unintended ways. This danger can only be minimized by continuing engagement and collaboration with "progressive forces" to the bitter end. This, of course is fraught with problems. It is not always simple to identify which are the progressive forces. Nor does one necessarily want to let their world view dominate one's own. Nevertheless, the alternative of staging politics from the academic pedestal is a risky venture.

Whatever its other outcomes engaging those one studies does compel recognition of one's interests as an intellectual, that politics is an inseparable part of every aspect of knowledge production. In light of the above accounts it is difficult to sustain the distinction between an interest-propelled process of discovery and an interest-free process of validation. The role of "observer" is no less entangled with contextually defined interests than the role of "participant." But by not engaging the world one studies one can eclipse the constellation of interests around the scientific process. Thus, although Wright's methodology leaves no space for systematically reflecting on the significance of engagement, this is not to deny that he is actively engaged. But it is an active engagement with a restricted group of academics, who share a common interest—the suppression of their interests as academics. They become neutral arbiters in the search for truth. Those "studied" partake neither in the production nor the consumption of knowledge so the interests of the academic remain unchallenged and hidden.

A strange dualism emerges from the realist perspective in which the scientist is the dispassionate seeker after truth whereas the beliefs of those being studied reflect their class, race, or gender. Paradoxically, Wright does recognize that intellectuals have interests too—he has written about them. And when he tries to explain why his theory has not drawn greater support, he writes, "support for Marxism as a social theory is not primarily a question of belief in its analytical and explanatory power. It is primarily a political question" (p. 45). He, on the other hand, founds his own commitment to Marxism precisely on its analytical and explanatory power. It is not simply that this puts him in a different (implicitly superior) category from almost every one else but the basis of that difference is illusory. Wright's own relentless rigor and honesty demonstrate the impossibility of demonstrating the scientific superiority of Marxism.

It is a trite observation that as academics we are no less subject to institutional pressures, hierarchies, and interests than anyone else. In the preface to *Classes* Wright declares that changes in his institutional position may have affected his work but he has tried to be self-reflective and to minimize the negative effects. Here Wright is uncharacteristically unrigorous. Indeed positivist knowledge has to be unrigorous about its own determination if it is to uphold its claims to universalism. Practical knowledge, on the other hand, compels and provides a basis for being rigorous about the determination of science by the context of its production, validation and consumption. Science is no less socially determined than any other knowledge. Within the university political struggles—be they over a nuclear weapons laboratory, unionization of clerical workers or teaching assistants, affirmative action, academic freedom, or the curriculum—are not a distortion of true knowledge production. Political struggles do not contaminate the pursuit of truth, they are the pursuit of truth. Science is a political process. But what sort of science is this? Let us now look at the theory–practice couplet from the standpoint of the development of theory. Let us focus on the advancement of Marxism as a body of knowledge.

7 From the Standpoint of Science

Wright recognizes a double determination of facts, on the one side by "real mechanisms" and on the other side by the conceptual apparatus and the interaction of subject and object. The elucidation of real mechanisms, I have argued, is an impossible task so I begin at the other end of the determination equation—knowledge shaped by the social and theoretical context of its production. What he regards as an annoying distortion, impeding our grasp of real mechanisms, I regard as the defining character of knowledge.

But, how do we choose between systems of knowledge deriving from different social and theoretical contexts? First, theories must explain commonly agreed experiences as well as being internally consistent. Conformity to such empirical controls and to technical rules still leave competing theoretical systems. Marxists have often argued that the superiority of Marxism rests in it being the "world view" of the proletariat—whose privilege it is to emancipate humanity. When the working class "betrays" this privilege by not embracing Marxism intellectuals deem it guilty of false consciousness. This is the very opposite of a knowledge based on engagement. It is not my solution.

The choice of a particular system of knowledge involves political, moral and aesthetic judgments as well as an empirical judgment. Objective knowledge cannot be reduced to knowledge in pursuit of empirical reality but stems from commitment to the theoretical framework one adopts to examine that reality. It is the anchor within Marxism that allows me to make sense of the experiences produced through engagement in the world, to turn those experiences into knowledge that can then be mobilized to advance Marxism. And by the advance of Marxism I mean the solution of the anomalies at the center of Marxism, the development of what I earlier called a progressive research program.

What do I mean by engagement with the world? I mean actively participating in the lives of those one studies. In historical work I am arguing for a dialogue with the past from the standpoint of involvement in the present. It means making the fact that we are simultaneously participant and observer in society an inescapable reality. That involvement grounds one in the real empirical interests of those being studied—the participants—at the same time that Marxism provides the necessary lens through which to interpret what one experiences through this engagement—a lens which also has an associated set of interests.

When I began working in a South Chicago machine shop, the overwhelming experience was how hard people were working—harder than seemed warranted by the ostensible rewards. From this emerged the question of how consent was organized on the shop floor. I asked my fellow workers why they worked so hard and they laughed at me, saying they weren't working hard at all. They were getting away with murder. How effortlessly they seemed to have accepted management's norms of hard work. What an effective means of exploitation! Perhaps, then, all the talk about the role of state, family and ideology to explain the dampening rather than deepening of class struggle is unnecessary—consent is manufactured at the point of production. Was this true of other factories, other capitalist countries, other periods of history, socialist societies? This was my second question. I conjectured that in socialist countries interests are organized very differently in the workplace. Working in a Hungarian steel mill I was struck by the way in which the organization of production systematically engendered opposition to socialism for failing to live up to its claims. Paradoxically it is in state socialism that workers, although hostile to socialism, actually act in defense of its principles.

The process of discovery is simultaneously a process of validation. Each moment of each day on the shop floor becomes a trial of one's conjectures, hypothesizing that people will react in particular ways to given situations and trying to resolve the anomaly when they don't. This can take place on a very micro level of everyday interactions or it can take place in a "social drama," sometimes provoked by one's own presence. For example, my friend János (who had spent time with managers in their offices and on the shop floor) and I wrote a paper which argued that in a socialist enterprise there is a bimodal distribution of functions among managers. Top managers have to bargain with the state for resources, subsidies, production profiles, etc. while shop floor management has to retain a lot of autonomy in order to adapt the exigencies of shortages. It means that the layers of middle management have no clear function and their redundancy is reflected in disruptive interference on the shop floor backed up with punitive sanctions, particularly fines.

According to the rules of the Hungarian Academy of Sciences if

János wants to publish case study material he must first submit the paper to the enterprise concerned. Well, we did and the Academy was informed that this was not an objective report and was damaging to the company. A representative of top management said that he actually would have liked the analysis had it been of another company but since they wanted to export steel to the West such an article in English wouldn't be to their advantage. [It would be difficult to hide the identity of the steel mill without losing essential detail in our exposition.] The paper was handed to middle management for their comment. It was ritually condemned at a meeting of thirty managers from the plant. We then received sets of written comments on our paper from middle managers, supposedly refuting what we had said. As far as we were concerned these comments only further convinced us that middle managers didn't know or didn't want to admit they knew the true character of work organization. One manager, who had been away when it all blew up, commented in front of another manager that he thought that the analysis was fine. The following day he was furiously berated in a meeting of managers, "We don't need people like you around here." Handing back one's work to those one studies is a way of learning one's interests as a scientist. But it is also a means of validating and developing one's explanations. Though don't expect anyone to like you for it. Don't expect any rosy consensus in the name of truth.

But does this mean we should rule out the use of surveys? The more the survey is abstracted from the context in which it is carried out the more skeptical I am about its use. Surveys that are administered to a community in which the sociologist is already involved are more meaningful than national samples that ride rough shod over diverse contexts. The results of surveys are often more revealing in the effects their use engenders than in the abstract responses to their questions. Let me offer a last example.

While studying for my MA at the University of Zambia I became actively involved in the newly established student Sociological Association. Colonialism had left Zambia with only a hundred university graduates and so the university was grooming a new elite. We thought that one of the functions of the Sociological Association could be to regularly tap student opinion. We did this with considerable success, using questions ranging from domestic and international political issues to the quality of campus food. In 1971 there was a demonstration outside the French Embassy over rights granted to South Africa to manufacture Mirage jet fighters. A battle with the police ensued, many students were arrested and one lay in hospital with a bullet in his thigh. Rather than endorsing student support for government anti-apartheid policy, President Kaunda admonished students and told them to leave matters of foreign policy in his hands. Piqued at this rebuff the executive of the student union signed an open letter to President Kaunda, accusing him of "hypocrisy" and "inconsistency." In response the ruling party organized massive demonstrations of solidarity with the President. Threats to invade the campus by party youth brigades led students to mobilize themselves behind their union executive and barricade themselves in. But the defenses were not strong enough to stop the military, paramilitary and riot police marching on to the campus at 4 a.m. and herding us out into a field at gunpoint. The student executive was expelled and the university was closed down for six weeks.

When classes resumed I and another student decided to run another survey of student opinion. Among other matters we were asking students for their opinion about the closure, who should make foreign policy, the nature of democratic politics, etc. Fielding the survey and publicizing the results generated a furious battle, revealing the true factions on campus and their connections to outside forces. The social and political structure of the student body was laid bare by the sociological investigation, not in its empirical results which revealed little, but through its social and political effects. From this perspective the social context is not a contaminating influence, a barrier to discovering those underlying mechanisms, but becomes the very object of investigation by examining the consequences of applying the survey instrument.

Don't get me wrong. I am not claiming that there is anything "revolutionary" in these examples. What is essential is that the methodology they embody is not incompatible with revolutionary commitment. I am only trying to defend a perspective that *can* be both scientific and revolutionary. Indeed it is a method in which revolutionary activity can give rise to the greatest advance in science. Revolutionary activity is activity that challenges the status quo in the most radical way and therefore reveals most vividly the lines of interests, the constellation of social forces resisting and promoting change. At the same time, the more revolutionary the intervention in society, the more it threatens to transform social and political structures and the more necessary is a science to guide it. At a moment when societal structures are at their most fluid, expanding the range of possible development, we also require a flexible theory to guide us through the uncertainty.

8 Conclusion

I can now return to my original question: what sorts of Marxism are appropriate to the present period? By claiming that theory too was a practice, "theoretical practice" cut the umbilical cord uniting Marxist theory to practical activity. It was designed to create a breathing space for intellectuals within the French Communist Party. It was taken over by some American academics to win a place for Marxism within the university. This was at a time when one could still talk about socialism in the United States with a straight face, when *Socialist Review* was still called *Socialist Revolution*, when the tide of popular struggles had not completely receded from the campus.

Theoretical practice now justifies a rigorous science at odds with radical politics. Political quiescence has cut Marxists adrift within the university to find a new equilibrium, one that is shaped by interests within the liberal university. Professionalization threatens to reduce Marxism to an ideology of intellectuals whose interests are systematically concealed by the veil of neutrality surrounding the pursuit of science. Venturing beyond the narrow community of Marxist academics and engaging people with other interests has two benefits, apart from the possibility of directly affecting change. It makes us aware of our interests as academics and it fosters the solution and generation of anomalies that define the Marxist research program. When the mountain doesn't come to Mohammed, Mohammed must go to the mountain.

Postscript

As ever committed to dialogue and truth Wright read the penultimate draft of the above essay. After making detailed criticisms he concluded as follows:

> The irony in much of your commentary is that many of the criticisms you raise could be raised equally by someone committed to a realist philosophy of science. I found nothing in your discussions of Zambia and Hungary or your comments on adjudication with Poulantzas unreasonable, but I also do not see them as representing some radical methodological alternative. Above all, aside from the specific issue of whether or not one should ever try to bring evidence to bear in arguments in favor of one theory (or concept) over another, I do not believe that there are great consequences in practice from our differences.

I have two comments.

First, examples chosen to illustrate features of one ontology can obviously be understood from within an alternative ontology. Nevertheless, from the same account our different frameworks draw different conclusions. Wright relegates the issues I raised in the Hungarian and Zambian examples to the province of "the sociology of knowledge"—how scientists discover knowledge, how participants respond to scientific knowledge. He sharply distinguishes the context-dependent *production and consumption* of knowledge from the context-independent *validity* of that same knowledge. I, on the other hand, am arguing that the very criteria distinguishing truth from falsehood are themselves contextually shaped. By withholding the academic context within which the correspondence theory of truth gains acceptance he gives it an aura of universality. Realist ontology and the correspondence theory of truth are thereby presented as natural and inevitable. Rival ontologies such as the one explored here and rival epistemologies such as the consensus view of truth (in which truth is what we agree to be true) or the pragmatic view (in which truth is what works) are not so much as mentioned. And so the consequences of his analytical Marxism (the inability to ever know whether one is approaching truth, the opposition of science and revolution, and the emphasis on adjudication at the expense of the examination of anomalies that face Marxism) are presented as the unavoidable if unpleasant facts of scientific life when in reality (!) they are products of a particular ontology and a particular epistemology.

Second, I leave it to the reader to decide whether there are significant differences in the way we practice Marxist science. But to the extent that there are similarities, this may not be because holding divergent theories of knowledge makes no difference but because we don't follow our prescriptions. On the basis of realism and a correspondence theory of truth alone I don't believe Wright would be able to defend his commitment to Marxism. In my own case, in order to persuade academic audiences of the validity of Marxism, I adopted their criteria of truth and falsehood. It was a defensive maneuver whose implications I have only slowly and dimly begun to recognize. While I think it imperative to continue the war on that front and here Wright's work is critical because it is consonant with conventional sociological practices, nevertheless the more urgent task is to try and practice the methodology I have proposed in this essay. To save sociology or to save Marxism—that is the question!

REPLY TO BURAWOY

Erik Olin Wright

I would like to briefly discuss three issues raised in Michael Burawoy's comments: the tension between commitment and skepticism in science and revolution; the relationship between knowledge and emancipation; and the relationship between a realist ontology and scientific knowledge.

1 The Tension Between Commitment and Skepticism

From early in its history, Marxism has been troubled by tendencies for Marxist theory to degenerate into Marxology. Debates over theoretical issues are often waged through an idiom of interpretation of *texts* of Marx (or Lenin or Stalin or Mao, depending upon the historical context). Scientific writings become viewed as sacred texts in which authoritative readings become the criteria for truth. This is the sense in which Marxism can become more like a theology than a science. Any defense of the harmonious "unity of theory and practice" needs to be able to account for the strength of this tendency within the Marxist tradition.

In my comments I suggested that this tendency reflects an inherent *tension* (not polar opposition, but tension) between the psychological states required for revolutionary practice and scientific activity. The former, I said, required absolute commitment; the latter, perpetual skepticism. Since Marxism was simultaneously the ideological foundation of revolutionary movements and the theoretical foundation of a social science, it embodies this tension and, in certain times and places, one mode or the other dominates.

The rhetoric with which I expressed this tension was perhaps somewhat overdrawn. It is certainly excessive to say that revolutionary movements require "true believers" instead of open-minded activists prepared to learn from their mistakes. The image I conveyed was of the revolutionary as fanatic, and while tendencies toward fanaticism may be inherent in revolutionary movements, revolutionary commitment itself does not entail fanaticism. And, as Burawoy points out, it is equally essential for the advance of Marxist science that theoreticians have passionate commitments. No one would ever be a Marxist simply from a dispassionate weighing of the evidence and argument in its favor, without extra-scientific commitments.

To say that scientists need deep commitments and revolutionaries need open-mindedness, however, is not to deny that a tension between these modes of thought exists. It may be true, as Burawoy suggests, that without dogmatism (or at least some degree of dogmatism) there is only chaos, but this does not eradicate the tension between the intellectual rigidity encouraged by dogmatism and the intellectual flexibility required to learn new things. What I described as the tension between revolutionary practice and revolutionary theory, therefore, may equally be a tension within the practice of revolutionary theory, but it remains a tension nevertheless.

2 Knowledge and Emancipation

Burawoy poses an interesting contrast between the view that "truth would serve the Marxist cause" and the view that "the ultimate grounding of Marxism is its truth." He believes that there was a time in which I believed the first of these statements, but that I am now committed to the second. Thus, if I came to believe that Marxism was not true—or, perhaps more precisely, that some alternative theoretical perspective was closer to the truth—then I would abandon Marxism.

Burawoy is correct in this conclusion: I would abandon Marxism if I came to believe that it was false relative to a rival theory *that attempted to explain the same things.* But the initial contrast he draws between truth serving the "Marxist cause" and Marxism being grounded in truth is a misleading one and leads to misinterpretations of the implications of this conclusion. I would reformulate the contrast by saying that I believe that truth serves the cause of *emancipation* (where emancipation is understood as the elimination of oppression, exploitation, domination) and that "Marxism" is the name I give to the emancipatory theory which I believe is closest to the truth. Thus while Burawoy is correct in saying that if I came to believe that Marxism was false (relative to a rival) I would indeed abandon it, this would not in any sense imply an abandonment of the moral and political cause of emancipation itself. Emancipatory interests are central to defining the kinds of questions I think are important to ask and thus the explanatory objects that a scientific theory to which I am committed should address. My commitment to these *questions* remains grounded in moral and political concerns, but my commitment to the specific concepts and explanations embodied in Marxist *answers* to these questions is based on my assessment of their truth relative to rivals.

This raises the issue of the relationship between emancipatory goals and scientific knowledge. Burawoy quotes Bhaskar as saying "the emancipatory potential of social science is contingent upon, and entirely a consequence of, its textual explanatory power." This, Burawoy says, is a form of idealism for it sees ideas as having a social force (an emancipatory potential) independently of the interests of actors. There are two comments I would like to make on this issue.

First, I agree entirely with Burawoy that the social efficacy of ideas is contingent upon the ways in which they resonate with interests. "Truth" *per se* has no effects. Contrary to Burawoy, however, I do not think that there is anything whatsoever inherent in a realist perspective on knowledge that implies that ideas should have an autonomous social effectivity. A realist would say that in order to understand the effects of ideas we must study the real mechanisms through which ideas work in the world. These mechanisms would include a range of psychological mechanisms (through which ideas are "heard" and incorporated into cognitive and motivational structures) and institutional mechanisms (through which ideas are disseminated). It is entirely plausible that as a general "law" in the sociology of knowledge we might decide that ideas have social impact only when they resonate with the interests of actors. This claim about the conditions for ideas to have causal weight in the world, however, does not follow logically from any epistemological premises. It is a substantive claim about how the world works, not an *a priori* philosophical assertion.

Second, I cannot defend rigorously my assertion that scientific truth in fact has emancipatory potential (when this truth "resonates with interests"). It could be the case, for example, that distortions and lies aid the cause of emancipation more than knowledge. It might be the case that people need illusions of grandeur, exaggerated beliefs in their historical efficacy, confidence in the ultimate triumph of communism, in order to engage in the practical sacrifices needed to accomplish even limited emancipatory transformations. A scientific analysis which convinced people that historical materialism was false (that is, that communism was not inevitable) might thus in fact reduce the chances for even partial emancipation. Since I believe that partial emancipation is preferable to no emancipation, it might therefore be the case that defending strong historical materialism (which I believe to be a false theory) could serve the cause of emancipation (or the "Marxist cause" if you prefer). Such a situation would pose a serious moral and intellectual dilemma for me: would I support ideas which I believed to be false when I also believed them to be emancipatory?

If the interests served by particular ideas become the essential criterion for their "truth," the above dilemma of believing certain ideas to be simultaneously false and yet emancipatory would be reframed as a conflict between two interests held by a theorist: their interests as academics (which leads them to adopt realist-type criteria for truth) and their interests as Marxists (which leads them to hold emancipatory criteria for truth). The theorist thus simply has to choose which of these interests is more important: is it more important to be an academic or a Marxist? As Burawoy says, "to save sociology or to save Marxism—that is the question."

This seems to me to be an unsatisfactory resolution of the dilemma. When I say that strong historical materialism is false what I mean is that I can marshal evidence and argument which, if presented to a revolutionary *who was willing to listen and to rationally weigh the issues*, would lead that revolutionary to reject strong historical materialism. It would not necessarily lead the revolutionary to reject revolutionary goals, but it would lead to a discrediting of the theory that such goals will inevitably be achieved because of the fettering of the development of the forces of production by capitalist relations of production. Of course, some people will not "listen" and rationally consider the evidence—they are dogmatic in a way that destroys rather than complements skepticism—and thus discredited ideas can remain durably believed. Nevertheless, it seems much more plausible to *explain* this by the analysis of various social and psychological mechanisms of belief formation—cognitive dissonance, wishful thinking, pressures to conform to institutionalized ideologies, etc.—than by the global epistemological claims that truth has meaning only in terms of interests and thus different truths are no more than direct expressions of different interests.

3 Realist Ontology

Burawoy's critique of scientific realism rests on a critique of its ontological position (that real causal mechanisms exist independently of the theorist) and its epistemological position (that we are capable of distinguishing the relative truthfulness of rival claims about the world). These two issues are joined, for the ability to adjudicate between rival explanations of the same theoretical object hinges on the existence of a "real world" independent of our thought, since it is this independence that makes the various strategies of adjudication plausible (experimental and quasi-experimental designs, criteria of internal consistency of concepts and data, etc.). Adjudication may still be fraught with difficulties, and in many cases it may prove impossible to decisively marshal evidence and arguments to differentiate rival explanations of the same phenomena, but nevertheless if the realist ontology is correct, adjudication becomes at least possible in principle.

Burawoy rejects the realist ontology by saying that in his perspective, "the world is neither external to us waiting to be mapped nor is it a figment of our imagination but exists in an inseparable relationship to us. The world does not exist outside our relationship to it" (p. 59). Particularly in the context of social science, there is a deep ambiguity in the collective personal pronoun used in this statement. Is the claim that the social world does not exist outside of *my* individual relationship to it, or that it does not exist outside of the relation of *people* in general to it? The latter statement seems to me eminently reasonable: the theoretical objects of social science are constituted by the relations among people and their practices, and thus the social world does not exist independently of our collective relationship to the world.

The former statement—that the social world does not exist independently of my personal relation to it—does not make sense to me. I believe that apartheid exists, that workers are exploited and that the US government is supporting right-wing movements around the world independently of my individual relationship to any of these particular social phenomena. I could, of course, be wrong about any of these beliefs, but whether or not apartheid, capitalist exploitation or support of right-wing movements exists is independent of me.

Furthermore, with the exception of a radically idealist epistemology, in *all* of the alternative epistemological positions mentioned by Burawoy—consensus views of truth, pragmatic views of truth, realist views of truth—the belief that the social world exists independently of my individual relationship to it would be considered "true." Burawoy's preferred epistemology is what he terms the consensus view of truth "in which truth is what we agree to be true" (p. 70). It would certainly be the consensual view of human beings in general (and certainly of human beings in modern capitalist societies of whatever class) that the social world exists independently of each individual person, and thus the realist ontology would be consensually validated. It is one thing to say that each person does not exist independently of the social world (since we are all constituted as persons within social interaction) or that the social world does not exist independently of people in general, and quite another to say that the social world does not exist outside of my individual relationship to it.

A realist ontology does not logically entail a realist epistemology—the view that real mechanisms exist in the world independently of our theories and our individual relation to the world does not imply the view that we are capable of differentiating the relative truthfulness of claims about those real mechanisms. But a realist ontology does imply that our descriptions of the world, and the theories we construct using these descriptions, are constrained *both* by the effects of these real mechanisms and by the concepts which we use to analyze them. This double constraint at least opens up the possibility for scientific adjudications between rival concepts and explanations of the social world.

3

Classes and Class Analysis

Guglielmo Carchedi

By transporting the concept of capitalism from its production relations to property relations and by speaking of simple individuals instead of speaking of entrepreneurs, he moves the question of socialism from the domain of production into the domain of relations of fortune—that is, from the relation between capital and labor to the relation between poor and rich.[1]

In recent years E.O. Wright has emerged as an influential sociologist of the left. In his most recent work, *Classes*, he undertakes a complete reformulation of his theory of social classes.[2] In this process of reconceptualization, Wright touches upon a number of issues which lie at the core of Marxist analysis. A review of *Classes* is thus an important occasion to clarify the issues and assess the consequences of choosing among the different, alternative, formulations of those issues. Thus, the importance and significance of the following discussion goes much further than the assessment of this work.

There are two dimensions to this work. A "biographical" one, which deals with the reasons for Wright's theoretical shift and with a comparison between his previous and his new conceptualization. In this review I shall not dwell on it. Rather, in what follows I shall focus on the second dimension, that is, on the characteristic features of Wright's new approach. Wright has a clear and immediate style of writing. He can present complex issues in an attractive way. He also undertakes a difficult task, that of providing empirical evidence for a Marxist theory of class. He should be given credit for this and the difficulty of the task should not be forgotten in assessing his results. But, unfortunately, and

---

1. R. Luxemburg, *Reform or Revolution*, in M.-A. Waters (ed.), *Rosa Luxemburg Speaks* (New York: 1970).
2. E.O. Wright, *Classes* (London: Verso, 1985).

contrary to Wright's own conviction, on the whole, his new conceptual apparatus does not constitute an advance compared with his previous one. I shall argue this by examining both his theory's internal difficulties and his claim to be faithful to Marx's political agenda and theoretical goals. Since a point by point substantiation of this claim would require a whole volume, I shall restrict myself to consider only some of the nodal points in Wright's theory.

Epistemology

Classes opens with a discussion of the "logic of concept formation." Concepts, says Wright, are produced by human beings, that is, by individuals. The production of concepts "takes place under a variety of constraints" (p. 20), that is, under both empirical and theoretical constraints. The latter are the theoretical suppositions which determine the range of possible concepts that can be produced. The former are the "real world" constraints and "operate through data gathered using the concepts of the theory" (ibid.). The key word here is "individuals." A critical remark should be made at once.

Wright's epistemology is individualistic, that is, it is based on individual producers of knowledge and thus on individual "actors." Within this theoretical constraint all one can do is to inquire into how classes affect individuals. However, the basic unit of analysis remains the individual, not classes. The difficulty with this kind of "micro-individual logic" is, as Wright is well aware, that it is unsuitable to explain "historical trajectories of struggle and chance" (p. 182). His answer is that people (individuals) are "systematically affected in various ways by virtue of being in one class rather than another" (ibid.) and that his theory explains the effects of classes on individuals better than rival interpretations do. Wright does not consider this result to be a definite proof of the superiority of his theory. However, he sees in this feature an element which lends more credibility to it than to other rival conceptualizations.

Whether Wright's theory is really a better explanation of the effects of class on individuals (as we shall see, he considers the effects on individuals' incomes and consciousness) depends on the validity of the method chosen. This is a question which will be considered later on. Let us assume, for the time being, that Wright's theory does fare better than alternative ones on the grounds Wright himself chooses. This does not show yet that his theory is a better explanation of "historical trajectories and change." But it is this latter which is the basic aim of the Marxist theory of classes, not Wright's problematic. From this perspective, the theoretical link which alone can lend meaningfulness to Wright's careful statistical research is the one which shows that the ability to explain individual features in terms of class positions is also a proof of the ability to explain social phenomena (and thus that the theory which fares better as an explanation of individual determinations by classes is also the one which is more suitable to explain class phenomena). But this is the link which is missing, this is the theoretical nexus which Wright has yet to provide. Personally, I believe that this is an impossible task. Once one starts with a "micro-individual logic," the only way to come up to the social level is by aggregation of individual units. But aggregation of individual units cannot explain the social, that is, what constitutes the units as units of a whole. This is not the place to elaborate on this theme. Here suffice it to mention that the burden of providing the missing theoretical link falls on Wright.

One point should be stressed, in order to avoid misunderstandings. It has been mentioned above that the basic focus of Marx's theory of class is social phenomena and change. This does not imply that the concern for how classes affect individual phenomena is illegitimate. On the contrary, the importance of this area of study cannot be underestimated. But one thing is to inquire into how social phenomena (for example, classes) affect micro-individual ones. This can be done only *after* the alternative theories have shown their merits on the basis of their ability to explain social phenomena *and change* them. Another is to suggest that, somehow, the ability to explain how individual phenomena are affected by social phenomena is an indication of the ability to explain the nature and laws of development of the latter and to bring about social change. This is methodologically illegitimate because one logic of explanation is substituted by another. Moreover, as the last section of this review will argue, in Wright's case this substitution is accompanied by the adoption of a method which has a built-in ability to explain social change, a method which requires a static concept of both structure and consciousness and a deterministic notion of the relation between them.

Exploitation

Having presented his epistemological frame of reference, Wright goes on to introduce what could be regarded as the major element of novelty in his new formulation of classes: the concept of exploitation. This concept is adapted from John Roemer's notion of exploitation and is thus influenced by game theory. Therefore, in what follows I will have to briefly comment on this type of application of game theory to the theory of classes.

For Wright class locations structure the objective interests of the actors (p. 145). One can find two notions of objective interests in this book. The first is that people "have an interest in reducing the toil necessary to obtain whatever level of consumption they desire" (p. 36). The second is that people have an interest in increasing their capacity to act (p. 28). The relation between these two notions of "objective interests" is unclear, just as it is unclear why the term "objective" is used here. In any case, it is around the former notion that Wright conceptualizes exploitative relations. The link is "game theory." In terms of this approach the following question is posed: "if one of the classes would disappear, would there be more consumption and/or less toil for the other class?" If this question is answered positively, then there is exploitation. More concretely, and by way of example, "the lord is rich because lords are able, by virtue of their class relations to serfs, to appropriate a surplus produced by the serfs" (ibid.). In this view, then, the rich are rich because they appropriate the fruits of the poor's toil. There is a causal link "between the wellbeing of a class and the deprivation of another" (ibid.). But this link (1) is at the level of appropriation/distribution and (2) is an ahistorical concept. On the contrary, Marx's concept of exploitation is at the level of production and is an historically specific concept. Let us see why.

In order to conceptualize a general notion of exploitation, Wright shifts his analysis from the level of production to that of distribution. For him exploitation is "an economically oppressive *appropriation* of the *fruits of the labor* of one class by another" (p. 77; emphasis added). But in so doing Wright loses sight of the specificity of capitalism: the fact that exploitative relations are first of all production relations. "In other words," says L. Colletti, "capitalist appropriation is not exclusively or primarily an appropriation of *things*, but rather an appropriation of subjectivity, of working energy itself, of the physical and intellectual powers of man."[3] Suppose that the capitalists would give back to the laborers the surplus they appropriated. This is an absurd example which I use only for didactical purposes, not to build a theory on it, as game theorists could do. In this case there would be no exploitation, in terms of distribution. Yet, at the level of production there would have been no change. The laborers might not be exploited any more in a distributional sense. But the nature of the exploitative relations at the level of production, the fact that the workers would still have no say as to what to produce, for whom to produce it, and how to produce it,

---

3. L. Colletti, *From Rousseau to Lenin* (New York: Monthly Review Press, 1972), p. 102.

would not have changed. Both the distribution and the production aspects of exploitation are necessary. But Wright's "game theory approach" simply erases the latter, specific, one. As a result, there is implicit in this approach to exploitation the notion that if the rich would disappear there could be an equitable redistribution of wealth produced *in the same way*, that is, in a capitalist way, under a system of capitalist production relations. The congeniality between game theory and reformist policies becomes then clear.

Wright's notion of explanation is not only distributional, it is also ahistorical. If one's starting point is that in all class-divided societies there is *appropriation* of surplus by one class from another, then a general concept of exploitation is found principally at the distributional level of analysis. If, on the other hand, one's starting point is that in all class societies there are classes which *produce* for other classes, then a general concept of exploitation is found principally at the level of production. At this level of abstraction there are no compelling reasons to prefer either one of these concepts. If, however, one wants to analyze *specific* types of exploitation (for instance, feudal as against capitalist exploitation) then one has to proceed from the distributional level to the level of production. In fact, a notion of exploitation based on production can be made immediately historically specific by inquiring into the specific forms of production relations. The same can be done for a notion of exploitation based on distribution (that is, how is the surplus appropriated in specific societies?) only if one disposes to begin with of a theory of how that surplus has been produced. For example, the distribution of surplus under capitalism is distribution of surplus *value*, of the surplus produced under specific relations of production. An historically specific theory of distribution presupposes an historically specific theory of production. Or, if one remains at the level of distribution, one cannot descend to the analysis of concrete forms of exploitation. All one can say is that in all class-divided societies there is appropriation of surplus.

It is often said that a distributional theory of exploitation can provide a general framework. This, it is proposed, can then be filled with an historically specific content (specific forms of exploitation) when specific societies are considered, much the same as a bottle can be filled with different types of wine. Unfortunately, in social theory, different wines come in different bottles. From the above, it is now clear that an analysis in terms of production relations, conceptualized as historically specific relations, and one in terms of distribution relations, conceptualized as ahistorical relations, *are antithetical because they are the result of, and presuppose, two antithetical methods of abstraction*. These two analyses exclude, rather than integrate, each other. One method, which is highlighted by Marx in the *Grundrisse,* is based on concentrating and focusing on the historical specificity of a socio-economic system. The other method, typical of bourgeois social sciences, is based on disregarding what is historically specific and focusing on formal, ahistorical similarities. In the case of exploitation, the focus of distribution presupposes *remaining* at the level of ahistorical similarities. It is because of this that Wright's and Roemer's concept of exploitation cannot be considered to be a general case under which the Marxian concept can be subsumed.

One of the novel features of Wright's new theory is that classes are rooted in three forms of exploitation: besides the traditional economic form (based on the ownership of capital assets), he considers also the exploitation rooted in the control of organization assets and in the position of skills or credential assets (p. 283). Wright himself has doubts about his new categorization. To these, I shall add two of my own.

First, ownership for Wright means "effective economic control" (p. 80). To own organization assets, then, means to be able to control them. But suppose somebody has an effective economic control of the organization of capital assets. How can then somebody else own those capital assets? This is possible only if by ownership of capital assets one means *legal* ownership. But this is inconsistent with Wright's claim that "the *basis* of the capital–labor relation should be identified with the relations of effective control (that is, real economic ownership) over productive assets as such" (p. 72). Or, to have the effective economic control of the organization of capital assets means in fact to be able to decide what to produce, for whom, and how; that is, it means to have the effective economic control of capital assets, to own them. The separation between ownership of capital assets and ownership of organization assets is meaningless since to control the organization of capital assets is to own them, in the effective, economic sense. To hold to this distinction would mean to reduce ownership to legal ownership, an absurd result in terms of Wright's problematic.

Second, it is equally impossible to uncouple skills from labor power as a separate "productive asset": the former are what makes the latter more or less skilled and thus more or less productive. Here, I shall not dwell further on this critique. I shall only consider one aspect of Wright's "skill exploitation" to indicate the width of the gulf separating Marx's and Wright's concept of exploitation.

Skills exploitation is based on credentials. "When credentials are operating, employers will bid up the wage of the owners of the credentials above the costs of producing the skills" (p. 76). This means that the owners of credentials (skills) exploit the nonowners. In terms of the Marxian labor theory of value, this only explains the payment of wages higher than the value of labor power due to a situation favorable to the sellers of labor power: in short, the laborers with credentials reduce their exploitation. In Wright's theory this is a case in which the laborers with credentials exploit those without credentials, that is, both other laborers and the capitalists.

Four more considerations can be made on Wright's use of game theory. First, the game theory approach explains at most the actors' behavior. It is thus powerless to explain the laws of motion of society: yet this is the core of Marxist analysis. The game theory approach is thus perfectly consistent with Wright's individualistic epistemology but both are inconsistent with a Marxist approach to social phenomena. Second, for Wright "the labor-transfer approach to studying exploitation and class is a powerful and compelling one under certain simplifying assumptions . . . [but] it runs into difficulty . . . when some of these assumptions are relaxed" (p. 67). It is because of these "complications" that a second strategy is introduced, the "game theory approach." One of the two. Either one does not relax those simplifying assumptions, and then there is no need for the game theory approach. Or one does relax those assumptions and then one cannot use the labor transfer approach and must use only the game theory approach. However, Wright seems to opt for a compromise. He uses the game theory approach but specifies that, to have exploitation, there must also be "the appropriation of the fruits of the labor of one class by another" (p. 74), that is, the appropriation of surplus product (p. 100). But this does not work. In fact, in this case, neither the product nor the surplus product can be measured in terms of labor. How can we know then that "a person consumes more than they produce" (p. 75), that is, that there is exploitation? How do we know, for example, how much a factory worker produces in the absence of a unit of measure in terms of labor? It would seem that Wright has to rely only on the game theory approach. But this implies two further difficulties.

Third, in Wright's game theory approach, "the essential strategy adopted for the analysis of exploitation is to ask if particular coalitions of players would be better off if they withdrew from this game under certain specified procedures in order to play a different one [that is, if they would be better off in an "hypothetically feasible alternative"]. The alternative game differs in the way the assets are allocated (p. 68). But there are no methodological guidelines in setting up the "hypothetically feasible alternative." Therefore, there is arbitrariness in both setting up this alternative and in interpreting the results. Take the unemployed. They are economically oppressed, says Wright, since they "would surely be better off under the counterfactual conditions of the withdrawal rules," but they are not exploited because they do not produce anything and thus cannot be expropriated of the fruits of their labor (p. 75). Wright does not say what this counterfactual condition is, nor can we find anywhere in his book the principles for envisaging such an alternative condition. Should we just let our imagination loose? Would they be better off if they withdrew from this society to form their own society? We do not know. Since they would have no capital assets, they might have to work more and consume less than in their previous situation (where they did not work but did consume something). This comparison implies of course that we are willing to disregard the objections raised in the second point. But let us assume that the unemployed would be better off. This means that they are economically oppressed. Now take the point of view of the employed. In the alternative situation (that is, without the unemployed) they too would be better off since they would not have to finance the unemployment benefits. Who is now oppressing whom? And, if we do not like the results of this "hypothetically feasible alternative" (whatever it might mean), what are the methodological reasons which allow us to discard it and to choose another one?

Fourth, as implied in what was just said, the game theory approach is built upon the analysis of phantastic models. These models are not a simplified depiction of reality, they are not models which encompass only the basic elements of reality. Rather, they are figments of the imagination, "fanciful examples" (p. 74), like the "credit-market island" and the "labour-market island" or the "hypothetically feasible alternative" to an existing situation. K. Kautsky remarked eighty years ago that bourgeois economics rests on the belief that "the best way to discover the laws of society is to disregard them completely."[4] Does not this summarize the nature of the game theory approach as well?

Finally, a few words on the labor theory of value. There are incontrovertible signs that Wright abandons it. Let me mention briefly four examples. First, organization, skills and capital are productive assets on a par with labor power. For the Marxian labor theory of value, on the other hand, only labor power is the source of value: other factors can only increase its productivity. Thus, Wright chooses a variant of the "factors of production" approach. Second, exploitation is "rooted in the monopolization of crucial productive assets" (p. 106). It is, in other words, the appropriation of the surplus product (p. 100) as a result of a monopolistic situation (p. 101). This is a purely redistributional concept. Third, the "value" of a commodity is the price it would have in conditions of perfect competition (p. 101). Value here is a price category, a misnomer. Fourth, wage is both the cost of producing skills in terms of

---

4. K. Kautsky, *Etica e Concezione Materialistica della Storia* (Milan: Feltrinelli, 1975), p. 112.

labor content (p. 70) and the price of the marginal product (p. 76) but not the tendential value of labor power. Wright quotes Roemer to the effect that "the labor theory of value should be dismissed entirely" (p. 99) without giving, however, his opinion on the matter. But what has just been said shows clearly that he too withdraws from it. The point of this critique is not that Wright casts off the labor theory of value. One is free to retain it or not. The point is that he replaces that theory with an eclectic mixture of elements of different theories while avoiding taking an explicit stand on it. This is unfortunate. The neo-Ricardian arguments, which seem to have made such an impact on Wright and which focus principally on the transformation problem, are unsound. As I show elsewhere (1984), Marx's labor theory of value is perfectly consistent.[5]

Classes

On the basis of what has been said above it is now easy to see that Wright's notion of exploitation does not disregard the ownership of the means of production. On the contrary, he raises ownership relations to the status of production relations. The game theory approach is not interested in what people produce, for whom, and how (the production relations). In this approach classes confront each other over the distribution of the product on the basis of property relations (that is, who owns the capital assets as well as the other assets, seen as property). In fact, "property relations of classes ... define classes ... by the productive assets which classes control" (p. 73). Ownership of the means of production is seen here as property, as distribution relations, not as production relations. And this cannot be otherwise since for Wright the class structure "constitutes the basic mechanism for distributing access to resources in a society, and thus distributing capacities to act" (p. 28).

But this is not all. Wright collapses classes (which should be defined in terms of production relations) into distributional groups (defined in terms of the distribution of assets) only for the bourgeoisie, the small employers, the petty bourgeoisie, and the proletarians. The first three categories own the means of production, the latter does not. However, Wright introduces eight more "classes," defined in terms of contradictory class locations. These locations have different degrees of ownership of organization and skill assets but do not own the means of

---

5. G. Carchedi, "The Logic of Prices as Values," *Economy and Society*, vol. 13, no. 4 (1984).

production. They are: expert managers, expert supervisors, expert nonmanagers, semicredentialed managers, semicredentialed supervisors, semicredentialed workers, uncredentialed managers, and uncredentialed supervisors (Table 3.3, p. 88). But, as it has been argued above, if the control of organization assets is simply the economic control (or real ownership) of capital assets and if skills are not separable from labor power as productive assets, the basis for deriving class relations from these categories collapses. We are then left with *occupational* groups, in no essential way different from the categories of stratification theory. Thus, in Wright's game theoretical approach classes are distributional and occupational groups with only a pale resemblance to Marx's original categories. If time and space allowed, it would be interesting to compare Wright's concept of classes with Weber's concept of "class situation."[6]

There are four problematic areas which Wright himself recognizes to be such and for which he admits not to "have entirely satisfactory solutions" (p. 92). The importance of these difficulties for his theory should not be underestimated and they, as Wright says, "may prove 'fatal' to the proposed concept of classes" (ibid.). One of these difficulties has already been alluded to: the identification of organization assets as a separate productive asset (force). Reasons of space prevent me from dealing with the other areas of difficulty. Suffice it to say here that Wright's answers are far from being convincing.

Class Structure and Class Consciousness

When it comes to testing his new theory, Wright inquires into the effects of class structure on individual incomes and consciousness. I shall disregard here the discussion of the effects of structure on income and will focus on consciousness. Basically, Wright constructs measurements of consciousness and relates them to his twelve classes by means of statistical tests. He uses "t-tests" to test the statistical significance of the difference in means between groups (p. 161). In slightly different words: he fills his class categories with occupational categories, constructs measures of class consciousness (on the basis of eight questions), asks a representative sample the relevant questions, and then applies statistical procedures to find out whether differences in consciousness can be explained by differences in class positions. It will come as no surprise that there is no difference here between this procedure and the one

---

6. M. Weber, *Economy and Society* (Berkeley: University of California Press, 1968), p. 302.

followed by a stratification analysis of consciousness. It could be objected, of course, that the difference is in the concepts, in the categories to which the procedure is applied, and that the procedure in itself is neutral. My view, on the contrary, is that Wright's application of these statistical procedures to the study of the relation between structure and consciousness (1) requires a static definition of both concepts, and (2) replaces dialectical thinking with deterministic thinking.[7] If these points can be substantiated, then Wright's basis for "empirically adjudicating contending class definitions" (already challenged above in the section on epistemology) is weakened on yet further grounds.

Consciousness

To begin with, Wright chooses attitudes as indicators of consciousness. He is aware of the weaknesses of this procedure but, nevertheless, chooses to disregard them (pp. 143ff and 188). I shall not repeat them here. Rather, I shall comment on the notion of consciousness employed by Wright. This is revealed by the respondents' answers to eight questions. On the basis of these answers, a measurement of consciousness is constructed, which goes from maximally procapitalist to maximally proworkers.

It will be immediately evident that this is an inherently static definition of consciousness, one which does not see consciousness in its concrete historical conjuncture. The question is not whether, according to a certain scale, a type of consciousness is always procapitalist or proworker, irrespective of the concrete situation. Rather, the question is whether that type of consciousness is a form of domination of one class over another under specific and concrete circumstances. For example, the first of Wright's eight questions is "corporations benefit owners at the expense of workers and consumers" (p. 146). A positive answer is supposed to reveal a proworker consciousness, a negative answer a procapitalist attitude. Is this right? Well, it all depends on the concrete situation. There are enough "anticapitalist" elements in European fascist ideologies to move a hypothetical fascist respondent to answer positively. This would hardly be a symptom of a proworker consciousness. Or, one can believe that "a main reason for poverty is that the economy is based on private profit" (Wright's fifth question; ibid.) without revealing a proworker attitude. This would be the case, for example, of a respondent's belief that there are no alternative feasible social systems and thus

---

7. On dialectical thinking and how it should be applied to social research, see G. Carchedi, *Class Analysis and Social Research* (Oxford: Basil Blackwell, 1987).

that poverty is inevitable. The real, ideological, content of such an answer is then procapital.

The issue here is not that one should be more careful in the formulation of questions nor that the number of questions seems to be extremely limited in relation to the task assigned to them. Even a different formulation or a greater number of questions would not answer the criticism that this method (1) assumes that there are questions whose answers always reveal a procapitalist (or proworker) attitude, abstracting from the ideological context of which they are part (a doubtful proposition), and (2) assumes that the simple addition of these answers gives us the contours of the individual respondent's consciousness.

This method, the addition of the parts in order to arrive to the whole, is diametrically opposed to that of Marx, which starts from the whole in order to explain the parts. In it the parts get their meaning from the whole and thus from their reciprocal interrelation. Consciousness should thus be seen as something in which it is the character of the whole which gives meaning to the parts, that is, as something in which the character of the whole is not given by the addition of the parts *and thus cannot be reconstructed by adding the parts* (the individual answers, in Wright's methodology). According to this alternative approach the same objectively determined consciousness (for example, ideology) is internalized by each individual in a different way.[8] However, all these individuals can be said to share that consciousness inasmuch as they share its dominant features, its class content. Thus, the task becomes that of *searching the dominant forms of consciousness in a specific situation*, those forms which are shared, in a variety of individual ways, by a number of individuals sufficient to make of those consciousnesses social phenomena, social forces. Even assuming that there are questions the answers to which always reveal a procapitalist or a proworker attitude, what is important: to discover this immutable form of consciousness or to discover the dominant forms of consciousness under the concrete circumstances, the changeable forms of ideological domination shared in their class content by a great number of individual forms of consciousness? It is clear that this latter view of consciousness is unsuitable for tests of statistical significance. Or, alternatively, if one chooses to measure consciousness as conventional sociology does, one has to adopt a static and 'micro-logical' notion of it.

---

8. See ibid., ch. 3.

Structures

But Wright conceptualizes structures too in a static manner, that is, in a structuralist fashion. Structuralism sees structures as crystallized realizations. A structure becomes a complex of positions (pigeonholes) to be filled by people. Structuralism does not see that the relation between structures and people is not one between pigeonholes and pigeons but one in which people are the personifications of the structure, of its inner contradictions, and thus can also be the agents of change. This is why *positions should be seen as processes* and thus as elements of a whole, as the expressions of definite relations but also, at the same time, of the dynamics inherent in those relations. For example, it is not structuralist to define the new middle class in terms of production relations and to stress that people filling those positions belong to the new middle class, provided that those positions are seen as the result of a specific dynamic and thus historical process. One could thus define the new middle class in terms of a contradictory combination of those elements of the production relations which define the two fundamental classes but, in the same breath, would have also to stress that the emergence of these positions is the result of the needs of capital accumulation. At the same time, the same needs subject those positions to a process of dequalification as soon as they realize themselves and this process is, in its turn, counteracted by the introduction of new techniques which create new, qualified, jobs in a constant process of tendential and countertendential phenomena.

More generally, a Marxist dialectical approach defines positions in terms of relations of production but also inquires into whether those positions are in the process of being qualified or dequalified, whether they belong to a production process subject to technological innovations or not, whether they are part of a process organized on the basis of, say, scientific management or of the human relations approach, whether they are part of a branch of industry being threatened by restructuring or one in the process of economic expansion, whether that category of agents has qualifications which match those required by the positions they fill, whether those qualifications are in the process of being brought down or up to the level required by those positions, etc. The study of structures does not lead necessarily to structuralism and is, needless to say, essential for class analysis. But the study of structures without dialectics cannot but fall into a structuralist, that is, static, analysis.

In short, the difference between a structuralist (Marxist oriented or not) and a Marxist dialectical approach is that the latter sees both consciousness and structures as processes, in their movement. From the point of view of dialectics, consciousness, seen as the dominant forms of class domination under specific circumstances, must be related to positions seen as the dynamic expression of production relations. Thus, both structures and ideologies must be seen *in their historical and conjunctural specificity.* They must be seen as representing (in a contradictory way) the interests of the different classes in the sense that *the ideological form of these interests is not fixed and predetermined* but changeable as the conjuncture, and thus the interrelation with all other social phenomena, changes.

If structures, positions, are seen not as a process but statistically, and if positions determine consciousness, then changes in class consciousness can only be determined by extrastructural, or nonclass factors. Alternatively, if changes in positions do occur, then Wright's approach must move directly from these changes to changes in consciousness without being able to examine *within the framework of class analysis* the role political parties, trade unions, schools, social movements, etc., have in the formation of *class* consciousness. As Leo Panitch convincingly argues, it is this kind of crude determinism which is at the basis of much contemporary, as well as past, reformism.[9]

The Relation Between Structures and Consciousness

As I have just hinted at, Wright conceptualizes the relation between structure and consciousness in a deterministic way. Let me elaborate on this. Within Wright's theoretical frame of inquiry, only structures determine consciousness. Of course, other factors, the so-called 'nonclass mechanisms' affect the concrete form taken by consciousness (p. 29), but they fall outside the explanatory power of the model; they only account for the deviations of these concrete forms from what should be the consciousness of the respondents as indicated by their positions and in a form independent of the historically specific conjuncture. Thus, somehow, positions account for the "pure" form of consciousness while the actual, concrete, form taken by consciousness is the result of both class determination (which accounts for this pure form) and of the nonclass mechanisms (which account for the deviations). In short, class determination is insufficient to explain concrete realizations. But a theory which relies on nonclass mechanisms for the explanation of the concrete form taken by phenomena—in this case, consciousness—cannot but fall into a view in which consciousness is somehow predetermined by the structure and in which the real, concrete form taken by social

---

9. L. Panitch, "The Impasse of Working-Class Politics," in *The Socialist Register* (London: Merlin Press, 1984–5).

phenomena falls outside class analysis's explanatory power. This tremendous, but unnecessary, constraint imposed on class analysis is nothing else but the result of having collapsed class determination into class determinism.

Wright attempts to escape this criticism by pointing out that class positions do not "strictly determine class outcomes, but only the probabilistic tendencies for such outcomes" (p. 186). This seems to cleanse this approach from its deterministic features, it seems to introduce the concept of tendency, a dialectical concept. But whether class positions explain the class consciousness of the respondents or the probability that the respondents have a certain consciousness, the fact remains that in Wright's scheme class position is the only determinant of these dependent variables, the only independent variable. As Wright puts it, "where deviations occur it is due to factors which are *contingent* relative to the effects of the positions themselves" (ibid., emphasis added). (Concrete examples of institutions through which these deviations take place are political parties, trade unions, schools, etc. (p. 251).) The addition of the probabilistic element does not change the deterministic character of the model in which there are dependent and independent variables into a dynamic one, in which there are determinant and determined social phenomena.

This is obviously not the place to discuss the dialectical method of analysis.[10] However, a few remarks are necessary to clarify the meaning of my critique. The dialectical method does not consider phenomena as dependent and independent variables. Rather, there are determinant and determined social phenomena. They all interact with, and modify, each other so that a certain instance's realization is the result of the interaction of all instances, determinant as well as determined. However, the determinant instance is "more important" than (that is, determinant of) the other instances. There are various interpretations of what "more important" means. One of them, the one to which I subscribe, is that a certain instance is determinant when it can be said to call into existence the other (determined) instances as conditions of its own supersession or reproduction. Structural determination, then, does not mean that the structure determines a certain form of consciousness and that this form is modified by other nonclass factors, so that the structure is accountable for a part (percentage) of a certain class consciousness. *Structural determination means that the structure determines the class content of a certain consciousness* (almost inevitably a contradictory content) and that the realization of, the concrete form taken by, that consciousness is

---

10. See Carchedi, *Class Analysis and Social Research.*

the outcome of the complex interrelation of all instances (determinant as well as determined) in their concrete, realized form.

For Wright structural determination does not mean that the determinant instance gives its class content to the determined ones; rather, for him structural determination becomes a separable step in the concrete realization, in the specific form taken by, the determined instances. But the "homogeneity of the effects generated by the structure" (p. 137), that is, class consciousness, is not something which can be observed empirically aside from the modifications produced on class consciousness by other "effects" generated also by the same structure. This is so because both the structure and the "effects" realize themselves in their specific form in a process of mutual interrelation. Wright does not seem to realize that the attempt to find out by statistical means the "pure" structural determination of consciousness is precisely the point where a dialectical view is replaced by a deterministic one, the point where the "reflection" (even if only a partial and distorted one) of the structure into consciousness is sought.

This can be easily seen if one considers that the greater the explanatory power of the model (that is, the match between positions and consciousness) is, the less relevant schools, parties, unions, etc., become for the formation (and thus for the explanation) of class consciousness. At the limit, a theory finding a perfect match between positions and consciousness would be the best theory in terms of Wright's problematic. This theory, however, would leave no room for the influence all other phenomena (both social and individual) have on class consciousness. Thus, the better a theory is, the less realistic it becomes; or, the best theory is also the least realistic. In short, the best theory leaves no room for human agencies in the production of class consciousness and thus in effecting social change. Again, this is a consequence of the structuralism implied in Wright's approach.

If this critique is accepted, then to inquire into concrete, realized cases of structural determination, into the "homogeneity of the effects generated by the structure," takes on a different meaning. The empirical observation that, say, 65 per cent of the incumbents of a certain type of positions have a certain ideology (consistent, somehow, with their structurally determined interests) does not mean that the other 35 per cent have another ideology due to extrastructural (or nonclass) factors. On the contrary, if the structure (due to its inner contradictory nature) generates its own (contradictory) conditions of reproduction or of supersession, then the 35 percent holding an "inconsistent" ideology do that for reasons no less structural than the ones explaining why the other 65 percent holds a "consistent" ideology, that is, they do that because of the influence on class consciousness of social phenomena other than the class positions of the individuals. The so-called nonclass mechanisms (that is, social phenomena nonspecific to classes as for example the oppression experienced by women and minority groups), become then so many conditions of reproduction or of supersession of the structure since they too are elements shaping the formation of class consciousness.

Thus, to inquire into the empirical relation between positions and consciousness is methodologically valid only if (1) both positions and consciousness are seen as processes, and (2) the relation between them is interpreted not in the sense that the discrepancy is due to nonclass factors (so that the less the discrepancy the higher the explanatory power of the theory) but in the sense that it too is an element of class determination, a result of class struggle. From Wright's "micro-logical" perspective, in which statistics are used to test whether differences in consciousness are due to differences in class positions, it is logical that what is not explained by class positions must be the result of nonclass factors. From the point of view of classes, in which dialectics is used to inquire into the relation between structures, that is, classes, and their realized conditions of existence or supersession, what is not a condition of supersession of the system (for example, a proworker ideology) is a condition of its reproduction (for example, a procapitalist ideology). Statistical tests of significance here are inapplicable. They are thus not neutral, they have a class content, because their application requires a redefinition of the dynamic concepts of ideology and structure into static ones as well as radical (micro-individual) reconceptualization of the relation between them.

This last remark raises an important question in class analysis: the conditions of applicability of certain techniques of social research. Let me consider another technique of social research on which Wright relies heavily in order to inquire into the respondents' class consciousness: the method of the interview. That this method can be applied within any type of logic of social research is a self-evident truth for the great majority of social researchers, no matter what their strategy of social research is. Yet there are reasons indicating that we should apply this method cautiously. When a worker is confronted by an interviewer, s/he is alone. Chances are that s/he would answer the same questions differently in a different situation, for example, in a workers' assembly. This is so not only because of psychological reasons (that is, because s/he is not alone with, and intimidated by, the interviewer but is part of a group, of a community) but also because of deeper epistemological reasons. In fact, in this collective situation, the individual worker becomes part of a process of collective production of knowledge in which his or her individual knowledge both is enriched by the collective one (through discussion with the other members of the community) and contributes to (and thus enriches) that collective knowledge.

But, it could be argued, this is the use of the questionnaire made by conventional sociology, and by Wright. The same method could be applied in a different situation, for example, during a workers' assembly. This is true. Yet, this application would not cancel the capitalist nature of this technique. The nature is given by the fact that this technique is an "acquisitive" tool of research, an appropriation by the researcher of the knowledge of the respondents, instead of being a process which also provides information, a process which shapes consciousness. It is this capitalist nature which makes this technique contradictory to socialist social research. This, however, does not mean that the method of the interview should never be used. This, as other methods of conventional sociology, can be used within a Marxist dialectical framework on condition that they can be immersed in this framework, if they are not incompatible with this framework, and on condition that their use is limited and subordinate to this framework. Let me elaborate on this latter point by providing a short example of the conditions under which the method of the questionnaire can be used to inquire into the determination of consciousness by structure.

First, we need a theory of classes which has been tested, verified, in terms of both its internal consistency and, especially, in terms of practice, in terms of its ability to explain *and change* social phenomena. This (and not statistical tests of significance) is the ground on which alternative theories should be compared and chosen, assuming, of course, that our main interest is, as Wright puts it, Marx's theoretical agenda and political goals.

Second, on the basis of this theory, we should identify positions within the social structure and analyze them as *processes*, as the contradictory result of a process of development. I have given an indication above of what elements to look for when conceptualizing positions.

Third, we consider ideologies. Three points must be made in this regard. To begin with, we consider ideologies not only in terms of what people say but also in terms of what people do (for example, voting patterns). Also, we do not look at ideologies as construed by the sociologist, not at the ideal type of what the respondents' ideology should be under any circumstances. Rather, we must look for actually existing, realized social phenomena (for example, a certain racist ideology). Then, the individual discrepancies, internalizations of that ideology become unimportant since they all share the dominant features, and thus the class content, of that ideology. Finally, these ideologies must be considered dynamically, as processes, as the contradictory result of a process of development.

Fourth, the relationship between structure and ideology should be looked at dialectically. That is, the concrete form taken by ideologies as social phenomena (disregarding the variety of individual internalizations) should be seen as conditions of either reproduction or of supersession of the concrete form taken by the structure, by positions.

Fifth, it is within this framework and only at this point that questionnaires can be used to inquire, for example, into how many of a certain position's incumbents share an ideology functional for the reproduction of the system (and thus, for example, contrary to their own interests) and how many share another ideology (functional for the supersession of the system and consonant with their interests).

This last point requires some further comments. The questionnaire can be used to study individual class consciousness but this must be done along lines different from those followed by Wright. Having identified, as mentioned above, those ideologies which have become social phenomena, we look at those which have penetrated the individual's consciousness. We only look at the dominant features, that is, we disregard the individual, particular ways they have been internalized. Then, from this point of view, an individual consciousness appears as the particular and contradictory internalization, at the individual level, of socially realized ideologies, all of them being conditions of reproduction or of supersession at the ideological level of the capitalist production relations. Therefore, the individual consciousness can be considered as an individual, that is, *potential* condition of reproduction or of supersession of the capitalist production relations, something which, because of this potentiality, can become an actual, socially realized, condition of reproduction or of supersession.

Since many social phenomena go into an individual's consciousness, an individual's *class* consciousness is formed by the internalization of all those phenomena, of all those conditions of reproduction or of supersession. Therefore, class consciousness is given not only by the individuals' ideas concerning, and attitudes towards, capital but also by the ideas concerning, and attitudes towards, unions, women, migrants, blacks, homosexuals, peace, etc. Or class consciousness is the consciousness of the need to abolish capitalism by substituting not only the capitalist *production* relations with different, socialist production relations, but also all other capitalist *social* relations (relations of subordination of women, colored people, etc.) with socialist social relations. If we do not follow this approach, we separate artificially the different fields of struggle for socialism, we foster (once more) a notion of class struggle as the struggle to replace a system of production relations by another system of production relations. This is a limited and ultimately self-defeating concept of class struggle.

Since all social phenomena influencing the individual's class consciousness change continuously, it is important to consider the individual forms of consciousness not as immutable, *a priori* forms which are modified by nonclass factors. Rather, they must be seen as the changeable forms social phenomena take at the individual level, as the contradictory potential conditions of reproduction or of supersession, the concrete form of which must always be inquired into. It is this form of consciousness which should be studied by using the questionnaire, it is this form of consciousness which should be related to positions, seen as moments in a process of historical development.

Thus, the questionnaire can be used in dialectical class analysis in spite of its class content (it is acquisitive) because it can be immersed into, and thus subordinated to, a radically different analytical approach. This is possible because the adoption of this technique does not force us to reconceptualize our notions of structure and consciousness. On the other hand, statistical tests of significance cannot be used within a dialectical approach to the study of the determination of consciousness by structure because these tests force us to reconceptualize these notions in a static and individualistic way. These tests are thus incompatible with a dialectical class analysis of the determination of class consciousness by structures. Therefore, whether a technique can be applied to dialectical class analysis (in spite of its class content) or not is a question which can be answered only by considering the specific features of each technique, only case by case: if the application of that technique does not require the static and individualistic reconceptualization of dynamic class phenomena, it can be immersed in the dialectical frame of analysis in spite of its class content, in spite of its being contradictory to it. If such a reconceptualization is required, then there is incompatibility between that technique and dialectical analysis.

To conclude, that Wright's theory fares better than rival ones only means that it explains better individual consciousness, a feature which, as Wright admits, is not a proof of being a better theory of social change. Wright advances a more limited claim: if his theory's explanatory power is no proof, it is perhaps an indication of its usefulness for a socialist strategy. But even this limited claim must be properly assessed. How useful can this theory be if it uses static concepts instead of dynamic ones, if it is based on a deterministic (instead of a dialectical) relation between them, if this relation is inquired into by exclusively using techniques of social research unfit to both research and form collective consciousness, and if it is to these techniques that this theory owes its credibility? In what measure can such a theory both analyze and influence social change, that is, the *movement* of history? If these questions are answered negatively, is this not the result of Wright having shifted to a terrain in which concern for social change is not built in any more into the logic of social research, a terrain alien to socialism no matter how one wants to define it? If this is the case, then Wright's rival theories, as he construes them, are not a relevant term of comparison.

Conclusions

This review has touched upon only some of the most important aspects of Wright's most recent work. My thesis is that Wright's approach is undermined by extremely serious internal difficulties. Only some of them have been mentioned in this review: the separation of the control of the organization of capital assets from the real, economic ownership of those assets as separate productive assets; the separation of skills from labor power also as separate productive assets; consequently, the collapsing of the concept of social class based on those separations; the methodological problems inherent in the game theory approach; consequently, the collapsing of the notion of exploitation based on this approach; the use of attitudes as indicators of consciousness; the extremely limited number of questions used to measure consciousness. These are all elements of a critique based on the internal consistency of Wright's new approach. But my critique has also a different dimension. My thesis is also that Wright has chosen a frame of reference in which the Marxist unit of analysis (classes) has been replaced by individuals; the Marxist labor theory of value has been replaced by an eclectic mixture of neo-Ricardian and neoclassical economics; the Marxist method of historically determined abstractions by the fantasies of game theory; the Marxist concept of classes rooted in production relations by a concept rooted in distributional and occupational categories; Marxist dialectics by determinism; and the Marxist concern for social change by the concern for the explanation of individual consciousness.

In opening his book, Wright remarks that his answer to the question "what constitutes a class?" is not the one Marx would have given if he had completed the last, unfinished chapter of the third volume of *Capital*. I agree. However, he also remarks that *Classes* proposes an answer faithful to Marx's theoretical agenda and political goals. With this, I could not disagree more. If the above conclusions are valid, then it is the meaning itself of Wright's enterprise which is called into question.

4

Class Theory: Still the Axis of Critical Social Scientific Analysis?

Uwe Becker

By now, some notion of class is common to most schools of social science. But only in Marxist social and political theory are the concepts of class and class struggle traditional analytical cornerstones. In Marxist analyses, history is the "history of class struggle"; economic class positions—under capitalism notably those of capital and labor—are the most important bases of collective action; class interests govern politics and ideology; as a political doctrine devoted to the working class. Marxism is founded on class theory. Engels wrote the classical formulation of this theory. In his view, Marx had

> discovered the great law of motion . . . according to which all struggles in history, whether they happen on a political, religious, philosophical, or any other ideological terrain, are indeed the more or less clear expression of struggles between social classes. The existence and therefore the collisions between these classes are conditioned by the development of their economic situation—by their mode of production.[1]

Although the various Marxisms have always differed considerably, for a long time fundamental criticisms of the centrality assigned to class and class struggle were stigmatized as "revisionist." For nearly a century, some version of the traditional view as expressed by Engels was canonical in mainstream Marxist theories. And the—at least implicit—

---

1. F. Engels, Foreword to the 3rd ed. (1885) of K. Marx, *Der achtzehnte Brumaire des Louis Bonaparte*, in *Marx–Engels–Werke* (hereafter *MEW*) vol. 8, (East Berlin: Dietz-Verlag, 1956–), p. 562.

assumption of an objectively socialist working class was a common feature of these theories.

Only recently, in the course of the so-called crisis of Marxism, has this heritage been questioned rigorously and on a large scale within Marxism itself. The past decade witnessed, as it were, the erosion of class theory and of other fundamentals of traditional Marxism. Class reductionism, economism, essentialism, and even obscurantism are now identified as serious defects in Marxist theory. As a result, Marxism in the mid-1980s has lost many of its traditional contours, and its central concern has shifted from the question of capitalist reproduction to themes like the periodization of capitalist modes of accumulation and comparative public policy research. However, the erosion of traditional Marxism was not always based on rational argument. To some extent this process is simply an uncritical intellectual adaptation to a changing socio-political context.

Erik Olin Wright's plea for the restitution of the "explanatory priority" of the concept of class based on an exploitation-centered approach and his insistence on objective class interests as the foundation for social-scientific critiques are thus a remarkable contrast. Wright's position provides the occasion to reflect systematically on the relevance of the concept of class in social and political theory. In the following, I outline recent theoretical developments regarding the explanatory status of the concept of class, consider Wright's theses, and then return to Marx to pose the question of the original basis for arguing the centrality of class. Finally, I discuss the question of objective interests and the relevance of investigations into class structure.

The main thesis of this article is that there is indeed a certain specificity of class, a specificity overlooked by both the adherents and the critics of the centrality of class. It stems from the structural dynamics of the relationship between capital and labor. Capital is compelled to accumulate, and labor is pressed to resist what I call the "logic of capital." The structurally dynamic character of the conflict between labor and capital renders the presence of this conflict in the history of capitalism plausible, and it defines a special quality of the respective class locations as bases for politico-ideological articulation and action. No *a priori* explanatory primacy, however, can be deduced from this specificity. Therefore, Wright's view has to be rejected. Furthermore, I argue that the notion of objective interests of the working class in socialism is not tenable. More generally, I reject Wright's assumption that the analysis of class structure provides the base for a critical social science.

Throughout this article, I try to argue along the lines of an empiricist, "naive" falsificationism. This means, in short, that I accept abstract propositions as generally valid only if they can be made plausible by corresponding descriptive propositions and by deductions on this lower level of abstraction. This method is empiricist because it assigns priority to the lower levels of abstraction, and it is naive because the supposed criterion of falsification is not an objective one. But the epistemological naivety is justified because in daily life we are condemned to assume that "true" knowledge corresponds to reality and that human beings are not only capable of producing this knowledge, but actually do so.

The Challenge to Tradition

Althusserian Rhetoric

The renaissance of the intellectual left in the late 1960s was character-ized by a critical stance toward Marxist orthodoxy. Although repre-sentatives of the older independent Marxism—for example, E.P. Thompson in Britain, J.-P. Sartre in France, and adherents of the Frankfurt School in Germany and the United States—had a great impact on this revival, probably the most prominent exponents of the academic Marxism that dominated the following years were Louis Althusser and Nicos Poulantzas.

In the tradition of Gramsci, one of the central objectives of their work was to attack economism and class reductionism, which they denounced as "deviation," "revision," and "bourgeois interpretation."[2] The central methodological points of departure for Althusserian Marxism were the postulates of "economic determination in the last instance" and of the "relative autonomy" of the superstructural "levels" of politics and ideology. To underline this approach, Althusser coined the concept of the class struggle as the "motor" of history. The development of pro-ductive forces is not the motor of history; rather the class struggle is, with its irreducible politico-ideological dimension, as Poulantzas pointed out in his 1968 work *Political Power and Social Classes*. For him, there are no inherent class interests in the economic structure and nothing like a "class in itself."[3] However, Althusser and Poulantzas never examined the fallacies of economism and class reductionism in detail.

---

2. See A. Gramsci, *Selections from the Prison Notebooks*, eds. Q. Hoare and G.N. Smith (London: Lawrence & Wishart, 1971), pp. 163ff; L. Althusser, *Lenin and Philosophy and Other Essays* (London: Verso, 1971), pp. 7, 19, 45; and Nicos Poulantzas, "The Problem of the Capitalist State," *New Left Review*, no. 58 (1969) p. 68.

3. N. Poulantzas, *Pouvoir politique et classes sociales* (Paris: Maspero, 1968), pp. 110–17.

The anti-economism of Althusserian Marxism marked a rupture in the history of Marxist thought. For the first time the explanatory status of the economy and of economic class positions was questioned, not just by isolated theorists, but by a whole generation of Western Marxists. Claims, however, are one thing; their realization is quite another. And, in fact, a closer look at Althusser's and Poulantzas's claims reveal them to be sheer rhetoric, or—to use Alvin Gouldner's phrase—"programmatic theatrics."[4]

Some examples may illustrate the aptness of this characterization. Without a class reductionist ascription of political objectives to economic class positions, it is impossible to say, as Althusser did, that Marxism–Leninism "represents the proletarian class struggle in theory" and that it "brings the social classes face to face with their truth."[5] Relatively autonomous processes of class formation or, more specifically, of the formation of political forces in such a conception can only be "deviations." The theses of "economic determination in the last instance" and of "relative autonomy," then, refer to real history but not to true history, which is the point of reference of the first.

The same can be said of Poulantzas. Starting from the proposed relative autonomy of politics and ideology and from the distinction between "class determination" on the structural level and "class position" in the politico-ideological conjuncture, he claims to evade an economist definition of class: "A social class is defined . . . by its place in the social division of labour as a whole. This includes political and ideological relations." But this is followed by: "A social class . . . may take up a class position that does not correspond to its interests, which are defined by the class determination."[6]

This construction is typical. Presenting structural class determination as the standard of true or objective class interests conflicts with the proclaimed relative autonomy of politics and ideology at this level. In order to function as a standard, they must be derived from economic positions. As a result, politics and ideology are only relatively autonomous in the conjunctural class positions, but here it is just this autonomy that makes conjunctural class interests deviate from true class interests. If class interests are true and thus correspond to class determination, conjuncture in such a case would be nothing more than a reflection of

4. A.W. Gouldner, "Stalinism? A Study of Internal Colonialism," in *Political Power and Social Theory*, vol. 1, ed. M. Zeitlin (Greenwich, Conn.: JAI Press, 1980), p. 244 n. 2.

5. Althusser, *Lenin*, pp. 19, 8, see also p. 100.

6. N. Poulantzas, *Classes in Contemporary Capitalism* (London: Verso, 1975), pp. 14, 15.

structure. Structure refers to true history; conjuncture—where the autonomy of politics and ideology is effective—to a deviation from true history. Intentionally or unintentionally, Poulantzas presents a Hegelian argument; he "is not denying economism, but merely complicating it."[7]

Ever present in Althusserian Marxism are the assumptions of a "properly" revolutionary socialist proletariat, determined by its economic class location, and of a "normal" course of history that would lead to the abolition of capitalism. In this essentialist construction, the continued existence of capitalism proved that the capitalists dominated the working class. Political power and ideological hegemony were the necessary conditions for the survival of capitalism. Its survival showed that these conditions existed; the state therefore could only be a capitalist class state, and the dominant ideologies could only be capitalist class ideologies. Everything was determined by class, and class was determined by economic location. But the (majority of the) actual working class in any given conjuncture deviates from this picture. A working class determined by its class location would have destroyed capitalism! Since, however, politics and ideology have the "function" of bringing about the "cohesion" of capitalism, conjunctural politics and the ideology of the working class necessarily have to deviate from proletarian "class determination" in the logic of Althusserian Marxism.

Radical Criticisms

Despite all criticial pretensions, the dominant Marxist social theory of the 1970s remained economist and class reductionist. Economist because political and ideological content was *a priori* ascribed to economic relations; class reductionist because social and political events were *a priori* reduced to class struggle. The late 1970s, then, witnessed a radicalization of the theoretical claims placed on the agenda by Althusser and Poulantzas. This development was represented by Barry Hindess, Paul Hirst, Ernesto Laclau, and Adam Przeworksi.

Apart from E.P. Thompson, Hindess and Hirst were perhaps the sharpest critics of the "isms" of Althusserian Marxism. In their view, classes have to be distinguished radically from political forces:

> The problem . . . is that when we turn to confront the dominant political issues and struggles of the day, "classes", categories of economic agents, are

---

7. P. Hirst, "Economic Classes and Politics," in *Class & Class Structure*, ed. A. Hunt (London: Lawrence & Wishart, 1977), p. 138; for a detailed presentation and critique of Poulantzas's theory, see B. Jessop, *Nicos Poulantzas: Marxist Theory and Political Strategy* (London: Macmillan, 1985).

not directly present in them. We encounter state apparatuses, parties . . .
trade union and employers' organisations, bodies of armed men, demonstrations, riotous mobs, etc., but never classes. . . . So much for the forces
acting in the political [domain], what about the issues at stake? Just as classes
are not political organisations, so political struggles do not occur in the form
of direct contests between classes for political hegemony, contests in which the
issue is the nature of the social relations of production: capitalism versus
socialism.[8]

The central thesis of Hindess's and Hirst's criticism is that there is no
necessary correspondence between classes and politics. Classes are
simply categories of economic agents. They "do not have given
'interests', apparent independently of definite parties, ideologies, etc.,
and against which these parties, ideologies, etc., can be measured."
Consequently, politics and ideology have their "conditions of existence,"
which are manifold, but they do not "represent" classes in any direct
form. The assumption of "some essential arena of class struggle beyond
politics," therefore, has to be rejected.[9]

The decisive difference between traditional Marxism, in its classic
version as well as in its Althusserian revision, and critics like Hindess
and Hirst seems clear. Where the former hold essentialist assumptions,
the latter reject them because they cannot see an empirical basis for
these assumptions. The critics' own approach is to present an elementary
description of a more complex social and political reality and to assume
the irreducibility of this complexity. This mode of argument holds true
for Hindess and Hirst—though they explicitly reject any empiricist
epistemology[10]—as well as for Laclau and Przeworski.

In contrast, Przeworski's theory leaves room for politico-ideological
"class formation" and for classes as political subjects. This difference,
however, is partly a question of the definition of class. Yet Przeworski's
emphasis on the irreducibility of social complexity is identical:

The organization of class as historical subjects . . . is not determined by the
places occupied by individuals within the realm of property relations. There is
no relation to be deduced here. The history of capitalism need not be a history
of class struggle . . . although it may happen to be that if workers and capi-

---

8. Hirst, "Economic classes," pp. 125–6.
9. Ibid., p. 131. See also B. Hindess, "Classes and Politics in Marxist Theory," *Power
and the State*, ed. G. Littlejohn et al. (London: Croom Helm, 1978), pp. 72–97; and A.
Cutler et al., *Marx's Capital and Capitalism Today*, 2 vols. (London: Routledge & Kegan
Paul, 1977–8).
10. B. Hindess and P. Hirst, *Mode of Production and Social Formation* (London:
Macmillan, 1977), esp. pp. 7, 20–21.

talists organize as such and if everyone struggles only in their capacity of workers or capitalists.[11]

And further:

The people who perpetuate their existence by selling their capacity to work for a wage are also men or women, Catholics or Protestants, Northerners or Southerners. They are also consumers, tax-payers, parents, and city dwellers. They may become mobilized into politics as workers, but they may also become mobilized as Catholic workers, Catholics or Bavarian Catholics.[12]

Przeworski never took part in the discourse of Althusserian Marxism. Laclau, by contrast, did, and his first attempts to criticize class reductionism still show the marks of the Althusserian approach. In his 1977 critique of Poulantzas's theory of fascism, he asserts that

every contradiction is overdetermined by class struggle. According to basic Marxist theory, the level of production relations always maintains the role of determination in the last instance in any social formation. This in itself establishes the priority of the class struggle.[13]

By the beginning of the 1980s and with direct reference to the "crisis of Marxism," however, Laclau (mostly in cooperation with Chantal Mouffe) began to develop a theory of political articulation in which the traditional "isms" of Marxism were banned. In 1985 this preliminary work culminated in the publication of *Hegemony and Socialist Strategy*.[14]

The central element of the "post-Marxist" theory of Laclau and Mouffe is the concept of discourse. They conceive political subjectivity as resulting from discursive articulation; that is, from processes of the "production of meaning." Articulation is a "discursive practice which does not have a plane of constitution prior to, or outside, the dispersion

---

11. A. Przeworski, "The Ethical Materialism of John Roemer," *Politics and Society* vol. 11, no. 3 (1982), pp. 293–4. Przeworski's initial contribution to the subject of class was his "Proletariat into a Class: The Process of Class Formation from Karl Kautsky's 'The Class Struggle' to Recent Controversies," *Politics and Society* vol. 7, no. 4 (1977): 343–401.

12. A. Przeworksi and J. Sprague, "Party Strategy, Class Ideology, and Individual Voting: A Theory of Electoral Socialism" (Paper prepared for the Colloquium on Class Formation, Paris: Sept. 1982).

13. E. Laclau, *Politics and Ideology in Marxist Theory: Capitalism–Fascism–Populism* (London: Verso, 1977), p. 108.

14. E. Laclau and C. Mouffe, *Hegemony and Socialist Strategy: Towards a Radical Democratic Politics* (London: Verso, 1985), p. 4: "we are now situated in a post-Marxist terrain."

of the articulated elements." Consequently, there does not "exist a constitution principle for social agents which can be fixed in an ultimate class core." According to Laclau and Mouffe, traditional Marxist concepts like objective interests lack "any theoretical base whatsoever," and the search for the "true" working class is a "false problem."[15] Meaning, political subjectivity, and collective action cannot be read off from structural positions; processes of discourse circumscribe an irreducible level of social constitution, and this is exactly what characterizes the "openness" of the social. Class locations are not even privileged bases for articulation. Race, sex, nationality, or anything else can have the same or greater importance in this respect. The base of articulation has to be found in the "plurality of diverse and frequently contradictory positions."[16] Class is just one of them, and nothing can be predicted about its relevance.

One could say that Hindess's and Hirst's criticisms lack a sustained constructive component; that Przeworski's concept of class is inconsistent; and that Laclau and Mouffe can be faulted for the confusion they create in defining the concepts of articulation and discourse,[17] as well as for the absence of empirical transparency in these concepts. Furthermore, all of these authors tend to exchange one extreme (economism and essentialism) for another (relativism and subjectivism). The lapse into subjectivism seems particularly apparent in the texts of Laclau and Mouffe, who reject the distinction between discursive and non-discursive aspects of social reality,[18] and thus tend to reduce this reality to processes of the constitution of meaning, which are based on meaning. In such a conception, any given structural context of action (and of discourse), whether constituted by discursive practice or not, is irrelevant.[19]

But however justified these criticisms may be, these authors reject the centrality that Marxism traditionally assigned to class.[20] Their writings pose the question of how class and class struggle ever came to be seen as

---

15. Ibid., pp. 83–5, 109.

16. Ibid., p. 84; for the "openness of the social," see p. 113.

17. At one point (*Hegemony*, p. 96), they define a discursive structure as "an articulatory practice"; elsewhere (p. 105) they call discourse the "structured totality resulting from the articulatory practice." Perhaps a structure can be a practice, but it makes no sense to say, as their definitions imply, that a structured totality resulting from a discursive structure is called discourse!

18. Ibid., p. 107.

19. For a similar criticism, see B. Jessop, *The Capitalist State* (Oxford: Martin Robertson, 1982), pp. 199–200.

20. More recently, the publications of, e.g., Isaac Balbus, Jon Elster, Anthony Giddens, Claus Offe, Frank Parkin, and Theda Skocpol point in the same direction.

relevant. Is it not evident that the concept of class lacks any special explanatory status?

Looking for Arguments for the Centrality of Class

Wright's Defense

In his 1985 publication *Classes*, Erik Olin Wright answered no to this question. *Classes* is above all devoted to problems of class structure. Although Wright certainly does not try to rehabilitate economism and class reductionism, he insists that Marxism must adhere to the centrality of class. According to him, this centrality has been undermined "by the shift to a domination-centered concept of class." This concept tends

> to slide into the "multiple oppressions" approach to understanding society. Societies, in this view, are characterized by a plurality of oppressions, each of which is rooted in a different form of domination—sexual, racial, national, economic, etc.—none having any explanatory priority over any other. Class, then, becomes just one of many oppressions, with no particular centrality to social and historical analysis.

To retain this centrality, Wright argues, Marxism has to opt for an exploitation-centered concept of class.[21]

The question, however, is whether the concept of class deserves centrality. Centrality, understood in a nonreductionist way, would mean, as Wright indicates, the explanatory priority of class. For him, therefore, the class structures should

> not only . . . be viewed as setting the basic limits of possibility on class formation, class consciousness and class struggle, but they also constitute the most fundamental social determinant of limits of possibility for other aspects of social structure. Class structures constitute the central organizing principles of societies in the sense of shaping the range of possible variations of the state, ethnic relations, gender relations, etc.

And, he adds:

> the claim is that class structures constitute the lines of demarcation in trajectories of social change . . . the thesis that class struggle is the "motor" of

---

21. E.O. Wright, *Classes* (London: Verso, 1985), p. 57. See also chapter 1 above, p. 8.

history, then, means that it is the conflict between actors defined by their location within class structures which explains the qualitative transformations that demarcate epochal trajectories of social change.[22]

Wright has to demonstrate that class structure is the most important determinant of human identity and that class struggle explains the basic features of society and history. And since it is impossible to demonstrate this in an all-embracing empirical way, Wright would make his claim plausible only if he could refer to some societal mechanism or to some fundamental social fact that generates the centrality of class and if he could illustrate such configuration by significant examples. Does he provide arguments of this kind?

To maintain the primacy of class, he says: "It is sufficient to argue that the class structure constitutes the central mechanism by which various sorts of resources are appropriated and distributed, therefore determining the underlying capacities to act of various social actors. Class structures are the central determinant of social power." Because class structure "distributes the basic access to the resources which determine human capacities to act," Wright argues, it establishes the "limits" within which "non-class mechanisms operate."[23] Is this a basic social fact, and is it really sufficient?

Marxism has always stressed the material dimension of social life and considered it fundamental because access to material resources determines the existential conditions of life, the standard of living, and hence, to a large extent, access to other resources like education, culture, information, and politics. This stress is certainly justified, and by themselves material factors explain many aspects of social differentiation. It is also true that class structure is the most global matrix for the distribution of material resources. The concrete distribution of these resources, however, reflects the various individual economic positions and circumstances of a population, which cannot adequately be described in class terms. Moreover—and Wright seems to endorse this view—the distribution of resources between the sexes, among nations and even regions, or among ethnic groups is not (primarily) a matter of class. Every

---

22. *Classes*, pp. 31, 32–3.
23. Ibid., pp. 312–2, 29. In an earlier publication ("Giddens's Critique of Marxism," *New Left Review* no. 138 [1983]), Wright mentions two further reasons for the primacy of class: (1) that it has "the greatest *existential* impact on human subjectivity" (p. 23); and (2) that "class relations have an internal logic of development" that is "articulated to the development of the forces of production" (p. 24). In my view, the first reason (which he himself critically undermines in that article) seems to be an aspect of his thesis that class structure limits the possible range of variation of other social dimensions. This could not be the case if class structure did not have a decisive impact on human subjectivity. The idea of the "internal logic" of class structure has entirely disappeared in *Classes*.

member of one of these categories may also be a member of one class and involved in particular class structures, but his or her *specific* capacity to act is determined by a complex configuration of *specific* relations.

But even if we accept the view that class structure is the central determinant of access to resources, a question remains: Does this fact "limit" the possible variations of non-class relations more than these relations limit the possible variation of class structure? Wright does not refer to any compelling mechanism that would substantiate his claim. As an illustration of his thesis, he mentions only male domination, whose persistence, he admits, cannot be explained by class structure. The historical possibility of the "elimination of institutionalized forms of male domination," however, must still be explained by the "transformations of class relations—the development of advanced forms of capitalist production accompanied by emerging elements of state production."[24] Here Wright obviously conflates class structure and the economy, and this again is not convincing.

The concept of the capitalist economy is much more comprehensive than the concept of capitalist class structure. The largely autonomous dynamics of capitalist development—which are irrelevant to Wright's argument—indeed cause change on other social terrains. These dynamics, which resulted in more change in the past two hundred years than anything in the preceding millennia, are determined not by the presence of private property in the means of production and the existence of wage labor, but by the combination of these production relations with production for largely anonymous, unregulated markets under a system of competition among capitalist enterprises. Historically, it was the unleashing of the market that brought about the "great transformation" toward a society that is condemned to change and develop by its elementary economic structure.[25] Apart from specific circumstances determining the rise and fall of national economies, long waves, and the business cycle, the structural dynamics of capitalism cause more or less continuous change in at least three dimensions: technology and productive knowledge; commodities and the material way of life; and social structure. The "transformation of class relations" is only one aspect of this dynamic.

Thus, as Wright recognizes, when in the past two decades, traditional

---

24. *Classes*, p. 59 n. 17.
25. See Karl Polanyi's famous *The Great Transformation: The Political and Economic Origins of Our Time* (Boston: Beacon Press, 1957), especially Part 2. One might object that capitalist markets are by no means unregulated. Indeed, there are thousands of regulations and restrictions. But none of these regimentations is comparable to the strict limitations of the precapitalist private markets in, for example, medieval Europe or China.

patriarchal relations have been questioned, this is because of new technico-economic demands, the proliferation of higher education, growing professionalism, and increasing socio-geographic mobility, as well as mass consumption and modern mass communication. In this erosion of traditional bonds, the changing class structure (the expansion of the middle classes) was but one link in a causal chain and not even a central one at that. Indeed, the historically unique dynamics of capitalism open up various possibilities of social change. Because of capitalism's power to penetrate, it can justifiably be seen as the central motor of social development in the modern world. Structure always limits as well as enables action, and capitalism tends to limit the range of possible social variation by generating functional requirements. But this argument does not resemble Wright's arguments for the "primacy of class."

Finally, Wright's universal thesis of the centrality of class struggle, especially with regard to periods of epochal change, seems to me very weak. If one defines epochal change as fundamental change in class structure, the choice of possible actors struggling for change is already restricted *by definition*. Many questions, however, remain. Are there always definite periods of epochal change? What if fundamental change occurs gradually, without any central and conscious struggle over class structure? Actually, both feudalism and capitalism rose gradually; we can identify the decisive steps only in retrospect. The bourgeois revolutions turned out to be a sort of class struggle, but not, however, a struggle between the relational classes of feudalism, the feudal lords and the peasantry. Moreover, these revolutions were first and foremost political revolutions. By contrast, the Russian revolution of 1917–19 changed the class structure, and the given class structure limited its possible range. But the latter is trivial and does not substantiate the centrality of class struggle. Were the opposing forces class forces, or popular versus ruling forces? Was the revolution initiated by class relations? And was the even more fundamental Stalinist revolution of 1928–30 determined by class structure and class struggle? Were the factions of the party classes; were the peasants who were stigmatized as "kulaks" a class? Or, as a final example, German fascism did not seriously affect class structure, but it did change social reality dramatically. The struggle of class-based forces was, no doubt, of great relevance in this process. But if the concept of class provides the central explanation, why did fascism rise only in Germany and—in a less dramatic form—in Italy?

In conclusion, Wright does not provide sustained arguments for his claim. So, more than ever, one has to ask why Marxism traditionally accorded centrality to the concept of class. What were the original arguments?

Marx's Materialist Account

Why did Marx assume that social relations, social action, and social change must be explained by the struggle of economically defined classes? His so-called political writings describe socio-political processes of his time, but contain no foundation for his claim concerning the universal explanatory status of class. Nor does his political economy provide this foundation; it is restricted to capitalism. The only thing one could expect from Marx, then, is a theory of the centrality of class within capitalism. And indeed, such a theory can be derived from his political economy.

Even with regard to capitalism, however, this theory refers only to a very limited field. Its central thesis holds that capitalist development will *in the long run* demote social positions other than class to historical irrelevance. In the long run people are *forced* to "make history" on the basis of their economic class location only. And it is the working class that is forced to destroy capitalism and to bring about socialism. That capitalism must necessarily give birth to socialism is an element of Marx's metaphysical teleology of history. But Marx's claim that the working class necessarily has to destroy capitalism is debatable. His arguments originate in his materialism, in which material force is the most important concept.[26]

In essence, Marx's theory of capitalism contains a two-class model. He defines classes as relational categories shaped by the relations between producers and the means of production.[27] In capitalism the "subjective" and "objective" factors of production are "divorced" and represented by wage labor and capital. For Marx the landowners—also mentioned as a separate class—and the small bourgeoisie are declining entities, and the new middle classes are not a serious theme. He deals only sporadically with the differentiation of wage-earners into industrial and "commercial," skilled and unskilled, and supervisory and executing workers.[28] This differentiation, as well as the distinction between productive and nonproductive wage laborers,[29] will have no impact on capitalist development. In the long run, uniformity will triumph.[30] The relevant classes, therefore, are the capitalists and the unified working

---

26. The following account draws heavily on U. Becker, *Kapitalistische Dynamik und politisches Kräftespiel: Zur Kritik des klassentheoretischen Ansatzes* (Frankfurt a/Main: Campus Verlag, 1986), pp. 15–45, 90–94.

27. K. Marx, *Das Kapital II* (*MEW* 24), p. 42.

28. See, e.g., *Das Kapital I* (*MEW* 23), pp. 351, 443, 697; *Das Kapital III* (*MEW* 25), pp. 311–12, 402; and *Theorien über den Mehrwert I* (*MEW* 26.1), p. 145.

29. *Theorien I*, pp. 145, 171; and *Theorien II* (*MEW* 26.2), p. 576.

30. *Kapital I*, p. 442; *Kapital III*, pp. 311–12, 402–3, 508.

class. Marx's definition of the working class is ambiguous: one could identify it with only the industrial working class, but if we follow the dominant logic of Marx's political economy, his working class has to be identified with more or less all wage-earners.

In Marx's theory, the "law of motion" of the capitalist mode of production will ultimately force the working class to destroy capitalism, and it is this principle that gives centrality to class struggle. Because of the strain of competition, capital has to maximize profit to develop productive forces, to create new products, and to enlarge the surplus value by lowering (relatively or even absolutely) the costs of the labor force, thereby increasing the rate of exploitation. All this determines the unique dynamics of capitalism, but it also threatens the material existence of wage-earners. People work for use values, but the logic of the capitalist orientation toward profit undermines this objective. Progress in production threatens job security, and reduced labor costs can imply lower wages, more working hours, a higher intensity of production, and diminished security on the shopfloor. Hence the relation between labor and capital is a structural opposition (in Marx's dialectical terminology, a "contradictory" relation) and therefore one of potentially permanent conflict.

Marx does not consider exploitation defined as a certain quantitative relationship as the source of class antagonism under capitalism. In his view, this antagonism originates in the overall *dynamics* of capitalist accumulation, in which the dynamics of exploitation are a central element. What is important for the current argument is that in his political economy Marx postulates a dramatic deterioration in living conditions for the working class in the course of capitalist accumulation. The development of productivity and, in conjunction, the swelling of the industrial "reserve army" and the increasing rate of exploitation will inevitably lead to the impoverishment of (large homogenized parts of) the working class. This is "the general law of capitalist accumulation,"[31] which in the long run will bring about a situation of generalized existential misery in which it will be irrelevant whether the wage-earners are of one nationality or another, men or women, Catholic or Protestant, young or old, villagers or city dwellers. The only base of political action that counts will be the wage-earners' class location: because of their class location they will be forced to overthrow capitalism.

Whether Marx argued for the absolute impoverishment of the working class is subject to academic dispute. Throughout his work he made contradictory remarks about the development of the material conditions

---

31. *Kapital I*, ch. 23, esp. p. 675.

of life of the working class. However, in central parts of his work, whenever he deals with epochal change, Marx does hypothesize the absolute impoverishment of the working class: see, for example the *Communist Manifesto, Labor and Capital, The Poverty of Philosophy,* and especially "Address on the Anniversary of *The People's Paper,*" "Inaugural Address to the IAA," and the final chapters of *Capital* Volume I. But, more important, Marx's emphasis on material necessities and historical laws would have no coherent base without a theory of the increasing misery of the working class. This theory is the only, though very limited, foundation for the extraordinary significance that Marx and traditional Marxists assign to class location and the class struggle.

Capitalist Dynamics and the Pressure to Class-Based Struggle

It is no secret that the crucial aspects of Marx's theory of the historical tendencies of capitalist accumulation are not tenable. His basic mistake was to raise certain abstract possibilities of development to the status of *the* tendencies of history, of long-term laws proceeding with "iron necessity."[32] Thereby he abstracts "from processes that affect predictions," and these abstractions "are bad abstractions."[33] Thus, in analyzing the process of capitalist accumulation, he treated the change in the composition of capital in favor of fixed capital—that is, the substitution of machinery for human power—as the determinant of the course of this process.[34] And on the basis of his investigation of this "factor," Marx arrived at the absolute impoverishment of wage-earners. The creation of new products—which in the labor market can compensate for increases in productivity—and, most important, the organization and struggle of the wage-earners to improve their material situation *within* capitalism, got no attention from Marx. It is precisely these factors, however, that are responsible for the fact that the working class is *not* forced to destroy capitalism. Hence, there is no economic development to diagnose here that in the long run consigns sexual, racial, national, religious, or sociogeographic positions to historical irrelevance.

Moreover, Marx's thesis of the increasing homogeneity of the working class has not proved to be true. On the contrary, capitalist development involves, as an inherent tendency—as a condition of the

---

32. Ibid., p. 12.
33. Przeworski, "Ethical Materialism," p. 299.
34. See *Kapital I*, p. 640.

technological and organizational division of labor—a growing differentiation of wage labor. The process of capitalist accumulation is
twofold: the tendency toward the polarization of labor and capital is
opposed by a tendency toward the individualization and fragmentation
of wage-earners. The existence of the so-called new middle classes is the
most tangible result of this development. The individualization and fragmentation of wage labor makes it evident that the concrete relation
between labor and capital is not simply a relation between the working
class and the capitalist class. Individual and collective economic
locations do not necessarily coincide.

Hence, critics like Hirst, Laclau, and Przeworski are right in contest-
ing the centrality that traditional Marxism accorded to class. However,
they tend to overlook the specificity which class location actually has as
a base for social articulation and political action. *The true kernel of
Marx's theory remains his stress on the structurally dynamic character of
capitalism.* The dynamics of capitalism make some sense of the theorem
of base and superstructure, because in capitalist society and only in capitalist society no other part of the social whole has overall effects
comparable to those of the economy. This dynamic, which is absent in
feudalism or other precapitalist modes of production (and which has
nothing to do with Althusser's "last instance"), is the locomotive of the
development of capitalist society. By continually reshaping class structure, human needs, and the material space of society, the economy
initiates change and adjustments in politics, ideology, and culture much
more than the latter influence the economy. In this sense, the capitalist
economy is the "base" for historical development. The notion of "superstructure," however, is questionable, because no economic mechanism
strictly determines politics, ideology, and culture.

A second kernel of truth in Marx's theory is his emphasis on the
structural character of the antagonism between labor and capital or,
more generally, between the human orientation toward use values and
capital's orientation toward profit. In fact, the logic of capital, the structurally imposed pressure to maximize profits and to lower costs, threatens the existence of the wage-earners and *structurally* pressures them to
struggle against this logic. The everyday struggle over wages and working conditions is an obvious expression of this pressure. In contrast to
nineteenth-century capitalism, the current struggle between labor and
capital in the North and West is not normally about existential subsistence. But without labor's resistance to the logic of profit maxi-
malization, there would not even be a relative guarantee of work, of
wage levels, of hours of labor, and of decent conditions on the shopfloor. Life would be a very uncertain affair, and labor would be a play-
thing of capital. Whereas people can manage the poverty resulting from

exploitation, they cannot manage the complete uncertainty of life expectations that the pure logic of capital would create.

It is the structural pressure on wage-earners to fight the logic of capital—and the impetus to struggle for more, which is fostered by capitalist expansion and by its continual reshaping of the consumers' needs— that explains why the conflict between labor and capital in capitalist society is *universal* and *nearly permanent*. No other front of conflict has such a comparably broad and indeed fundamental, existential basis as that between the orientation toward use values and the orientation toward profit—of which the struggle between labor and capital is the central and primary form. No other front of conflict has a comparable historical record. The structural pressure to conflict involved in the relational capitalist class locations is their distinguishing feature. This does not prove the overall explanatory "centrality" of class, but it certainly does substantiate a characteristic of the relational class locations as bases for articulation and political action. The structural pressure to conflict establishes the peculiarity of the struggle between labor and capital.

This structural antagonism between labor and capital is a concrete reality. But it is an abstraction because its manifestation in struggle depends on many factors. First, the capitalist class locations overlap the hierarchical division of labor, which differentiates and fragments the wage-earners.[35] This makes the capitalist class structure more complex, and it implies that not all individual wage-earners are threatened by the logic of capital in the same way and to the same extent. The result is that the antagonism between labor and capital usually does not lead to a struggle between two class collectivities. Further, it cannot be deduced from the structural antagonism between labor and capital how the struggle between these two poles will be settled. Hindess and Hirst are right here: the struggle between labor and capital is a struggle between political forces. These forces are based not only on the relational class locations but also on individual economic locations, on ideological traditions like the distinction between the prestige of manual and mental labor, on age, on sex, and on other positions. All these factors are effective in their own right. Finally, political articulation—resulting from the processes of socialization, manipulation, and learning from experience— is an irreducible level of social reality.

To conclude, the confrontation between labor and capital is distinguished by its structural dynamics, but this does not justify the general

---

35. Capital is also differentiated, but that is of lesser exemplary relevance in the present discussion.

claim that class locations have a particular explanatory force. Class struggle is not the motor of the history of capitalist society. If there is any such motor, and only in the sense of the central initiator of societal change, it is the dynamics of the capitalist economy, of which the structural antagonism between labor and capital is only one aspect. Capital is compelled to accumulate, and labor is pressed to fight the logic of capital accumulation. Because of its elementary existential dimension, therefore, the conflict between capital and labor is a universal and nearly permanent feature of capitalist society. Theorists like Hindess and Hirst and Laclau and Mouffe tend to overlook this specificity. The capital–labor conflict, to be sure, has a central place in capitalist history. Evidently, the history of the distribution of profits and wages or the development of important parts of welfare legislation are rooted in the power relations between the two poles of the capitalist antagonism. But in the explanation of the various histories within capitalist society, such as the rise of fascism or the "cultural revolution" of the 1960s, the antagonism between labor and capital has no *a priori* centrality.[36]

It follows that the concept of class struggle is useful only in the sense of a struggle between class-based (political) forces initiated by problems originating in the dynamics of class relations. The concept of class formation should be considered in the same way. Class formation—in its emphatic sense as the politico-ideological formation of an economic class as a class—refers only to a theoretical possibility. What really exists is the formation of class-based forces such as social-democratic or Catholic unions. The concept of class consciousness is problematic. Does it refer to any given awareness members of a class have of class structure and the interests that articulate within this structure? The point of reference in this case would not be class but the individual. Or does the concept of class consciousness refer to the extent that members of a class express the objective interests that can be derived analytically from their class locations? Such an interpretation is acceptable only if the concept of objective class interests is viable.

Class Structure, Objective Interests, and Critical Social Science

In traditional Marxism the concept of class does not have "explanatory

---

36. This does not mean that the capital–labor conflict explains the commonalities among capitalist nations. To a certain extent this may be the case. But for the rest, these commonalities originate largely in common traditions (Christianity, for example) and in the tautological fact that all the capitalist nations are capitalist.

priority" only. Marxism has always claimed to be a critical science or, in Engels's words, the theory of "scientific socialism." In this context the concepts of class, particularly of objective class interests, and of class structure as the basis for these interests are of central importance. Marx's goal in his political economy was to offer the "theoretical foundation" of communism[37] through an analysis of the process of capitalist accumulation, which would necessarily both define antagonistic objective interests and lead to the realization of the objective interest of the working class in socialism/communism. In this teleological theory, *critique* was a synonym for the analysis of the direction of capitalist development. Whatever values might have guided Marx's investigation, in his own judgment, his theory was only an "organ" of real history.[38]

With the shift of the overall problematic of Marxism from social change to social reproduction, the relevance of the notion of objective interests changed. It came to serve as a criterion for the determination of "deviant" class consciousness and as a justification of the socialist/communist party's claim to be a scientifically led "avant-garde" of the working class. And in "actually existing socialism," the objective interests of the working class for the party and the related state apparatus even serve to justify repressive measures against the working class and the whole population. This evolution of the idea of objective interests should, at the very least, be reason enough for a careful use of this concept, which intrinsically tends to distinguish between those who claim to have objective knowledge and those who do not know their own "true" interests.

There has been limited discussion in Marxism of the validity of the concept of objective class interests. As long as economism, class reductionism, and a teleological view of history were dominant, the validity of the notion of the objective interests of the working class in socialism was largely—especially in the tradition of Georg Lukács's theory of "objective class consciousness"—taken for granted.[39] In Althusserianism, the concept of objective interests was absent because it was considered a feature of "historicism" and subjectivism, but the Althusserian critique remained ambiguous. In the course of the recent crisis of Marxism, however, the concept of objective interests more or less withered away as an aspect of the "bad isms" of traditional Marxism. In criticizing Wright, Laclau and Mouffe say simply that this

---

37. See his letter to Lassalle of February 6, 1849 (*MEW* 39, p. 618).
38. See *Elend der Philosophie* (*MEW* 4, p. 143).
39. See Georg Lukács, *Geschichte und Klassenbewusstsein* (Berlin: Malik-Verlag, 1923), pp. 57–93.

concept "lacks any theoretical basis whatsoever" and that it "becomes meaningless" if one abandons the "privileging [of] certain subject positions."[40] To these authors, a systematic elaboration of their criticism does not seem necessary. The question is whether Wright, with his new, exploitation-centered approach, does provide tenable arguments for the restitution of the concept of objective class interests, and particularly for his claim that the working class has an objective interest in socialism.

A Short Outline of Wright's Approach

Wright's points of departure are neither teleological nor Leninist. But he is one of the few Western Marxists who explicitly pay attention to the concept of objective interests. His basic assumption is that people "have an 'objective interest' in increasing their capacity to act." And "insofar as the actual capacity that individuals have to make choices and act upon them—their real freedom—is shaped systematically by their position within the class structure, they have objective class interests based on this real interest in freedom."[41] The analysis of class structure, therefore, is of crucial importance, for it has to locate the structural bases of these objective class interests.

In Wright's view, the suitable criteria for determining class structure are the relations of exploitation. In contrast to domination, he asserts, "exploitation intrinsically implies a set of opposing material interests."[42] Following the theory of John Roemer, he conceives exploitation as denoting a causal relationship between the wealth of one person, group, or class and the poverty of another person, group, or class. The cause of exploitation is seen in the unequal distribution of productive assets, of which the main examples are private ownership of the means of production, control over organizations, and possession of skills. Exploitation through property assets—the classical item of Marxism—refers only to a special case in Roemer's and Wright's general concept of exploitation, and defines—with regard to capitalism—the classes of labor and capital. Organizational assets (prototypically belonging to managers and supervisors) and skill assets (prototypically belonging to experts) define the location of the new middle classes. These locations, however, are "contradictory locations," because the wage-earners involved are capitalistically exploited on the one hand but are skill or organizational

---

40. Laclau and Mouffe, *Hegemony*, pp. 83–4.
41. Wright, *Classes*, pp. 28, 249.
42. Ibid., pp. 56–7.

exploiters on the other hand.[43] The true working class, then, consists of those wage-earners who are exploited both by capital and by the new middle classes. Wright calls them "uncredentialed non-managerial employees."[44]

In Roemer's view, however, exploitation is not just a causal relationship between wealth and poverty. He has a second criterion: A coalition S, in a large society N, is exploited if and only if:

(1) There is an alternative, which we may conceive of as hypothetically feasible, in which S would be better off than in its present situation.

(2) Under this alternative the complement to S, the coalition $N-S=S'$, would be worse off than at present.[45]

Wright bases his theory of objective class interests on this construction. Since the capitalists would be worse off and thus have a diminished capacity to act by the elimination of private property, they have an objective interest in the reproduction of capitalist relations. The working class, by contrast, would be better off in a society in which "each worker receives his or her per capita share of society's total productive assets."[46] This class, therefore, has an objective interest in changing society in this direction. It also has an objective interest in the abolition of skill and organizational differentials. The opponents of the working class in this respect are the new middle classes, who have an objective interest in maintaining these differentials. On the other hand—and this characterizes their contradictory location—they share the workers' interest in the elimination of private ownership of the means of production.[47]

In sum, capitalists have an objective interest in capitalism; the new middle classes seem to have an objective interest in a mode of production resembling "actually existing socialism," which Wright calls "statism";[48] and the working class has an objective interest in what Marxism traditionally describes as full communism, that is, a society characterized by "radical democratic control over the physical and

---

43. Ibid., p. 87.

44. Ibid., p. 182. For present purposes, it is sufficient to distinguish between capitalists, the middle class, and the working class. It should be mentioned, however, that Wright in his detailed investigation develops a map of seven or even twelve classes. The seven classes are employers, petty bourgeois, managers, supervisors, non-managerial experts, skilled workers, and workers.

45. J.E. Roemer, *A General Theory of Exploitation and Class* (Cambridge, Mass.: Harvard University Press, 1982), p. 194.

46. Ibid., p. 69.

47. For this argument, see ibid., pp. 68–70, 285.

48. Wright does not say this explicitly, but it can be deduced from his argument.

organizational resources used in production."[49] And according to
Roemer and Wright, it is the prospect of hypothetically feasible alternative modes of production in which the exploited would be better off
that makes the labor transfers from labor to capital and from the working class to the new middle classes exploitative, for "it only makes sense
to talk about exploitation if the exploited would be better off in the
absence of exploitation."[50] And precisely because the exploitation-
centered approach "contains within itself the notion of alternative forms
of society," the concept of class based on the theory of exploitation "has
a particularly sustained critical character."[51]

Hypothetically Feasible Alternatives as the Basis of Critical Science?

Before trying to answer this question, I will briefly comment on certain
features of Wright's (and Roemer's) theory of exploitation that are not
directly related to the problems in the critical science Wright intends to
develop.

First, Roemer's and Wright's concept of exploitation is a purely
quantitative one that refers to the unequal distribution of income by
labor transfers. According to this theory, capitalist exploitation is
nothing more than a special case of the general concept. This, however,
is questionable; capitalist exploitation is much more than the enrichment
of one class through the labor of another class. And the picture of the
struggle between labor and capital drawn by Roemer as a "class struggle
between poor workers and rich capitalists" seems unrealistic—even as a
model.[52] Aiming at analytic relevance should at least imply that models
pretend to say something about reality. And this is possible only when
the models are not fictitious but consciously idealized constructions of
reality.

Capitalist exploitation is the private appropriation of the socially
produced surplus in which use is determined by production for profit. It
intrinsically involves a dynamic relationship between the exploiters and
the exploited. Roemer and Wright disregard this specificity and offer a
theory in which capitalist, skill, and organizational exploitation are
equally relevant to the concept of class structure. With this concept of

49. *Classes*, p. 287.
50. Ibid., p. 68.
51. Chapter 1 above, p. 42.
52. J.E. Roemer, "New Directions in the Marxian Theory of Exploitation and Class,"
Politics and Society vol. 11, no. 3 (1982), p. 275.

exploitation, one can strive for the abolition of capitalist income exploitation even within the context of capitalism. The logic of capital would not necessarily be touched in a democratized capitalism without capitalists.

Wright's arguments for skill exploitation are also not convincing. His thesis is that "people with scarce skills receive incomes above the costs of producing those skills."[53] Are these costs a compelling criterion? Is not productivity that is intensified by qualification a more appropriate criterion for the valuation of someone's work and income? In any case, this question seems to be much more complex than Wright suggests, as is the connection between exploitation and class structure. There are many forms and degrees of exploitation, of enrichment by the labor of others. And we would have multifarious classes if all exploitative relations constituted class relations. But which exploitative relations constitute class relations and which do not? Wright does not provide any clearcut criterion here.

Further, I doubt that a domination-centered approach "weakens the link between the analysis of class locations and the analysis of objective interests." The human capacity to act is restricted as much by domination as by exploitation. If the concept of objective interests is viable, the oppressed have an objective interest in changing their situation. Wright seems unaware of the arbitrariness of any theory of class structure. The differentiation of wage labor does not involve any objective classificatory criterion. And where society does not provide such a criterion by itself, we have to make a substantiated choice. But this choice is always governed by our analytical objectives.

I question, finally, the idea that exploitation can be determined as exploitation only in the light of a "hypothetically feasible" alternative. If there is no such alternative, Roemer and Wright argue, exploitation has to be considered necessary. I think that this is wrong because the social conditions that possibly make exploitation necessary for the moment are never fixed once and for all. And since all social arrangements are in principle changeable, *each definition of social reality potentially contains a hypothetically feasible alternative.* Thus, hypothetical feasibility is not a specific classification criterion at all. Moreover, people first define their social situation and value it as worth maintaining or changing. Only after this—however preliminary—judgment do they think about the actual, not the hypothetical, feasibility of change.

But, and this is the central question of this section, does the criterion

---

53. *Classes*, p. 70.

of hypothetically feasible alternatives justify the thesis that the exploitation-centered approach "contains within itself the notion of alternative forms of society" and that it, therefore, "has a particularly sustained critical character"? Is it possible that an imaginary criterion, "a construction of thought experiment,"[54] provides the basis for a critical social science? How? Would it not be necessary that the alternative be truly feasible? Roemer and Wright do not answer these questions. Roemer concedes that the abolition of capitalism "will alter institutions and incentives in such a way as to make the exploited agents worse off instead of better off,"[55] whereas Wright's argument is not consistent. On the one hand he adheres to the concept of (only) *hypothetically* feasible alternatives, and on the other hand he characterizes the "possibilities for transformation" of capitalism as "immanent" possibilities of the "given society."[56]

In any case, the meaning of socialism or communism that is central in this respect remains unclear. What is needed is an elaboration of the *concrete* possibilities *and* difficulties of the transformation toward a democratically organized society in which exploitation would be eliminated or at least radically reduced and in which other capitalist excesses like waste and environmental damage would disappear. How to avoid an all-embracing bureaucratization, how to combine democracy and efficiency, and how to combine the market with planning—these are some of the questions that have to be discussed in the light of the experiences of actually existing socialism. Only such a discussion, which would extend far beyond a discussion of the problem of incentives,[57] could sustain the particularly critical character of Marxism.

Objective Class Interests: A Viable Concept?

Is it possible to infer objective interests from class structure? What makes interests objective? Without going into an epistemological discussion about the notion of objectivity, there are two principal possibilities: objective interests could be defined (1) as interests that are objectively *imposed* on someone, as in the case in Marx's original theory; or (2) as the objective purposive rationality that can be deduced from someone's situation. The latter is Wright's version of objective interests. "If workers had a scientific understanding of the contradictions

---

54. Cf. A. Carling, "Rational Choice Marxism," *New Left Review* no. 160 (1986), p. 50.

55. Roemer, *General Theory of Exploitation*, p. 241.

56. Chapter 1 above, p. 42.

57. Wright, *Classes*, pp. 120–21.

of capitalism" he once wrote, "they would in fact engage in struggles for socialism."[58] The rationalistic construction of objective interests is bound to some fundamental premiss. The objectivity of objective interests understood as objective rationality, then, depends on: (1) the validity of the premiss; (2) whether the premiss is without rivals; and (3) the possibility of realizing the deduced rational interests.

Wright's premiss is that people have an objective interest in increasing their capacity to act. I do not know whether this is an interest at all. But I will accept Wright's assumption as a premiss of critical social science because there is some indication that the interest to increase the capacity to act is an inherent aspect of the motives of human action. One can, however, construct other, and what is more important, conflicting premisses; for example, the tendency of people to reduce or at least to minimize risk. This interest seems to me as fundamental as the interest in increasing the capacity to act. And since the attempt *to increase* the capacity to act carries with it the risk that one may become worse off, it no longer makes sense to infer objective interests from this premiss. The very notion of "increase" becomes relative and conditional. Interests, or to be more exact, "instrumental interests,"[59] lose their logical contours in the context of complex configurations of premisses. Their determination, then—supposing it is rational—becomes *a practical problem in which people have to weigh several factors.*

This problem is much more difficult when we realize that people are not only workers, skill exploiters, or capitalists, but also individual assembly-line workers, electricians, supervisors, teachers, technical experts, or managers. Wright restricts his concept of contradictory objective interests to the middle class, that is, to those wage-earners occupying a contradictory class location But why not extend this concept to all wage-earners, except perhaps the top managers? If increasing the capacity to act is the premiss or the fundamental interest and if rationality is the criterion for defining objective instrumental interests, why then should we deny the assembly-line worker an objective interest in becoming a supervisor or technical expert? Thus, he or she also has contradictory interests. And these interests may become even more contradictory when gender and age as well as specific

---

58. E.O. Wright, *Class, Crisis, and the State* (London: Verso, 1978), p. 89.
59. Although interests are always bound to preceding premisses, it is perhaps useful to distinguish between intrinsic or fundamental interests, which can be considered premisses of human action, and instrumental interests. Wright made this distinction in his paper "Agency and Class Interests," which was presented to the Colloquium on Class Formation in Paris, September 1982. The interest in increasing the capacity to act, then, is a fundamental interest; the workers' interest in socialism an instrumental interest.

personal conditions are taken into consideration. Does it make sense to stress the objectivity of all rational interests that can be deduced from someone's social and economic locations, when these interests are contradictory? And, moreover, does it make sense to talk about the *objective* interest of the working class in socialism, when the chances and possibilities for realizing people's fundamental interests are tenuous in socialism? It may be possible to construct an objective interest in a better world or even in paradise. The concretization of these abstract interests, however, is a matter of historical subjectivity and struggle.

Against this background socialists and critical social scientists are not justified in speaking of an objective interest of the working class in socialism. And if there is no objective interest in socialism, the concept of class consciousness loses its raison d'être. The only thing critical social science can do is to offer an interest in socialism as a *possible rationality worthy of discussion.* The feasibility of an efficient, nonbureaucratic, and nonrepressive socialism, in which the people's capacity to act would increase, however, would have to be shown. And in this respect Wright and most Marxists have nothing to tell us.

Conclusion

The relevance of class structure is more limited than Wright assumes. Class structure is certainly an important, and moreover, as in the case of labor and capital, a specific base of political articulation. Knowledge of it should be part of the basic knowledge of social science. The starting point of the analysis of the class structure of capitalist society should be the overlap of economic polarization and fragmentation. The inevitable subdivision of the overly abstract class of wage-earners into working class(es) and middle class(es) is determined not just by objective criteria like income. The lines of class demarcation are also always determined by the purpose of the analysis, and therefore they are to a certain extent arbitrary.

The analysis of class structure can be used neither for the determination of "take-off areas" of teleological historical processes nor for the determination of objective rational interests, and it is not *the* basis of critical social science. Our society is, among other attributes, a capitalist, industrial, patriarchal, racist, and bureaucratic society, and it is organized in nation-states. To all these dimensions of reality correspond different social-scientific points of departure. Capitalism refers to the most basic dimension of our society, and the dynamics of capitalism initiate its historically unique development. But this does not devalue the other dimensions of reality as autonomous points of departure. Critical social science does not have a "natural" addressee. This, in conjunction with the failure of all attempts to provide an objective or emphatically "scientific" base for the critique of society, necessitates a more modest assessment of critical social science.[60]

---

60. After spending more than a decade on the development of an objective, normative criterion of social critique, even Jürgen Habermas adjusted his theory in his monumental *Theorie des kommunikativen Handelns* (Frankfurt a/Main: Suhrkamp, 1981). One can only try to make norms "plausible," he writes (vol. 1, p. 199). See pp. 132–33, 417.

PART II

Theoretical Issues

Symposium on *Classes**

NEW DIRECTIONS IN CLASS ANALYSIS
Val Burris

Among Marxist theorists, the class position of salaried managers and professionals has been the focus of long and heated controversy. The reasons for this preoccupation are not hard to identify. As salaried professionals, most theorists are themselves members of this group. Their concern has thus been motivated by an interest in self-understanding, if not by an inflated sense of their own importance. Apart from this is the genuine ambiguity of these positions. Given their heterogeneous composition, salaried managers and professionals pose some of the most difficult problems for the classification of persons according to their place within the social relations of capitalist production. Disagreements over the nature of the class structure have therefore focused on this stratum. Finally, because of their increasing numbers relative to other occupational groups, salaried managers and professionals have figured prominently in speculation regarding the transformation of the class structure. Critiques of earlier theories of class and projections of the future of class society have therefore placed salaried managers and professionals at the center of attention.[1]

---

*This was originally held as a panel, coordinated by Rhonda Levine, at the 1987 annual meeting of the American Sociological Association.

1. M. Oppenheimer, *White Collar Politics* (New York: Monthly Review Press, 1985), pp. 45–84; V. Burris, "The Discovery of the New Middle Class," *Theory and Society*, vol. 15, no. 3 (1986), pp. 317–49.

Recent attempts to clarify the class location of salaried managers and professionals have generally found the traditional Marxist definition of class (ownership versus nonownership of the means of production) an insufficient criterion for the assignment of class positions. By this criterion, wage and salary workers at all levels would be defined as proletarians—a view that does not square easily with the distinctive social characteristics and political behavior of the more privileged strata of salaried employees. Contemporary Marxists have therefore proposed alternative criteria by which to locate these positions within the class structure and clarify their relationship to both the capitalist and working classes.

One of the most provocative and far-reaching of such attempts to reformulate the Marxist conception of class is that presented by Erik Olin Wright in his book *Classes*.[2] In this brief presentation, I wish to comment upon what I see as the strengths and weaknesses of this new formulation and to situate it in relation to a variety of alternative perspectives. At the outset I should say that this is an impressive book. Wright tackles the most complex issues and presents them in a fashion that is unequaled for its clarity and precision. He is not afraid to alter his previously stated positions, and he openly acknowledges and explores the problematic aspects of his own arguments. While I am generally critical of Wright's new perspective, these positive qualities should not be forgotten during the comments that follow.

The Theory of Contradictory Class Locations

To understand the reasoning behind Wright's new conception of class structure, we must begin with his earlier theory of contradictory class locations—the theory which guided his work prior to the publication of *Classes*. Wright's theory of contradictory class locations is one variant of a more general strategy for the analysis of intermediate classes in capitalist society. I shall refer to this as the "Marxist-structuralist" approach to class analysis. What is common to the different variants of this approach is the notion that the capital-labor relation—the basic class relation of capitalist society—is not a unitary relation, but the articulation of several component relations. As the correspondence between these component relations is less than perfect, the possibility exists for class locations which simultaneously occupy a *superordinate* position on one dimension of the capital-labor relation and a *subordinate* position

---

2. E.O. Wright, *Classes* (London: Verso, 1985).

on others. These locations, combining characteristics of the proletariat and the bourgeoisie, are interpreted as an intermediate class or stratum within capitalist society.

Carchedi, Poulantzas, and Wright present three variants of this approach. Carchedi distinguishes between the ownership and functional aspects of the capital-labor relation.[3] Positions which are subordinate from the standpoint of ownership, but nevertheless participate in the function of capital (which Carchedi defines as the control and surveillance of the labor process) are classified as belonging to the "new middle class." Poulantzas decomposes the capital-labor relation into three components: its economic aspect (productive versus unproductive labor), its political aspect (supervision versus nonsupervision), and its ideological aspect (mental versus manual labor).[4] He argues that wage- and salary earners who occupy a superordinate position on any of these three dimensions should be excluded from the proletariat and classified as part of what he calls the "new petty bourgeoisie." Wright in his earlier theory, decomposed the rights and functions of capital into their ownership aspect (control over investments and resource allocation) and what he referred to as the relations of "possession"—that is, day-to-day control over the physical means of production and the labor process.[5] Salaried employees who do not own the means of production, but nevertheless retain significant powers of possession (either as managers or as semiautonomous experts), were classified by Wright as occupants of "contradictory class locations." Such positions, Wright argued, belong neither to the proletariat nor the bourgeoisie, but are objectively torn between opposing class positions. What was distinctive about Wright's contribution to this debate was (1) his coining of the felicitous term "contradictory class locations" to capture the nature of these positions, and (2) his claim that these positions did not constitute a discrete class as much as a heterogeneous stratum, of which two main clusters (managers and experts) could be distinguished.

Various criticisms have been raised against this approach to the analysis of intermediate class positions. First, we may note a number of objections to the specific criteria of class position given by different theorists. Generally speaking, most critics have found Poulantzas's definition of the nonproletarian pole of class relations to be too broad, resulting in an overly restricted notion of the working class. Conversely, Carchedi has been criticized for defining the functions of capital too

3. G. Carchedi, *The Economic Definition of Social Classes* (London: Routledge and Kegan Paul, 1977).

4. N. Poulantzas, *Classes in Contemporary Capitalism* (London: Verso, 1975).

5. E.O. Wright, *Class, Crisis and the State* (London: Verso, 1978).

narrowly, ignoring the nonsupervisory aspects of capitalists' domination over workers, and thereby underestimating the dimensions of the new middle class. Wright's model has been better received, although some critics have questioned the emphasis it places upon abstract class structures as opposed to concrete class subjects, and the appropriateness of the autonomy criterion by which Wright defines the class location of salaried experts.

At a more general level, two kinds of criticisms have been leveled. First, questions have been raised about the importance that these models attach to *authority* relations in the identification and analysis of intermediate class locations. Weberians like Parkin have interpreted this as a tacit acceptance of the Weberian premises of the independent importance of power and domination as bases of social cleavage, in contrast to the traditional Marxist emphasis on relations of property and exploitation.[6] Wright, in his new book, takes this criticism to heart, arguing that relations of property and exploitation have indeed been pushed to the background in recent Marxist analyses of the class structure. In a self-criticism of his own former position, he now maintains that it was an error to attempt to solve the problem of intermediate classes by incorporating relations of domination into the Marxist definition of class. From a Marxist standpoint, Wright argues, the introduction of such class criteria as the exercise of supervisory authority or autonomy from supervision creates two types of problems. First, such relations do not, in and of themselves, imply any necessary asymmetry of class interests. Second, incorporating relations of domination and subordination into the definition of class obscures the distinctiveness of class oppression by placing it on the same plane as numerous other forms of domination—sexual, racial, national, etc. This renders problematic the basic Marxist claim of the explanatory primacy of class relations in the analysis of social conflict and change.

A second general criticism of this approach is that it is focused too narrowly on the immediate production process and ignores other important dimensions of class relations. Weberians have been especially critical of the tendency of Marxists like Wright to treat market relations and distributive conflicts as mere epiphenomena. Theorists like Giddens, Parkin, and Collins have argued that the class position of salaried managers and professionals can be better understood from the standpoint of distributive relations and have proposed a variety of

---

6. F. Parkin, *Marxism and Class Theory: A Bourgeois Critique* (New York: Columbia University Press, 1979).

models in which skills and credentials are seen as the defining character-istics of intermediate classes.[7]

Wright's New Model of Class Structure

The new conception of class structure proposed by Wright in *Classes* can be seen as a response to these two general lines of criticism. His objective, in a nutshell, is to reconceptualize both authority and market relations and incorporate them in the definition of class in a manner which preserves the centrality of the Marxist concept of exploitation. To this end, Wright now argues that class must be conceived exclusively as an ownership relationship, rather than a complex unity of ownership and domination relations. Building on the work of Roemer, he maintains that exploitation is essentially a product of the unequal distribution of property rights in the means of production.[8] Relations of domination and subordination may enhance or reinforce such exploitation, but they are basically incidental to its operation.

As far as salaried managers and professionals are concerned, the key conceptual shift in Wright's new model can be described as follows. Whereas previously he conceptualized capitalist relations of exploitation as a complex articulation of ownership and domination (control) relations and identified intermediate strata by their contradictory position on different aspects of this mode of exploitation, he now dispenses with domination relations, reduces exploitation to a property relation, and argues that intermediate strata are distinguished by their contradictory positions on different modes of exploitation. The dominant form of exploitation in capitalist society, Wright argues, is that based on the private ownership of the material means of production, but there are also subsidiary forms of exploitation which derive from the unequal distribution of other productive assets. One such asset is skills—especially those whose supply is artificially restricted by credentials. A second is what Wright calls "organization assets," by which he means control over the conditions for the coordination of labor. Within this framework, salaried intermediaries are distinguished from the proletariat by their ownership of one or the other (or both) of these subsidiary

7. A. Giddens, *The Class Structure of the Advanced Societies* (New York: Harper and Row, 1973); Parkin, *Marxism and Class Theory*; R. Collins, *The Credential Society* (New York: Academic Press, 1979).

8. J. Roemer, *A General Theory of Exploitation and Class* (Cambridge, Mass.: Harvard University Press, 1982).

assets. Such differentials in skill and organization assets, Wright argues, enable them to exploit the labor of other workers, even as they themselves are exploited by capitalists.

This new theory of class structure has obvious continuities with Wright's earlier theory of contradictory class locations. The class location of salaried intermediaries can still be viewed as "contradictory" in the sense that they occupy both dominant and subordinate positions on different criteria of class position. What is different is the claim that these criteria represent different modes of exploitation, not just different aspects of a single, complex mode of exploitation. Descriptively the new theory also yields roughly equivalent class groupings. On the boundaries of the working class stand two kinds of contradictory class locations. The first are salaried managers, which Wright now distinguishes by their ownership of organization assets rather than by their control over the physical means of production and the labor of others. Second are non-supervisory experts, which Wright once distinguished by their autonomy, but now argues are distinguished by their ownership of skill assets.

At first glance, this reformulation would seem to answer the two main criticisms outlined earlier. First, it dispenses with the problematic (allegedly Weberian) notion of domination as a criterion of class position. This reaffirms the distinctiveness of the Marxist concept of class and, according to Wright, enables him to specify the interests of intermediate classes more clearly. Their interests both within capitalism and with respect to various noncapitalist alternatives can now be analyzed, he says, in terms of their "material optimizing strategies given the specific kinds of assets they own/control".[9] Second, it broadens the Marxist definition of class beyond the narrow confines of the production process to encompass those market relations, such as skill differentials and credential-based privilege, that were previously the exclusive purview of Weberian theory.

Should we then accept this new formulation of the Marxist concept of class? I think not. As I shall argue shortly, Wright's resolution of the twin problems of his previous model of class is accomplished mainly by definitional fiat, and his reassertion of the primacy of exploitation is achieved only by embracing a manifestly untenable notion of the nature of exploitation in capitalist society.

Consider first Wright's concept of "organization assets" as a basis of exploitation. Wright argues that the coordination of the technical division of labor is itself a source of productivity. This is plausible. He

---

9. Wright, *Classes*, p. 91.

further argues that organization can therefore be viewed as a productive asset which is controlled by managers and which enables them to exploit the labor of those who are without such assets. This claim is much more dubious. In what sense can organization be treated as an "asset" akin to property or skills? Wright admits that the asset of organization cannot be owned in the same way as property or skills; it has no existence apart from the positions within which it is exercised and cannot be transferred by its owner from one use to another. The ownership of organization assets is therefore indistinguishable from the exercise of hierarchical authority. Operationally, the two concepts identify identical class groupings. What then is gained by redefining the exercise of hierarchical authority as the ownership of organizational assets?

The crucial difference, it seems to me, is that the first view treats authority over the production process as a relation of domination which is ultimately *subordinate* to capitalist property ownership, while the latter defines it as a *separate* kind of property relation. From the standpoint of class interests, the first view interprets the privileges of managers as a dividend which they reap because of their strategic importance to the process of capitalist exploitation, while the latter treats them as the fruits of a form of exploitation which is independent of (and potentially *antagonistic* to) capitalist exploitation. The latter perspective, in my opinion, is problematic for at least two reasons. First, it posits a degree of conflict between capitalists and managers, which is in striking contrast to their actual political behavior. Second, it assumes that the economic returns to managerial status exist mainly because of the contribution of managers to productivity—a one-sided view which downplays the unproductive role of managers in enforcing the extraction of surplus.

Wright's concept of skill-based exploitation poses similar problems. As with exploitation based on organization assets, Wright maintains that the rewards accruing to credentialed employees reflect the greater contribution of more skilled employees to the total social product. This is similar to the argument of "human capital" theory, and there is unquestionably a partial truth to this proposition. But Wright's wholesale acceptance of this view ignores a wealth of empirical evidence demonstrating the tenuousness of the relationship between credentials and productivity or between productivity and market rewards.[10] On this question, the more cynical outlook of those Weberians like Parkin and Collins, who see credentials as an essentially arbitrary political/ ideological mechanism for restricting market opportunities, while one-

---

10. S. Bowles and H. Gintis, *Schooling in Capitalist America* (New York: Basic Books, 1976).

sided in its own way, nevertheless captures a truth that is missing in Wright's analysis.[11]

Wright's claim that credential exploitation can be viewed as *independent* of capitalist exploitation is also questionable. Credentials (or the lack thereof) are certainly important as a mechanism mediating between class positions as "empty places" within the social division of labor and social classes as concrete collectivities with a degree of intergenerational continuity. They may also serve as a barrier that reduces the exploitation of certain salaried occupations below what it would be otherwise, although I think this can easily be exaggerated. But, as any Ph D who has driven a cab for a living can attest, credentials are basically valueless unless they provide entry into occupational positions that entail strategic responsibilities, are not easily rationalized, and therefore command special compensation. The nature and distribution of such positions is certainly influenced by the structure of labor markets, but is it also and more fundamentally conditioned by the powers and interests invested in the private ownership of the means of production. The precariousness and dependent status of skill-based privilege is demonstrated nowhere more clearly than when the interests of capital dictate the deskilling of once privileged occupations as a means of increasing the rate of exploitation.

Like his redefinition of hierarchical authority as the ownership of organization assets, Wright's concept of skill-based exploitation is intended to appropriate for Marxism the conceptual terrain of Weberian theory, without abandoning the fundamental principles (as he understands them) of a Marxist perspective. Once again, however, this is achieved mainly by definitional fiat. Concerned to establish the Marxist pedigree of his new perspective, Wright argues that Weberians treat skills and credentials from a "culturalist" standpoint (that is, in terms of the meaning systems that shape social action), whereas he conceptualizes them from a "materialist" standpoint (that is, in terms of objective patterns of exploitation that exist independently of the subjective states of actors). This, I believe, is both a caricature of the Weberian perspective and an undue restriction on the kinds of analysis that can properly be called "Marxist." As Marxists themselves have shown, what passes for skill in a given society or what is certified by credentials is very much a social construction and therefore dependent upon the subjective states of actors.[12]

---

11. Parkin, *Marxism and Class Theory*; Collins, *The Credential Society*.

12. Bowles and gintis, *Schooling in Capitalist America*; M.S. Larson, *The Rise of Professionalism* (Berkeley: University of California Press, 1977).

Conclusion

As these comments are intended to be of an exploratory character, I shall not attempt to present a full-blown alternative theory of class that addresses all of the problems touched upon above.[13] I would, however, like to offer some suggestions about what I think might be some more promising directions for theoretical development. First, let me say that I think that Wright's attempt to refocus our attention on the concept of exploitation is entirely appropriate, and indeed is the most important theoretical contribution of the book. If the Marxist concept of class has anything distinctive to offer to the analysis of social cleavage in capitalist society it is certainly the notion that material interests rooted in relations of exploitation define the fault lines along which epochal struggles for social transformation take place. Moreover, it must be admitted that continuing controversies over Marx's labor theory of value raise numerous questions regarding the traditional Marxist concept of exploitation and call for renewed theoretical work in this area.[14] I would strongly reject the proposition, however, that Roemer's game-theoretical concept of exploitation offers a fruitful starting point for such efforts. More promising, I would argue, is an open and unashamed attempt to explore the possibilities for rapprochement between Marxist class analysis and the more materialist versions of Weberian theory.[15] This, I believe, is what Wright is surreptitiously doing in his new book, despite his best efforts to cover his tracks with strained redefinitions of familiar Weberian concepts.

In my opinion, Roemer's concept of exploitation is deficient for at least two reasons. First, it is based on a wholly inappropriate form of abstraction—inappropriate in the sense that it abstracts away from not merely contingent, but absolutely *fundamental*, aspects of exploitation as it actually occurs in capitalist society. Like the deductive models of neoclassical economics, Roemer's method disregards what is historically specific about capitalist society and focuses on formal, ahistorical similarities. Second, his method of conceptualizing exploitation is entirely arbitrary in that it is possible to posit the existence of diverse forms of exploitation on the basis of thought experiments that are constrained only by the imagination of the theorist (for an elaboration of

---

13. See V. Burris, "Class Structure and Political Ideology," *The Insurgent Sociologist*, vol. 14, no. 2 (1987), pp. 5–46.

14. See I. Steedman *et al.*, *The Value Controversy* (London: Verso, 1981).

15. See V. Burris, "The Neo-Marxist Synthesis of Marx and Weber on Class," in N. Wiley (ed.), *The Marx–Weber Debate* (Newbury Park, Calif.: Sage Publications, 1987).

these criticisms, see Kieve and Carchedi).[16]

In opposition to Roemer and Wright, I would insist that capitalist relations of exploitation cannot be specified independently of the relations of domination through which they are maintained and reproduced. Neither can they be specified independently of certain market relations that are essential to the appropriation of surplus, but which are not entirely given by the structure of ownership and production relations. Most basically, for capitalist exploitation to take place, workers must be subjected to competition from a reserve army of labor to drive down the value of their labor power, and jobs must be rationalized and/or subjected to surveillance in order to ensure that the labor expended exceeds the value of the wage. Whatever one might hypothesize as possible in the Robinson Crusoe world of Roemer's thought experiments, neither of these conditions are incidental to the process of exploitation as it actually occurs in capitalist society.

If class positions are to be defined according to their place within the process of exploitation, then it follows that they must be specified by a *combination* of ownership, authority, and market relations. I think one is justified to treat the ownership element as the dominant relation within this ensemble and the one which gives coherence to the overall process of exploitation. This I take to be the basic premiss of a Marxist theory of class. The difficult task is to bring these elements together in a manner which recognizes the specificity of authority and market relations, while also grasping their dependence upon the relations governing the allocation of the material means of production—that is, capitalist property ownership. The more one-sided versions of Marxist theory err by ignoring this specificity and treating authority and market relations as epiphenomena. Weberians, on the other hand, grasp the distinctiveness and practical importance of authority and market relations, but theorize these in a manner that exaggerates their autonomy from ownership relations. Wright's error, I believe, is that while sensing the importance of authority and market relations for class analysis, but still wishing to be loyal to what he considers to be the fundamentals of Marxist theory, he has attempted to force these relations into the conceptual straitjacket of property ownership which seriously distorts his understanding of their operation. In a perverse way, he rejects what is most valuable in Weberian theory (the specificity of authority and market relations and their importance for the concrete

---

16. R.A. Kieve, "From Necessary Illusion to Rational Choice?," *Theory and Society*, vol. 15 (1986), pp. 557–82; G. Carchedi, "Classes and Class Analysis," Chapter 3 above.

experience and behavior of class subjects) in order to embrace what is most problematic (a multidimensional model of separate and independent bases of exploitation).

If space allowed, I believe I could demonstrate an exactly parallel tendency on the part of certain Weberian theorists to force Marxist concepts into a restricted Weberian framework—for example in Dahrendorf's attempt to reduce all class relations to authority relations or Parkin's claim that capitalist property ownership can be reconceptualized as merely another form of market closure.[17] But that will have to be the subject of another paper.

I recognize that these arguments leave some of the problems that motivated Wright's new theory unresolved. Seeking to incorporate authority and market relations within the Marxist concept of class does indeed complicate the analysis of class interests and undermine some of the traditional arguments for the primacy of class. Nevertheless, I believe that it is better to confront these problems at an empirical level than to sweep them under a theoretical rug. If the perspective I have advanced means that the material interests of intermediate classes are less clear-cut than they might appear if classes were defined exclusively by property ownership, then I say that this is but a reflection of the complexity of the contemporary class structure. And, if it means that the Marxist concept of class is less radically distinct from other bases of privilege, such as race or nation, then I say that this is to be welcomed, for it may help to overcome the persistent difficulties Marxists have had in applying their conceptual framework to these important issues.

---

17. R. Dahrendorf, *Class and Class Conflict in Industrial Society* (Stanford, Calif.: Stanford University Press, 1959); Parkin, *Marxism and Class Theory*.

EDUCATION, EXPLOITATION, AND CLASS CONSCIOUSNESS

Arthur Stinchcombe

By p. 135 in Erik Wright's book *Classes*, we have not yet confronted any data, nor any particular societies, socialist or capitalist, any subgroups of workers known by common names like "plumbers" rather than by a series of minuses and pluses in a conceptual table.[1] Even then, the first table is twenty-nine pages later, p. 164. For an old-fashioned positivist like me, that's a long time without contact with the world, with a flow of facts of some kind. So I will start my comments at the wrong end of the book, with the first big results in the empirical chapters.

The big result in Chapters 5–7, is, I believe, the direct complement of the first big finding that established Wright's reputation. That finding was that class position (relations of ownership of the means of production or authority over labor power), added explanatory power to education and occupation that were the staple of the status attainment literature. The principal result of the tables in Chapters 5–7 is that education adds explanatory power to all sorts of class position definitions.

It might seem, if Wright did not write 164 pages first, that this means that the correct position is a little of this, a little of that: a little Marxism, a little "social stratification." So what Wright has to show in the first part of the book is that there is a good argument that the superior returns to education in various kinds of societies are exploitative. He ends up doing that by claiming that the main returns are to credentials, not to any difference in competence that education makes.

Although Wright relies on Roemer for an extended definition of exploitation, this is not the position that Roemer took in his work.[2] Even if there were truly superior productivity of people with increased education, Roemer would regard their having to work less for a given standard of living, or to work the same for a higher living standard, as exploitation. Further, if education is only a certification system which functions as a gigantic IQ test, and if IQ increases productivity, then Roemer would still regard the resulting greater income of people with college degrees as exploitation. So agreeing that higher education of,

---

1. E.O. Wright, *Classes* (London: Verso, 1985).
2. J. Roemer, *A General Theory of Exploitation and Class* (Cambridge, Mass.: Harvard University Press, 1982).

say, college professors are exploitative does not depend on the argument
that the returns to education or IQ are pure monopoly earnings, earned
only by keeping other people out of the job.

It seems to me to be a good socialist position that people should not
be able to live better than others because they are smarter, or just
because we as a society create positions in which they can live the life
required to learn to be truly productive. Roemer argues that one can
(and should) construct a definition of exploitation in which income or
leisure advantages both of brightness, and of the opportunity to learn to
be more highly productive than others, is exploitative. This distinguishes
Roemer, and perhaps Marxism, from the position of the Fabian socialist
George Bernard Shaw who argues that it is acceptable even under
socialism for talent to earn exceptional rewards. Wright, while not
agreeing with Shaw's position, also seems to want not to take Roemer's
position. For Wright, the exploitative position of educated people is a
position of credential monopoly. I am not willing to allow him that
rhetorical advantage for this book, because I would like to take away the
economic privileges that go with the genetic advantages in productivity
as well.

But to return to those 135 to 164 pages before letting us look at the
data. It takes a lot of talk to get us to forget that the relation of education to economic success and even class consciousness was a big finding of bourgeois sociology. If you are given a table on p. 4, with no
complicated theoretical introduction, in which the independent variables
are an index of education, authority, and property relations (p. 150), the
first thing that will pop into your head is W. Lloyd Warner or August
Hollingshead and their index of socioeconomic status. So we have all
those pages to convince us that having many years of education is essentially the same sort of thing as owning the means of production, rather
than the same as having high SES or the same as contributing to status
attainment.

How does it come about that education is as closely related to
working-class consciousness as ownership of the means of production or
authority in the workplace, in both the United States and Sweden? This
does seem to me to be a central thing we need to explain. We might
possibly explain the higher incomes of people with higher education by
their higher productivities. But here we have a general scale of attitudes
that clearly poses a series of questions about working class invasion
of managerial and ownership prerogatives (the six attitude questions
are given in notes on p. 263), and we find that even controlling
for managerial and ownership position, educated people are a lot
more conservative, less working-class conscious, than uneducated
people.

It seems to me that showing that one can form a definition of exploitation in which earning more money because of education is exploitative
does not really answer this question. It does seem to me however that
the fact that the educated who are otherwise equal in authority and
ownership do earn more money is likely to be crucial in explaining their
attitudes (and of course their behavior in strikes, their bargaining strategies in the civil service, and so on).

The first explanation I would suggest is that the class conflict in
modern societies is no longer about capitalism but about income distribution. What is distinctive about Swedish social democracy is not that
capitalists earn a lot less than they do elsewhere, but that all the rich
earn much less (especially after taxes, but actually before taxes as well)
than they do elsewhere. The argument then is that, wherever class
conflict was to be found in Marx's day, it is now to be found in the field
of exchange, not relations of production, and that it now has to do with
income tax rates and social security and health service tax rates and the
sizes of social security pensions for people who earned different
amounts before retirement, and the like.

The reason income does not predict class consciousness as well as
class position is because lifetime earnings are better predicted from class
position than from evanescent variations in last year's paychecks. To put
it another way, the first explanation is that class conflict today is over
governmental redistribution from the rich to the poor, rather than from
capitalists to workers. Consequently class positions which give people
the notion of where, in the long run, their taxation and pension interests
lie are good predictors of class consciousness. It is not because we teach
experts to be conservative in college, or because they hold precarious
monopolies, that their consciousness is not favorable to the working
class. It is because the working class is today trying to get their incomes,
not their profits.

A second possible explanation I will call "technocratic anti-
anarchism." Some of the questions by which class consciousness is
measured ask about one's reaction to workers throwing a wrench in the
works. Managers want things to run well because that is their job, and
capitalists want things to run well because that gives them higher profits
and because disruption is a powerful device for extracting higher wages
and benefits. But perhaps technocrats are natural adherents of what
used to be called in France the "parties of order." Their higher status is
based on their usefulness in planning things, not on their superiority at
collective bargaining, nor at functioning flexibly in times of disruption
and anarchy.

A third possibility departs from class analysis altogether, at least as I
understand Wright's use of class. Bourdieu analyzes the behavior of

highly educated people, controlling for money capital holdings.[3] He finds a great many matters of taste on which the educated differ markedly from the rich and from the workers. He argues that these matters of taste are essentially status claims. These status claims are often fairly unsuccessful in the income market, so I suppose they are oriented toward prestige in consumption. The educated go for Andy Warhol and Bertholt Brecht rather than boulevard theatre, for Braque and Goya rather than Renoir or Watteau, left bank galleries rather than right bank galleries, all of which distinguish them from the rich. Theatre rather than TV, opera rather than Tchaikovsky or Bizet, the "Well Tempered Clavier" rather than "Rhapsody in Blue," galleries rather than photography, distinguish the educated from workers. I'm sure the dimensions will sound familiar everywhere in the Western world. The question is, what do they have to do with Wright's measure of class consciousness?

One possibility is that attitude toward trade unions, especially their seamier, conflict-oriented side, is simply a cultural symbol. I have been in several countries during times when all the newspapers carried on as if there were serious class conflict going on, and as far as I could see daily life was not disturbed except that sometimes business executives and higher bureaucrats couldn't get a plane to go to a conference. Nobody really went cold or without electricity because of the long coal strike in England, for example—at least nobody I am likely to know when I go there. So what trade unions may be in the life of an educated person is merely a particularly interesting actor in the drama that we read on the front pages, a cultural object.

I am reminded of Bernard Beck's comment when asked why Colonel North was a hero in the United States: he said it had to do with the script that was played out on TV. Most Americans disapprove of many of the things he did, just as they would disapprove of most of the things John Wayne did on the screen if he did them in real life. But like John Wayne, Colonel North was cast as a hero in the script, whether or not you really believe in standing tall and shooting things up. Similarly, the trade unions and working-class conflict groups in Wright's questions may be simply cast as the representatives of low culture in the scripts we read in the newspaper, even though their low culture in economic conflict doesn't win any more economic advantages than, as college professors, our dignified proof to the dean that our salary is lower than the average of people of our distinction. So collective bargaining and class conflict is perhaps a symbol like the "Rhapsody in Blue," which educated people reject as "without distinction."

---

3. P. Bourdieu, *Distinction: A Social Critique of the Judgment of Taste* (Cambridge, Mass.: Harvard University Press, 1984).

To turn to a more minor matter, I do not think that it was necessary for Wright to bring up heavy guns of not being able to predict class consciousness very well to dismiss the silly distinction between "productive–unproductive" labor. Consider the bank clerk as an "unproductive" worker. Almost all of us pay a bank clerk to make up the monthly summary of our checking account, by agreeing to take a lower rate of interest on checking account money than we could get if we put what we weren't going to spend in savings (and carried cash for expenditures), or else simply by paying a fee. If those clerks aren't being productive, why are we willing to pay them to do it for us?

In this case, it is not because we need to have them help us exploit others. It's when we don't use much bank clerk labor, in the money market account, that we are exploiting labor in the classical Marxist sense.

Similarly, a big share of the advertising expense of the beer industry goes to pay the salaries of baseball or soccer stars. One can doubt whether baseball stars really communicate a lot to us about the true qualities of Budweiser without going so far as to argue that they are unproductive of the amenity of civilized life that we would want to have in a socialist society.

Of course we may think of buying nationally advertised beers rather than good old local beers that we used to buy, before TV modernized baseball, as an *inefficient* way of taxing us for paying baseball stars' salaries. But a good part of advertising revenue goes to people who produce values, on the diamond or pitch, that workers want, and would want under socialism. So it seems to me that they can't be considered "unproductive."

Baseball stars may not be very working-class conscious (though their unions have sure done them a lot of good), but that would not be sufficient to show that it is our business to define them as non-productive because they facilitate the economic concentration of brewers by making up an attractive background for a beer ad.

A CRITIQUE OF WRIGHT'S THEORY OF CONTRADICTORY CLASS LOCATIONS

Peter F. Meiksins

Erik Olin Wright's *Classes* is an ambitious book which raises a wide range of questions for Marxist theory.[1] The rational-choice model of exploitation which he adapts from John Roemer's work has become the center of a burgeoning controversy.[2] Wright's work also is an inter-vention in the growing debate regarding the relationship between Marxist and Weberian theories of class.[3] It will not be possible here to do justice to the many questions this complex book raises. Instead, this paper will focus on an aspect of *Classes* that has, thus far, received rela-tively little critical discussion: the class "map" which results from Wright's new analytical framework.

Like most neo-Marxist class theories, Wright is particularly concerned to make theoretical sense out of the growing "middle class" of nonmanual labor in contemporary capitalist societies. In his earlier work, he argued that many of these strata occupy "contradictory class locations" that straddle the major classes in capitalist society.[4] Wright now rejects the theoretical framework on which this argument was based. Because it focused on relations of domination rather than exploitation, his earlier approach tended, in his view, to weaken the link between the analysis of "class locations" and the analysis of objective interests (p. 56). It also tended to slide into the "multiple oppressions" approach to society, in which class appears as merely one among a variety of social cleavages, none of which is particularly central to the

---

1. E.O. Wright, *Classes* (London: Verso, 1985).
2. See A. Carling, "Exploitation, Extortion and Oppression," *Political Studies*, vol. 35 (1987), pp. 173–88; G. Carchedi, "Classes and Class Analysis," chapter 3 above; E.M. Wood, "Rational Choice Marxism: Is the Game Worth the Candle?," *New Left Review*, no. 177; P. Meiksins, "New Classes and Old Theories: The Impasse of Contemporary Class Analysis," in R. Levine and J. Lembcke (eds), *Recapturing Marxism: An Appraisal of Recent Trends in Sociological Theory* (New York: Praeger, 1987).
3. See V. Burris, "The Neo-Marxist Synthesis of Marx and Weber on Class," in N. Wiley (ed.), *The Marx–Weber Debate* (Newbury Park, Calif.: Sage Publications, 1987); F. Parkin, *Marxism and Class Theory: A Bourgeois Critique* (New York: Columbia University Press, 1979); P. Meiksins, "Beyond the Boundary Question," *New Left Review*, no. 157 (1986), pp. 101–20; Meiksins, "New Classes and Old Theories."
4. E.O. Wright, *Class, Crisis and the State* (London: Verso, 1978).

process of historical development (p. 57). In his new work, he seeks to overcome these problems by placing the concept of exploitation squarely in the middle of his analysis.

However, Wright contends that simply "parroting" the basic Marxist notion that capitalism is built on the exploitation of wage-labor by capital leaves unanswered many questions about contemporary class structure. The simple polarization that would seem to be implicit in the classical Marxist notion of exploitation has not developed. Consequently, "it has become more difficult to sidestep the theoretical problem of the gap between the abstract polarized concept of class relations and the complex concrete patterns of class formation and class struggle" (p. 9). He therefore rejects a "two-class" model of capitalist society, returning instead to his earlier notion that there is a range of "contradictory class locations" between the bourgeoisie and the proletariat.

Two theoretical arguments are central to Wright's new analysis of class. First, he argues that it is the dynamics of exploitation that make certain locations contradictory. Replacing the traditional Marxist analysis of exploitation with a modified version of John Roemer's "rational-choice" model,[5] he argues that contemporary capitalist societies embody three distinct modes of exploitation—traditional capitalist exploitation, rooted in the control of alienable assets; skill exploitation, rooted in the differential distribution of skills and credentials; and organization assets, rooted in unequal control over the structuring of the process of production. These coexisting forms of exploitation produce a far more complex class structure than Marx anticipated. In addition to a number of intermediate "class locations" for each type of exploitation (for instance, petty bourgeois property owners who are neither exploiters nor exploited), there exists a range of "locations" which are exploiting along one dimension of exploitation while exploited along others. For example, managers and supervisors, although they lack control over alienable assets and may, thus, be said to be exploited by capitalists, also exploit in the sense that they benefit from their control over skills and/or organization assets (pp. 86–7). Wright places particular emphasis on this last type of "contradictory class location"; just as the bourgeoisie emerged as a contradictory class location within feudalism, so has the class of managers and bureaucrats emerged within capitalism as "a principle of class organization which is quite distinct from capitalism and which potentially poses an alternative

---

5. J. Roemer, *A General Theory of Exploitation and Class* (Cambridge, Mass.: Harvard University Press, 1982).

to capitalist relations" (p. 87).

Second, he insists that a Marxist class analysis which discussed only class locations would be incomplete. Citing Adam Przeworski and other neo-Marxist theorists, Wright contends that there is no simple correspondence between class location and actual patterns of class formation: "The class structure may define the terrain of material interests upon which attempts at class formation occur, but it does not uniquely determine the outcomes of those attempts" (p. 123). This is particularly true of "contradictory class locations," given the highly complex pattern of class interests their location in capitalist social structure produces (p. 124).

Wright's new analysis of contradictory class locations may be criticized on at least three grounds. First, questions can be raised about the redefinition of exploitation on which he bases his argument that contradictory class locations are contradictory. Second, his contention that contradictory class locations such as bureaucrats and officials represent a possible non-proletarian challenge to capitalism may be criticized on both theoretical and historical grounds. Finally, Wright is unable to put into practice the notion that there is no simple correspondence between what he calls "class location" and "class formation." Indeed, one can argue that his own analysis of class conflict places him very close to the position which he is trying to criticize. Ironically, a more thoroughgoing analysis of the relationship between "class formation" and "class location" might have led Wright to question the need for a theory of contradictory class locations. It may well be that a subtle, historical approach to the development of class conflict, coupled with the *traditional* Marxist analysis of exploitation may provide more insights into the nature of class in contemporary capitalist society.

Exploitation

In referring to various types of non-manual labor as "contradictory class locations," Wright is going beyond the mere proposition that certain types of labor are privileged, or that the category of non-capitalists is differentiated and disunited. He is asserting that these "locations" are qualitatively different, in class terms, from the proletariat as it has been traditionally defined. This assertion is rooted in his insistence that these groups are, in some sense, exploiters.

The theory of exploitation on which Wright bases this new theory of "contradictory class locations" represents a fundamental departure from the traditional Marxist analysis of exploitation.

Wright rejects the traditional Marxist view that exploitation should be defined as the appropriation of surplus labor. In its place, he develops a definition of exploitation in terms of per capita shares of the total social pie. If an individual or group receives less than their per capita share of the available social assets, they are economically oppressed. Exploitation requires that the oppressing class benefit at the expense of the oppressed, that the welfare of the exploiting class depend upon the work of the exploited class (p. 75). He goes on to suggest that exploitation really means appropriation of the fruits of someone else's labor, or its equivalent, consuming more than one produces (pp. 75-6). It is the antagonism inherent in this interdependency that is the foundation of class and class struggle.

On the basis of this definition, Wright suggests that there is more than one type of exploitation in capitalist society, as we have already seen. It is the existence of these multiple exploitations that is the key to "contradictory class locations", since one can be an exploiter along one dimension and exploited along another. Wright's argument, therefore, stands or falls on whether he can establish that these multiple exploitations exist.

There are a number of theoretical problems with Wright's analysis of multiple exploitations, especially his discussion of skill exploitation and organization asset exploitation. In his discussion of the former, Wright suggests that credentialed workers benefit at the expense of those who lack them. Those who possess credentials have artificially restricted the availability of certain skills, thereby obliging employers to pay them wages that exceed the value of their "marginal product." It follows, therefore, that they are appropriating the labor of someone else (p. 76). But, is this the case? Wright offers no proof that the holders of credentials are, in fact, receiving wages in excess of their "value." He is dismissive, for example, of the possibility that the skills possessed by those who have credentials make them more productive, so that they are entitled to higher wages (p. 77). Nor does he demonstrate that credentials always regulate the supply of labor in such a way as to ensure that wages are "too high." Is it not possible that credentials may, at least at times, keep the market for certain skills from being flooded, preventing the cheapening of labor below its actual "value"? In other words, it is not at all clear that credentialed workers are necessarily exploiters of the uncredentialed. Had Wright attempted to analyze the distribution of the social product in capitalist society, this would have become immediately obvious. And, if some (or all) of the credentialed are not exploiters, then their class location may *not* be different from that of those who lack such credentials.

Furthermore, and more fundamentally, Wright's discussion of skill passes rather lightly over an important aspect of Marx's analysis of the capitalist labor process. As Marx pointed out, capitalism tends to create collective labor processes within which *groups* of workers, not individuals, are engaged in the production of value and surplus-value.[6] Different individuals within the labor process may be more or less highly rewarded; but, it is the group, not the individual that is exploited. From Wright's point of view, the more highly paid portions of the collective laborer would be viewed as exploiters of those with whom they "cooperate" in producing surplus-value. Yet, their relationship is a fundamentally cooperative one whose primary beneficiary is a third party—the *capitalist* exploiter. This is obscured by Wright's willingness to equate distinctions of skill with the capitalist exploitation of wage-labor.

Wright's discussion of organization assets is unsatisfactory in a different way. He explicitly includes this concept in his analysis of exploitation in order to deal with Soviet-type economies (pp. 78–9). Yet, he also asserts that, under capitalism, one may distinguish organization asset exploitation from capitalist exploitation. Certain "class locations" may be exploiters in one sense but not in the other; hence, organization assets may also be the basis for contradictory class locations.

Most Marxists would concede that those who determine the organization of the labor process are probably in the position of being exploiters of other people's labor. However, as Carchedi has pointed out, it is not at all clear that this is in any way distinct, at least under capitalism, from traditional capitalist exploitation.[7] Wright is not talking here about the classical problem of ownership vs control over the means of production. Rather, he is talking about the structuring of production itself. But, if someone controls the means of production, as capitalists do, they *automatically* control organization assets. As innumerable examples from history will show it is rare indeed to find a situation where those who *did not* control the means of production could successfully structure production in ways opposed by those who did.[8] And, if control over organization assets is not distinct from capitalist property, why does Wright postulate it as a distinct form of exploitation under capitalism?

These are only a few of the possible objections to Wright's analysis of multiple exploitations. The central point, however, is that he is not able to ground his theory of contradictory class locations in a coherent

6. K. Marx, *Capital* (Harmondsworth: Penguin/NLR, 1976).

7. Carchedi, "Classes and Class Analysis", above.

8. For example, in the case of the scientific management movement, see P. Meiksins, "Scientific Management and Class Relations: A Dissenting View," *Theory and Society*, vol. 13 (1984), pp. 177–209, and M. Calvert, *The Mechanical Engineer in America, 1830–1910* (Baltimore: Johns Hopkins Press, 1967).

analysis of exploitation. Consequently, his view that these locations are qualitatively different in class terms is called into question. He is certainly correct to point to differences of rank and skill and to note that these inequalities may become the basis for various forms of social conflict. But, he gives us no theoretical justification for seeing these distinctions and conflicts as more than forms of differentiation and disunity within the polar classes of capitalist society.

New Classes?

In *Classes* and in his recent collaboration with Bill Martin, Wright adds a new political wrinkle to his analysis of contradictory class locations.[9] In his original argument, the political significance of contradictory locations lay in their ambiguity, in their being "torn" between the two warring camps of bourgeoisie and proletariat. This point is retained in Wright's new formulation; but he adds to it the suggestion that the development of multiple exploitations, especially organization asset exploitation, may signal the rise within capitalism of post-capitalist class relations. In other words, those contradictory class locations which are exploiters in organization asset terms may be seen as a kind of proto-class that may develop into a ruling class in a post-capitalist society (Wright is less sure that skill exploitation can be seen as the basis for future *class* relations (p. 85)). The proletariat, then, may not be the only "gravedigger" of capitalism, from Wright's point of view. It will not be possible to consider all of the implications of this argument, which clearly bear on the class nature of Soviet-type societies. However, it is important to ask whether this makes sense as an analysis of *capitalist* class structure.

Wright's primary theoretical justification for his argument lies in his contention that skill exploitation and organization asset exploitation are not forms of capitalist exploitation. Each mode of production, according to Wright, is constituted by one primary mode of exploitation. Thus, capitalist exploitation is the basis of one mode of production, while organization asset exploitation is the basis of another. Modes of production, however, are abstract constructs—these "pure" types of exploitation do not exist as separate entities in actual societies, or social formations, to use Wright's term. When one descends to a lower level of theoretical abstraction and examines actual societies, one finds combinations of different modes of production, and, therefore, exploitation

9. E.O. Wright and B. Martin, "The Transformation of the American Class Structure, 1960–1980," *American Journal of Sociology*, vol. 93, no. 1 (1987), pp. 1–29.

(pp. 109–14). By arguing in this way, Wright is able to suggest that each form of exploitation is distinct and that each represents an alternative exploitative logic, by definition. It follows, therefore, that different types of exploiters may come into conflict when they encounter one another within hybrid social formations (hence the parallel he draws between the bourgeoisie under feudalism and experts and bureaucrats under capitalism).

Thus, Wright implies that, just as feudal social relations produced the capitalist, capitalist social relations created new, potentially contradictory exploiting classes. Yet, it is unclear in what sense the development of skill distinctions or the organization of the process of production contradicts capitalism—or creates groups who, by themselves, pose a substantial threat to capitalism. This is particularly true of organization asset exploitation. Clearly, the creation of hierarchically organized production process, the detailed division of labor, etc. is no threat to capitalism. Rather, they are the historical *product* of capitalism, very much a part of the development of large-scale, organized capitalism. And, as has already been suggested, it is virtually impossible to distinguish between capitalist exploitation and organization asset exploitation under capitalism. Under the circumstances, it is indeed hard to imagine, as Wright himself notes, conditions under which cadres of high managers and bureaucrats, who hold significant organization assets, might be led to reject the capitalist system which they control and from which they clearly benefit. For these groups, at least, the organization of the production process creates no contradictory dynamics.

One suspects, however, that Wright has in mind lower and middle managers and experts when he makes this argument. He suggests that a weakened capitalism, one that is no longer able to deliver the goods to such middling types, might spawn opposition—he speculates that managers and bureaucrats might be attracted to anticapitalist forms of statism in cases when capitalism seemed to be failing. This might become the basis for a new type of society in which organization asset and skill exploitation superseded capitalist exploitation as the dominant form of exploitation (pp. 90–91). Leaving aside the question of whether their modest control over organization assets makes them exploiters, let us ask how middle managers, bureaucrats, and experts would be likely to react if capitalism were to founder in this way. It is quite possible that they might be attracted to the idea of *modifying* capitalism in the direction of greater state planning and coordination, perhaps a kind of "managed capitalism" *à la* Felix Rohatyn. But, this hardly makes them anticapitalist, nor does it distinguish them from the large numbers of capitalists and even proletarians who have favored such ideas in times of crisis. On the other hand, the idea of an *anticapitalist* movement of intellectuals, managers, and bureaucrats is hard to imagine. What would such a movement advocate? Either it would have to be a democratic socialist movement, in which case both the working class and "middle-class" experts would be potential constituencies. Or, it would have to call for the creation of Soviet-type economies in which public ownership is combined with strong, centralized, undemocratic control over the economy. The idea that a manager or intellectual in an advanced capitalist society would find this an attractive way to "cash in" their organization assets strains the imagination to the breaking point.

Skill exploitation does, at first glance, appear to be contradictory to capitalist exploitation. Thus, it has frequently been noted that capitalism has leveling tendencies and seeks to destroy skill barriers and bottle-necks because they tend to raise the price of labor. And, it has frequently been the case that employees have resisted the worst conse-quences of capitalist exploitation by establishing skill and credential barriers.

It does not follow from this, however, that skill is a fundamental threat to capitalism. To begin with, we must remember that capitalists have also fostered skill distinctions at times. And, it may be that this is actually useful to the capitalist order. As Richard Edwards reminds us, a labor force divided by skill, rank, and credentials is in certain ways easier to control than a mass of undifferentiated labor.[10] Moreover, as Larson has pointed out in her analysis of professionalism, the logic of "credentialism" may also help to support the basic ideals of capitalist ideology, especially its individualism and its justification of inequality.[11]

Even if this were not true, it needs to be added that it is hard to imagine a conflict between the pretensions of skill and the logic of capi-talist exploitation that would pose a fundamental threat to the capitalist system. Conflicts over skill tend to divide rather than to unite. And, the politics of skill is not incompatible with capitalism—all it requires is that merit be rewarded better. Capitalists have generally been able either to accommodate such demands (as with the organizational professions[12] and certain types of skilled labor) or to defeat those demands it was unwilling or unable to meet.

Under the circumstances, it should not surprise us that the historical record holds very few examples of significant middle-class technocratic or statist movements. Despite a large literature which has treated the

10. R. Edwards, *Contested Terrain* (New York: Basic Books, 1979).

11. M.S. Larson, *The Rise of Professionalism: A Sociological Analysis* (Berkeley: University of California Press, 1977).

12. See P. Whalley, *The Social Production of Technical Work* (Albany, NY: State University of New York Press, 1986).

intermediate strata as naturally technocratic, managers, engineers, professionals and others have been notably unenthusiastic about such ideas.[13] On the contrary, they have either supported capitalism resolutely, hoping to better themselves within the system. Or, when opposition to the status quo has developed, it has tended to take forms reminiscent of certain kinds of working class resistance (for example, quasi-craft unions in the case of American engineers, or various forms of social-democratic politics in the case of British white collar and public sector workers).

In sum, there is little evidence that contradictory class locations spawn distinctive anticapitalist ideologies, nor is there strong theoretical justification for supposing that they will do so in the future. There are real conflicts and divisions set up by the hierarchical organization of production and the dynamics of skill. But, unhistorical arguments which imply that managers under capitalism want to, or may at some point want to, become Soviet-style managers do not advance our understanding of these social relations.

Class Location and Class Formation

Finally, we come to Wright's discussion of the contingent relationship between "class location" and "class formation." He insists that there is no immediate correspondence between class location and the actual patterns of class conflict that develop in real historical situations. This is particularly true of contradictory class locations, where material interests are complex and variable. But, it is also true of unambiguous class locations—it is always an open question how people will react to and perceive their material interests in concrete situations.

There is nothing fundamentally wrong with this theoretical view of class and class conflict. However, in practice, Wright's analysis of class has much more in common with the view of which he is critical than with his own theoretical framework. Consider his analysis, with which he attempts to justify his theoretical argument about class locations, of the differences in class sentiment between Sweden and the United States.

Wright hypothesizes that class consciousness should vary monotonically along the dimensions of his exploitation matrix (p. 251). That is, one would expect to find that levels of pro-working-class sentiment

---

13. See, for example, P. Meiksins, "The Myth of Technocracy: The Social Philosophy of American Engineers in the 1930s," paper presented to SHOT Conference, Pittsburgh, 1986.

should increase as one moves from unambiguously exploiting locations to contradictory class locations to unambiguously proletarian locations. And, his results appear to bear him out—working-class sentiment is stronger in working-class locations in both Sweden and the United States.

However, Wright also notes that this association was much stronger for the United States. In Sweden, pro-working-class sentiment had a broader base, extending into segments of the workforce with significant skills and/or organization assets. Indeed he presents evidence that many Swedish contradictory class locations identify with the working class more than do American proletarians. However, he explicitly rejects any suggestion that this undermines his analysis of class locations: "This does not imply that the objective basis of conflicts of interests among wage-earners in different classes has disappeared, but simply that their common interests as capitalistically exploited wage-earners have assumed greater weight relative to their differential interests with respect to organizational and credential exploitation" (p. 279). In effect, we are asked to conclude that procapitalist sentiment among proletarians is the result of the contingency of the process of class formation, while procapitalist sentiment among contradictory class locations is the result of objectively complex class interests. Similarly, pro-working-class sentiment among proletarians is the result of their unambiguous working-class interests, while pro-working-class sentiment among contradictory class locations develops only under certain highly contingent historical circumstances.

It should be obvious that there is a theoretical inconsistency in this form of argument. Moreover, there is more than a hint here of the mechanical "mirror-image" model of class consciousnesss of which Wright is so critical. That is, Wright *expects* to find more proletarian sentiment in proletarian locations than in contradictory class locations. When the results are more complex, for instance, when Swedish contradictory class locations are more pro-working class than American proletarians, he is forced to bend one part of his theoretical framework in order to retain the rest.

Ironically, had Wright stuck to his theoretical guns, he might have been able to interpret his data more consistently. Thus, had he employed a really *developmental* approach to class consciousness, in which "class locations" only established pressures and limits to which their "occupants" react, Wright's data would make more sense.[14] Thus, we could argue that class consciousness starts in a relatively undeveloped form for

---

14. R. Williams, *Marxism and Literature* (Oxford: Oxford University Press, 1977).

all employees. Occupational solidarity, the effort to protect skill, even individual forms of resistance contain a *germ* of class consciousness which may develop into something broader. The fact that a type of employee does not identify with the broader working-class movement, thus, does not necessarily mean that they are structurally different. It may only mean that the "germ" of class consciousness has not developed, or has developed differently, for historical reasons—state policy, ideological counterpressures, divisions and conflicts within the working class, etc. It thus becomes possible to explain the greater working-class orientation of the Swedish "contradictory class locations" as evidence of their having *developed* the germ of a class consciousness inherent in occupational consciousness into a larger sense of class. Similarly, the lower level of working-class identification among American "proletarians" is the result of the different history of class conflict in the United States. In sum, such an approach allows us to understand the ambiguous attitudes of *all* kinds of employees without ignoring the element of working-class consciousness inherent in them.

Conclusion

We are thus returned to the question of whether a theory of contradictory class locations is needed at all. Erik Olin Wright, and other influential new left theorists, have relied on this and similar formulations, arguing that there is no other way to make sense, within a Marxist framework, of the large numbers of non-manual workers in contemporary capitalist societies. The arguments outlined here, while in no sense meant as a complete analysis of contemporary capitalist social structure, are intended to call this assumption into question. Undoubtedly, the complexities of contemporary class structure pose many problems for Marxist theory; many questions do remain unresolved. However, it is not at all clear that the theory of contradictory class locations helps us to understand these complexities. Indeed, it may very well be that the answers lie in the *other* issue Wright raises—that is, the complex and contingent historical process through which capitalist relations of production shape actual patterns of class conflict. Perhaps it is in this direction that future theoretical and historical analysis should move.

WORK RELATIONS AND THE FORMATION OF CLASS CONSCIOUSNESS

Johanna Brenner

Careful, rigorous and honest struggle with theoretical issues is the hall-mark of Erik Olin Wright's work. *Classes* is no exception.[1] In its clarity of exposition, in its provocative ideas, in its comparative analysis of Sweden and the United States, this book makes a substantial contribution.

Wright consistently emphasizes the "probabilistic" relationship between class location on the one hand, class affiliation and action according to class interests on the other. Still, he contends that class consciousness systematically connects to objective interests arising from locations in a class structure. Managerial/supervisory workers and expert/semicredentialed workers will tend to have different world views because their interests differ from those of proletarians on two counts: (1) they enjoy higher incomes as a result of an exploitative transfer from other workers within capitalism, and (2) they have the potential to become a dominant class in alternative societies: statism or socialism.

Wright is right to look for underlying structural determinants of different world views, but, I think, wrong in how he has defined them. First, I think it important to recognize that even the most proletarianized workers still have short-run interests within capitalism that divide them from each other. Unskilled workers, just like skilled workers, can improve or maintain their position within the system by using strategies which put them in antagonistic relationships with other workers. Whatever their long-run interests, any given group of workers will have a set of short-run interests that do not lead to class-based world views. So, for example, private sector workers, experiencing a real decline in their standard of living and unable to take on their own employers, have supported tax decreases and cuts in public spending as a strategy to improve their own incomes, even at the expense of public sector workers and recipients of public services.

It is true that certain conditions, the militant organization of important sections of the working class, economic crisis, etc., help to

---

1. E.O. Wright, *Classes* (London: Verso, 1985).

change this set of interests by making particularistic and narrow strategies less possible and by making broader and more political forms of organization more possible. Thus, where public sector workers are well organized and there is a strong anti-racist movement, private sector workers might come to see that they have more to gain by affiliating with public sector workers to demand shifts in spending from the military to social services, corporate tax increases, control on the export of capital and so forth. The strength of trade union organization and the breadth of working-class political organization mediate experience and consciousness, but not only, as Wright says, because they provide different interpretations of experience. They also change the character of experience itself. Workers who fail to act in class conscious ways are not failing to understand their "real" interests, but are rather acting in terms of one set of interests, their immediate interests under given historical conditions, rather than in terms of another set of interests, the long-run benefit of an alternative.

However, short-run conflicts of interests among workers get constructed in different ways. And some conflicts are more enduring and difficult to overcome than others. This, it seems to me, was useful about Wright's earlier conceptualization of contradictory class locations which utilized two dimensions of actual work relationships: whether or not individual workers controlled the conditions of their work and whether or not their work put them in domination relations with other workers. This approach, whatever its weaknesses (and I think Wright has laid them out rather well), focused on how social relationships within production might define different experiences which in turn would produce different world views. There was a dynamic and social/historical element that is missing in Wright's current framework.

Attention to social relationships seems to me not only useful but very much in line with the classic Marxist argument that day-to-day experiences of conflict and cooperation at work could lead workers to take up kinds of affiliation, organization, action, militance that would in turn provide the experiential basis for the development of broader revolutionary vision. Marx argued that the proletariat is the historical bearer of a socialist revolutionary project not only because workers would benefit from ending their exploitation under capitalism (that is, it is in their "interest" to end capitalism), but because their experiences within capitalist production might allow them to imagine a society based on collective, democratic control over production as an alternative to capitalism.

Wright argues against his earlier conceptualization of contradictory class location on the ground that neither worker autonomy nor domination relations specify particular antagonistic economic interests. To take the example of managers: he says that unless we can show that

managers dominate labor in their own interests and not only in the
interest of capitalist owners, there is no reason to distinguish managerial
employees from other workers. As an alternative, Wright argues that
managers exploit other workers through their effective control of what
he calls organization assets. Managers have a claim on the surplus
because they control the coordinated cooperation among producers in a
complex division of labor.

Yet, it is not at all clear to me how managers are able to appropriate a
piece of the surplus for themselves through control over the coordination and planning of production separate from capitalist property
structures. Indeed, I find convincing Wright's earlier argument that
managers' relatively higher wages are a "loyalty dividend" paid out of
the surplus in order to insure that they carry out their control functions. (Of
course, managers in the upper tier may acquire large amounts of capital, in
which case they are no different from capitalist employers proper and so
present no analytic difficulty for traditional Marxist class theory.)

I would argue that it is more reasonable and useful, in differentiating
managers from workers within capitalism, to say that they have a different relationship to the capitalist surplus extraction process. Managers
and supervisors do not exercise authority simply to coordinate production but do so within a context in which the goal of production is
profit and the means to that goal is the extraction of surplus labor.
Managerial direction of other workers therefore has a two-sided character: on the one side, in coordinating production managers and supervisors may be performing tasks that are socially necessary labor; on the
other side, since production is being coordinated within constraints set
by the need to make an average rate of profit, managers also have to
control and discipline the workforce. Managers may exercise authority
in order to coordinate the labor process or they may exercise authority
in order to control workers—and often they do both at once. But these
are two distinct kinds of authority (and a failure to distinguish them
underlies Weberian claims about the inevitable connection between a
complex division of labor and bureaucratic hierarchy). Positions within
the labor process that synthesize information or coordinate different
aspects of production may exist without coercion, resting on the consent
of those receiving direction. On the other hand, a manager's capacity to
set the pace of work faster than what the workers themselves desire,
requires the right to discipline and rests on capitalist class relations. (In
making this point and in the following argument I'm relying very much
on Bob Carter's Capitalism, Class Conflict, and the New Middle Class. [2]

---

2. B. Carter, Capitalism, Class Conflict, and the New Middle Class (Boston: Routledge
and Kegan Paul, 1985).

However, he should not be held responsible for my formulations.)

Wright's definition of modes of production in terms of dominant forms of exploitation and exploitation in terms of effective control of productive assets leads him to separate the organization of the production process from the distribution of the product. On this basis, he can argue that managers exploit labor not as agents of capital but in their own interest and through their control of the labor process. However, this separation between structures of production and appropriation is unwarranted, since the organization of technology and the division of labor are always limited by the structures through which a surplus is appropriated. Even in feudalism, where the peasant household/community organizes production without interference from the landlord, feudal institutions affect the way that production is organized. For example, the inalienable character of both land and labor power limit concentration and centralization of the means of production, investment in technological innovation, and so forth.

The division of labor within production is only in part determined by a given level of technological development—presumably the same under socialism, capitalism, or statism. Much of the technology of production in both capitalist and statist society, including the particular division of tasks, the way that expertise is developed and practiced, the way that productive activities are coordinated, reflects the given social relations of production and would be different in a socialist society. In capitalism, the drive toward accumulation socializes production, including the evolution of a complex division of labor, but only in ways appropriate for the continued extraction of surplus labor.

Managerial tasks that involve giving direction in order to integrate and coordinate the labor process and to provide specialized knowledge are usefully distinguished from the authority exercised to discipline and control. But coordination tasks in themselves cannot be a base for exploitation, for the extraction of surplus labor. Exploitation does require discipline and control. However, under capitalism, the managerial tasks of discipline and control must be exercised toward the end of producing an average rate of profit. (I would also argue that the requirements of capitalist accumulation constrain the organization of production within the state in similar, although not as direct ways, but that point will have to be left aside here.)

By the same argument, I think that Wright's definition of the statist mode of production is less satisfactory than his earlier approach. In *Classes* he defines statism as the extension to the whole society of managerial control over coordinating production. In his article, "Capitalism's Futures", Wright asserted that in both statist and capitalist societies managers are in similar positions: they direct production but under constraints, in particular decisions about the allocation of investment, over which they have no control.[3] In capitalism, the allocation of investment is determined by the market, capital flowing to the most profitable areas. In statism, as Wright previously argued, the allocation of investment is determined directly in a process of political negotiation among bureaucratic sectors adjudicated by the highest decision-making bodies of the state. "The ruling class in a statist society is thus defined by those positions within the relations of bureaucratic domination that control the basic allocation of means of production and distribution of the social surplus. This implies that vast numbers of positions within the bureaucratic structure of the state economic apparatuses are *not* in the ruling class" (p. 98).

This argument suggests that managers might not have an objective interest in the statist alternative to capitalism and do not exploit other workers independently of capitalist exploitation. Yet, whatever their long-run interest in a democratic socialist alternative to capitalism, within capitalism, that is outside of a revolutionary transformation of the system, managers and supervisors must carry out, to a greater or lesser extent, control functions which do place them in an antagonistic relationship to other workers. The degree to which the jobs of lower-level supervisors involve them in control functions varies according to both management policies (the greater or less centralization of control/supervision) and the level of organization and combativity of the workers they are supposed to supervise. Thus, both their experience in work, their relationships with other workers, and their actual interests (for example, whether they have more to gain than to lose from cooperating with those they supervise) will also vary. None the less, most supervisors and managers, most of the time, however pressed by capital, will find themselves to one degree or another in an antagonistic relation to other workers. These real relationships within production can lead them to organize, when they do, separately from other unions and can open them up to technocratic/statist ideologies.

An analogous argument can be made in regard to the work of many professional and technical workers who do not exercise direct managerial authority. I think Wright is correct not to try to find a single dimension that differentiates both these workers and managers/supervisors from other occupational groups. (This is a problem with the work of other new middle-class theorists such as Poulantzas and Carchedi.) Still, I'm not convinced by his argument that these workers exploit others through a credential monopoly which raises their pay

---

3. E.O. Wright, "Capitalism's Futures," *Socialist Review*, no. 68 (1983).

above what it would be in a free market. Unskilled unionized workers make more money than nonunionized workers, but none of us I think would want to argue that they are exploiting nonunionized workers. Wright rejects his earlier emphasis on work autonomy as defining the contradictory location of these employees. He argues that, unlike the (petty bourgeois) self-employed professional or artisan, the autonomy of salaried professional/technical workers or skilled workers is generally highly contingent and therefore a weak criterion for class locations, as these ought to designate fairly stable and structurally determinate properties of positions within the social relations of production. I agree with Wright's critique of his former definition of these workers as in a contradictory location between the petty bourgeoisie and the working class.

However, I think that there are characteristics of their work that do distinguish them from other nonmanagerial employees. They possess knowledge that other workers don't have and that often supplies the conditions and *direction* for the work that other workers do. This may be in part a necessary aspect of the technical division of labor—that is, of the need for specialized knowledge. But it is also the result of their own actions aiming to monopolize knowledge as a labor market strategy and the result of management actions aiming to reduce management's dependence on its employees. As members of a collective labor process, workers with expertise have no reason to differentiate themselves from other workers, to refuse to share their knowledge, or to be hostile to having the goals of their work set by the associated producers rather than by an employer. As possessors of knowledge, knowledge workers have no particular interest in organizing themselves apart from other workers. Nor do they have a reason to resist identifying with the class of producers whose collective labor is exploited by capital. On the other hand, as competitors on a labor market, these workers can improve their standard of living by excluding others from access to their knowledge. But this labor market strategy will itself have implications for the social relationships these workers enter into at work. Insofar as this set of workers judge that their own higher salaries depend on their monopolization of knowledge, they have a consistent interest, within capitalism, in maintaining their exclusive control over knowledge and in adopting an elitist ideology which justifies that control. This interest in protecting their position within the labor market encourages their commitment to defending their exclusive control over certain kinds of decisions, reinforces the hierarchical character of their relations with other workers, and can therefore lead them to resist attempts by other workers to expand and democratize decision-making. It will encourage them to insist on their distance from other workers and discourage their identification with the trade union movement. It will also tend to attract them to a technocratic/statist alternative to capitalism. I would argue that analogous sets of pressures characterize many service professionals' relationship to other workers and to their clients, most of whom will be working class.

Workers with specialized skills are also subject to tendencies toward proletarianization. However, the impact of proletarianization on consciousness has historically varied. Sometimes, proletarianized workers have been in the forefront of militant class confrontations (for instance, the shop stewards' movement in early twentieth-century England). But many times proletarianization has led them to organize primarily to restore old prerogatives, thus to a kind of trade unionism that is in a very uneasy alliance with the rest of the trade union movement.

Defining class location in terms of exploitation interests and measuring exploitation by income, Wright is forced to assert an overly abstract connection between objective interests and consciousness. There is nothing in his definition of class location that theorizes the process through which workers develop their world views. Work relationships are not the only determinant of consciousness. However, it seems to me that they are a significant structural dimension differentiating experience and thus leading to different ways of understanding the world. Attending to them can provide one point of entry for analyzing changing consciousness.

EXPLOITATION, IDENTITY, AND CLASS STRUCTURE: A REPLY TO MY CRITICS*

Erik Olin Wright

Most of the criticisms raised in this symposium on *Classes*[1] can be grouped under two general headings: (1) criticisms which question various aspects of my analysis of exploitation, although not necessarily rejecting the general claim that class structures should be defined with respect to mechanisms of exploitation; (2) criticisms which question the definition of class structure exclusively in terms of exploitation and argue that the concept of class must also capture the idea of common lived experiences. Both of these clusters of criticisms touch on fundamental issues in class analysis. In what follows I will try to respond to these criticisms in the spirit of clarifying and advancing the conceptual issues at stake rather than simply defending the arguments I have made in the past.

Class and Exploitation

It will be helpful to recapitulate briefly the core argument in my analysis of class structures. Classical Marxism contains a well-developed concept of the fundamental classes of the capitalist mode of production—capitalists and workers—but does not provide a satisfactory way of conceptualizing what in common language is called the "middle class." I proposed the following solution: actual capitalist societies should be understood as containing a variety of forms of exploitation, not simply capitalist exploitation as such. While these noncapitalist forms of exploitation may be structurally subordinated to capitalism—indeed, this is what is entailed by calling the society "capitalist"—nevertheless, they can still provide the material basis for secondary forms of class relations. The "middle classes" can then be understood as locations in the class structure which are *exploited* in terms of capitalist mechanisms of exploitation, but *exploiters* in terms of one or more of these secondary mechanisms of exploitation.

---

*I would like to express my gratitude to Michael Burawoy for refusing to let me sidestep certain crucial theoretical problems in an earlier draft of this paper.

1. E.O. Wright, *Classes* (London: Verso, 1985).

More concretely, I argued that "actually existing capitalism" contains two secondary forms of exploitation: exploitation based on the control over organizational assets and exploitation based on the ownership of monopolized skills, most notably where these are legally certified through "credentials".[2] The middle class, therefore, consists of wage-earners who are organization and/or skill exploiters.

Three general objections to this formulation have been advanced in the papers commenting on *Classes*: first, while the ownership of skills or credentials may reduce the rate of capitalist exploitation, they should not be thought of as a distinctive mechanism of exploitation in their own right; second, organization assets cannot be distinguished from capitalist property itself, and thus cannot be the basis for a distinctive mechanism of exploitation; and third, regardless of the issue of whether or not managers and professionals are exploiters, their class interests are so deeply linked to those of the bourgeoisie that it makes no sense to regard them as in a distinct class with latently anticapitalist tendencies at all. They may be junior partners of the bourgeoisie, but they are not part of some "contra-dictory class location" as I suggest. Let us look at each of these issues.

Skill Exploitation

Arthur Stinchcombe questions the claim that the higher incomes that go to people with high levels of skills or talents can be considered "exploit-ation." As an alternative he suggests that such higher income basically reflects the higher levels of productivity of wage-earners with high levels of skills. For various reasons one might want to criticize inequalities in income based on differential productivity, but this should not be conflated with exploitation—the unjust transfer of labor from one econ-omic agent to another.[3]

---

2. It is important to note that the argument is not that the possession of skills *per se* constitutes a basis for exploitation. Skill exploitation is based on the restriction of the *supply* of particular skills, through one mechanism or another, so that the price of those skills (that is, the wage of the skilled labor power) is above its costs of production. Credentialing is the most important institutionalized mechanism of such monopolization, and thus I generally identify skill exploitation with credentialism.

3. This is obviously a highly truncated general definition of "exploitation." The use of the adjective "unjust" is intended to distinguish exploitations from gifts (since gifts also involve the transfer of labor from one agent to another), but this obviously simply displaces the problem to establishing appropriate criteria for the unjustness of a transfer. Throughout *Classes* I adopt a modified version of John Roemer's concept of exploitation; J. Roemer, *A General Theory of Exploitation and Class* Cambridge, Mass.: Harvard University Press, 1982. The core idea is that exploitation involves two critical elements: (1) the material welfare of exploiters are at the expense of the material welfare of the exploited; and (2) the material welfare of the exploiter depends upon the labor or effort of the exploited. Cri-terion 1 alone defines economic oppression. The two criteria together define exploitation.

The issue, then, is whether an income differential which reflects productivity differences can still constitute exploitation. I think that it can. Consider the following imaginary world: every person is allocated an equal amount of land, but different land has different degrees of fertility and is suitable for growing different crops. Also imagine, for simplicity, that everyone in this imaginary world wants to consume the same bundle of crops (the only things produced in the world). I happen to have a parcel of land that can grow a crop that few other parcels can grow and which also turns out to be very desirable. Everyone else is willing to trade large quantities of their produce for mine. What happens in this world? I discover that, *given my private ownership of this land,* I can obtain the commodities I wish to consume by working many fewer hours than people on other land. Everyone ends up with the same consumption (by the assumption of the story), but I have to work fewer hours to get it. This, I would argue, is appropriately described as a situation in which I am able to exploit other producers by virtue of my ownership of the special land.[4]

The story I have just told could, of course, also be described by saying that my land is more productive than other land since the products from it will have a higher equilibrium price (or, equivalently, that the land itself would have a higher market value if it were traded). The higher income I receive (in the form of less work for the same consumption) is simply a return to the higher productivity of the land, but is exploitative none the less.

Now let us change the example a bit: instead of land of differential fertility, let us say that everyone is given one "unit" of labor power (themselves), but this labor power has differential *talents*, where we consider talents to be innate attributes of individuals acquired through the "genetic lottery." Talent in this sense is analogous to the natural fertility of land: it allows particular skills to "grow" with the expenditure of less effort (and other inputs). Because of the unequal distribution of talents, some people are able to obtain a given level of consumption by expending less labor than others (or, equivalently, to obtain higher levels of consumption by expending the same amount of labor). This seems to me to be parallel to the case of the differential fertility of the land: the private ownership of talents enables the talented to potentially appropriate the labor of the untalented. This is not to deny the claim that people with talents are more productive—indeed, if they were not, their talents could not be cashed in for exploitative appropriations of the

---

4. This story is a slight variant of a model from Roemer, *A General Theory.*

labor of others.[5] This higher productivity may help to legitimate and mask the exploitation, but it does not render the transfer of labor, if it occurs, nonexploitative.[6]

Talents, as defined here, are genetic endowments. In the analysis of the middle class, however, I have talked of skill or credential exploitation, not "talent exploitation." Credentials, in these terms, can be viewed as a socially institutionalized mechanism of artificially creating talents. A "talent" is a scarce genetic endowment that enables people to acquire valued skills. A credentialing institution is a mechanism that allows some people to acquire a valued skill and not others. The result is that the acquired skill is scarce just as it would have been if it was strictly the result of differential talents. To be sure, the owner of that skill may be "more productive" in the sense that they have a skill that is valued in market.[7] But the inequalities that are generated by that ownership, as in the earlier case of land, should still be treated as potentially exploitative.

Now, this does not imply that all income inequalities linked to skill differentials necessarily reflect exploitation. It takes time and effort to acquire skills, and part of the income of a skill owner is simply a reflection of the costs of producing the skill itself. Furthermore, in many instances, people have to accept lower incomes during the training period in which skills are acquired and, again, part of the higher income of a skilled wage-earner reflects the "discounted" value of such foregone earnings. The exploitative element in the wage of a skilled wage-earner, then, is that part of the wage which directly reflects the monopoly control of the supply of the skill. One form of such monopolization is

---

5. Throughout this discussion I will ignore the problem of what is sometimes called unproductive labor—labor that is expended in capitalist production but which does not produce anything of value. I am assuming that all labor power is deployed productively, but that different units of labor power are more or less productive. I do not think that the issues under discussion here are affected in any interesting way by the problem of unproductive labor, since unskilled, fully proletarianized labor power can also be unproductive in the sense defined above. The unproductive/productive distinction, therefore, does not bear on the problem of the status of skilled labor power with respect to exploitation.

6. A talented person who makes things for his or her own consumption much more productively than others is not exploiting anyone. The exploitation comes when this production is used to appropriate the labor of others through exchange.

7. It is important to stress that contrary to Burris's construel of my argument (see p. 163) I am not suggesting that skill or credential holders are actually more productive physically in the sense of contributing more to the total social product. The activities of a lawyer involved in corporate mergers may actually reduce the total social product and thus be negatively productive in social terms, and yet highly valued in the market because of their "productivity" for the capitalist. All that is entailed by the argument is that their labor power is more valued on the market and that this greater valuation results in exploitative transfers.

rooted in "natural" talents; another—and I believe more important—form is based on credentials. The result is a monopoly *rent* component of the wage. This rent component is potentially a form of exploitation.[8]

Why do I say simply "potentially"? This is an important wrinkle in the argument: the existence of monopoly rents in the wages of skilled/credentialed labor power is a *necessary* condition for such wage-earners to be exploiters, but it is not a *sufficient* condition. The monopoly rent indicates (by definition) that skilled wage-earners are able to appropriate part of the social surplus in their wage. But since the laboring activity of the skilled wage-earner is also contributing to that surplus, this need not imply that the skilled wage-earner is appropriating the labor of anyone else. The privileged position of skilled wage-earners in the labor market, in short, may simply give them the "privilege" of appropriating their own surplus.[9]

It is not an easy matter to establish whether or not this rent component of the wage is sufficiently large to constitute a genuine transfer of surplus to skill owners, and thus to constitute exploitation. To sort this out we would need a way of measuring the contribution of a given wage-earner to the social surplus and then compare this to the amount of surplus embodied in that person's wage. If all labor power was completely homogeneous, this would not be such a difficult matter—contribution to the surplus would be measured directly by the labor time expended by workers in the production of the surplus. But how should the value of the surplus be measured under conditions of heterogeneous labor?

---

8. To say that skills/credentials constitute a distinct mechanism of exploitation in capitalist societies does not imply that the empirical effects of skill exploitation in capitalism occur independently of the capitalist context in which they occur. Burris seems to believe that to postulate a distinct mechanism one must also be committed to the view that this mechanism produces empirical effects autonomously from the effects of capitalist institutions (see p. 163). This is simply not the case. Burris is entirely correct when he writes: "The nature and distribution of such positions [positions in which credentialed labor power is employed] is certainly influenced by the nature of labor markets, but it is also and more fundamentally conditioned by the powers and interests invested in the private ownership of the means of production" (p. 164). This is, indeed, what it means to describe the society as "capitalist"—that capitalist interests, powers and imperatives structure the opportunities for all economic agents in the society. But this does not imply that what I have termed skill exploitation has no effects of its own. In late feudalism, for example, one could have said the same thing about the powers and interests of feudal lords with respect to the opportunities for capitalist investment, and yet this would not have implied that the capitalist mechanisms did not exist. Skill exploitation in capitalism is deeply structured and constrained by capitalism, but this does not demonstrate that it is no more than an effect or reflection of capitalist exploitation.

9. This description of the logic of exploitation mechanisms for credential owners is consistent with the theoretical position that they are "petty bourgeois"; the petty bourgeoisie consists of those producers who are neither exploiters nor exploited—that is, they are able to appropriate the surplus which they produce.

There is no simple answer to this question. If a type of labor power is in permanent short supply because of scarce talents or institutionalized credentials, and thus is highly valued in the market, does this mean that it creates more "value" in an hour of labor time than a type of labor power in abundant supply? From the point of view of "subjective theories of value" the answer is obvious: a scarce input into production of whatever sort creates more value precisely because it is subjectively more valued (that is, in greater demand and thus commands a higher price). In such a perspective, the problem under discussion disappears: highly valued labor produces additional value exactly equivalent to the wage it commands in the market, and thus it is meaningless to say that the wages of such labor power are exploitative.

Marxists, however, generally reject such subjectivist views.[10] A change in the effective market demand for a particular kind of labor power should not, in and of itself, change the amount of labor value it produces per unit time, even if it will affect the prices of the commodities produced by that labor power. Imagine the following situation: a particular kind of highly trained credentialed labor power capable of producing ten units of commodity X per day is very scarce and in high demand. It therefore commands a very high wage and, accordingly the commodity X commands a high price. Now the monopoly control of the training is broken, the supply increases and the wage drops to the point that it simply covers the costs of reimbursing the costs of training. But nothing else changes: the physical productivity of the trained labor power is the same and thus still produces ten units of X per day. Only now, X is much cheaper. In a subjectivist theory of value, this labor power is now less productive—it produces less value than before— whereas in an objective theory of value, the amount of objective value remains unchanged since the real inputs into production remain unchanged. If one rejects a subjectivist theory of value, therefore, the only reason why trained labor power might produce more labor value per hour of current work is that part of the past labor of training is embodied in the value of the products currently produced by skilled labor power.[11]

---

10. Even Marxists who reject the labor theory of value are hesitant to accept a full-fledged subjectivist view of value. They reject the labor theory of value because, once the assumptions of homogeneous labor and homogeneous capital are relaxed, it is no longer internally coherent, but in general Marxists still argue for some sort of objective, real-cost based theory of value.

11. In traditional Marxist language this means, in effect, that part of the "socially necessary labor time" of producing a particular commodity is the socially necessary labor time of training the labor power itself. Training time is thus amortized over the useful life of the skill in question by being "transferred" to the commodities produced using the skill.

Because highly trained labor power does contribute more to the social surplus than unskilled labor power, it is entirely possible that the higher incomes of many credentialed wage-earners do not embody any genuine exploitation of others. They would still be a *privileged* social category, and thus it might be appropriate to call them a distinctive *stratum* within the working class, but they would not be properly described as exploiters and thus would not have a distinctive class character. This is basically the theoretical position advocated by Meiksins and Burris.

Classical Marxist accounts of exploitation in capitalism finessed this problem by assuming homogeneous labor. Possible labor transfers among wage-earners were thus ignored; the only issue was the transfers of surplus labor (or surplus value) from wage-earners to capitalists. But in the world in which we live labor power is not homogeneous and massive income differentials exist among wage-earners. One way or another this has to be accommodated within the general discourse of Marxist theory, and how it is accommodated affects the way in which the class structure of capitalism is viewed.

We thus have two broadly different theoretical solutions to the problem of the class character of highly skilled/credentialed labor power: in one, such wage-earners are at least potentially exploiters, potentially appropriating the labor of others through their monopolization of a particular scarce social resource, and thus occupying a contradictory location within class relations; in the other, they are a privileged stratum of the working class, able to reduce their rate of capitalist exploitation by appropriating part of the surplus which they produce. How can we choose between these alternative theoretical solutions? There are good arguments that can be brought to bear on both approaches, and I certainly do not think that there is an unambiguous case for the solution I have proposed. There are, however, several lines of reasoning which might support the concept of skill exploitation.

First, the main upshot of the above discussion is that in many cases it is difficult to decide in practice whether or not a given position involves skill exploitation. As Roemer has demonstrated, however, the same ambiguity exists for capital-based exploitation as well: there is a grey area of self-employed small owners for whom it is ambiguous whether or not they are exploiters.[12] The difference between the skill case and the

---

12. In Roemer's analysis, such small owners are potentially exploiters through unequal exchange in the market, even if they hire no labor power. Petty bourgeois self-employed producers with relatively large amounts of capital are able to appropriate the surplus of others by exchanging their products for those produced under less capital-intensive technologies. Once they own sufficient capital to become employers, however, there is no ambiguity in their exploitation status: all capitalist employers are necessarily exploiters.

capital case in Roemer's analysis is that for the latter there is a clear criterion for when this ambiguity disappears: once a capital-owner owns sufficient capital to employ wage-earners, that owner becomes an exploiter. This is the basis of Roemer's important Class-Exploitation-Correspondence-Principle: under conditions of homogeneous labor, all wage-earners are exploited and all employers are exploiters. There is no corresponding transparent criterion for when a skill owner becomes a skill exploiter. The "grey area" in which it is ambiguous whether or not a skill owner is an exploiter is thus not only potentially quite large for skill exploitation but there is no direct indicator of its boundaries. This does not, however, imply that unambiguous skill exploiters cannot be identified. In particular, no matter how one counts the training time of high-paid professionals it is hard to see how they would fail the test of being net appropriators of the surplus labor of workers.[13] These conceptual problems, however, may undermine the usefulness of the concept of skill exploitation for the empirical specification of class structures.[14]

Second, it can be argued that the social surplus is a jointly produced surplus of a collectively organized process of production. While individuals contribute their time and energy to this process, it is impossible to meaningfully define individual contributions to that surplus, and thus any individual, private appropriation of the social surplus is a form of exploitation. Wage differences that reflect different costs of producing and reproducing different kinds of labor power, therefore, would not be exploitative, but any other differential would be.[15]

---

13. Take, for example, a doctor whose work life is forty years and, let's assume, that the training time embodies forty years of training—surely a large overestimate. Assuming that the training does not have declining value over time (and thus it is evenly amortized over the work life of the doctor), this would mean that in every hour of current labor the doctor contributes two hours of labor value to the total social product. Further, imagine that the doctor works ten hours a day, thus contributing a total of twenty hours of labor values to the social product a day. If the income of this doctor was the equivalent of only twenty hours of abstract labor value a day, then he would not be an exploiter. Even with these exceptionally liberal assumptions, however, most doctors will be consuming more labor values than they contribute.

14. Skill assets, like capital assets, are essentially a continuous variable: in both cases an individual can own incrementally increasing amounts of the resource. The critical difference is that in the case of capital, once this quantity surpasses a certain threshold, the owner is in a position to hire others: the quantitative variation thus constitutes the basis for a qualitative shift in the nature of the social relations. There is no corresponding qualitative shift in the social relations in which owners of skills enter the production process that could provide the basis for an unambiguous demarcation between skill privileges and skill exploitation. As I have argued in *Classes*, this lack of a qualitative relational criterion corresponding to skill exploitation may undermine the claim that skill exploitation is a dimension of class structures.

15. If one accepts these arguments, then the normative principle "equal income returns to equal effort" is the nonexploitative income distribution among wage-earners, rather than "equal income returns to equal contribution," since contribution is no longer, in general, identifiable with isolated individual labor.

Third, following the work of John Roemer, one can argue that the surplus-transfer notion of exploitation should be abandoned altogether since the concept of surplus-transfer becomes so ill-defined under conditions of heterogeneous labor. The test for exploitation, then, is basically whether or not the welfare of one group is *at the expense* of another; the issue of whether or not there are actual labor transfers between the groups does not enter the analysis.[16]

Organization Exploitation

Some of the same issues raised around the problem of skill exploitation could be raised for organization exploitation as well. One might argue that managers are not the beneficiaries of exploitative transfers of surplus at all; they occupy strategic jobs within firms, positions within which their decisions can have a massive impact on the overall productivity of the enterprise. Their higher incomes, therefore, could simply reflect the size of their "productive contribution."

Most radical class analysts would reject this kind of neoclassical economics defense of high managerial incomes. While it is undeniable that actions of a top manager might result in massive increases (or decreases) in the surplus produced within a capitalist firm, most radical theorists would still insist that the surplus is actually produced by the laborers who make the products. Managerial labor is, at most, a small component of the total labor embodied in those products. Radical class analysts, therefore, in general accept the idea that the income of managers, particularly higher level managers, is exploitative. The issue in dispute is whether managers should be seen as participating indirectly in capitalist exploitation itself or, alternatively, whether they should be seen as exploiters based on their control of organizational resources.

In the treatment of managers as beneficiaries of capitalist exploitation,

---

16. Roemer adds a number of other conditions to his formal definition of exploitation which I will not review here. The important point is that he tries to maintain the notion of exploitation as a condition which produces inherently antagonistic material interests without insisting that the antagonism is based on actual surplus transfer. It should be noted that in more recent work Roemer has seriously questioned whether Marxists should worry about exploitation at all; J. Roemer, "Should Marxists Be Interested in Exploitation?" in J. Roemer (ed.), *Analytical Marxism* (Cambridge: Cambridge University Press, 1986). He now argues that the fundamental arguments against exploitation by Marxists ultimately amount to arguments against inequalities of resources as such, and that the rhetoric of exploitation simply confuses the matter. Marxists, in his view, should defend their normative commitments directly on egalitarian principles rather than indirectly via the problematic concept of exploitation. I believe that such a conceptual move undermines one of the core explanatory concepts in Marxism. Exploitation is explanatory not just because it reflects inequalities, but because of the ways in which it attempts to map interdependencies of antagonistic interests.

they are viewed as simply holders of powers delegated to them by their employers. If they are loyal lieutenants, then they will receive some of the spoils of capitalist exploitation. But as lieutenants they control no autonomous mechanisms of exploitation at all. In the alternative approach, on the other hand, capitalists are seen as being forced by the level of development of the forces of production and the social character of production in advanced capitalism to create managerial hierarchies. The powers of managers, however, should not be viewed as simply nominally "delegated," as if they were revokable at will by capitalist owners. Rather, these powers are built into the social organization of production in such a way that they give managers some measure of real autonomy and power. This constitutes the basis for their organizational exploitation.

As in the case of skill exploitation, I do not think that the case for organization exploitation is unambiguous. It may well be that the privileges of managers should be viewed entirely as derivative from capitalist exploitation. The essential opposing argument is that the exploitative transfers to managers can exist even in the absence of capitalist exploitation. In a society within which private ownership of the means of production has been eliminated—that is, means of production could not be sold on a market and individuals could not accumulate capital—managers could still occupy positions within which they were able to extract surplus labor from workers. And this could be true even if managers did not monopolize any particular scarce skills and were thus not skill exploiters in the sense discussed above.

How is this possible? Basically the argument is this: people who control organizational resources—the basic planning, coordinating and integration of productive activities—occupy what I have called "strategic jobs." These are jobs in which it matters a great deal for the overall productivity or profitability of the organization how responsibly and conscientiously the job is performed.[17] Because of managerial control over information flows and the extreme interdependence of managerial actions, these are also jobs in which it is very difficult for anyone outside of the managerial hierarchy itself to effectively monitor the performance of individual managers. The combination of the strategic importance of these jobs and the ineffectiveness of external surveillance means that

---

17. As in the case of skills and productivity, there is no assumption here that managerial activity actually contributes to physical productivity. All that matters is that this labor is strategically important for the economic performance of the organization. Such activity can be, of course, profoundly "unproductive" in material terms (for example, where managerial activity is directed towards speculation or simply increasing the capitalist exploitation of workers).

managers are in an excellent position to extort wages out of proportion to the costs of producing managerial labor power. Of course, such higher wages are legitimated as "incentives," but this is simply the ideological mask for exploitation, much as the need for profit incentives is an ideological mask for capitalist exploitation.[18] The abolition of private ownership of the means of production does not in and of itself eradicate this strategic power of managerial labor, and thus in state socialist societies managers and bureaucrats are still able to exploit.

Now, in spite of this argument, it remains the case that in capitalist societies there is a sense in which capitalists, not managers, "own" the organizational assets of production. The capitalist hires at least the very top managers and the capitalist—not the manager—can decide to destroy the organization assets by eliminating the organization as a whole. In the same sense, capitalists "own" the jobs occupied by credentialed wage-earners. A credential as such does not generate exploitation; the credential owner must be hired into a job which requires that credential in order for the credentialed employee to acquire the wage within which skill exploitation occurs. It is thus true, as Burris and Meiksins have argued in different ways, that in capitalism the wages of both managers and credentialed wage-earners are "derived" from capitalist revenues.

However, even though the exploitation from which managers and credentialed wage-earners benefit is systematically tied to capitalist exploitation, it does not follow from this that these exploitations are reducible to capitalist exploitation. They can have real effects of their own even if, in a capitalist society, they invariably take the form of payments out of capitalist profits. The fact that such exploitations can exist in the absence of private ownership of the means of production at least lends some support to the claim that they should be treated as distinct exploitations in capitalism as well.

---

18. Incentives are not inherently indicators of hidden exploitation. It may take the expectation of higher incomes, for example, to induce people to undergo a long and unpleasant process of training to acquire a skill. If this is fundamentally reimbursement for the effort and foregone earnings of training, the "incentive" would not constitute exploitation. Or, it may take incentives to get people to do unpleasant work—to pay them for the "disutility" of particularly toilsome labor. If in these cases there are no barriers to entry into either training or unpleasant work—anyone is able to accept the bribe if they want—then the incentives are not exploitative. But when a person says, "I will not act responsibly unless you pay me more," and you pay the person more because they have the power to harm you if you don't, the "incentive" is simply a mask for the use of power to extort income.

Class Interests

Ultimately the most serious objection to the concept of skill and organization exploitation as the basis of particular kinds of class locations is not
based on technical arguments concerning the existence of strategic rents
or monopoly rents in wages, but rather concerns the question of the
basic class interests of managers and professionals-technocrats. Peter
Meiksins has expressed this problem most forcefully when he argues that
it is basically unthinkable that managers or intellectuals in advanced
capitalism could ever adopt an autonomous class project.[19] Either they
would support some version of capitalism, perhaps reformed and
rationalized in various ways, or under extreme conditions they might
support some kind of democratic socialism embodying a working-class
project. In neither case would they have their own project for the reconstruction of society. Similar themes are raised by Burris and Brenner.

Again, I take these criticisms seriously and I do not feel that I can
offer a decisive defense of the theoretical position I am advocating. I do
not, however, think that the arguments I have made "strain the imagination to the breaking point.[20] To clarify my position, I would like to
discuss two issues: first, the mechanisms within capitalism that tie the
interests of the middle class to the bourgeoisie; and second, the sense in
which "middle classes" in capitalism potentially could support an anticapitalist, antiproletarian class project.

Within capitalist societies there are two central mechanisms which
systematically link the material interests of the middle classes to the
bourgeoisie. First, one of the distinctive features of middle-class jobs is
their location within orderly career structures, either as part of
managerial hierarchies, or as part of professional hierarchies. To a significant extent, the reproduction and enrichment of such career structures depends upon the profitability and vitality of capital accumulation.
This is most obviously the case when such career structures are directly
located within capitalist corporations, but it is also true for career structures in the state since the funding of state employment through taxation
is at least in part contingent upon accumulation.

This interest in capitalist profits and accumulation, of course, is not
unique to middle-class wage-earners; as Adam Przeworski has argued,
so long as workers have to live in a capitalist society, they also have an
interest in profitability and accumulation.[21] While the middle classes

19. See pp. 179–81.
20. See p. 180.

may disproportionately benefit from capital accumulation, all wage-earners have such a material interest.

The second mechanism which ties the middle class to capitalist interests, on the other hand, is much more specific to their class situation. The argument that the middle classes are exploiters through secondary mechanisms of exploitation implies that their incomes will tend to be much higher than the costs of producing and reproducing their labor power. This means that, compared to the working class, they will have relatively high levels of discretionary income, income left over after they have provided for their basic expenses of living. The existence of such discretionary income opens the possibility that middle-class wage-earners are able to save and, more importantly, invest their surplus income. In other words, they are able to capitalize the income they receive through exploitation. In the course of a middle-class career this can result in the accumulation of a quite considerable portfolio of capitalist assets which, in effect, directly integrates the middle class into the bourgeoisie. While the unearned income generated by such capital assets will rarely equal the wage income of a professional or manager at the peak of their careers, it nevertheless links them to the capitalist class in a direct and systematic way that rarely exists in the working class itself.

So long as people in the middle class are able to capitalize their surplus income and count on a career trajectory firmly underwritten by capitalist accumulation, it is hardly surprising that in general they support capitalism. This is in part what it means to say that capitalism is a *hegemonic* system: it is able to effectively tie the class interests of various subaltern classes, in this case the middle classes, to the interests of the capitalist class. This is similar to the situation of merchant capitalists in feudal society: so long as they were able to "feudalize" their capitalist exploitation (that is, buy into the feudal class in various ways) they generally supported feudalism. It was only in the period of the long crisis of late feudalism, in part perhaps stimulated by the expansion of capitalism itself, that the bourgeoisie became stridently antifeudal. Similarly, in the case of the middle classes of advanced capitalism: their procapitalist orientation is likely to be eroded only under conditions where a long-term stagnation occurs which seriously erodes the ability of people in the middle class to capitalize their surplus income and which threatens the reproduction of middle-class employment in the state and private sectors. It is even possible to imagine corporate managers

---

21. The argument is not that workers have an interest in capitalism over socialism, but rather, given the continuation of capitalism they have an interest in capital accumulation rather than stagnation. See A. Przeworski, *Capitalism and Social Democracy* (Cambridge: Cambridge University Press, 1985).

supporting various kinds of statist alternatives to corporate capitalism if
capital was rapidly disinvesting, managers were losing their jobs, etc.

Meiksins argues that under such long-term crisis conditions, the only
plausible political reform program of intellectuals, managers and
bureaucrats would be some modification of capitalism involving greater
state planning and coordination, but not anything genuinely anticapitalist. The only alternatives to such "managed capitalism" that he
entertains would be democratic socialism (in which case they would be
basically supporting a working-class project, not a middle-class project)
or "Soviet-type economies in which public ownership is combined with
strong, centralized, undemocratic control over the economy." This latter
alternative is so unattractive to all actors that it is impossible to imagine
a mass-based movement in the middle class adopting it as a political
goal. In Meiksins's view, therefore, the middle class would either put its
political support behind a basically bourgeois-class project of reformed
capitalism or a working-class project of democratic socialism. In either
case it would not have its own class project, and therefore should not be
considered a "class."

I do not think that Meiksins has correctly posed the alternatives.
Under the specified conditions of long-term stagnation and crisis of
capitalist hegemony, it is possible that the working class and the various
segments of the middle class might form a coalition to struggle for something people would call "democratic socialism," as Meiksins suggests,
but this common discourse is likely to mask rather different—and deeply
conflicting—visions of an alternative society. In one vision of democratic
socialism, it is a society which is deeply antimeritocratic and antihier-
archical. Not only would the principal means of production be under
"democratic control" rather than privately owned, but hierarchies within
production would be severely curtailed in favor of radical participatory
democracy at the point of production, and meritocracies would be
dramatically eroded in favor of popular control over and access to training and certification of specialized skills. In the second vision, "democratic socialism" would be democratic in the familiar bourgeois
sense—civil liberties, elected officials, due process—and it would be
socialist in the sense of the state owning the principal means of production, but would retain hierarchies and meritocracies in production.
These would, undoubtedly, be legitimated on the grounds of rewarding
people for their contribution to society (meritocracy) and the responsibility and importance of their work (hierarchy), but would nevertheless
protect the exploitative inequalities that define the material interests of
the middle class.

The kind of society that would actually emerge if a democratic
socialist project of a coalition of the working class and the "middle class"
were successful would probably embody in significant ways the distinc-

tive class interests of skill exploiters and organization exploiters. Even under conditions of sustained capitalist crisis, antimeritocratic, anti-elitist, radical democratic socialism is unlikely to have a broad base in the middle class. What is more plausible, therefore, is that under these hypothetical conditions, the middle class would be mobilized behind the more statist, hierarchical and meritocratic vision of socialism. Struggles over these hierarchies and meritocracies would be at the center of class struggles in such a society.

These claims on my part are highly speculative. Meiksins is correct that "the historical record holds very few examples of significant middle-class technocratic or statist movements." The response that this simply reflects the long-standing hegemonic strength of capitalism in the advanced industrial societies sounds like special pleading. However, one could equally well point to the weakness of revolutionary democratic socialist movements in the working class as proof that the working class in advanced capitalism is also not properly a class in fundamental opposition to the bourgeoisie. Working-class anticapitalism, when it occurs at all in developed capitalist countries, tends to take social democratic and statist forms, forms which embody much of what I have characterized as middle-class anti-capitalism (that is, they do not challenge exploitation based on hierarchy and meritocracy). What the historical record of advanced capitalism really demonstrates is the profound difficulty of any social category consistently defining a political project radically opposed to capitalism. When such projects do become articulated, they tend to embody in complex ways the specific class interests of a variety of subordinated classes within capitalism.

Class and Identity

I would now like to turn to an entirely different set of issues. Throughout the development of my work on class I have resolutely insisted that class should be understood fundamentally as a concept revolving around the problem of antagonistic material interests based on exploitation.[22] While I have devoted considerable energy to trying to figure out how those interests are constituted, what kinds of relations are most central

---

22. "Material interests," as I will use the term, are interests with respect to toil, leisure, and consumption. I have generally argued that material interests should also be thought of as "objective" interests, that is, that it makes sense to say that people have objective interests in improving their material well being (in the above sense). This does not mean that people have an inherent or objective interest in maximizing consumption (or income) *per se*, but simply that if given the choice between two different trade-offs between toil, leisure, and consumption, people have an objective interest in the more favorable trade-off.

to determining class interests, how different aspects of class interests are combined, and so on, I have always taken it as axiomatic that the most crucial thing which all members of a given class share in common is common material interests.[23]

It is because of this preoccupation with class and material interests that I sought to reconstruct the concept of the "middle class" around the problem of exploitation. Exploitation is a preeminently interest-centered concept and is certainly at the heart of Marxist conceptions of class. It therefore made intuitive sense to try to understand the middle class as occupying a distinctive kind of position within processes of exploitation, for this would define them as having a distinctive commonality of material interests.

Johanna Brenner's critique of my approach to class structure rests, in part, upon the view that classes should not simply be defined with respect to interests, however those interests are conceptualized. She concludes her essay by writing:

> Defining class locations in terms of exploitation interests and measuring exploitation by income, Wright is forced to assert an overly abstract connection between objective interests and consciousness. There is nothing in his definition of class location that theorizes the process through which workers develop their world views. Work relationships are not the only determinant of consciousness. However, it seems to me that they are a significant structural dimension differentiating experience and thus leading to different ways of understanding the world.[24]

In my approach, the crucial thing which all members of a class share in common is fundamental objective material interests. The theory of exploitation, then, provides the basis for understanding the mechanisms which generate that commonality of interests in opposition to the interests of other classes. In Brenner's argument, in contrast, members of a class also share in common a pattern of *lived experiences* and the theory of workplace relations and practices provides the basic understanding of the mechanisms which generate that commonalty of experience:

> Attention to social relationships seems to me not only useful but very much in line with the classic Marxist argument that day to day experiences of conflict

---

23. To talk about "common" material interests implies being situated in a common manner to the underlying mechanisms which generate material welfare. Two people with the same actual income may not be in the same class since to be in the same class they would have to share a common relation to basic income-producing mechanisms.

24. See p. 190.

and cooperation at work could lead workers to take up kinds of affiliation, organization, action, militance that would in turn provide the experiential basis for the development of a broader revolutionary vision. Marx argued that the proletariat is the historical bearer of a socialist revolutionary project not only because they would benefit from ending their exploitation under capitalism (i.e. it is in their "interest" to end capitalism), but because their experiences within capitalist production might allow them to imagine a society based on collective, democratic control over production as an alternative to capitalism.[25]

Class structures, in Brenner's argument, are characterized both by a particular distribution of exploitation-generated material interests and of labor process-generated lived experiences. An account of both interests and experience is essential for class structural analysis: the commonality of material interests within a class helps to explain the inherent tendency towards conflict between classes; the commonality of lived experience is essential for explaining why members of class tend to develop common *identities*, without which there would be no inherent tendency for solidary action and class struggle.[26] Exploitation is central to explaining what classes struggle over; common experiences are central to explaining their collective capacity to struggle at all. The category "workplace relations and practices" is therefore analytically parallel to "exploitation": both are meant to designate an underlying mechanism which generates particular effects—objective material interests and lived experiences—which, in turn, are constitutive of the concept of class. Both exploitation and workplace relations/practices are themselves structured by the social relations of production characteristic of capitalism, but they need not correspond to each other perfectly.

One possible implication of Brenner's comments is a new general way of specifying the theoretical status of the "middle-class."[27] The category "middle class" could be seen as representing a particular disjunction between interest-mechanisms and experience-mechanisms: they share with all wage-earners a common set of exploitation-generated interests opposed to capitalism, but they have a distinctive set of workplace experiences which produce a systematically nonproletarian form of

25. See p. 185.
26. I am using the term "identity" in a very broad sense to encompass the self-understanding of people of who they are and how they fit into the social world.
27. Brenner does not explicitly play out these implications for the analysis of the middle class in the class structure, and I am not sure that she would in fact endorse them as I have elaborated them here. Nevertheless, I think that the analysis I propose is a logical extension of her comments.

identity.[28] More specifically, Brenner suggests that this is the best way of understanding the division between workers on the one side and managers and professionals on the other. Managers and supervisors, she writes,

> must carry out, to a greater or lesser extent, control functions which do place them in an antagonistic relationship to other workers. The degree to which the jobs of lower level supervisors involve them in control functions varies according to both management policies . . . and the level of organization and combativity of the workers they are supposed to supervise. Thus, both their experience in work, their relationships with other workers and their actual interests . . . will also vary . . . These real relationships within production can lead them to organize, when they do, separately from other unions and can open them up to technocratic/statist ideologies.[29]

She makes an analogous argument for professionals: their immediate conditions and practices of self-direction and control of knowledge within the workplace generate lived experiences and corresponding identities which set them apart from other workers. For both managers and professionals, then, the decisive feature of their structural location which differentiates them from the working class is not their material interests *vis-à-vis* capitalist exploitation, but the nature of the daily experiences generated within the process of production that shapes their identity.

One way of situating this alternative strategy of specifying class structures within the classical Marxist tradition is in terms of the contrast between alienation and exploitation as foundational concepts for class analysis. The different immediate lived experiences that Brenner emphasizes can be thought of as generated by different locations with respect to the process of alienation. The control over knowledge and self-direction within work characteristic of professional labor processes could be understood as involving incomplete alienation. The managerial work of domination, control, surveillance, on the other hand, can be thought of as labor that produces and reproduces alienation in workers in the

---

28. This formulation is similar to my earlier conception of the middle class as a contradictory location within class relations in which there was a noncorrespondence between the relations of domination and the relations of exploitation; *Class, Crisis and the State* (London: Verso, 1978). Capitalists were considered exploiters and dominators, workers as exploited and dominated, and managers as dominators and exploited. In Brenner's formulation, the emphasis is less on domination *per se* than on the workplace experiences generated by the totality of workplace relations and practices. Domination would constitute one aspect of these relations, but not necessarily the decisive one.

29. See p. 188.

labor process. More generally, then, the middle class could be defined as individuals who are proletarianized with respect to exploitation but nonproletarianized (or only incompletely proletarianized) with respect to alienation.

- In the traditional Marxist vision of the historical trajectory of capitalism, there is a systematic tendency for these two dimensions of class structure to progressively correspond. Capitalism simultaneously brings ever-broader sectors of economic activity under a regime of capitalist exploitation and deepens the conditions of alienation within the capitalist labor process. In the essential Marxist teleology of history, then, the workplace experiences that generate collective identities progressively coincide with the exploitation relations that generate material interests. In these terms, the persistence, and perhaps even the intensification, of the disjunction between exploitation and alienation, constitutes the social basis for the existence of a middle class in capitalist societies.

This general line of reasoning in class analysis is in keeping with a variety of recent work in class theory. There is, of course, a long tradition in mainstream sociology in which the concept of "social" class is linked to issues of common lifestyle which is closely tied to the issue of common subjectivity and identity, presumably rooted in some structuring of common lived experiences. More significantly for radical class analysis, the attempt to integrate the problem of common experiences and identity formation into the concept of class finds a resonant cord in the work of Pierre Bourdieu.[30] Bourdieu attempts to elaborate a view of class around the dual concepts of class *habitus* and *capital*. A class habitus is defined by a set of common *conditions* in everyday life which produce common *conditionings* experienced by people and which, in turn, generate a common set of internalized *dispositions* to act in particular ways. These dispositions range from *tastes* (the central preoccupation of Bourdieu's book, *Distinction*) to receptivities to particular ideological appeals and calls to action. In Bourdieu's analysis, a class habitus is not simply constituted within the workplace, but in community, schools, families, and other institutions as well. These institutional settings generate lived experiences (conditionings) over the life cycle which reinforce certain modes of thought and action and undermine others. As in Brenner's argument, the decisive criteria which distinguish classes are thus not reducible to differences in their material

---

30. For a good review of Pierre Bourdieu's work on class theory (*Distinction* (Cambridge: Harvard University Press, 1984), "The Social Space and the Genesis of Groups," *Theory and Society*, vol. 14, no. 6 (1985) and "What Makes a Social Class?" *Berkeley Journal of Sociology*, vol. 22 (1987)), see R. Brubaker, "Rethinking Classical Theory: The Sociological Vision of Pierre Bourdieu," *Theory and Society*, vol. 14 (1985), no. 6, pp. 723–44.

interests (based on their control over different kinds of capital in Bourdieu's analysis), but must include differences in their habituses as well.[31]

A general reconstruction of the concept of class structure along the lines proposed by Brenner is an important, and potentially powerful, alternative to approaches such as my own which more narrowly elaborate the concept of class structure around material interests. To be convincing, such an approach needs to construct a clearer abstract concept of the commonalty of workplace experiences that are constitutive of different class positions in capitalism. In the case of exploitation-centered concepts of class structure, there is a systematic, abstract, deductive logic to the specification of what it is that all members of a given class have in common: all workers in capitalism are exploited through capitalist mechanisms of exploitation; all capitalists are exploiters. Of course, there is great variation within classes in what I have called elsewhere *immediate* interests—interests determined by particular markets, particular working conditions, particular forms of competition, etc.—but members of a given class share common *fundamental* interests, interests over how the basic property relations of the society should be organized.[32] What is needed, then, to construct a concept of class structure which is, in part, based on workplace relations and practices and not just exploitation, is a parellel abstract specification of "fundamental" and "immediate" commonalities of workplace experiences.

What is the abstract dimension of workplace experiences that is shared in common by workers in a nineteenth-century textile mill, a contemporary Japanese auto factory, and a Swedish high technology factory in which worker teams are given high levels of collective autonomy? In his comparative research on the organization of industrial work, Michael Burawoy has defined a number of different "factory regimes": market despotism, patriarchal regimes, hegemonic regimes.[33]

---

31. Brenner's arguments are also in keeping with Michael Burawoy's emphasis on what he calls the "relations in production" in constituting the working class; *The Politics of Production* (London: Verso, 1985). In his view a class cannot be defined simply in terms of a set of "empty places" within the relations of production (the relations which generate exploitation in my terms), but must include a specification of the relations in production, the relations within which the daily experiences of social interaction in production are created.

32. Stated in somewhat different terms, immediate interests are interests defined within a particular set of rules of the game; fundamental interests are interests over what game should be played (that is, what should be the mode of production). See Wright, *Class, Crisis and the State*, pp. 88–91.

33. M. Burawoy, *The Politics of Production*.

We can say that in each of these cases the workers are capitalistically exploited, but what *precisely* defines the fundamental commonalty of their lived experiences within work? If we simply say that they are "dominated" within work and lack full control over what they produce and how they produce it, then this does not distinguish their lived experiences from those of workers in many noncapitalist systems of production (for instance, workers in the Soviet Union). If we try to define the forms of domination in a less vague way, then it is hard to encompass all of the cases that we would want to consider "capitalist".

Because of these difficulties in defining adequately the distinctively capitalist form of workplace experiences, for the moment, I continue to have reservations about the ultimate fruitfulness of this conceptual strategy. While I think that the substantive problem of identity-formation is important and, furthermore, that the micro-experiences within the daily practices of work are likely to be an important determinant of class identities, nevertheless I am not persuaded that the best way of advancing class analysis is to subsume these processes under the concept of *class structure* itself. The alternative is to define classes in terms of a structural map of material interests (based on exploitation or some other account of material interests) and then to treat the problem of lived experiences as an independent source of variation within classes rather than as a criterion for class as such.

Now, if one were convinced of the traditional, teleological version of the Marxist theory of history, then there would be a good reason for insisting that the structural map of relations of exploitation and the map of workplace lived experiences should be combined into a single concept of class structure in spite of the difficulty of constructing a rigorous abstract concept of such experiences. Such a class concept would capture the immanent, dynamic tendencies of the system as a whole in a powerful and elegant manner. If, however, one is skeptical about the strong teleological versions of the Marxist theory of history and question the existence of any immanent tendency for these two dimensions of class to coincide, then merging them into a single concept is likely to hinder, rather than enrich, the development of class theory. Under these theoretical conditions it is better to have two distinct concepts—one of class structure centered on exploitation and interests, and one of class experience, centered on workplace practices and the formation of identities. Instead of seeing the linkage between these two concepts as having some immanent necessity, the problem of their interconnection could then be treated as a theoretical problem in its own right in which a considerable degree of variability and even indeterminacy is allowed.

6

A Revolution in Class Theory*

Philippe Van Parijs

Many Europeans in my generation—among them some of my closest friends—have never had a "real" job. They have spent their adult life alternating between the dole and precarious, often government-sponsored jobs. And as they grow older, they have less and less hope that their situation will ever improve. The stark contrast between their position and, say, my own or that of most of my readers—a safe job with a decent wage, career prospects, pension rights, sizable perks and so on—has made me increasingly uneasy, not least because the dark side of this contrast has been growing with the arrival of each new cohort on European labor markets. If this deep split has, as I have come to believe, become a permanent feature of welfare-state capitalism, there is at least some intuitive appeal in looking at it as a cleavage between two classes.

Yet, faced with this phenomenon, standard class analysis has little to say. The central class divide in our capitalist societies, it says, is between capitalists and workers, between the owners of the means of production (and their agents) and those who operate the latter in exchange for a wage. Within this framework, the unemployed are classified as "virtual" workers, who just happen to be temporarily out of work. Like "actual" workers, their central complaint is the capitalists' monopoly of the means of production. And their struggle to improve their lot cannot but merge with the pursuits of the labor movement. If this were all class analysis could offer in the present context, it would be worrying indeed since it is unpleasantly reminiscent of bourgeois apologetics at the time

*Earlier versions of this paper were presented at the international seminar "Recent Developments in Class Theory and Class Analysis" (Amsterdam, April 1985) and at the Dutch political scientists' annual meeting (Amersfoort, June 1986). I am particularly grateful to Leo Apostel, Sue Black, Johannes Berger, Mino Carchedi, Jos de Beus, Michael Krätke, Mary Nolan, Adam Przeworski, Ian Steedman, Robert van der Veen, Jenny Walry, and Erik Wright for useful comments and discussions.

of the incipient labor movement, when the spokesmen for capitalist interests attempted to convince workers that the only privilege that mattered was landownership and that, therefore, the only real fight was against landowners.

Is class theory, as developed in the Marxian tradition, bound to become the "scientific" guise of welfare-state capitalism's established working class? Or can it be revised and extended to provide an illuminating critical analysis of social relations in contemporary capitalist countries? I believe that it can, but that extensive alterations in the standard class-theoretical framework are required. Some key ingredients for the needed reconstruction have recently been adduced by Erik Olin Wright on the basis of John Roemer's theory of exploitation.[1] My main aim, in this paper, is to rephrase and generalize the Roemer/Wright approach in such a way that it can be fruitfully applied to the issues raised above.

In the first two sections, I spell out the distinctive formal features of this approach, and, in the third and fourth sections, I show how its most radical extension can cover domination as well as exploitation, and sex or race as well as "productive" classes. Even when restricted to exploitation and to productive assets, however, the Wright/Roemer approach can accommodate the notion of organizational classes, Wright's most original contribution, and the closely analogous notion of job classes (discussed in the fifth and sixth sections, respectively). In the last two sections, I argue that the concept of job classes provides an essential tool for understanding the specific class structure of welfare state capitalism and the new class struggle, which will, under some conditions, develop on the basis of that class structure. Some recent contributions to the microeconomics of unemployment and the emerging debate in Europe on the "universal grant" will prove to be of crucial importance for this discussion.

What Do We Want Classes to Be?

Conceptual discussions are pointless if we do not specify what job we want the concept under discussion to perform. Here I take it for granted that the purposes of class theory are not primarily normative. Consequently, we do not need to try to make sense of the claim that we must

---

1. See E.O. Wright, *Classes* (London: Verso, 1985); idem, "A General Framework for the Analysis of Class Structure," chapter 1 above; J.E. Roemer, *A General Theory of Exploitation and Class* (Cambridge, Mass.: Harvard University Press, 1982); and idem, "New Directions in the Marxian Theory of Exploitation and Class," *Politics and Society*, vol. 11 (1982): 253–88.

strive for a classless society—even though the class concept we end up selecting may be such that we can defensibly maintain that classes ought to be abolished. Instead, I assume that we are searching for a class concept that is

1. relevant to the explanation of *consciousness* (ideology, values, attitudes) and/or *action* (lifestyle, political behavior, social conflict).[2]

What, then, is a class explanation of consciousness or action? I submit that the explanatory variable must at least be

2. *hierarchical*, in the sense that one can meaningfully say that one class is "superior" to another.

In other words, class has something to do with inequality. Moreover, the explanatory variable must also be

3. *discrete*, in the sense that belonging to a class is not just a matter of degree.

In other words, even if class is defined by reference to some gradient (income, wealth), there must be some nonarbitrary border. These two conditions are still very liberal. They would be met, for example, by a classification that grouped people according to whether they can curl their tongues or according to whether they lived above or below sea level.

The class-theoretical research program is, of course, more distinctive than this. It is rooted in a materialistic conception of history and hence requires classes to be defined in "materialistic" terms. This can be understood in two distinct senses. One may mean that classes must be

4. concerned (by definition) with the distribution of *material advantages* and burdens, that is, of (*a*) income and work, but also possibly of (*b*) exercise of and submission to power.

---

2. As Jon Elster (*Making Sense of Marx* (Cambridge: Cambridge University Press, 1985), pp. 335–6) notes, Marx himself primarily used the concept of class to explain collective action. Marx also tended to view the explanation of behavior by class in terms of a simple convergence between the class map and the behavioral map of a society (see J. Elster, "Three Challenges to Class," in *Analytical Marxism*, ed. J.E. Roemer (Cambridge: Cambridge University Press, 1986), section 2). In both respects, the present characterization of the class-theoretical research program is broader: it leaves room for class explanations of individual behavior, and it allows for a more complex causal link between class and behavior.

or that they must be

> 5. rooted (by definition) in the *property relations* that characterize the mode of production concerned.

Property relations refer, for example, to the feudal rights enjoyed by the lords over their serfs or to the capitalists' private ownership of the means of production. Under either interpretation, this requirement of materialism implies that classes must be "objective," in the sense that belonging to a class is a matter of situation rather than of consciousness or action.[3] If class were a matter of consciousness or action, class explanations, given the nature of the facts they are meant to explain, would tend to become tautological.

Very schematically, it could be said that conventional definitions of class meet either condition 4 or condition 5, but never both. The conventional exploitation definition (workers versus profit earners) meets 4*a*. The conventional domination definition (workers versus their bosses) meets 4*b*. And the conventional ownership definition (workers versus the wealthy) meets 5. As we shall see, Wright's new concept of class has the advantage of simultaneously meeting 4 and 5, while elegantly generating a set of hierarchical and discrete classes that do not give rise to the "embarrassment of the middle classes." In other words, Wright's concept is materialistic in both senses mentioned above as well as hierarchical and discrete, and, unlike conventional definitions, it does not generate large intermediate categories that are hard to put to explanatory use. The method Wright uses to achieve this remarkable result is directly inspired by John Roemer's "game-theoretical" concept of exploitation.[4] Let us carefully examine what it consists in.

The Logical Structure of Class Explanations

In the third part of his *General Theory of Exploitation and Class*, Roemer defines exploitation with the help of a "withdrawal game." A

---

3. There is no lack of "subjective" definitions of class in this sense among authors who explicitly distance themselves from the Marxist tradition. See, for example, in the last section, the grounds on which Dahrendorf and Gorz refuse to grant class status to the unemployed.

4. And *not* by Roemer's own class concept, to which I return below. What I here call the Roemer/Wright approach to class (based on Roemer's game-theoretical treatment of *exploitation*) must not be confused with what I call below (see especially note 14) the Roemer/Elster approach to class (based on Roemer's "endogenous" analysis of *class*).

group is *exploited* (or *exploits*) if its members would become better off (or would become worse off) as a result of withdrawing from the economy. By varying the rules to which this withdrawal must conform, one can generate a number of institutionally specific types of exploitation. Feudal exploitation, capitalist exploitation, and socialist exploitation are distinguished by, respectively, whether the withdrawers are allowed to depart with their initial share of all assets, their per capita share of alienable assets (wealth), or their per capita share of inalienable assets (skills). Unfortunately, this formulation in terms of withdrawal games leads to a number of counterintuitive consequences, especially as we relax the restrictive assumptions of a perfectly competitive economy with income-maximizing agents within which Roemer conducts his argument.[5]

Such difficulties can largely be resolved, however, if one interprets Roemer's game-theoretical definition as a simple conceptual *test* to check for exploitation under highly idealized circumstances (perfect competition, constant returns to scale, no incentive effects). The *definition* of exploitation, however, is to be phrased directly in terms of the *causal* influence of the distribution of various assets on the distribution of income (or of income–leisure bundles). In feudal exploitation, distribution of ownership over *people* affects the distribution of real income. In capitalist exploitation, the unequal distribution of ownership of the *means of production* influences the way incomes are distributed. And in socialist exploitation, it is the unequal distribution of *skills* that plays a causal role in shaping the distribution of income.[6] To this list, Wright adds *organizational* exploitation, which can analogously be defined by reference to the influence of an unequal distribution of organizational assets on the distribution of income. He accordingly defines as many classes as there are combinations of exploiter or exploited statuses according to these various definitions.

This general concept of class beautifully meets the various desiderata set forth in the previous section. It is hierarchical and discrete in the sense specified there: the nonarbitrary boundary between classes is determined by asking who would be better off and who would be worse off if the type of asset under consideration were equally distributed. It is also materialistic in the sense of both conditions 4 and 5. Since it refers

5. See the *Politics and Society* (vol. 11 (1982)) symposium around Roemer: "New Directions in the Marxian Theory of Exploitation and Class."

6. For a more detailed justification of this reconstruction of Roemerian exploitation, see R.J. van der Veen and P. Van Parijs, "Entitlement Theories of Justice: From Nozick to Roemer and Beyond," *Economics and Philosophy* vol. 1 (1985), pp. 69–81; and P. Van Parijs, *What (If Anything) Is Wrong with Capitalism* (forthcoming), ch. 4.

to the distribution of income, it is clearly concerned, by definition, with material advantages. And since it refers to the distribution of assets, it is rooted, by definition, in the structure of property relations that characterizes a mode of production.

The logical structure of the class-theoretical research program is thereby given a new, and rather attractive, shape. Contrary to simplistic presentations, class theory does *not* attempt to derive whatever aspect of consciousness or action it aims to explain (E) from the distribution of material advantages (M), using the simple causal scheme: $M \rightarrow E$. Nor does it attempt to derive its explanandum (E) from the distribution of a particular type of asset (A^*)—for example, the alienable means of production—to which it would give a special privilege at all times and places, using the simple causal scheme: $A^* \rightarrow E$.

Rather, the class-theoretical research program consists in first asking, within a given historical context, which type of asset (A) exerts a major influence on the distribution of material advantages (M), and in next conjecturing that the control of that type of asset (A) therefore constitutes a major factor in the explanation of whatever aspect of consciousness or action one wants to explain (E), in particular of those aspects that command the future of the mode of production (attitudes and behavior with respect to property rights).[7]

Hence, the underlying causal scheme can be represented as $(A \rightarrow M) \rightarrow (A \rightarrow E)$. In other words, a class explanation entails the existence of three causal links. If the first link $(A \rightarrow M)$ were absent—for example, if all material advantages were distributed by a lottery—there would be no classes. If the third link $(A \rightarrow E)$ were absent—if the assets that shape the distribution of income did not shape consciousness and behavior— the class explanation would be straightforwardly falsified. Moreover, even if the assets that shape the distribution of income also shape those aspects of consciousness and behavior that interest us, the class explanation may still be false; the truth of such an explanation requires the assets to shape consciousness and behavior *because* they shape the

---

7. As Mino Carchedi pointed out to me, this provides a neat interpretation of the old Althusserian distinction between "dominance" and "determination in the least instance." Which type of asset—and hence which class struggle—is dominant $(A \rightarrow E)$, varies from one mode of production to another, but is determined throughout history by an invariant criterion. This criterion gives dominance in this sense to whichever type of asset most powerfully influences the distribution of material advantages $(A \rightarrow M)$. For a formally analogous but substantially different interpretation of Althusser's "determination in the last instance," see P. Van Parijs, "From Contradiction to Catastrophe," *New Left Review*, no. 115 (1979), pp. 87–96; and idem, "Marxism's Central Puzzle," in *After Marx*, ed. T. Ball and J. Farr (Cambridge: Cambridge University Press, 1984), pp. 88–104.

distribution of income—that is, it entails the existence of the central causal link in the formula given above.[8]

Thus, class is now defined in terms of income inequality.[9] But class so defined differs fundamentally from an income group, not just because the definition turns a continuous distribution into a discrete classification (those who would be better off and those who would be worse off if assets were equalized), but mainly because it filters out any aspect of the income distribution resulting from choice or change rather than from the unequal distribution of some asset.[10] Class divisions are therefore closer to inequalities in the control over assets. However, belonging to the exploiting class (with respect to some particular asset) is not equivalent to having more than the average amount of that asset since assets may be left dormant instead of being used "productively" to generate income. The owner of dormant assets would not be made worse off by asset equalization. The possession of assets is a potential and is turned into class membership only when this potential is used.

---

8. Note that the truth of $M \rightarrow E$, though sufficient for the truth of $(A \rightarrow M) \rightarrow (A \rightarrow M)$, is by no means implied by it. Class theory, as characterized here, is not committed to asserting that assets affect behavior *because* assets affect income *and* income in turn affects behavior. Singly or in combination, the three causal links that class theory consists in asserting do not even entail that income affects behavior or that there is any statistical correlation between income and behavior. For an old, but still very useful clarification of this point, see H.L. Costner and R.K. Leik, "Deductions from 'Axiomatic Theory,'" *American Sociological Review*, vol. 29 (1964), pp. 819–35.

9. Talking about an asset-based income inequality is just a convenient shortcut. Unequally distributed ownership of asset A can conceivably affect income, and exploitation can therefore be present, even though income is distributed in a perfectly equal way. This can happen because the influence of asset A on income could (by a fluke) be exactly offset by the influence of other assets (whose ownership would need to be inversely correlated with that of A) or by the play of individual preferences and luck.

10. One's present assets may result from past chance or choice. When assets are distinguished from choice and chance as major influences on income, some time scale is implicitly brought in. Restricting ourselves to the two extreme possibilities, we must decide whether the equalization thought experiment that enables us to determine which class someone belongs to should operate on "initial" or on "current" endowments. In the case of wealth, for example, should one equalize what people have received and can still be expected to receive (leaving out choice and chance) over their whole lifetime? Or rather, should one equalize the wealth people happened to have, say, at the beginning of this month? For explanatory purposes, one major advantage of the first option is that it enables class theory to discriminate between the young with good and bad ("structural") prospects, instead of lumping (nearly) all of them together into the wealth-exploited class. One major advantage of the second option is that it puts into the wealth-exploiting class those who have accumulated wealth through a combination of choice and chance (that is, hard work, persistent thrift, and good luck), while putting those whom chance and choice have left with very little of their initial assets into the wealth-exploited class. Realizing the importance of the time scale selected does not blur the distinction between assets on the one hand and choice or chance on the other hand. But it does make it necessary to specify whether reference to initial assets or reference to current assets makes the concept of class more fruitful as far as the explanation of consciousness and action is concerned.

Class, Domination, and Exploitation

Erik Wright describes the move to this new concept of class, inspired by
Roemer's approach to exploitation, as a shift from a domination-based
to an exploitation-based concept of class. The gist of his move, however,
is just as compatible with the former as with the latter.[11] There is no
reason why, in the logical structure spelled out above, one should restrict
the interpretation of material advantages (M) to income, or even to
income–leisure bundles,[12] and hence leave out *power*, construed as the
(successful) giving of commands. Just as we can distinguish between
capitalist exploiters and the capitalistically exploited in terms of whether
they would have less or more income (with an unchanged amount of
labor) if wealth were equalized, could we not distinguish between capitalist dominators and the capitalistically dominated in terms of whether
they would have less or more power if wealth were equalized?[13] And
what applies to wealth-based inequalities can easily be extended, *mutatis
mutandis*, to inequalities deriving from the unequal distribution of other
types of assets. What is central to a Roemer-inspired approach is the fact

---

11. Moreover, Roemer's concept of exploitation itself arguably has little to do with
exploitation, as the term is commonly understood. I argue elsewhere (see "Exploitation and
the Libertarian Challenge," in *Modern Theories of Exploitation*, ed. A. Reeve (Los
Angeles: Sage, 1987), section 2; and, more fully, *What (If Anything) Is Wrong with
Capitalism*, ch. 2) that any defensible explication of our (or indeed Marx's) notion of
exploitation must fulfil at least three conditions: A exploits B only if (1) B works, (2) A
gets a benefit from B, and (3) A exerts power over B. Not one of these conditions is
fulfilled by Roemer's definition, which allows a nonworker to be exploited—for example,
someone choosing to live austerely on the meager interest yielded by a smaller than average
capital endowment is, according to Roemer, capitalistically exploited. Roemer's definition
also allows for two autarkic communities to exploit and be exploited because of unequal
endowments, even though neither of them derives any benefit from or exerts any power
over the other. Hence, although I shall for convenience continue to do so below, using the
term *exploitation* to refer to Roemer's concept is misleading. So, too, if only for this
reason, is describing Wright's redefinition of class as a shift to an exploitation-based
concept. In the text, however, I ignore this semantic issue.

12. Agents may trade income off against leisure, and the unequal distribution of assets
may therefore substantially affect the distribution of material advantages by generating
massive inequalities in leisure time while hardly affecting the distribution of income.
(Imagine, for example, a society in which people choose to work just enough to get a
subsistence income and some of whose members control an amount of wealth just sufficient
to give them that income without working at all. In such a situation, wealth equalization
would not make anyone better or worse off in income terms. It would only lead some
people to work less (or to take on more attractive jobs) and other people to work more (or
to take on less attractive jobs) than before, in order to maintain the same income level. For
formal models along these lines, see Roemer, *A General Theory*, part 1.) To take this
possibility into account, one needs only to modify the counterfactual exercise slightly.
Instead of simply asking whether people's incomes would increase or decrease as a result of
asset equalization, one must now ask this same question *assuming that* everyone keeps
doing the same job for the same length of time.

that it focuses on the causal link between assets and material advantages and not on the particular type of material advantage it happens to select.

Of course, for such an extension of the class concept to be of any use, we need a well-defined concept of power. In particular, we need a concept that lends itself to measurement at least to the extent that it is in principle possible to say whether someone's power would be increased under various hypothetical arrangements. Note, however, that this implies no more than an *intra*-personally comparable and ordinal—though ultimately one-dimensional—concept. (We do not need to be able to say how much power an agent has or whether he/she has more power than another, but only whether his/her power increases or decreases.) Note, too, that income, especially but not exclusively in a nonmonetary economy, is not an unproblematic concept either. (Think, for example, of the fuzzy notion of a perk: Should the enjoyment of a large desk or thick carpets, and not just that of a company car and business meals, count as part of a manager's income?)

Furthermore, the concept of power we need has to be analytically distinct from the various asset concepts. This may seem particularly tricky in the case of ownership rights over people, of control over the state, and of organizational assets. The intuition that needs to be worked out, however, is that these assets—just like the ownership of wealth and skills—are titles or rights, to be enforced by legal or customary sanctions, whereas power, as a material advantage derived from one's ownership of assets, consists in actually getting one's commands obeyed, shaping what is produced and how. The test for analytical distinctness is that one must conceivably be able to hold those assets—to be a feudal lord or a manager—without actually giving the orders that the holding of these assets entitles one to give, just as the test for the analytical distinctness between wealth and income is that one must conceivably be able to be rich without earning any income.

If these conceptual difficulties can be solved—and I believe they

---

13. Consider a hypothetical situation in which all incomes are equal, not by virtue of people's preferences (some of them would like to earn more than the equal-income share), but by virtue of the system's basic rules: taxes are collected in such a way that both the post-tax return on capital and the post-tax wage rate are zero. (For a description of such a system and an argument that it could work, see J. Carens, *Equality, Moral Incentives and the Market* (Chicago: University of Chicago Press, 1981), part 1.) In such a situation, the wealth-equalization test (whether in its simpler version or in the modified version described in the preceding note) would lead to the conclusion that, even though wealth is very unequally distributed, there is no wealth-based exploitation. At the same time, wealth-based domination may be ubiquitous. Those who own the factories get no post-tax return on their capital, but they may well exert considerable power over the workers they hire, even though the latter find their jobs so attractive that they are willing to take them at a zero net wage.

can—the result will be a dual concept of class that extends Wright's concept while preserving the key feature of Roemer's notion of exploitation (the systematic connection between assets and material advantages). In other words, what Roemer's insight prompts is not a shift from a domination-based to an exploitation-based concept; it just happened that, being interested in exploitation, he naturally focused on one particular type of material advantage—namely, income. Rather, what Roemer's insight prompts is a shift from definitions of class phrased either simply in terms of material advantages or simply in terms of assets to a definition phrased in terms of the causal link between advantages and assets. If asset-based power is as worthy of a place in a materialistic approach as asset-based income, there is no reason why such an approach should emphasize exploitation over domination.[14] For the sake of simplicity, however, the rest of this paper is almost exclusively concerned with exploitation.

The Radical Extension: Race and Sex as Class

Turning our attention from material advantages to assets, we can similarly ask why Wright restricts assets to the four rights he lists: over people, over means of production, over skills, and over organizational assets. To give this question a rigorous answer, let us first turn to Roemer's original discussion of exploitation. Most of it focuses on two types of assets, wealth and skills (which he sometimes contrasts as alienable versus inalienable productive assets). There is nothing surprising about this selection. In a perfectly competitive market economy—the sort of economy most of Roemer's models are about—income, at equilibrium, is determined by marginal product. In such a context, only those

---

14. As mentioned earlier (note 4), Wright's concept of class, based on Roemer's concept of exploitation, differs from Roemer's concept of class, recently taken over and generalized by Jon Elster (*Making Sense of Marx*, section 6.1). Roemer (*A General Theory*, chs 2 and 4) defines class (in a capitalist society) in terms of whether people's optimal course of action consists in selling their labor power, in hiring someone else's labor power, or in being self-employed (or a combination of these). This is not a purely behavioral definition, but a *modal* definition in terms of a relation between people's assets (which determine, jointly with people's preferences, what is their optimal course of action) and their overt behavior. It can be generalized to any type of economy: "A class is a group of people who by virtue of what they possess are compelled to engage in the same activities (working or nonworking, renting or hiring land, capital or labor, giving or receiving orders) if they want to make the best use of their endowments" (Elster, *Making Sense of Marx*, p. 331; see also idem, "Three Challenges to Class," section 2). Why not adopt this general definition instead of the one used in the present paper?

It is important to note, first of all, that the above definition uses the expression "compelled" in a very weak and unusual sense: being compelled does not consist in having no other option or in having no other tolerable option, but simply in having no better option. In this sense, a Rockefeller who plays at being a proletarian is not just someone who does something (selling his labor power) he is not compelled to do, but ipso facto also someone who does not do something (hiring workers) that he is "compelled" to do. Such people are absent from Roemer's models. But there are many of them in the real world: people who fail to optimize—for example, by hiring no one when, given their endowments (and imputed preferences), they should, or by remaining idle when optimality (on their part *and* on everyone else's) would require them to work. This leads to a dilemma. Either we define classes in terms of what people are "compelled" to do, whether or not they actually do it, in which case we end up with "workers" who have never worked and "employers" who have never hired anyone—not a promising point of departure for treating the issues mentioned at the beginning of this paper—or we define classes as categories of people who do something they are compelled to do (or, somewhat more strongly: people who do whatever they are compelled to do *because* they are compelled to do it). In this case, we end up with huge gray areas containing many more than one crazy Rockefeller. This dilemma, which does not arise with the Roemer/Wright approach, points, in my view, to a serious defect in the Roemer/Elster general concept of class and provides a major reason for rejecting it.

Elster, however, objects to the Roemer/Wright approach on two distinct grounds. First, he claims, an exploitation approach is bound to be either too coarse-grained or too fine-grained. Too coarse-grained, if classes are just a matter of exploiting or being exploited— which prevents us from distinguishing between capitalists and landowners, for example. Too fine-grained, if classes are made a matter of degree of exploitation, which does not give more or a basis for a nonarbitrary discrete classification than does income distribution (see Elster, *Making Sense of Marx*, 323–4). However, the Roemer/Wright version of the exploitation-based approach allows us to make as many qualitative distinctions as there are types of assets we want to distinguish. Moreover, it provides—no more but no less than the Roemer/Elster approach—a nonarbitrary device for turning the continuous distribution of assets into a small number of discrete categories.

Second, Elster (*Making Sense of Marx*, p. 328) argues that "exploitation status does not serve as a motivation for collective action, since no one in a society knows exactly where the dividing line between exploiters and exploited should be drawn." Note again, however, that this applies much less to the Roemer/Wright exploitation concept than to the standard one (in terms of net value appropriation). It is, of course, in most cases extremely difficult to assess whether someone's income would be higher or lower than it is now if all assets of a given type were equalized. How much income some individual ends up with depends on the complex dynamics of incentive effects, on possibly counterintuitive price effects, and on the individual's own preference structure. But Roemer's exploitation criterion abstracts from these intricacies and must do so (see Van Parijs, *What (If Anything) Is Wrong with Capitalism*, ch. 4, for a more detailed discussion), in such a way that it comes down, in practice, to simply checking whether the individual concerned owns more or less than the average amount of the type of asset under consideration. For most types of assets and most individuals, which side of this dividing line they are on should be pretty clear. Indeed, this criterion is likely to apply unambiguously in many more cases than the Roemer/Elster criterion, as soon as one fully takes into account that the latter is not a behavioral definition but a modal one: one cannot determine someone's position by looking at what (s)he does; one needs to look at what (s)he has and work out in this light what is optimal for her/him to do. Many cases will, of course, be unproblematic (you cannot rent out land if you have none, or hire workers if you cannot provide them with tools), but the number of uncertain cases cannot but be greater under this criterion than under the Roemer/Wright exploitation criterion. Consequently, if Elster's objection were sufficient to destroy his target, it would be more than sufficient to blow up the position from which he is shooting. (Roemer's proof of a systematic correspondence between class and capitalist exploitation does not invalidate this conclusion. The correspondence derives from the connection between wealth on the one hand and both class and exploitation in Roemer's sense on the other hand. But since Roemer's class partition is more fine-grained than his exploitation partition, it is clear, even in this particular case, that class status is harder to assess than exploitation status.)

items that "contribute to production" can affect the distribution of income. *Skills* are simply all those productive items that cannot be detached from their bearers (and hence cannot be sold), whereas all other productive assets can be sold and are therefore subsumed under the concept of *wealth*. The real world, of course, only vaguely resembles this simple picture. Many systematic income differences—that is, differences that do not stem from choice or chance—cannot be accounted for by differences in skills or wealth, in however broad a sense.

Indeed, Roemer speaks about feudal exploitation in precapitalist societies and about status exploitation in socialist societies precisely to denote deviations from the income distribution that competitive markets would tend to generate. Whereas *feudal* exploitation occurs whenever feudal bondages affect the distribution of income, *status* exploitation occurs when special privileges (in income terms) accrue to someone because of membership in the communist party or position in the bureaucractic hierarchy.[15] The intuition behind feudal exploitation differs from that behind status exploitation in two ways: feudal exploitation is a personal relationship, and it is determined by birth, whereas those exploited by virtue of their lack of status in a socialist society need not be personally related in any way to their exploiters or prevented by virtue of their birth from acceding to the position of status exploiters. However, Roemer's wealth (or capitalist) exploitation covers cases in which there is a personal relationship involved (the exploitation of a wage worker by her/his employer) as well as cases in which there is nothing of the sort (two unequally wealthy autarkic communities), whereas his skills (or socialist) exploitation covers both the case of innate talents and that of acquired skills. Neither of the two differences between feudal and status exploitation can therefore consistently be used by Roemer as a basis for turning them into two distinct types of exploitation on a par with wealth and skills exploitation. Rather, to be consistent, one should construe feudal exploitation as a variety of status exploitation and define the latter—in a purely negative fashion—as income inequality stemming from the unequal distribution of "nonproductive" assets.

The plausibility of this reconstruction is enhanced if one considers that, according to Roemer, status exploitation can occur under capitalism as well.[16] The so-called internal labor market makes for a hierarchy of wages within large firms that could hardly be said to mirror inequalities in skills and marginal products. In order to secure loyalty to

15. See Roemer, *A General Theory*, pp. 199–202, 243–7.
16. See ibid., p. 247.

the firm and strong work incentives under imperfect competition, promotion systems have been set up in such a way that income is strongly affected by seniority and by past performance. To take an extreme case, the best-paid job (which one only gets after a certain number of years in the firm and/or if one is believed to have worked harder than anyone else) might be one in which no skill is exerted and whose productivity is zero (say, sitting in a deep armchair smoking cigars and gazing through the window). Even a perfectly competitive capitalist economy with rational profit-maximizers—though not, of course, a perfectly competitive economy of independent producers—could contain such jobs.[17] Whether one can attain such positions, that is, whether one can become a status exploiter, may, of course, depend on the skills one possesses and has exerted in the past. But this does not turn status exploitation into a variety of skills exploitation, just as the fact that one's current wealth is the result of the past exertion of one's skills does not turn wealth exploitation into a variety of skills exploitation.

There are, of course, many other dimensions of status exploitation in this purely negative sense, most of which can be viewed either as constraints on the free operation of the market or as responses to imperfect information or transaction costs. For example, my Belgian citizenship gives me a number of income advantages over citizens of some other countries because citizenship determines, to a significant extent, where one is allowed to settle, which jobs one can apply for, or what benefits one is eligible for. Similarly, the fact that in some remote past I got a degree—perhaps to certify that I had acquired some skills that have now eroded away—also enables me to get higher benefits and better-paid jobs.

Moreover, a significant part of what is usually called sexual or racial *discrimination* can be given an analogous interpretation. True, the concept of productive skill could be stretched to cover the facts that a male executive does not risk career interruption by pregnancy or that a black shop assistant may turn away racially prejudiced customers. True too, much discrimination takes the form of the indirect influence of race or sex on income via selective access to skill acquisition. There is little doubt, however, that this attempt to reduce sex and race either directly

17. For a subtle attempt to reconcile marginal-product payment (as far as career profiles, not synchronically given incomes, are concerned) with internal wage hierarchies, see, however, J.M. Malcomson, "Work Incentives, Hierarchy, and Internal Labour Markets," *Journal of Political Economy*, vol. 92 (1984), pp. 486–507. If all internal wage hierarchies can be analyzed in this way, intra-firm "status exploitation" vanishes as soon as the appropriate time scale is selected.

to skill or indirectly to factors commanding skill acquisition leaves a considerable residue. Equally skilled men and women and blacks and whites frequently get unequal rewards because of their sex or race, even though they would not in a perfectly competitive economy.[18] In other words, there is specifically racial and sexual exploitation. Being (at least) as innate as feudal exploitation and as impersonal as citizenship or degree exploitation, both are varieties of status exploitation as defined above.

The notion of status exploitation then simply covers all types of income inequality attributable neither to change nor to choice nor to inequalities in wealth or skills. Given the heterogeneity of this residual category, it is presumably wise not to define a single status-class divide (in terms of who would be better off and who worse off if the impact of status on income were neutralized). Rather, there should be as many class divides as there are factors systematically affecting the distribution of material advantages. The inhabitants of developed countries and those of the Third World, graduates and the uneducated, males and females, blacks and whites, can then constitute pairs of classes just as much as those who own considerable wealth and those who do not.[19] Which of these class divides is most relevant in a particular historical context simply depends on which factors most powerfully affect the distribution of income and power.

Productive Assets and Organizational Classes

Wright, however, explicitly and firmly resists this radical extension of the Marxist notion of class, on the grounds that the materialistic class concept we are after should be concerned only with inequalities in material welfare stemming from unequal ownership of the *productive forces*.[20] This restriction cannot be justified, I believe, by the expectation

18. A tricky case arises when the causal link between, say, sex and income, is not provided by legal restrictions or collective bargaining power, but by preference schedules (in the broadest sense, encompassing normative expectations, gender ideology, and the like): think of "the belief of male workers, employers and women workers themselves that here existed a woman's job and a woman's rate" (J. Lewis, "The Debate on Sex and Class," *New Left Review*, no. 149 (1985), p. 114). Exploitation is an asset-rooted, and hence not a preference-rooted, inequality of income. But what if asset differences generate differences in preferences?

19. In some contexts, it may be equally meaningful to differentiate wealth classes as well. For example, when land has a special standing and cannot readily be exchanged against other forms of wealth (produced means of production), it makes sense to speak of land classes.

20. Wright, "A General Framework," section 3.

that the distribution of productive assets, in this sense, universally affects the distribution of material advantages more powerfully than race or sex, for example. Nor can it be justified by the belief that income or power inequalities deriving from inequalities in productive endowments are more objectionable or more conducive to ill feelings than, say, sex-based or race-based inequalities. To justify it, one needs to confine the explan-andum of class theory to consciousness or action related to a change in the mode of production, the latter being defined in terms of property rights over the productive forces. Classes in this restricted sense cannot be expected to provide the sole basis for a materialistic theory of consciousness and action in general. But it can sensibly be argued that such a restriction is warranted if our primary aim is to understand why a society moves from one mode of production to another because classes in this restricted sense partition society into different categories precisely according to whether they have a (*prima facie*) interest in a different mode of production.

Even if we accept this restriction, however, the Roemer/Wright approach can still yield a significant broadening of conventional class analysis along the assets dimension. How serious this restriction is depends on how narrowly the notions of productive forces and, hence, of mode of production are conceived. From the previous section, one might expect "productive" classes to be defined in terms of wealth and skills exploitation and the residual category of status exploitation to be ejected from the realm of class. In addition to wealth classes and skills classes, however, Wright allows for classes defined by feudal exploitation—on the grounds that labor power is a productive force—as well as for classes defined by organizational exploitation—on the grounds that organization is a productive asset distinct from wealth and skill. Can this be sustained?

Take feudal exploitation first. Either one does *not* view the feudally exploited as part of the lord's property and interprets feudal exploitation as the serf's obligation to pay a due (in labor, goods, or money) to the lord. Such an obligation, as protected by custom and enforced, if neces-sary, by force, is bound to involve an influence on income distribution that is not reducible to wealth exploitation. But it plainly constitutes a standard case of *status exploitation* in the above (purely negative) sense. Although the lord's status can legitimately be construed as an asset—it is vested in him by the prevailing structure of property rights and commands access to material advantages—it cannot be regarded as a productive asset, that is, something that, on a par with the means of production and the skills of labor power, contributes to the social product.

Alternatively, one may interpret feudal exploitation as an inequality of income that derives from the fact that some people own, at least in part, some other people and hence their labor power (on the slavery pattern). Feudal exploitation then becomes one aspect of wealth exploitation, along, say, with income inequality generated by the unequal ownership of horses. However, there is a sufficiently significant qualitative difference between such human wealth and other types of wealth to justify our assigning societies in which the ownership of other people is allowed (partial or total slavery) and societies in which it is banned to different modes of production. (Similarly, a society that bans the private ownership of land though not that of other material means of production may be said to have a mode of production distinct from the one obtaining in a society in which all nonhuman goods can be privately appropriated.) The need to explain changes in the mode of production would then make it mandatory to allow for feudal (and possibly land) classes in this sense, instead of lumping everything together under the single heading of wealth classes. To sum up: if, as Wright insists, classes have to be defined in terms of income inequalities stemming from unequal control over productive forces, then either feudal classes are not classes at all or they constitute a subtype of wealth classes, though one that may deserve separate treatment.

An analogous reduction to wealth exploitation is out of the question in the case of Wright's most novel category, *organizational exploitation.* Organization assets consist in "controlling the technical division of labor, the coordination of productive activities within and across labor processes."[21] There is no doubt that the way in which the division of labor is organized can affect productivity to a tremendous extent and that those who do this organizing are thereby enabled to appropriate considerable material advantages (both in terms of income and, almost by definition, in terms of power). But it does not follow that organization assets constitute a distinct type of productive asset. Here again, two interpretations are possible. One could view the task of organizing the labor process as the exertion of a particular kind of skill. In a capitalist economy, this constitutes the specific job of the entrepreneur, who takes economic initiatives and brings capital and labor together to produce commodities. It is true that the entrepreneur's rewards cannot be reduced to capitalist or wealth exploitation: an entrepreneur might conceivably operate entirely with borrowed money. It is also true that such rewards are very different, under capitalism, from most rewards for skills, insofar as they tend to be eroded by imitation and competition and have completely disappeared from (notional) equilibrium situ-

---

21. Ibid.

ations.[22] Yet, however peculiar the skill and however precarious the way in which it is rewarded, such organization exploitation is, under socialism even more than under capitalism, just a special case of skills exploitation.

There is, however, another interpretation that does justify a distinct treatment. Imagine a situation in which the job of organizing production does not require any particularly scarce, valuable skill. If the person who happens to do it were replaced by any other able-bodied worker, there would be no noticeable difference. Nonetheless, the job is an essential one, and if it were not done, economic performance would be disastrous. This gives incumbents of such positions—on a par with the possessors of skills and wealth—a potential base for claiming material advantages, providing property relations are such that incumbency is firmly established. The essential difference between organization assets and skills concerns the nature of the sanction they confer on their holders: the disturbance of the production process in one case, the withdrawal of a precious input in the other. To the extent that market forces rule, the sanction associated with organization assets is kept within narrow bounds, as its use—the disruption of production—would threaten the very source—profits booked by selling the product—of the material advantages potentially accruing to those using it. Hence, returns to organization will be under constant pressure to disappear unless they are reinvigorated by the exertion of innovative skills. Under monopolistic capitalism, however, and even more under centrally planned socialism, organization assets are given considerable leeway to shape the distribution of material advantages.

Consequently, unlike feudal exploitation, organizational exploitation cannot be subsumed under either of Roemer's two types of productive-asset exploitation (based on wealth and skills) or dumped into the residual category of status exploitation. Organization assets do affect production, though not in the same way as "withdrawable" factors of production. It makes sense, therefore, to incorporate them into the definition of a mode of production. And Wright's fourfold distinction (human means of production, material means of production, personal skills, organization) can be preserved as a meaningful and provocative conjecture about the sequence of dominant class divisions from slavery to bureaucratic socialism.

---

22. See the Austrian School's analysis of entrepreneurial profits (for example, I.M. Kirzner, *Competition and Entrepreneurship* (Chicago: University of Chicago Press, 1973).

Jobs as Assets and the Microeconomics of Unemployment

Without questioning Wright's restriction to productive assets (in his fairly broad sense), however, I want to argue that this typology is badly defective because it is blind to what tends to become the central class divide under what I shall loosely call welfare-state capitalism. Persistent involuntary unemployment provides my argument with its most natural point of departure. By definition, someone who is involuntarily unemployed is someone who possesses all the qualifications required to fill existing jobs and would be willing to do so for a wage lower than that paid to current incumbents. Consequently, the very existence of involuntary unemployment establishes that the holding of jobs influences the distribution of material welfare in a way that is not reducible to the influence of skills. But if involuntary unemployment is a purely transient phenomenon, both for society as a whole and for the individuals affected, the possession of a job cannot be viewed as a significant asset. This is, of course, exactly what standard models of perfectly competitive market economies imply. Such economies constantly tend toward an equilibrium state in which all those wanting to work have a job and earn a wage equal to their marginal product. Wealth and skills, in such a context, are highly important assets, but the holding of a job does not constitute an asset at all.

In contrast with this standard approach, some recent developments in economic theory (radical as well as mainstream) have endeavored to establish the possibility of equilibrium involuntary unemployment, even under perfectly competitive conditions. One of them, the so-called insiders–outsiders approach, is directly relevant to our present purposes.[23] It attempts to answer the riddle of persistent involuntary unemployment—Why don't firms accept lower bids from outsiders instead of paying more than the market-clearing wage to their current employees?—by pointing (primarily) to the importance of hiring, training, and firing costs. Replacing an insider by an equally qualified, equally paid outsider is an expensive operation for a firm: severance pay to the worker being replaced, advertisements to find someone else, interviews, health checks, time spent teaching the job to the new recruit, initial mistakes due to lack of experience, and so forth may amount to a considerable cost that the firm saves by keeping its current employee.

---

23. See, for example, R. Solow, "Insiders and Outsiders in Wage Determination," *Scandinavian Journal of Economics*, vol. 87 (1985), pp. 411–28; A. Lindbeck and D.J. Snower, "Explanations of Unemployment," *Oxford Review of Economic Policy*, vol. 1 (1985), pp. 34–59, sections 3 and 4; and idem, "Wage Setting, Unemployment, and Insider–Outsider Relations," *American Economic Review*, vol. 76 (1986), pp. 235–9.

This provides the insider with possibly ample room to maneuver to negotiate a wage exceeding both the outsider's reservation wage and his/her own.

How ample this room is depends on the size of the costs involved, and these in turn are largely a matter of institutional framework. The incentive for a firm to keep a worker at a wage significantly higher than what the unemployed would be willing to accept is, for example, much stronger if sacked workers are entitled to two years' severance pay than it is if the firm owes no compensation to the dismissed worker. How much of the maneuvering room thus created the workers will actually use depends on their bargaining power. Even a worker bargaining individually, with quitting as her/his sole weapon, may be able to win in higher wages a substantial portion of what it would cost the firm to replace her/him by an outsider. Collective bargaining and the use of such weapons as strikes and work-to-the-rule further enhance this ability, up to the point where insiders appropriate nearly all the firm saves by keeping them rather than hiring outsiders.[24]

It follows that some involuntary unemployment can be expected at equilibrium in any market economy relying on wage labor—there are always some hiring and training costs that will give rise, through the mechanism sketched above, to a discrepancy between the equilibrium wage (no endogenous pressure to change) and the market-clearing wage (demand matches supply). But this discrepancy, and the corresponding level of involuntary unemployment, will become significant only as the "right to one's job" becomes institutionalized in various ways—in particular through statutory severance pay and recognition of the right to strike. Insofar as such a right is a central specific feature of welfare-state capitalism, this form of capitalism is inevitably characterized by a sizable amount of involuntary unemployment and, hence, of material inequality deriving from the unequal distribution of job assets.

This conclusion receives further support from another, quite distinct, development in the microeconomics of unemployment, the so-called efficiency wage theory. The central question is the same as above: What prevents market forces from eliminating involuntary unemployment? Why don't capitalist firms take advantage of underbidding by adequately qualified unemployed workers? The answer, however, is very different. This theory does not appeal to the difference between the bargaining positions of insiders and outsiders, but to the fact that productivity is affected by the wage level and that, therefore, the lowest

---

24. If they appropriated the whole of it, it would become in the firm's interest to sack everyone and recruit a new lot of workers from the pool of the involuntarily unemployed.

possible wage is not necessarily the profit-maximizing one. There are at least two reasons why this may be the case and, correspondingly, two main variants of efficiency wage theory.[25] The soft, Maussian variant claims that the profit-maximizing wage is higher than the market-clearing wage because workers who feel well treated by an employer from whom they receive a wage significantly higher than their reservation wage respond to this gift with a countergift in the form of keen performance.[26] The hard, Hobbesian variant claims instead that the firm's optimal wage rate exceeds the market-clearing rate because raising the workers' pay above what they could easily get elsewhere if sacked enhances their welfare loss in the case of dismissal and hence their incentive not to shirk.[27] As pointed out by proponents of both variants, the central claim of efficiency wage theory can also be expressed using the Marxian distinction between labor and labor power: paying as little as possible (the market-clearing rate) for a time unit of labor power (with given skills) generally does not amount to paying as little as possible per unit of labor effectively performed since a higher payment per unit of time may enable the capitalist, for either of the reasons mentioned above, to extract from each unit of labor time a significantly greater amount of actual labor.[28]

It follows that, even in the absence of any attempt by insiders to take advantage of their superior bargaining position, the capitalists' profit-maximizing behavior drives a wedge between equilibrium wages and reservation wages, thus turning involuntary unemployment into an intrinsic feature of any capitalist economy. Here again, however, this feature can be expected to grow more significant with the development of the welfare state. Carl Shapiro and Joseph E. Stiglitz, for example, point out that one of the implications of their (Hobbesian) model is a positive relation between the unemployment rate and unemployment

25. Here I ignore other possible rationales for the causal connection between wage rate and productivity: impact on physical productivity (workers can work better when they are better fed), recruitment of more productive workers (whose reservation wage is higher), impact on the rate of turnover, etc. See J.M. Malcomson, "Unemployment and the Efficiency Wage Hypothesis," *Economic Journal*, vol. 91 (1981), pp. 848–66; and Lindbeck and Snower, "Explanations of Unemployment," section 3.

26. See G.A. Akerlof, "Labor Contracts as Partial Gift Exchange," in his *An Economic Theorist's Book of Tales* (Cambridge: Cambridge University Press, 1984), pp. 145–74.

27. See especially Malcomson, "Unemployment"; C. Shapiro and J.E. Stiglitz, "Equilibrium Unemployment as a Worker Discipline Device," *American Economic Review*, vol. 74 (1984), pp. 433–44; and S. Bowles, "The Production Process in a Competitive Economy: Walrasian, Neo-Hobbesian, and Marxian Models," *American Economic Review*, vol. 75 (1985), pp. 16–36.

28. See Akerlof, "Labor Contracts," p. 147; and Bowles, "Production Process," pp. 19–20.

benefits (or other welfare payments). The reason for this is not, as conventionally asserted, that high benefits slow job search and thereby boost voluntary unemployment, but rather that high benefits soften the sanction of dismissal by reducing the welfare differential between being employed at a given wage and being unemployed. The higher the benefits, the theory predicts, the higher the efficiency wage, and hence (other things remaining equal) the higher the level of unemployment.[29] It hardly needs saying that this expectation is further strengthened if, as is usually the case, benefits are financed out of wages. Consequently, insofar as the development of the welfare state can be construed, at least in part, as a rise in the level of benefits (say, as a proportion of GNP per capita), efficiency wage theory warrants the expectation that welfare-state capitalism will be endemically plagued by a particularly high level of involuntary unemployment.[30]

This is not the place to discuss how well these two approaches fit the available data on unemployment, how many of these data they explain, or to what extent they compete with or supplement other accounts based, for example, on the deficiency of aggregate demand or on rationing. If the analysis stemming from either of the above approaches is correct, however, the distribution of (irreducible) job assets significantly affects the distribution of material welfare in any capitalist economy—as opposed to a market economy without wage labor—and this influence becomes ever more significant as the welfare state develops, whether in the form of an increasingly entrenched right to one's job or (somewhat paradoxically) in the form of a rising level of unemployment benefits. One can accordingly define a *job exploiter* (a *job exploited*) as someone who would be worse off (better off) if job assets were equally distributed, with the distribution of skills remaining unchanged and all efficiency effects being assumed away.[31] Job exploi-

---

29. See Shapiro and Stiglitz, "Equilibrium Unemployment," p. 434. The net effect of an increase in benefits is not just the sum of the voluntary unemployment generated in one way (search theory) and of the involuntary unemployment generated in another way (efficiency wage theory) since higher benefits may turn a significant part of the earlier involuntary unemployment into voluntary unemployment.

30. Ironically this means that the attempt to compensate those who suffer from the lack of job assets leads to an increase in the number of those who lack them *and* suffer from this lack. The fact that unemployment benefits reduce the number of the involuntarily unemployed (and the involuntariness of their unemployment) *with a given number of jobs and given wages* is perfectly compatible with their boosting considerably the number of the involuntarily unemployed, once the effects of higher (efficiency) wages and fewer jobs are taken into account.

31. Job asset equalization is not to be confused with the equalization—or neutralization—of what Wright (*Classes*, p. 76) calls *credentials.* Both the "ownership" of jobs and the restriction of access to certified skills can be viewed as posing "barriers to entry"

tation thus defined provides a further item on Wright's list of class divisions. Like feudal, capitalist, skills, and organizational exploitation, it denotes a way in which the unequal control over some productive forces generates inequalities in the distribution of material welfare.[32]

The Class Structure of Welfare-State Capitalism

Just how significant is this job class division under advanced welfare-state capitalism? Does the unequal distribution of job assets generate inequalities in material welfare to anything like the same extent as the unequal distribution of capital does? Is there any sign that it affects consciousness and behavior, in particular collective action aimed at changing the corresponding property relations? Should a class struggle between those endowed with a job and the jobless be expected to play an increasingly prominent role under welfare-state capitalism?[33]

To tackle these questions, let us first ask in which counterfactual situation the material welfare of the millions of West Europeans who are currently receiving unemployment or welfare benefits would be most enhanced: in a situation in which capital income were equally divided among all adults or in a situation in which labor income were equally shared among all those wanting to work? There is no doubt as to the answer: the unemployed would gain much more from a redistribution of jobs than from a redistribution of wealth.[34] Admittedly, this is only a

---

and thereby enabling employed workers to appropriate more than the return to their skills that would occur in a pure market model. Like skills, however, and unlike job assets, credentials are attributes that individuals can take from one job to another and that one may, therefore, want to subsume under a broadened version of skills.

32. One might conceivably deny "job classes" the dignity of classes on the grounds that jobs do not really constitute productive forces in the sense in which people, land, tools, and skills do. However, such a denial cannot be sustained once organizational assets have been allowed. Job assets and organizational assets are closely analogous. Both types of assets can exert a significant influence only to the extent that the rule of "market forces" is constrained—hence their absence in standard neoclassical models. Both presuppose the exertion of some skills, but neither reduces to skill ownership. Insofar as they are carefully distinguished from the provision of the skills they presuppose, neither of them can be said to "contribute to production" in a strict sense, even though the control of both types of assets can profoundly affect production, if only through the nuisance value they confer on those who possess them.

33. For interesting analyses of the specific nature of class relations under welfare-state capitalism quite different from the one proposed here, see M. Krätke, "Klassen im Sozial-staat" [Classes in the welfare state], *Prokla*, vol. 58 (1985), pp. 89–108; and J.W. de Beus, "Schept sociale zekerheid een nieuwe klasse?" [Does social security generate a new class?], in *De reconstrueerde samenleving*, ed. idem and G.A. van Doorn (Boom, Netherlands: Meppel, 1986).

very rough estimate of the significance of job assets. On the one hand, it overestimates that significance quite considerably by assuming skills to be evenly distributed between the employed and the unemployed. Although the gap between the educational level of the average worker and that of the average unemployed person has narrowed strikingly in the past ten years of massive unemployment,[35] it is still far from having closed completely. Consequently, the simple test described above captures the effect of some redistribution of skills as well as of job assets. On the other hand, there are also a number of reasons why this test greatly underestimates the real impact of job assets. First, it completely ignores the indirect incomes associated with having a job, mainly pension rights, to which the unemployed fail to gain entitlement. Second, it reduces the material welfare derived from having a job to the wage attached to it. But being unemployed does not just mean a cut in one's standard of living. It also means a loss of social integration and self-respect, which badly affects the material welfare of the people affected—most notoriously their health.[36]

Most important, however, this test completely ignores the unequal distribution of job assets *among the employed.* There is, of course, a world of difference between a part-time, casual, poorly paid job and a full-time, well-protected, and well-paid one. Some of the differences simply reflect the fact that people are at different stages in their careers. Others directly reflect inequalities in skills or inequalities in the control

---

34. In a typical welfare-state capitalist society such as Belgium, the officially unemployed have an average monthly income of about $390 (1982 figures). If (delcared and undeclared) post-tax capital income were distributed equally among all adults, each of them would receive an estimated additional $120 every month, bringing their income up to $510. The average monthly income of employed people is $740. If all jobs (and their incomes) were divided equally among all those wanting to work, each would get $690 (total income from work or benefits divided by the number of people currently employed or claiming benefits). For the officially unemployed, this amounts to an average increase of $300 per month, that is, more than double the increase they can expect (statically speaking, of course) from an egalitarian redistribution of wealth. The difference would be even larger if the unofficially (but involuntarily) unemployed had also been taken into account: most of them get far less than the average $390 of the officially unemployed, and many of them (mostly housewives) receive nothing at all. For them, of course, the income gains from the redistribution of paid work would be even greater. (I thank Paul-Marie Boulanger for helping me work out these estimates on the basis of Belgium's national accounts figures.)

35. See, for example, A. Vanheerswynghels, "Les jeunes, leurs chômages, leurs emplois," *La Revue Nouvelle* (Brussels), vol. 85 (1987) pp. 403–10, for the case of Belgium.

36. Such effects are well documented by numerous sociological studies; see, for example, M. Jahoda, P.F. Lazarsfeld, and H. Zeisel, *Die Arbeitslosen von Marienthal* (Frankfurt: Suhrkamp, 1975 [1933]); A. Sinfield, *What Unemployment Means* (Oxford: Martin Robertson, 1981); and D. Schnapper, *L'Epreuve du chômage* (Paris: Gallimard, 1981).

over organizational assets. But many, possibly most, of the differences are irreducibly rooted in what happens to be the distribution of "ownership" over jobs. Both the insiders–outsiders approach and efficiency wage theories predict wage differences among workers with identical skills; for example, as a function of intersectoral differences in hiring and firing costs or in the cost of monitoring performance.[37] Whether the underlying mechanism involves the unequal bargaining power attached to different jobs (insiders–outsiders approach) or the unequal interest the employer has in paying more than the reservation wage (efficiency wage theories), it is the holding of the job itself that is the source of the relevant material advantages.

One implication of this remark is that it is not just the unemployed who would gain from an equalization of job assets. Another is that even the purely static impact of such equalization becomes difficult to assess with any precision. Such an overall assessment is required, however, if one is to be able to compare the current significance of class divisions based on different types of assets. To establish that the job divide has now become more significant than the class divide, it is not enough to show that the jobless would gain more from a redistribution of jobs than from a redistribution of wealth—just as showing that the propertyless would gain more from the latter than from the former would not suffice to establish that capital ownership remains the central determinant of the class structure. What needs to be shown is that a greater share of the interindividual variation in material welfare can be (causally) explained by the distribution of job assets than by the distribution of capital assets. Needless to say, these remarks do not pretend even to start seriously investigating the empirical validity of this conjecture. But they suffice to show, I hope, that at least in some of the most developed welfare-state capitalist countries, the claim that the job class division has become the central component of the class structure makes enough sense for such an investigation to be worth undertaking.

The New Class Struggle

Suppose that, for some countries at least, such a claim can be established. Should one then expect the central class struggle under welfare-state capitalism to be one between those with a stable, decently paid job and those deprived access to such a job, rather than, say,

---

37. See, for example, Malcolmson, "Unemployment," p. 849; and Shapiro and Stiglitz, "Equilibrium Unemployment," p. 434.

between capitalists or manager-entrepreneurs and workers? For this to happen, a movement of the *job poor*—the unemployed and the casually employed—needs to get off the ground and formulate a coherent social project that would remove the property relations from which they suffer. But however deep the job class divide, is there not ample ground for skepticism about the possibility of mobilizing the job poor into collective action and of giving such action a coherent positive objective?

Even if the job poor are a class in the objective sense considered here, many argue that they will never become a class in a subjective sense; that is, that they will never acquire class consciousness or organize class action.[38] The unemployed and casual workers form a heterogeneous group, which they are unaware of belonging to, let alone proud to belong to. Dole queues, unlike factories, do not lend themselves to the sort of interaction that can lead to collective demands and actions. Unlike workers, who can strike, the unemployed have no weapon they can use in support of their claims. Those among them who are able to organize and mobilize the others are "good" enough to get a real job and leave the class.[39] All these arguments point to genuine practical obstacles in the way of the rise of a movement of the job poor. The most serious obstacle, however, may be of an ideological nature. What is the social model, the change in property rights, that the job poor should be fighting for in order to abolish or reduce inequalities stemming from the unequal distribution of job assets?

In a way, centralized socialism provides the most straightforward answer to this question. Only a system in which the means of production are centrally controlled could in principle ensure that job assets are equally shared by all those wanting to work. However, even leaving aside the possible cost in terms of other values (such as freedom), the risk that even the asset poor may end up worse off as a result of the implementation of such a system (taking all dynamic effects into account, not just the static effects considered when applying the criterion for exploitation) is now broadly perceived in our societies as an overwhelming one. Indeed, the notion that centralized socialism has a seriously adverse effect on efficiency gains further credibility if a legal

---

38. See, for example, Ralf Dahrendorf's ("Für jeden Bürger ein garanteirtes Mindesteinkommen," *Die Zeit*, January 17, 1986, p. 32) unambiguous statement: "The unemployed are not a class"; or André Gorz's (*Farewell to the Working Class* (London: Pluto Press, 1983), part 3) description of this category as a "non-class of non-workers."

39. For a beautiful firsthand report and an illuminating analysis of many of these difficulties, see B. Jordan, *Paupers: The Making of the New Claiming Class* (London: Routledge and Kegan Paul, 1973); and idem, "Basic Incomes and the Claimants' Movement" (paper delivered at the First International Conference on Basic Income, Louvain-la-Neuve, Belgium, September 1986).

right to a (decent) job is made an intrinsic component of it—as it needs to be in the present context.[40]

Instead of dwelling on this controversial, but academic, issue, let us ask whether there is an alternative; that is, whether there is any way of drastically reducing job asset-based inequalities within the framework of a decentralized economy, either capitalist or market socialist. A general and significant cut in maximum working hours (with matching cuts in gross wages), as advocated in Europe by some of the unions and parties that claim to have the interests of both employed and unemployed workers at heart, may seem to fit the bill. However, both theoretical considerations and empirical data on the history of work-sharing policies raise doubt about their ability to do much to solve the problem of mass unemployment without such a heavy loss in efficiency that even their "beneficiaries" would end up worse off.[41]

Instead of trying to equalize job assets, one may then (reluctantly) turn to neutralizing the effects of their unequal distribution—just as the working-class movement has turned away from the objective of social-izing capital to that of raising the share of wages. In the case of job assets, however, this sort of strategy seems to contain an internal contradiction. By increasing the incomes of the jobless—unemployment benefits and welfare payments—is one not bound, by virtue of the mechanism sketched above in connection with efficiency wage theories, to increase their numbers? When trying to improve their current, dis-advantaged station, the jobless would then be forced to worsen their chances of leaving it. Given that this strategy does nothing about the nonpecuniary advantages of having a job—or about inequalities among the employed—the net result of any effort in this direction will soon become an increase in job-related inequalities in material welfare.

This quick run through three possible objectives for a movement of

---

40. This is one implication of the efficiency wage theories presented above, as pointed out, for example, by J. Elster, "Is There (or Should There Be) a Right to Work?" in *Democracy and the Welfare State*, ed. A. Guttman (forthcoming), section 5.

41. For a well-documented, sympathetic, but sobering assessment of the chances of work-sharing politics in a broad sense, see J.H. Drèze, "Work Sharing: Some Theory and Recent European Experience," *Economic Policy*, vol. 3 (1986), pp. 546–619. To indicate briefly the nature of the difficulties I believe lie at the core of the working time-reduction strategy, let me ask four questions: How can you significantly reduce the working time of the low paid without either pushing them below the poverty line or pricing them out of their jobs by raising their (relative) hourly wages? How can you absorb most of the jobless in those trades in which unemployment is high without creating unmanageable bottle-necks—as well as sizable rents—in many other trades? How can you be fair to wage workers without imposing costly controls on the working time of the self-employed? And how can you impose compensatory new hirings without inducing useless (and possibly fatal) hiring and training costs in many firms that are currently hoarding labor?

the job poor may suggest that such a movement is doomed for lack of any coherent positive project. But what about the following, fourth possibility, which is now coming to the fore in those European countries in which an organized unemployed movement has more or less managed to get off the ground?[42] The proposal is to give every permanent inhabitant, whether waged, self-employed, or jobless, a completely unconditional "universal grant" or "basic income" sufficient to cover at least fundamental needs.[43] At first sight, this is no more than a slight variant of the previous strategy for attenuating the pecuniary inequalities generated by the unequal distribution of jobs. However, there are a number of crucial differences, one of which is particularly relevant in the present context. An adequate universal grant does not mean just a reduction in the cost of not having a job. It also means that everyone is now given the real possibility of creating, alone or with others, her/his own job. Why? Because the very notion of what constitutes a (paid) job is substantially altered since fundamental needs are unconditionally covered. A job no longer needs to be an activity yielding an income sufficient to cover at least these needs; creating one's own job, therefore, no longer requires an amount of capital out of proportion to what the vast majority can afford.[44] Even with a substantial universal grant, however, job assets could still be very unequally distributed among the employed (including the self-employed). Nevertheless, whether under capitalism or, *mutatis mutandis*, under market socialism, the universal-grant strategy offers the unemployed (and "poorly employed") movement a way of attempting to systematically reduce the privilege conferred by job assets while expanding (unlike the previous strategy) the circle of those with access to a job. Moreover, through a general increase in every individual's bargaining power on the labor market, it also means a gradual erosion of the inegalitarian impact of job assets among the employed.

---

42. See, for example, Hogenboom and Janssen, "Basic Income and the Claimants' Movement in the Netherlands"; and P. Rosemeyer, "Basic Income and the Unemployed Movement in Western Germany" (papers delivered at the First International Conference on Basic Income, Louvain-la-Neuve, Belgium, September 1986); and P. Albert, "Un système pur redonner la dignité aux chômeurs: l'allocation universelle," *Partage* (journal of the French Unemployed Union), vol. 31 (October–November 1986), pp. 19–21.

43. This proposal is not new, of course. What is new is the broader perspective in which it has been put (see R.J. van der Veen and P. Van Parijs, "A Capitalist Road to Communism," *Theory and Society*, vol. 15 (1986), followed by six comments and the authors' reply) and, above all, the intense interest and broad support it is beginning to attract throughout Europe (see P. Van Parijs, "Quel destin pur l'allocation universelle?", *Futuribles* (Paris), February 1987, pp. 17–31.

44. See the various arguments in favor of basic income from the viewpoint of small firms and the self-employed, well summarized in B. Nooteboom, "Basic Income: A Basis for Small Business" (paper delivered at the First International Conference on Basic Income, Louvain-la-Neuve, Belgium, September 1986).

If the argument sketched in the preceding paragraph is correct, the ideological obstacle to class struggle along the job-asset dimension is now removed. What about the practical obstacles mentioned earlier? There are good grounds for believing that something like the introduction of a universal grant—first at a modest level and without total replacement of current social transfers—is itself the key condition for the building of a strong movement in the service of the strategy described above. Such an institution would provide those wishing to set up an organization along these lines with the minimum amount of financial security and undisturbed leisure they need for this purpose. More important, it would homogenize a large number of people currently split into numerous categories with no perceived common interest (the registered unemployed, welfare claimants, low-paid workers, housewives, students, pensioners on a low pension). And it would dramatically curtail the current vulnerability of the unemployed movement to upward mobility (getting a job would no longer amount to leaving the group) and to stigmatization (no need to be ashamed of receiving what everyone receives).[45] In stating that the existence of something like a universal grant is the key condition for the building of a strong movement pursuing the universal-grant strategy, I am not implying that the latter is stuck in a vicious circle. The degree of universality of the grant system that is here claimed to be a prerequisite for the building of a strong job-poor movement and—even more so—the grant levels involved can fall far short of those such a movement should aim for.

Is there any chance that this prerequisite will be met anywhere on earth in the foreseeable future? One favorable factor is the current crisis of the welfare state. On both the left and the right, there is widespread frustration and discontent with its complexity, intrusiveness, administrative cost, and frequent counterproductivity. This provides a background on which a plan for radical reform has a fighting chance. But who is going to fight, given that it cannot be the movement that the success of this fight would make possible? It is hard to believe that the basic impulse will come from mainstream parties on the right or on the left, whose interests are too closely linked to those of big business and the established trade union movement. My guess is that the only serious

---

45. This conjecture gets some empirical support from the fact that countries—most typically the Netherlands—where support for the basic-income strategy is comparatively widespread, especially among the unemployed organizations, are also those countries in which welfare-state benefits are most universal (child benefits, basic state pensions, minimum guaranteed income, etc.). See the country-by-country survey presented at the First International Conference on Basic Income, to be published in *The Economics and Politics of Basic Income*, ed. A. Miller (forthcoming).

hope in the near future lies in the emerging Green parties' ability both to survive and to bring this demand to the forefront of their platforms. The importance these parties attach to solving the unemployment problem without counting on the resumption of rapid growth and the relative value their typical members ascribe to "leisure" (including unpaid work) as against "consumption" (of purchased goods) combine to make it likely that most of their members will find the idea of a universal grant most congenial and well worth fighting for.[46]

Whether this fight will prove successful, I do not know. Nothing in the extended framework for class analysis developed in this paper enables us to say whether it will. What this framework has made possible is the identification of a new class divide that has—I conjecture—become even more important than the standard division between capitalists and workers in those capitalist societies in which the welfare state is most developed. This identification has prompted questions about the conditions under which class struggle along these lines could take shape. Tackling these questions has, in turn, led to a novel interpretation of the historical significance of the European Green movement. If this line of thinking is, even approximately, on the right track, the revolution set in motion by the Roemer/Wright approach amounts to much more than academic hairsplitting. It is of central importance for a proper understanding of the fate of Western societies.

---

46. This is no political fiction since most European Green parties now include the proposal of a universal grant in their platforms, as has the Green–Alternative Fraction in the European Parliament. For more details, see Van Parijs, "Quel destin"; and idem, "L'Avenir des écologistes: Deux interprétations," *La Revue Nouvelle* (Brussels), vol. 83 (1986), pp. 37–48.

7

Constructing the (W)right Classes*

David Rose and Gordon Marshall

In *Classes* Erik Wright offers his second major contribution to neo-Marxist debate on social class.[1] In effect, this new text incorporates both an autocritique of his earlier theory of contradictory class locations, and a new theory of such locations, together with empirical investigations based on this new theory using data drawn from Wright's own survey of the American population and a similar one conducted in Sweden. While we have some reservations about Wright's new model, we wish at the outset to compliment him on producing a highly lucid account, not only of his own ideas but of those of others who have influenced him. We must also register an interest since we are colleagues of Wright's in the International Project on Class Structure and Class Consciousness which he has organized in his usual indefatigable manner since 1978.

1

The last twenty years have seen not simply a resurgence of Marxist thought in academic sociology, to the benefit of all sociologists, but a major reevaluation of Marxism by its proponents. This reevaluation has aimed at filling in some of the lacunae left by Marx himself,[2] as well as attempting to fit the theory to the realities of late twentieth-century capitalist societies. Both these themes come through strongly in Wright's work. However, as sociologists of a non-Marxist persuasion it has often

---

*We would wish to thank Howard Newby for comments on an earlier version of this paper and Ted Benton for a number of useful discussions during its preparation.

1. E.O. Wright, *Classes* (London: Verso, 1985).

2. See, for example, the comments of P. Anderson, *Considerations on Western Marxism* (London: Verso, 1976), and T. Benton, *The Rise and Fall of Structural Marxism* (London: Macmillan, 1985).

appeared to us that the revisions required in Marxist theory in order to fill in the gaps, and accommodate the theory to the contemporary situation, have involved such major departures from orthodox Marxism as to make it difficult to know what it is that is any longer distinctive about it. Again Wright's new book is an example of this.

Of course, debates in academic Marxism are always easy to decry from the outside.[3] However, we prefer to take the view that sociology progresses through debate between rival approaches. Hence, we intend to examine Wright's new class theory with a view to seeing more clearly what it is that is at issue between his theory and that of non-Marxists. We must stress that it is only Wright's version of Marxism which concerns us here, since some recent Marxist contributions make the point that both Marxists and non-Marxists alike have presented accounts of Marxism which are at considerable variance with what Marx himself said. For example, Rattansi has argued that the orthodox account of Marx relies too much on *The Communist Manifesto*, and too little on a careful reading of Marx's more considered analyses in *Capital* and *Theories of Surplus Value.*[4] According to this perspective the class polarization thesis has been overemphasized to the neglect of Marx's recognition of the importance of the emerging middle classes. Wright appears to take a more unreconstructed view than Rattansi and so our comments must address themselves to the former's version of Marxist theory.

2

Despite our involvement in Wright's international project we were never convinced by his original thesis of contradictory class locations.[5] Briefly, in the original theory, Wright argued that in each mode of production certain basic social classes are defined by being completely polarized within the relevant social relations of production. For example, under capitalism the working class is wholly dispossessed of the means of production, must therefore sell its labour power to the bourgeoisie and is hence both exploited and dominated by it. However, in the case of the

3. Witness, for example, the work of F. Parkin, *Marxism and Class Theory: A Bourgeois Critique* (London: Tavistock, 1979).

4. A. Rattansi, "End of an Orthodoxy? The Critique of Sociology's View of Marx on Class," *Sociological Review*, vol. 33, no. 4 (1986), pp. 641–69.

5. See E.O. Wright, *Class, Crisis and the State* (London: Verso, 1978), and G. Marshall *et al.*, "Class, Citizenship and Distributional Conflict in Modern Britain," *British Journal of Sociology*, vol. 36, no. 2 (1985), pp. 259–84.

social formation rather than the mode of production, certain complications arise. In real capitalist societies there are subordinate modes of production, especially that of "petty commodity" production. This latter case accounts for the existence within capitalist societies of a petty bourgeoisie. Equally the processes which constitute capitalist societies do not wholly coincide. For example, not all the functions of capital are performed by capitalists. Managers may have effective control of capital assets whilst also being employees. In this sense managers can be seen as simultaneously occupying two class positions. Managers are, like workers, exploited by capital; but they also dominate workers. They occupy contradictory locations within class relations. Figure 1 summarizes the original model.

Figure 1   Wright's Original Class Model

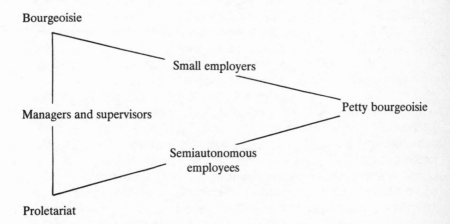

Capitalist mode of production   Simple commodity production

Bourgeoisie

Small employers

Managers and supervisors   Petty bourgeoisie

Semiautonomous
employees

Proletariat

Wright's new approach has the same starting point as the previous one: the need for Marxist theory to come to terms with the "middle classes." Unlike writers such as Rattansi, Wright takes the view that it was not only in the *Communist Manifesto* but also in his more considered analyses that Marx made clear his view concerning the increasing polarization of capitalist societies. Since the historical record has so far negated such a view, Marxists must therefore confront the issue of the "middle classes" or, as Wright euphemistically puts it, "it is no

longer assumed that history will eliminate the conceptual problem"
(p. 9). In order to elucidate his argument, Wright notes first the distinction between class analyses which focus on class structure and those
which focus on class formation; and, second, the different levels of
abstraction used in class analysis. His definitions of class structure and
class formation are themselves instructive. Class structure is defined as a
"structure of social relations into which individuals (or in some cases,
families) enter which determine their class interests" (p. 9); class formation of organized collectivities within that class structure on the basis
of the interests shaped by that class structure' (p. 10). Class structure
deals with relations between classes and class formation with relations
within classes. The levels of abstraction used in class analysis are the
familiar trinity of mode of production, social formation and conjuncture.
Within all the possible forms of analysis available on these bases, Marx
concentrated on class structure within the pure capitalist mode of
production; class alliances in the social formation; and concrete class
organizations in the conjuncture. Neo-Marxism has attempted to fill in
the gaps by theorizing the social formation and the conjuncture, and by
examining how class structure translates into the formation of collective
actors. At this level neo-Marxist and non-Marxist class analysis share
many features in common and hence debates have become more fruitful
between them. Moreover they have reached similar conclusions. Marxists now know what non-Marxists have long known, namely that class
formation is not "given" by the structure, but that there is a "complex
and contingent . . . relation between class structure and class formation"
(p. 14). Interestingly, Marxists such as Wright have arrived at these
conclusions using their own version of the type of middle-range theories
long used by neo-Weberians.

However, Wright is no longer satisfied that his first attempt at
middle-range theory was adequate. In order to explain why this is so,
Chapter 2 is devoted to an account of the development of the idea of
contradictory locations, as well as an autocritique of this concept. Given
Wright's desire to produce a middle-range form of Marxism, his first
task was to identify what he saw as the irreducible elements of Marx's
abstract theory of class, since any more concrete theory would need to
be consistent with these. Six such elements were identified: the primacy
of class structure over other class processes; the idea of class structure as
the central organizing principle of societies; the notion that class is a
relational concept and not a gradational one; that the social relations
which define classes are antagonistic; that exploitation is the objective
basis of antagonistic interests; and that exploitation is itself based in the
social relations of production. Wright then reviews the process by which
he arrived at the idea of some positions being simultaneously in two

classes and in that sense contradictory locations within class relations. It was this concept which he operationalized for his empirical work.

Wright now offers several criticisms of this initial conceptualization, although in effect, as he notes, they are all a part of the same problem. For those of us who believed that a major weakness of the original model was that it was too economistic, Wright on the contrary believes it was not economistic enough. The original concept of contradictory locations was underpinned by a theory of *domination* rather than one of *exploitation.* This resulted in class being merely one element rather than *the* element in social stratification. Hence Wright's self-appointed task is to return exploitation to centre stage. This he proceeds to do in Chapter 3 by way of an adaptation of the work of one of the leading rational choice Marxists, John Roemer.[6] Wright seeks to transform the concept of contradictory locations through a modification and extension of Roemer's work on exploitation. Having identified his failure to place exploitation at the centre of class analysis as the chief defect of the earlier model, Wright uses some of Roemer's insights on exploitation to rectify this. However, Wright does not thereby adopt a rational choice model, for unlike Roemer he is not prepared to abandon all aspects of the labor theory of value in favor of a game theoretic view of exploitation. Nevertheless, since Roemer's work is apparently central to Wright's new theory, it is necessary to consider the former before returning to the latter.

3

In common with older Marxist theorists, Roemer regards exploitation as involving a causal relationship between the incomes of different actors. However, his particular interpretation of exploitation is at odds with that of classical Marxism.[7] Roemer treats the organization of production as a game. His strategy is to ask whether particular players in the game

---

6. For recent critical discussions of game theoretic Marxism, see S. Lash and J. Urry, "The New Marxism of Collective Action," *Sociology,* vol. 18, no. 1 (1984), pp. 33–50; J. McCarney, "A New Marxist Paradigm?," *Radical Philosophy,* vol. 43 (1986), pp. 29–31; J. Holmwood, "The Games Marxists Play," *Network,* vol. 34 (1986), pp. 14–15.

7. In fact Roemer has produced two models of exploitation. The first was based on a labor transfer approach, but he found that he had to make too many simplifying assumptions for such a model to work. Hence he developed the game theoretic approach in order to overcome the problems which arise when the simplifying assumptions are relaxed. It is this second version of exploitation which Wright finds attractive (though in need of modification) because "it allows for a particularly elegant way of characterizing the different mechanisms of exploitation in different types of class structure" (*Classes,* p. 68).

would be better off if they were to withdraw from the game in favor of an alternative one. Hence, exploitation is a situation in which a coalition of actors have a hypothetically feasible alternative where they would be better off (and their complement, the exploiting coalition, would be worse off) if the former withdrew from the game. Four such situations of exploitation are identified by Roemer: feudal, capitalist, socialist, and status. Each form of exploitation is defined in terms of a withdrawal rule. Under feudalism peasants would be better off and lords worse off if the former withdrew with their personal assets, that is, were freed from feudal obligations. This rule is the test of whether feudal exploitation exists. The test of whether capitalist exploitation exists is a situation in which capitalists would be worse off, and workers better off, if the latter withdrew with their per capita share of society's productive assets. Under socialism exploitation exists where a "coalition" would be better off, and its "complement" worse off, if the former left the game with its per capita share of inalienable assets, for example, its skills. Finally, status exploitation exists where a coalition would be better off, and its complement worse off, if the former exempted itself from the dues to status. Here Roemer is thinking of exploitation through state bureaucracy.

What does such a game theoretic version of exploitation offer a more orthodox Marxist such as Wright in his attempt to rework the concept of contradictory locations in class relations? One obvious attraction is that Roemer's view of exploitation is materially grounded in property relations:

> The asset-exploitation nexus depends in each case upon the capacity of asset holders to deprive others of equal access to that asset. . . . On the one hand, inequalities of assets are sufficient to account for transfers of surplus labor; on the other hand, different forms of asset inequality specify different systems of exploitation. Classes are then defined as positions within social relations of production derived from the property relations which determine the pattern of exploitation. (p. 72)

This argument presents a challenge to any definition of class based on domination within production, such as Wright's original model. For Roemer domination is subordinate to exploitation, so that "domination *within* the production process or within the labor process does not enter into the definition of class relations" (ibid.). This is an argument that Wright now accepts: domination is relevant to aspects of class formation but "the basis of the capital–labor relation should be identified with the relations of effective control (that is, real economic ownership) over productive assets as such" (ibid.). However, Wright clearly had some difficulties in accepting the thrust of Roemer's argument because it seemed to blur the difference between Marxist definitions of class and Weberian definitions. Weberian definitions were "market-based" definitions of class, whereas Marxist definitions were "production-based." The reputed advantage of the latter was that production was more "fundamental" than exchange, and therefore production based concepts had more explanatory power than market based ones.

What now seems clear to me is that definitions of classes in terms of property relations should not be identified with strictly market based definitions. Property relations accounts of classes do not define classes by income shares, by the results of market transactions, but by the productive assets which classes control; which lead them to adopt certain strategies within exchange relations, and which in turn determine the outcome of those market transactions. (pp. 72–3)

Of course, as Wright acknowledges, this amounts to saying that the contrast between Marxist and Weberian definitions of class cannot be subsumed to the distinction between exchange and production. Having satisfied himself of this Wright is content to use Roemer's insights concerning exploitation as 'the basis for elaborating a comprehensive framework for analyzing class structure in general and for reconceptualizing the problem of the middle classes in particular' (p. 73).

However, Roemer's model does not satisfy Wright as it stands. He finds Roemer insufficiently economistic—or faithful to classical Marxism—because of the way in which the latter has completely abandoned all aspects of the labor theory of value. According to Wright, Roemer's theory "allows us to assess inequalities that are the result of causal interconnections between actors [but] lacks the additional force of the view that the inequalities in question are produced by real transfers from one actor to another" (p. 74). Thus the first of three criticisms Wright has of Roemer is that the latter has mistaken exploitation for simple economic oppression. This Wright finds acceptable to the degree that it produces a class concept which defines a set of objective material interests, but unacceptable in so far as it does not make clear how "the welfare of the exploiting class depends upon the work of the exploited class" (p. 75). Whereas, for Roemer, it is the withdrawal rules which define exploitation, for Wright exploitation is a combination of economic oppression with appropriation.

Wright is also critical of Roemer's concept of feudal exploitation. Roemer considers only two types of productive asset, namely, physical or alienable assets and skill or inalienable assets. Wright, following Cohen,[8] wishes to include labor power as a productive asset too. In

---

8. G.A. Cohen, *Karl Marx's Theory of History: A Defense* (Princeton: Princeton University Press, 1978).

capitalism each person owns one unit of labor power, but under feudalism serfs have less than one unit and lords have more than one because of the existence of corvée labor. Hence, for Wright, the withdrawal rule for feudal exploitation involves leaving the game with one unit of labor power rather than with one's personal assets. It is not physical assets which are unequally distributed in feudal societies but labor power. This reformulation also allows Wright to produce a symmetrical analysis in which feudal exploitation derives from unequal distribution of assets in labor power and leads to the class relation between lords and serfs; capitalist exploitation is based on the unequal distribution of alienable assets and produces the class relation between bourgeoisie and proletariat; and socialist exploitation is based on the unequal distribution of inalienable assets (skills) and results in the class relation between experts and workers. In this recasting of feudal exploitation, therefore, Wright has removed the nonmaterialist basis of Roemer's withdrawal rule (freedom from obligations of personal bondage) and has replaced it with a materialist one (labor power as a productive asset). He proceeds in similar fashion when dealing with the concept of status exploitation.

Mention of the concept of status is somewhat akin to waving a red flag at a bull for most Marxists—and Wright is no exception. Wright argues that status "has no necessary relationship to production at all" (p. 79), and therefore is inadmissible to any Marxist account of class. His economistic solution to the problem of the Roemerian concept of status exploitation is to replace it with one of organizational exploitation. He wishes to see organization as a particular type of productive asset and so arrives at the view that each type of class structure is precisely typified by the principal asset which is unequally distributed: under feudalism it is labor power; under capitalism, the means of production; under statism, organization; and under socialism, skills.

In this manner Wright is able to produce a typology of assets, forms of exploitation and class structure by which feudalism, capitalism, statism, and socialism can be defined in terms of the principal asset that is unequally distributed, the mechanism of exploitation involved and the polarized class system which results. At this level, with the modifications described above, Wright follows Roemer—the four forms of exploitation correspond to four modes of production. It is here, however, that Wright abandons the idea of an association between forms of exploitation and modes of production, in order to derive his new class model for contemporary capitalist societies. Just as the petty bourgeoisie were introduced into his earlier model as a class of a subsidiary mode of production to the CMP, so now Wright claims that the principal asset which is unequally distributed within any particular mode of production is not the *only* asset which is so distributed but merely the *prime* basis of exploitation. In other words, within any given system, assets other than the primary one may be the basis of exploitation. For example, in capitalism the principal asset exploited by capitalists is ownership of the means of production, and this is the defining feature of the system. Nevertheless capitalists may also exploit workers through their control of organizational assets. Thus it makes sense to produce a class typology which incorporates all the assets which are unequally distributed in the four modes of production identified. As Wright observes, he is not concerned with delineating abstract mode of production concepts, but rather the class structure of contemporary capitalism, especially as far as nonpolarized positions are concerned:

> Since concrete societies are rarely, if ever, characterized by a simple mode of production the actual class structures of given societies will be characterized by complex patterns of exploitation relations. There will therefore tend to be some positions which are exploiting along one dimension of exploitation relations, while on another are exploited. . . . Such positions are what are 'typically referred to as the "new middle class" of a given system'. (p. 87)

Thus Wright has not only modified Roemer's analysis but has also shifted it from a concern for different modes of production to the idea that all the exploitation processes operate simultaneously within real capitalist societies. Indeed, when all Wright's amendments to the original theory are taken together, they seriously undermine Roemer's project. Certainly it is not clear to us why, in order to produce a theory based on exploitation, Wright needs Roemer's work at all. After all, exploitation within the labor theory of value (in the manner which Wright wishes to use it) has a long, if suspect, pedigree. Why introduce a new and controversial version of the concept simply in order to reject its novel elements in favor of some more orthodox version? Moreover, as another of his critics has observed, if we take Wright's arguments on their own terms, it is not clear how all exploitation processes "can be part of the same system—that there can be a constant tendency of the reduction of skilled to average labor (proletarianization) at the same time as a constant tendency of the creation of skills and social closure around them and a constant ideological factor in managerial incomes".[9] Perhaps we should not take Marxist economics any more seriously than Wright seems to have taken Roemer's game theory?

9. Holmwood, "The Games Marxists Play," p. 15.

4

The result of this extended exercise in conceptual excavation is the erection of the twelve-class model illustrated in Figure 2. There are now six contradictory locations: that is, cells 4 to 8 and cell 10 represent different "middle-class" positions, while cells 9 and 11 are marginal working-class positions. Of course, these are now to be seen as "contradictory locations within exploitation relations" and from the viewpoint of history some are more important than others, as we shall see.

As we can see from Figure 2, Wright's "middle classes" are internally differentiated according to the amount of organizational assets and skill/credential assets they possess, though they share the common feature of nonownership of the means of production. This latter feature obviously characterizes the proletariat too but they are equally "negatively privileged" with regard to organizational and skill/credential assets. While we are thus presented with a variety of contradictory locations within exploitation relations, nevertheless it is Wright's opinion that some contradictory locations are more important than others. Within capitalism managers and state bureaucrats occupy the principal contradictory location by virtue of the fact that "they embody a principle of class organization which is quite distinct from capitalism and which potentially poses an alternative to capitalist relations" (p. 89). State managers in particular are singled out. In a statement calculated to give a whole new meaning to the phrase "the managerial revolution," Wright observes an important consequence of his new scheme for conceptualizing the middle class, namely

> that it is no longer axiomatic that the proletariat is the unique, or perhaps even universally the central, rival to the capitalist class for class power in a capitalist society. That classical Marxist assumption depended upon the thesis that there were no other classes within capitalism that could be viewed as the "bearers" of a historical alternative to capitalism. What (Figure 2) suggests is that there are other class forces within capitalism that have the potential to pose an alternative to capitalism. (ibid.)

After a brief defense of this heresy for the benefit of fellow Marxists, Wright also concedes "that the process of class formation and class struggle is considerably more complex than the traditional Marxist theory has allowed" (p. 91). Amen to that.

Having introduced his new class model, Wright next examines some of the implications of his new approach. For example, in examining the relationship between his theory and various alternative class theories, he confronts the fact that the former has come very close to what he himself had previously regarded as neo-Weberianism. In many respects, of

Figure 2 Wright's New Class Model

Assets in the means of production

Owners

Nonowners

		Organization assets
1 Bourgeoisie	4 Expert manager	7 Semicredentialed manager	10 Uncredentialed manager
2 Small employer	5 Expert supervisor	8 Semicredentialed supervisor	11 Uncredentialed supervisor
3 Petty bourgeoisie	6 Expert nonmanager	9 Semicredentialed worker	12 Proletarian

+   >0   −

+   >0   −

Skill/credential assets

course, it has. Indeed Wright hardly bothers to contest the fact that there are similarities between aspects of his approach and that of the self-confessed bourgeois sociologist Frank Parkin. Wright searches for a way out of this embarrassment. He realizes he cannot maintain the view that Weber's theory of class is market based while that of Marx is production based, for he now accepts that both use production-based definitions. The real difference for Wright is more subtle than this. Weber makes the mistake of viewing production from the vantage point of the market because he fails to make the distinction between a mode of production and a social formation. This is, of course, because Weber and his followers resolutely refuse "to treat historical development as a trajectory of qualitatively distinct forms of class structure" (p. 108). However, by not accepting the historicism of Marxism Weberians avoid the kinds of problem Wright has to face when, later in the argument, he confronts his general framework with the Marxist Theory of History and has to proceed upon yet another rewrite of what the latter means. We are told that it is a "probabilistic statement," "a sequence of historical possibilities," but that "the actual transition from one form (of society) to another . . . may depend upon a whole range of contingent factors that are exogenous to the theory." Finally he challenges three traditional theses of historical materialism. According to Wright, Marxists must now question the view that "socialism is the immanent future to capitalism" (consistent with his "managerial revolution"); they must no longer assume that the proletariat is "the only bearer of a revolutionary mission within capitalism"; and it must be recognized that socialist societies involve exploitation, too. Despite such revisionism he tries to rescue the theory of history from these not inconsiderable problems by asserting that history remains progressive, so that "while capitalism may no longer be thought of as the last antagonistic form of society in the trajectory of human development (nevertheless) the progressive character of the trajectory is maintained" (pp. 114–18, passim). If the Marxist theory of history means nothing more than that history is "progressive," how then does it differ from the Whig theory?

Having thus emasculated the Marxist theory of history, Wright's comments on the relationship between class structure and class formation make interesting reading, for once again he is forced to concur with the long held opinions of neo-Weberian class theorists. Accepting that the relationship between class structure and class formation is not as straightforward as described in classical Marxism, Wright is forced to the conclusion that "the class structure may define the terrain of material interests upon which attempts at class formation occur, but it does not uniquely determine the outcome of those attempts" (p. 123). This seems to us a welcome concession to reality. Wright can see that his new model provides "the material basis for a variety of *potential* class formations" and hence that "class structure does not generate a unique pattern of class formation." Thus, "it is only through the specific historical analysis of given societies that it is possible to explain what kind of actual formation is built on that foundation" (p. 124). Since these comments (and virtually all of his others) are addressed to fellow Marxists one can but wonder whether some of them have ever read or taken seriously the more sophisticated form of neo-Marxist class analysis.

Both feminist sociologists and more traditional theorists of stratification will be disappointed by Wright's short section on women in the class structure. While recognizing that Wright could not cover all the implications of his theory in detail, what he has to say in this section makes no real advance on the inadequate treatment given to gender and class in *Class, Crisis and the State*. In terms of his new model, gender can be seen as relevant to skill and organizational assets or as a part of feudal exploitation, but none of these possibilities is dealt with in depth. As in his previous book, Wright argues that the housewives of workers are in the working class in relation to capital and a variety of possible classes in respect of their husbands; and that women are not a social class simply by virtue of male oppression. This somewhat cursory consideration of class and gender does become surprising given the later empirical material in *Classes*. Jumping ahead in Wright's argument for a moment, we discover in later chapters that just over 60 percent of the working class in both Sweden and the United States are females; and that 52.8 percent of employed females in the United States and 59.6 percent in Sweden are classified as proletarian. As Wright notes, "the image which is still present in many Marxist accounts that the working class consists of male factory workers simply does not hold true any longer" (pp. 197–8). Further evidence provided by Wright shows the inferior mobility chances of working-class females. A cynic might be tempted to argue, after reading Wright's cursory treatment of gender and then examining his class and gender data, that all of these are not unconnected with his pessimism about the possibilities of working-class revolution.

With his discussions of the implications of the new approach to contradictory class locations Wright concludes the theoretical part of *Classes*. The second half of his book concerns empirical investigations using the new approach. There are three principal issues dealt with in Part 2. First, Wright attempts an empirical adjudication between his own theory and rival Marxist accounts, and especially that of Poulantzas.[10]

---

10. N. Poulantzas, *Classes in Contemporary Capitalism* (London: Verso, 1975).

Secondly, Wright uses his theory to make a comparison between the class structures of the United States and Sweden; and finally he examines the thorny problem of the relationship between class structure and class consciousness.

5

In the empirical adjudication of rival Marxist theories of class Wright is particularly concerned to examine the "boundary problem" between the middle classes and the working class. Any class model involves the claim that units in a given class should be more like one another than like units in any other class "*with respect to whatever it is class is meant to explain*" (p. 137). One of the key features that a Marxist theory is attempting to explain is, of course, class conflict, so that a definition of the working class in such a theory is a statement about a line of demarcation in class conflict. With such reasoning Wright arrives at a means for adjudicating between rival theories:

> If definitions are propositions about lines of demarcation for homogeneous effects, then this suggests that the appropriate strategy . . . is to focus on those cases where one definition places two positions on different sides of the line of demarcation whereas the rival definition treats them as homogeneous. (pp. 137–8)

The data that Wright uses to make his adjudication are from his own national survey of class structure and class consciousness in the United States. As he points out, this survey was especially constructed to test rival Marxist accounts of social class and so is eminently suited to his purpose. Or is it?

Wright himself acknowledges the problems of using *individual level* survey data to compare rival Marxist *class* theories but in defending his strategy he is once again brought close to the type of reasoning long used by non-Marxist class theorists. By its very nature Marxist class theory has addressed itself to macro social processes, yet the dependent variables Wright is forced to use in his empirical analysis are at a micro level. Wright argues that this need not be considered an insuperable problem, if it is recognized that Marxism must relate its macro theory to a micro theory of individual outcomes, for example, to show that individual behavior is not random with respect to class. Moreover, it would be extremely difficult to produce the necessary data for an adjudication at the macro level. However, there remain some problems with the particular dependent variables Wright wishes to use. So far as class consciousness is concerned, the available data from the survey is atti-tudinal, and therefore there are the usual caveats about the relationship between such data and class consciousness. Wright's view is that atti-tudes cannot be regarded as merely epiphenomenal but that they do have real consequences for class action. Indeed he uses neo-Weberian logic for this view in what sounds very like a restatement of the kind of theory of action used in much British social stratification research:

> Class location is a basic determinant of the matrix of objective possibilities faced by individuals, the real alternatives people face in making decisions. At one level this concerns what Weber referred to as the individuals' "life chances," the overall trajectory of possibilities individuals face over the life cycle. In a more mundane way it concerns the daily choices people face about what to do and how to do it.
>
> The objective alternatives faced by individuals, however, are not directly transformed into actual choices or practices. Those objective alternatives must be perceived, the consequences (both material and normative) of different choices assessed, and a specific alternative chosen in light of such assess-ments. . . . (Hence) subjectivity *mediates* the ways in which the objective conditions of class locations are translated into the active choices of class actions. While the objective social context of choice is clearly important in this explanation, I would argue that the subjective mediation of choices . . . is an essential part of the process as well. (pp. 144–5)

While we would wholeheartedly concur with this view, there still remains the question as to whether attitude items will yield valid infor-mation about this process. This is, in fact, the only type of information Wright has available. It takes the form of seven Likert items of a kind familiar from British surveys in the 1960s and 1970s (for example, "Corp-orations benefit owners at the expense of workers and consumers"); and one more complex item in which respondents were presented with the scenario of a strike over wages and working conditions and asked to say, without any other information being provided, which of four outcomes they would prefer. These ranged from total victory for the strikers to their total defeat. The problems of such items are well known. We cannot accept that they tell sociologists much about anything.[11]

---

11. See G. Marshall, "Some Remarks on the Study of Working-Class Consciousness," *Politics and Society*, vol. 12, no. 1 (1983), pp. 263–301. At this point we must declare an interest. During the period in which the American survey was being designed, we and others tried to persuade the American team not to use these items as a way of measuring class consciousness. However, they were retained. In the interests of comparative research we included them in the British pilot survey, but respondents were irritated by them. They found the Likert items too simplistic and the more complex item on the strike scenario impossible to answer without knowing more details than were offered.

Hence, we find ourselves in agreement with Wright's logic concerning the importance of subjectivity, but at odds concerning the measures of class consciousness used in the US survey.

The final operationalizations which Wright explains concern class structure variables, both his own and those of rival theories. His own theory involves finding measures for the three forms of asset which define the new class model. To measure assets in the means of production simply involves making a distinction between owners and nonowners and then differentiating within the category of owners. This is performed in what Wright admits is a crude way in terms of numbers of employees. Capitalists are defined as owners with ten or more employees; small employers have from two to nine employees; and the petty bourgeoisie one employee or none. Employees are then differentiated in terms of both of the other assets. Organizational assets are defined in terms of an individual's relation to supervision and decision making in his or her organization. Three categories emerge from this: managers, defined as people who have direct involvement in decision making and real authority over subordinates; supervisors, who lack decision-making powers but do have real authority over others; and nonmanagers, who have neither supervisory nor decision-making powers. Finally skill/credential assets are defined. This dimension caused Wright some problems, since a credential means nothing unless it is exploited. As Wright notes, a PhD in English is not exploiting his/her credentials if employed as a taxi driver. Simply to measure credentials is inadequate: they must be matched to jobs. Wright therefore includes job traits in the operationalization of this asset. This is done in terms of the use of both an aggregated occupational variable and, for certain occupations, a measure of job autonomy. The three categories in terms of skills/credentials which Wright produces are "experts," "skilled employees," and "non-skilled." The experts are all professionals, and managers and technicians with college degrees; skilled employees include teachers, craftworkers, managers, and technicians without degrees, and sales and clerical workers with both degrees and high autonomy; the nonskilled are all other sales and clerical workers and all manual and service workers. However, it is not clear why certain occupations are assigned to particular categories. Why, for example, are teachers not regarded as experts?

Without detailing Wright's subsequent analysis, he finds his own model superior to its rivals. Of course, he recognizes that many fellow Marxists will not accept the validity of the adjudication. Others might wish to reject its micro-individual basis. Once again, however, Wright's self defense brings out a logic which many non-Marxists would be happy to use:

even if the concept of class structure is centrally preoccupied with . . . macro historical and dynamic problems, there are, after all, real people who are systematically affected in various ways by virtue of being in one class rather than another. (p. 182)

Wright also recognizes the inherent problems of a strictly positional view of class structure and states his preference for a trajectory approach. Ironically, this is the very argument that has been used against Marxists by (among others) Stewart, Prandy, and Blackburn.[12] Indeed, the example quoted by Wright is their very example, although this is insufficiently acknowledged: "Proletarianized white collar jobs that are really pre-managerial jobs should therefore not be considered in the same location within class relations as proletarianized jobs which are not part of such career trajectories" (pp. 185–6). In the end Wright accepts that class is a "probabilistic" concept, so that "a full account of class structure . . . has to include some kind of recognition of these proba-bilistic trajectories" (p. 186). In such ways Wright gives much ground to his non-Marxist critics and brings his analysis very close to theirs.

The final empirical chapters of *Classes* treat issues of class structure and the relationship between class structure and consciousness. Wright attempts to test the robustness of his new model for the problems under investigation. There is not the space here to examine these chapters in detail since this would require setting Wright's model against alternative concepts of class and class consciousness, something we are pursuing in forthcoming publications. However, his general purpose in Chapter 6 is mainly a descriptive one, involving a comparison of the similarities and differences between the class structures of Sweden and the United States in terms of the new exploitation-centered concept of class. Some attempt is made to account for the differences observed, although the main explanation offered—that similarities result from a similar econ-omic system and differences from different political systems—is rather lame. Wright does make some speculative comments which go beyond this but he acknowledges that much detailed work remains to be done.

Wright's examination of class consciousness begins with an extended review of different approaches to the problem. He favors a definition of class consciousness which "identifies it as a particular aspect of the concrete subjectivity of human individuals . . . as an explanation of indi-vidual actions and choices" (p. 245). Such an approach is, of course, most suited to the survey data he has available. As previously noted,

---

12. A. Stewart, K. Prandy, and R.M. Blackburn, *Social Stratification and Occupations* (London: Macmillan, 1980).

however, the attitudinal items which are used to operationalize class consciousness are suspect. Hence, although Wright is able to show that "class attitudes are polarized in the ways predicted by the exploitation-centered concept" (p. 278), his model needs to be subjected to a more rigorous test than his data provide.

6

Obviously in a book of this range and ambition there are many points on which one is challenged to cross swords with the author. We can only here take up two general points and leave our more detailed analysis of Wright's model to our own future empirical analyses. Probably the major point of note is the extent to which Wright has produced a theory which yet again blurs the distinctions between neo-Weberian and Marxist analyses of class structure. Wright has effectively rejected a wholly structural account of class. The aim of his class analysis is not simply that of identifying class locations, as these are determined by relations of production, but to raise issues concerning class formation, and hence of agency and process. We have already offered a number of examples from *Classes* to illustrate this and we have noted his stated preference for a trajectory view of class. He has also opened up the whole issue of how far individuals do in fact share common interests and engage in collective action in a way unusual for a Marxist of his persuasion. All of this is to the good. However, it does produce some occasional strains in his arguments.

For example, his definitions of class structure and class formation tend to sit uneasily alongside the new approach developed in the text. Class structure is defined in terms of what needs to be demonstrated if Wright is to follow the logic of his own arguments: "a structure of social relations into which individuals . . . enter *which determine their class interests*" (p. 9, our emphasis) is surely a definition which begs the question. Whether class interests can ever be said to be determined by a structure of positions in an unmediated way is highly dubious. Moreover this definition would appear to leave aside the issue of the conditions under which class interests emerge. We would argue that definitions of class structure in terms of people's supposed real interests tend to ignore precisely the kinds of questions which Wright now wishes to open up for examination.

Similarly his definition of class formation is at odds with his subsequent comments concerning the relative openness of social processes. For Wright class formation is "the formation of organized collectivities within [the] class structure on the basis of the interests shaped by that class structure" (p. 10). But how can this be consistent with a trajectory view of class? Surely the precise purpose of such a view is to ask *whether* classes are "identifiable as social collectivities with which individuals and families retain the same class positions over time."[13] Wright's implicit model of structure → interests → class formation is too crude to bear the weight of his own insights. As Goldthorpe has argued, class formation must be shown to exist at the demographic level before it can be expected to exist in any sociocultural sense, or provide a basis for collective action. To produce a model of class structure consistent with a set of theoretical propositions is only the first step in the process. It is for this reason that Goldthorpe has observed that "little value can attach to attempts, such as those of structural Marxists, to treat problems of class formation and class action without reference to the extent of class mobility."[14] Hence we would argue that Wright is only partially facing the problematic issues concerning classes as collectivities. In particular he must find a way of squaring his structural map with his preference for a trajectory view. Certainly he appears to see some of the problems, for shortly after offering his definitions of class structure and class formation he notes that "the process of class formation is decisively shaped by a variety of institutional mechanisms that are themselves 'relatively autonomous' from the class structure and which determine the ways in which class structures are translated into collective actors with specific ideologies and strategies" (p. 14). Thus it is not class structure alone which determines people's interests nor is it the only factor affecting class formation. It is precisely for this kind of reason that Lockwood[15] has pointed to the importance of the citizenship order of modern societies in his criticisms of Marxist class theories, yet nowhere does Wright refer to Lockwood in his text.

This brings us to our second general criticism of *Classes*. The book is largely addressed to a Marxist audience and this may, therefore, account for the irritating way in which Wright presents the long-held views of non-Marxist sociologists as if they were fresh insights. Some examples of this have already been offered but perhaps the most egregious concerns Wright's discovery of the importance of credentials and organizational position in any understanding of modern stratification systems. After all it was Weber who originally investigated the coincidence of these two

---

13. J.H. Goldthorpe, "Social Mobility and Class Formation: On the Renewal of a Tradition in Sociological Enquiry," paper presented to the ISA Research Committee on Social Stratification and Mobility, Amsterdam, 1983, p. 15.
14. Ibid., p. 20.
15. D. Lockwood, "The Weakest Link in the Chain? Some Comments on the Marxist Theory of Action," *Research in the Sociology of Work*, vol. 1 (1981).

factors in his writings on bureaucracy, and it is Goldthorpe and Stewart, Prandy, and Blackburn who have developed this approach more recently.[16] Not only did Weber refer to the "bureaucratization of capitalism, with its demand for expertly trained technicans, clerks, etc." but he also noted that:

> If we hear from all sides demands for the introduction of regulated curricula culminating in specialized examinations, the reason behind this is, of course, not a suddenly awakened "thirst for education," but rather the desire to limit the supply of candidates for these positions.[17]

Indeed we are tempted to go further in our comparison of Wright and Weber. Surely Wright's use of credential and organizational assets to differentiate among the propertyless is not so different from Weber's view that the propertyless are differentiated from one another "according to the kind of services that can be offered on the market" and "that the kind of chance in the *market* is the decisive moment which presents a common condition for the individual's fate."[18] Or to put the matter more bluntly, organization assets and credential assets are aspects of work and market situations respectively.[19]

In the final analysis, however, we agree with Wright that the ultimate test of any class theory must be in terms of whatever it is that theory is trying to explain. We are not essentialists. Part of our future intention will be to subject this new theory to the same kinds of empirical adjudications which Wright himself uses, except that we shall make the comparison with non-Marxist theories. But this will not be without its problems, one of which is illustrated in Table 1. Wright has criticized Goldthorpe for the latter's inexplicit theorization of his class model and his over-reliance on occupational coding to operationalize it. However, the operationalization of Wright's model also requires the use of an aggregated occupational variable, derived from the American official classification system, in order to produce his credential assets variable. Before receiving from Wright details for constructing this variable, we assumed that we could use the OPCS definition of socioeconomic group as a proxy. This was because Wright's aggregated occupational variable

---

16. J.H. Goldthorpe, "On the Service Class: Its Formation and Future," in A. Giddens and G. MacKenzie (eds), *Social Class and the Division of Labour* (Cambridge: Cambridge University Press, 1982); Stewart, Prandy, and Blackburn, *Social Stratification and Occupations.*

17. M. Weber, *Economy and Society* (New York: Bedminster Press, 1968), pp. 999–1000.

18. Ibid., pp. 927–8.

19. See D. Lockwood, *The Blackcoated Worker* (London: Allen and Unwin, 1958).

distinguishes similar groups of occupations to the OPCS socioeconomic variable. The American variable requires the grouping of professional occupations together, craftworkers together, clerical workers, and so on. Similarly socioeconomic group has categories for employed professionals, for skilled workers and junior nonmanual workers. With some careful recoding of our data, it appeared we could at least approximate the American variable. Indeed, we believed that in some respects SEG, in combination with our details of respondents' credentials, would allow the production of a credential assets variable which allowed for finer distinctions than the American equivalent. However, we did not anticipate that the differences between the use of SEG and of the American variable would be very large. Yet, as Table 1 shows, there is a marked difference in the resulting class maps of Britain according to which collapsed occupational variable is used.

It can be seen that there are considerable discrepancies across all categories of nonowners, and most especially for cells 9 and 12. Because we have not yet been able to examine the discrepancies in detail, we cannot say whether it is merely coincidence that Wright's measure produces a larger working class. However, Table 1 does point to the difficulties of assuming, as Wright seems to have done, that any occupational coding will be relatively neutral in its effects when applied to the derivation of a sociological model of class. We wonder how far Wright has considered this problem. While there are no simple solutions, given that all official measures of occupation have their own difficulties, Wright's approach does seem somewhat cavalier. When discussing the details of variable constructions in an appendix, Wright notes that "the coding of occupational title . . . [is] entirely conventional and straightforward and [does] not require any specific commentary" (p. 314). But this is hardly a satisfactory statement unless it is also shown that there are no problems with the American official scheme for coding occupations which might affect the production of a sociological model of class. It is certainly the case that Goldthorpe was able to use the British scheme in his model only after combining occupational title with a measure of employment status, following a prolonged study of the problem. Thus it is not occupational title which determines a person's Goldthorpe class, yet it *is* occupational title (along with qualifications, and in some classes job autonomy) which determines one dimension of Wright's model. Moreover, we discovered some very real problems when we tried to translate our occupational data into the American scheme, due to the national differences in classifications. When we add to this the number of occasions on which Wright has to concede the inadequacies of other key measures, much of his empirical argument must be subject to some reservations.

Table 1 Distribution of UK Labor Force into New Wright Classes According to (1) Socioeconomic Group and (2) American Occupational Variable

Assets in the means of production

Owners (%)	Nonowners (%)		
1 Bourgeoisie (1) 2.0 (2) 2.0	4 Expert manager (1) 5.2 (1) 5.6	7 Semicredentialed manager (1) 8.7 (2) 7.9	10 Uncredentialed manager (1) 2.9 (2) 3.2
2 Small employer (1) 4.5 (2) 4.5	5 Expert supervisor (1) 1.6 (2) 2.2	8 Semicredentialed supervisor (1) 4.3 (2) 3.8	11 Uncredentialed supervisor (1) 3.5 (2) 3.4
3 Petty bourgeoisie (1) 6.0 (2) 6.0	6 Expert nonmanager (1) 2.1 (2) 4.1	9 Semicredentialed worker (1) 22.4 (2) 14.4	12 Proletarian (1) 36.9 (2) 42.9

Organization assets: + (> 0) $-$

Skill/credential assets: + (> 0) $-$

There can be little doubt that *Classes* will prove to be as influential and controversial as Wright's earlier contribution to Marxist class theory. Certainly we look forward to examining his new model in much greater detail in our future work. At this stage, therefore, our conclusions can only be preliminary. However, the new model appears superior to the previous one at the conceptual level. Indeed, it seems to us it is the most sophisticated of all the recent neo-Marxist attempts to come to terms with the realities of contemporary capitalist societies. As usual, Wright is admirably clear in setting out his arguments and spelling out the details of his analysis. In this respect he provides an example for others to follow. Moreover, given that he is a distinguished and influential adherent of a tradition which has been unsympathetic to research of the kind he pursues, Wright is all the more to be congratulated on producing *Classes* and facing the problems of middle-range theory. Whatever the differences others may have with him, he ensures we need not talk past one another, and thereby presents a challenge to us all.

PART III

Reconsiderations

Rethinking, Once Again, the Concept of Class Structure*

Erik Olin Wright

At the core of Marxian class analysis is the claim that class is a fundamental determinant of social conflict and social change. In trying to
defend and deepen this intuition, contemporary Marxist theorists have
been torn between two theoretical impulses. The first is to keep the
concept of class structure as simple as possible, perhaps even accepting a
simple polarized vision of the class structure of capitalism, and then to
remedy the explanatory deficiencies of such a simple concept by introducing into the analysis a range of other explanatory principles, such as
divisions within classes or between sectors, the relationship between
work and community, or the role of the state and ideology in shaping the
collective organization of classes. The second impulse is to increase the
complexity of the class structural concept itself in the hope that such
complexity will more powerfully capture the explanatory mechanisms
embedded in class relations. Basically, these alternative impulses place
different bets on how much explanatory work the concept of class structure itself should do: the first strategy takes a minimalist position, seeing
class structure as at most shaping broad constraints on action and
change; the second takes a maximalist position, seeing class structure as
a potent and systematic determinant of individual action and social
development.[1]

*I would like to express my thanks to Julia Adams, Ron Aminzade, Robin Blackburn, Sam
Bowles, Johanna Brenner, Lisa Brush, Michael Burawoy, Val Burris, Ira Katznelson, Lane
Kenworthy, Michael Mann, Scott McNall, John Roemer, Joel Rogers, Ivan Szelenyi, and
Philippe Van Parijs for their extraordinarily helpful comments on an earlier draft of this
essay.

    1. Of course, there is in principle no inherent incompatability between these two strate-
gies. Indeed, a fully developed class analysis should combine in various ways an elaborated
conceptualization of class structure with an account of the interactions of that structure
with various kinds of nonclass mechanisms. Nevertheless, in actual practice, most theorists
in the Marxist tradition who engage the problem of class analysis have adopted one or the
other of these strategies, either using a fairly thin concept of class structure but worrying a
lot about the mediations of other mechanisms, or worrying a lot about the problem of class
structure and paying relatively little systematic attention to nonclass determinants.

My work on class has pursued this second strategy. In my theoretical discussions of class structure I have been preoccupied with the problem of the "middle class," with elaborating a class structure concept that would give a coherent and systematic theoretical status to nonproletarian employees. My conviction was that conceptually clarifying the structural location of the middle class was essential for understanding the process of class formation in contemporary capitalism. Above all, I felt it was essential for understanding the problem of the formation of coalitions of classes and segments of classes around radical democratic and socialist political projects. This led to the introduction of the concept of "contradictory locations within class relations" and subsequently, the reformulation of that concept in terms of a multidimensional view of exploitation. The theoretical aspiration was that these reconstructions of the concept of class structure would enhance its explanatory power by more adequately representing the complexities of class interests in capitalist societies and, accordingly, making it possible to map more systematically the variations in class structures across capitalist societies and the impact of those variations on processes of class formation.

That aspiration has yet to be fulfilled. While I do feel that progress has been made in the conceptualization of class in the past decade, nevertheless the goal of producing a class structure concept which is at one time theoretically coherent and empirically comprehensive remains elusive. In what follows I will try to lay out a general agenda for the further development of the concept of class structure which, hopefully, will help to bring us closer to this goal.

Section 1 begins the discussion by briefly situating the concept of class structure within the broader agenda of class analysis and examining some metatheoretical considerations that affect the analysis of class structure. In particular, it will be helpful to clarify the distinction between abstract and concrete concepts and between macro- and micro-level concepts of class structure.

Section 2 discusses at a fairly abstract level what is the theoretical object of the concept of "class structure": what is it that classes have in common that justifies calling them "classes." In particular, I will defend the decision to treat objective material interests as the central commonalty of class.

Section 3 will then assess the strengths and weaknesses of my two principal solutions to the problem of constructing a concrete map of the class structure of capitalist societies grounded in an account of class interests. The upshot of this discussion will be that neither of these strategies provides a completely satisfactory solution to the conceptual problem of the middle class.

Section 4 will briefly explore the attractions, and limitations, of the neo-Weberian alternative to the entire enterprise of reconstructing a Marxist concept of the middle class.

Section 5 will then explore a different way of adding complexity to the concept of class structure from those embodied in my various class structure typologies. My work has been based on the view that the central problem to solve is the location of the middle class within the class structure, where class structure is understood as a structure of "empty places" filled by people. Here I want to suggest a different type of elaboration, namely the various ways in which individual lives are tied to such a structure of positions. This will lead to a framework in which the link between individuals and class structures is viewed as organized around three axes: individual class *locations,* class *networks,* and class *trajectories.*

On the basis of these new complexities, section 6 returns to the problem of the middle class. While I cannot offer a new synthesis, I will try to elaborate an agenda of issues and theoretical directions in terms of which such a synthesis might be generated.

1 Class Structure in Class Analysis

The concept of "class structure" is only one element in a broader theoretical enterprise that can be called "class analysis." Other elements include class formation (the formation of classes into collectively organized actors), class struggle (the practices of actors for the realization of class interests), class consciousness (the understanding of actors of their class interests). The task of class analysis is not simply to understand class structure as such but to understand the interconnections among all these elements and their consequences for other aspects of social life.

My discussion in this essay will be largely restricted to the problem of class structure. This is not because I believe that class structure is always the most important explanatory principle within class analysis. It could certainly be the case, for example, that variations in class formations across time and place may be a more important determinant of variations in state policies than variations in the class structures associated with those class formations. Rather, I will focus on class structure because it remains *conceptually* pivotal to clarifying the overall logic of class analysis. To speak of *class* formation or *class* struggle as opposed to simply *group* formation or struggle implies that we have a definition of "class" and know what it means to describe a collective actor as an instance of class formation, or a conflict as a class conflict instead of some other sort of conflict. Elaborating a coherent concept of class structure, therefore, is an important conceptual precondition for developing a satisfactory theory of the relationship between class structure, class formation and class struggle.[2]

Underlying this preoccupation with clarifying the concept of class structure is a particular view of the relationship between the problem of *concept formation* and *theory construction*. My assumption is that the explanatory capacity of the theories we construct depends to an important extent on the coherence of the concepts we deploy within them. When concepts are loosely constructed and vaguely defined, then it is much more difficult for the knowledge generated within a theory to have a cumulative character to it. Our capacity to learn both from our explanatory successes and our explanatory failures depends in important ways on the clarity and coherence of the basic categories used within those explanations. This does not imply that we cannot begin to study the world empirically and construct general theoretical explanations until we have a completely coherent inventory of concepts; but it does imply that critical element in the advance of our capacity for theory construction is the elaboration of our basic concepts.

The central thrust of my work on class structure has been to try to produce, within a broadly Marxist theoretical framework, a class structure concept capable of being used in analyses of micro-level processes at a relatively low level of abstraction. Why this preoccupation? It was driven by two overarching questions. First, how can we best explain the empirical variations in patterns of class formation across advanced capitalist societies? Second, under what conditions are class formations likely to embody projects of radical social change? My assumption was that the elaboration of a concept of class structure that was both relatively concrete and specified at the micro level of analysis was necessary to deepen our understanding of the causal relationships among class structure, class formation, class consciousness, and class struggle. More specifically, I felt that any viable democratic socialist politics in advanced capitalist societies must contend with the problem of the formation of durable political coalitions between segments of the "middle class" and the working class. Overly abstract and macro-level concepts of class structure did not seem to provide the categories necessary for exploring the problem of forging such coalitions in the process of class formation. In order to study in a politically relevant way class formation in

---

2. The assumption here is that the concept of class structure imparts the essential content of the adjective "class" when it is appended to formation, consciousness, and struggle. Class formation is the formation of collective actors organized around class interests within a class structure; class struggle is the struggle between such collectively organized actors over class interests; class consciousness is the understanding by people within a class of their class interests. In each case one must already have a definition of class structure before the other concepts can be fully specified.

advanced capitalism, therefore, I felt it was necessary to produce a class structure concept that was much less abstract than existing concepts and more suitable for micro-level analysis.[3]

In order to situate this effort at concept formation, it is necessary to clarify what it means to produce a concept at a relatively "concrete" level of abstraction which is directed towards the relatively "micro level" of analysis.

Levels of Abstraction   While all concepts are abstract in the sense that they are mental constructions distinct from the "real objects" which they attempt to represent, nevertheless, concepts differ in their degree of abstraction or concreteness.[4] The meaning of the expression "degree of abstraction" can be clarified by introducing the distinction between "types" and "tokens" in the construction of concepts. The term "token" refers to the individual, concrete instances of some theoretical object— let us say, for example, my pet dog Micah. The term "type," on the other hand, refers to the more general theoretical categories under which this specific token could be classified: golden retrievers, dogs, mammals, animals, living things. Within a given conceptual hierarchy, a more abstract concept is one that constitutes a classification of the variable forms of the less abstract concepts. Thus the concept "dog" is more

---

3. My initial belief, when I began this work in the late 1970s, was that solving the problem of the middle class was the most important conceptual task in advancing our understanding of class formation in advanced capitalism. I therefore gave priority to this task over, for example, examining the institutional conditions for class compromise as in the work of Adam Przeworski, or the impact of changing forms of the labor process on working-class formation, as in the work of Michael Burawoy, or the political conditions for the collective organization of labor, as in the work of Joel Rogers. While I continue to believe that solving the conceptual issues in class structure analysis is important, I no longer feel that this provides the key to understanding the more general problem of variations in class formation and possibilities for the creation of radical coalitions. For discussions of class formation that do not emphasize class structure, see Michael Burawoy, *The Politics of Production* (London: Verso, 1985) and "Marxism without Microfoundations: A Review of Adam Przeworski's Work," *Socialist Review* (1989); Adam Przeworski, *Capitalism and Social Democracy* (Cambridge: Cambridge University Press, 1985) and "Class Production and Politics: A Reply to Burawoy," *Socialist Review* (1989); and Joel Rogers, "Divide and Conquer: Further 'Reflections on the Distinctive Character of American Labor Laws,'" *University of Wisconsin Law Review* (1989), and *Organizing Interests: Post-war US Labor Policy and the Future of American Unions* (working title; forthcoming, Basic Books).

4. In describing a concept as "representing" a real object, there is no implication that it is a simple *reflection* of that object, as in the metaphor of a mirror reflecting reality. Concepts are always active mental constructions, produced through a set of practices by people attempting to understand the world. While to a greater or lesser extent these constructions are constrained by the real objects which they attempt to represent—that is, if the world were different, the concepts which attempt to represent the world would be different—they are never simple reflections of those objects. For a discussion of this kind of "realist" approach to the status of concepts, see *Classes*, pp. 20–24.

abstract than the concept "golden retriever" (because a golden retriever is one of many types of dog), but less abstract than the concept "mammal." In these terms, within a given conceptual hierarchy, concrete concepts are nested within abstract concepts.

It is important to emphasize that a more "abstract" concept is not *less real* than a more concrete concept, at least in the sense of attempting to identify real causal mechanisms. To describe my pet dog Micah as a mammal is to identify causal mechanisms that are just as real as those mechanisms captured by the description "golden retriever." Depending upon the specific theoretical question one is asking, the appropriate level of abstraction of the type-concepts used in the answer will vary, but in each case they are attempts at specifying explanatory mechanisms.[5]

Within the Marxist tradition, at the most abstract level, the concept of class structure attempts to differentiate distinct modes of production, for example capitalism and feudalism. More concrete concepts, accordingly, attempt to capture the ways in which the class structures vary over time and place within a given type of society.[6] One of the central objectives of my work on class structure has been to generate a concept capable of mapping in a nuanced way concrete variations in class structures across capitalist societies.

Micro/Macro Levels of Analysis   The distinction between micro and macro concepts refers to the level of aggregation of social phenomena to which the concept refers. As a macro-level concept, class structures are meant to describe a crucial property of whole societies. When Marxists say, for example, that the private ownership of the means of production acts as a powerful constraint on potential policies of the state, they are generally making a macro-structural argument about the effects of the capitalist class structure on state institutions.[7] As a micro-level concept,

---

5. Far from being "less real" than concrete concepts, there is a certain sense in which for many explanatory problems it is often the case that the causal mechanisms identified by more abstract concepts can be thought of as more "fundamental" than the mechanisms identified by more concrete concepts. Thus, the mechanisms defined by the concept "dog" are more fundamental than those defined by the concept "golden retriever" in explaining a wide range of empirical properties of the specific token, Micah, where "more fundamental" means determining the limits within which the more concrete mechanisms operate.

6. In terms of the use of *words* in discussions of class structure and levels of abstraction, sometimes Marxists use the expression "social relations of production" to refer to the mode of production level of abstraction, and reverse the term "class structure" for more concrete levels of analysis. Thus a (concrete) class structure consists of combinations of (abstract) relations of production, but the term "class structure" is not itself applied to the more abstract level. This is parallel to the distinction between elements and compounds in chemistry: compounds are specific combinations of elements. In the present discussion I will use the term "class structure" to refer to the theoretical object of the structural analysis of classes at whatever level of abstraction.

on the other hand, class structures define a set of "locations" filled by individuals. To be in a class location is to be subjected to a set of mechanisms that impinge directly on the lives of individuals as they make choices and act in the world. There is some debate, as we will see in section 2 below, over what is most salient about these micro-mechanisms attached to the locations within class structures: should they primarily be thought of as determining the material interests of individuals? or shaping their subjective understandings of the world? or determining the basic resources they have available to pursue their interests? In any event, to develop a concept of class structure at the micro level of analysis is to elaborate the concept in terms of such mechanisms that directly affect individuals within class locations.

The micro–macro distinction should not be confused with the abstract–concrete distinction. While it often seems that micro-analysis is more concrete than macro-analysis—since it deals with apparently concrete entities, "individuals"—one can perfectly well develop very abstract concepts for dealing with micro-analyses (as is often done in rational-actor models) or quite concrete concepts for dealing with macro-analyses (as occurs in many historical-comparative analyses of institutional development).

The Marxist concept of class structure has traditionally been constructed most systematically as a highly abstract macro-structural concept. Class structures were defined in terms of models of pure modes of production (slavery, feudalism, capitalism, communism) and used to understand the broad, macro-structural dynamics of social development. This is not to say that Marxists have failed to engage in concrete or micro-level class analyses. However, typically the class structure concept deployed in such analyses has tended to be directly imported from the more abstract macro-structural arena with relatively unsystematic amendments to make it suitable for concrete, micro-analysis.

The overarching objective of my work on the concept of class structure has been to elaborate this concept in ways that would enhance its analytical power both in concrete analyses and in micro-analyses. The goal was to generate a repertoire of class structure concepts that could be used both for comparative historical and institutional analyses of

---

7. To describe this as a macro-structural claim does not imply that the explanation of the relationship between class structure and state policies can be adequately developed strictly at the macro level of analysis. The actual working out of this relationship undoubtedly would involve at least some reference to the micro circumstances of state policy makers, capitalist investors, workers, and other actors within this structure of relations.

variations in the class structures of capitalist societies and for the analysis of the impact of class on the lives of individuals within those societies.

This concern with elaborating a class structure concept at the micro
level has led some critics to see my work as embracing principles of
"methodological individualism."[8] This is, I think, an incorrect judgment.
While much of my work has been concerned with elaborating the
concept of class structure in such a way that it enables us to analyze, in a
relatively fine-grained way, the diverse ways in which individual lives
intersect class structures, I have never argued that class structures are
reducible to the properties of individuals, which is an essential claim of
methodological individualism.[9] If Marxist class analysis is to advance, it
is essential that it develop what is sometimes called "microfoundations," but this does not imply that all of the causal processes in
class theory can be adequately represented at the level of individuals and
their interactions. The task is to understand the ways in which macro-
structural contexts constrain micro-level processes, and the ways in
which the micro-level choices and strategies of individuals can affect
macro-structural arrangements. To accomplish this task requires
developing class structure concepts at both the macro and micro levels
of analysis.

In attempting this kind of task, one must decide how unified a
conceptual field one should try to achieve. One aspiration is to establish
a set of rules for producing new concepts such that the micro and macro
concepts and the abstract and concrete concepts are theoretically integrated under a common logic. In this approach, while the specific class
structure concept one adopts will depend upon the kind of question one
is asking—one might use a simple polarized class structure concept for
understanding the epochal dynamics of capitalism as a mode of production and a highly differentiated class structure concept with contradictory class locations for the analysis of coalition formation within class
struggles in advanced capitalist societies—the different class structure
concepts are all integrated within a unitary conceptual logic. Alternatively, and more modestly, one can adopt a more eclectic and pragmatic strategy which is willing to acknowledge that different kinds of
class concepts may be more or less appropriate for different explanatory

---

8. For examples of this kind of critique, see G. Carchedi, "Classes and Class Analysis,"
in this volume, and Paul Kamolnick, *Classes: A Marxist Critique* (Dix Hills, New York:
General Hall, 1988).

9. The core of methodological individualism is not simply the concern with micro-
analysis, but the claim that macro-phenomena are in principle fully explainable by micro-
mechanisms (or, equivalently, that macro-phenomena are reducible to micro-phenomena).
For a critique of this claim, see my essay with Elliott Sober and Andrew Levine, "Marxism
and Methodological Individualism," *New Left Review*, no. 162 (1987).

tasks. It could be the case, for example, that Weberian class concepts work best for micro-analyses or concrete analyses of institutional variations across capitalist societies, whereas Marxist concepts work best for the analysis of broad epochal transformation.[10]

My ambition has been to achieve as high a level of theoretical integration among these various class structure concepts as possible, on the assumption that if such integration is achieved then the explanatory capacity of Marxist class analysis would be enhanced. This means that I have attempted, if not always completely consciously, to apply systematic rules to the derivation of new class structure concepts from the abstract concepts at the core of Marxist theory. As we shall see in more detail in section 3 below, the basic strategy I adopted for moving from the abstract to the concrete is to see concrete class structures as consisting of different combinations of the class relations defined within abstract class structure concepts. Thus, for example, we can abstractly define the class relations of capitalism and feudalism and then describe a concrete class structure as a particular form of combination of these abstractly defined relations. The basic strategy I have used for developing a more differentiated micro concept of class structure has been to elaborate the ways in which class relations are embodied in specific *jobs*, since jobs are the essential "empty places" filled by individuals within the system of production. The traditional assumption of Marxian class analysis is that every location in the class structure was in one and only one class. In contrast, I have argued that individual jobs can, in different ways, have a multiple, and sometimes even contradictory, class character.

Taking these two rules together in principle provides a way of linking the abstract macro concept of class structure rooted in the analysis of

---

10. In a personal communication on an earlier draft of this paper, John Roemer argued that it was probably hopeless to generate a general definition of class structure that would be appropriate for all explanatory tasks: "I think you take a somewhat Platonic stance in this paper, which I think is unnecessary or a bit naive. That is, your presupposition is that either (1) there does exist a perfect definition of class, and each of your two proposals is but an imperfect approximation to it, or (2) there does not exist a perfect definition of class, in which case Marxist theory is fundamentally flawed. To the contrary, I would argue that it is probably the case that there exists no perfect definition of class (perfect in the sense of performing 'correctly' in all applications), yet the Marxist insight of thinking in terms of class is a great one. . . . The cost of taking this viewpoint is that there is no automatic way of deciding whether the Marxist tool is better than Weberian theory, for example; for the latter too must be viewed as a tool that performs well in some cases and not in others. One must simply ask which tool seems to perform better on the most important jobs." In Roemer's view, then, there is no particular justification for believing that a unified class structure concept is possible, or at least that it will have more explanatory power than a collection of rather distinct class concepts deployed for specific explanatory purposes.

modes of production to the concrete and micro concept of class structure rooted in the analysis of individual lives. In the actual elaboration of
my conceptual strategies, however, I have not been able to sustain such a
neat and coherent conceptual space. In various ways, as we shall see,
arbitrary elements have entered the analysis—arbitrary in the sense of
not being tightly derived from the abstract concept itself.

In what follows I will try to reflect on the successes and failures of this
attempt at generating Marxist concepts of class structure that are both
more concrete and more oriented to micro-level analyses than the traditional mode of production class structure concept. This assessment,
hopefully, will point the direction towards further elaborations.

2 What Do Classes Have in Common That Make Them Classes?

Class structures, for most Marxists anyway, are thought to designate real
mechanisms, causal processes that exist independently of the theorist.
The concept of class is not meant to be simply an arbitrary, analytical
convention invented by the theorist. To define a class, therefore, is to
make a claim about the nature of these mechanisms.[11] Mechanisms are
effect-generating processes.[12] To identify a mechanism is to give an
account of the way it produces specific kinds of effects. One crucial
aspect of the theoretical content of the concept of class, therefore,
concerns the specification of the kinds of direct effects that class structural mechanisms are thought to produce.

-----

11. Two methodological points need to be made here. First of all, what is at issue here
is not the use of the *word* "class," but the status of the concept itself. The use of words is
obviously a matter of convention. The claim here is that the theoretical concept designated
by that word is meant to designate a real mechanism. In this sense, the definition of the
concept class structure can be *incorrect*, not simply *unhelpful.* Second, I am not claiming
that the only legitimate kind of concept in social theories is one which attempts to represent
real mechanisms in this way. For certain analytical tasks, strictly conventional, heuristic
concepts may be entirely appropriate.

12. To say that mechanisms are effect-generating processes does not imply that
mechanisms invariably generate *empirically observable* effects. Since, to use the formulation of Roy Bhaskar, the world is an open system consisting of many distinct mechanisms
operating simultaneously, it is always possible that the presence of one mechanism can
block the effects of another. This does not deny that mechanisms can be viewed as effect-
producing processes (or, in Bashkar's terminology, as *event*-producing processes), but
simply that the effects never appear as discrete events in our empirical observations. Our
observations (which Bhaskar refers to as "experiences") are always constituted by con-
catenations of many intersecting events. To identify a mechanism is therefore to identify an
effect-producing process which will have a tendency to be embodied in one way or another
in empirical observations, but the actual empirical realization of that tendency may depend
upon a variety of other contingencies. See Roy Bhaskar, *A Realist Theory of Science*
(Brighton: Harvester Press, 1975), and *The Possibility of Naturalism* (Brighton: Harvester
Press, 1979) for an elaboration of this conception of mechanisms.

While it is a commonplace in the Marxist tradition to say that class structures are defined by the "social relations of production," and specific classes within that structure are defined by their location within those social relations, there is much less agreement on which of the various effects generated by the relations of production are the most central to the concept of class. If the social relations of production constituted a simple mechanism which generated a single kind of effect, then this problem would not arise. But the concept "social relations of production" encompasses a complex set of interconnected mechanisms which generate a variety of effects, and there is no general agreement about how these are linked to the concept of class structure. One of our first tasks, therefore, is to try to sort out the kinds of effects that are generally seen as giving theoretical content to the concept of class structure.

Clarifying this issue is important both for understanding how the concept of class structure figures in class analysis in general and for our specific task of producing a more concrete, micro-level concept of class structure. The broader explanatory objectives of class theory hinge on an adequate understanding of the effect-producing mechanisms constituted by class relations. The concept of class figures in the explanations of many sorts of phenomena: state policies, social conflict, wars, ideologies, illness, voting behavior, etc. In each case, the explanatory power of class depends upon the immediate effects class mechanisms are thought to produce. For example, when we say that class structures figure in the explanations of state policies there is always, at least implicitly, a claim that class structures directly generate effects—perhaps material interests of key actors, perhaps consciousness, perhaps resource constraints on alternative strategies—which in turn explain (in conjunction with other mechanisms) state policies. Even if the actual explanation of policies involves many other factors and many contingencies, so that policies cannot be *reduced* to class, there must still be some rudimentary claim about the necessary effect-producing mechanisms of class in order for class to figure systematically in the explanation.

Clarifying the nature of the effect-producing mechanisms implicated in the concept class structure is also important for the project of elaborating a more differentiated repertoire of class structure concepts. If we want to construct a class structural concept at a lower level of abstraction than the perfectly polarized structure of class relations within pure "modes of production," it is necessary to have an explicit account of these effect-producing mechanisms, since it is only in terms of such mechanisms that we can evaluate the consistency of the new concrete concepts with respect to the more abstract ones. Without an explicit account of these mechanisms, we would be unable to know whether our more concrete concepts were indeed concrete *class* structure concepts or, perhaps, concrete concepts of some other more abstract theoretical object (such as stratification categories or occupational groups). In order for the attempt at building the more concrete class structure concept to be coherent with the more abstract concept, an explicit understanding of the mechanisms identified with class structure is essential.

In these terms, Marxist treatments of class structure can be seen as emphasizing one or more of three types of effects: material interests, lived experience, and capacities for collective action. While theorists generally do not use precisely this language, implicit in most elaborations of the concept of class structure is one or more of these kinds of class-generated effects. In each case, these effects are seen as directly generated by class structural mechanisms as such and, therefore, as providing the basis for the theoretical relevance of the concept of class. This does not mean, it must be stressed, that class by itself is thought to explain subjective understandings of material interests, or the forms of consciousness rooted in lived experience or the actual struggles of collectively organized actors. These empirical phenomena, like all empirical phenomena in a complex "open system," to use Roy Bhaskar's formulation, will be shaped by the joint operation of many distinct mechanisms, not simply class structural mechanisms.[13] What is being claimed, however, is that to the extent that class is explanatory of empirical phenomena, it is explanatory by virtue of the way class mechanisms generate material interests, or lived experiences, or collective capacities.

I will argue that of these three possible bases for the specification of class mechanisms, material interests provides the most coherent basis for the elaboration of concrete, micro-level concepts of class structure. Before explaining why I feel this is the case, it will be useful to briefly examine the logic of each of these positions.

2.1 Material Interests

Class is sometimes viewed as an answer to the question "Who gets what and how do they get it?" The social relations of production determine a set of mechanisms through which people obtain access to material resources and the social product which is produced using those resources. Two critical kinds of material interests are bound up with these mechanisms: first, interests with respect to *economic welfare,* and second, interests with respect to *economic power.* Before discussing each

---

13. See Bhaskar, *A Realist Theory of Science.*

of these, a brief comment on how I will use the term "interests" is needed.

Intrinsic and Instrumental Interests   In the analysis of interests it is important to make the distinction between what can be called *intrinsic* and *instrumental* interests. Intrinsic interests refer to the ends of actions, the goals that one is trying to accomplish through particular strategies. Instrumental interests, on the other hand, refer to interests organized around the necessary means for accomplishing those ends. Thus, for example, a particular level of consumption can be thought of as an intrinsic interest—it is a goal sought for its own sake; whereas improving one's market position for the acquisition of income is an instrumental interest.

In discussions of class interests the primary concern is instrumental interests. Take the question of economic welfare which we will discuss below. In terms of the *ends* specified by economic welfare—high standards of living, lower toil (unpleasant work), more leisure, etc.—there is no basic difference in the interests of individuals within different classes. Everyone, regardless of class, has an intrinsic interest in improving economic welfare. When we look at instrumental interests, on the other hand, there are big and systematic differences across classes. To improve their economic welfare, workers have to engage in quite different strategies, both as individuals and as members of a collectivity, from capitalists. The claim, for example, that workers have an interest in socialism whereas capitalists have interests opposed to socialism, means (among other things) that socialism constitutes a reorganization of society within which the welfare of workers would be improved while the welfare of capitalists would decline. Individuals in both classes have the same interest with respect to welfare as such, but they differ in their instrumental interests with respect to the means of realizing this interest. The interests which are most relevant for understanding the differences among classes, therefore, are these kinds of instrumental interests.

Economic Welfare   Economic welfare, in this context, is not equivalent to income or consumption. Rather, it refers to the total package of toil–leisure–income available to a person. Thus, to say that people have an "objective interest" in enhanced economic welfare, does not mean that they have an objective interest in more consumption as such, but simply that, all other things being equal, they have an objective interest in having superior trade-offs between toil–leisure–consumption. If given the choice between a package of 8 hours of toil plus 8 hours of leisure plus $40 of income and 6 hours of toil plus 10 hours of leisure plus $50 of income, then the latter package is an objective improvement in economic welfare.

To say that people within a given class share common interests with respect to economic welfare does not mean that they all, necessarily, have the *same* level of actual economic welfare. Some workers may be relatively affluent, others may be poor. Indeed, it is quite possible for people with the same level of income to have quite distinct and even opposed class interests, if the income is generated through different mechanisms. Workers and petty bourgeois farmers may have very similar levels of income, but quite different class interests. Class interests with respect to economic welfare are determined by what a person must do to achieve a given economic welfare, that is, by the welfare-generating mechanisms, not by the outcome itself. To talk about common class interests, then, means that people in a given class, by virtue of their relationship to the underlying mechanisms embedded in the social relations of production, objectively face the same broad structure of choices and strategic tasks when attempting to improve their economic welfare—that is, the package of toil–leisure–income available to them.

Economic Power   The social relations of production do not simply distribute, through a set of mechanisms, economic welfare to individuals; they also distribute a crucial form of power: control over the surplus product.[14] While there are many difficulties in a precise definition of the surplus product since much of it may take the form of earned incomes, loosely we can define the surplus product as that part of the total social product that is left over after all of the inputs into production (both labor power and physical capital) have been reproduced.[15] The control of the surplus product fundamentally determines

---

14. In an earlier draft of this paper I had restricted the discussion of material interests entirely to the problem of interests in economic welfare. This was in keeping with the thrust of my argument in *Classes* in which exploitation was defined, following Roemer, in terms of the causal interdependencies of the welfare of exploiters with the deprivations of the exploited. Joel Rogers (personal communication) pointed out that this preoccupation with individual material welfare missed one of the central aspects of class structures, namely the way they shape what he would call *political* interests, namely interests over the control of economic power resources. While in other contexts (such as the analysis of state policies in capitalist societies) I have emphasized this issue, it was largely absent from my specific discussion of class structure.

15. The difficulty in the specification of the "surplus" arises because of problems in defining the "costs of reproduction" of labor power. These costs certainly cannot be equated with actual employee incomes, since for reasons we will discuss in section 3.1 below, the wages and salaries of certain categories of employees embody appropriations of parts of the surplus product.

the nature of economic investments and consequently the form and character of economic development. Because of the centrality of investments to a broad range of social goals, the control over the surplus can also be considered a central mechanism constraining social and political alternatives in general.[16] As many commentators have stressed, the private, capitalist control over the surplus imposes a pervasive limit on the potential exercise of democratic political power in a capitalist society.[17]

As in the case of the argument about interests with respect to economic welfare, class interests with respect to economic power are based on the underlying mechanisms which determine access to the surplus, not simply on the outcomes themselves. In early capitalism, for example, a feudal lord and a capitalist could control the allocation of the same amount of surplus, but since their ability to appropriate this surplus is rooted in different mechanisms of appropriation (feudal rents and capitalist profits) they would have different class interests. In a complementary manner, the class interests with respect to economic power of serfs and workers would be different. More controversially, a similar argument can perhaps be made about the mechanisms underlying the appropriation of surplus by credentialed professionals, corporate managers, and state officials in contemporary capitalism. In any case, the central point here is that material interests are bound up with basic questions of social power and not merely individual economic welfare.

This dimension of the commonality of class interests is particularly salient for the problem of linking macro and micro levels of class structure analysis. The kind of economic power generated by the control over the surplus affects the overall, macro-structural development of a society, not simple the fate of the individual who exercises that power. Since the core of the explanatory project of macro-level class analysis centers on large-scale processes of institutional change, understanding

---

16. In neoclassical economics it is argued that capitalists do not actually have any meaningful *power* with respect to the allocation of investments, since they are driven by competition to invest in the most profitable way. That is, their apparent control of the surplus is really illusory. If any actor has real power in this system, it is consumers, who by their market choices dictate where investments will move. Two things are worth noting in this approach: first, since consumers vote with dollars—one dollar, one vote—it would still be the case that exploitation would enhance the economic power of exploiters by virtue of their purchasing power. Exploiters would have many more votes in the market than would workers. Second, since exploiters have control over the decision of whether to consume or invest the surplus they appropriate, this too represents an exercise of power. Workers do not have that choice. Thus *even if* we adopt the highly questionable view that the decisions about *where* and *how* to invest are totally determined by "the market," nevertheless the appropriation of the surplus by capitalists constitutes an appropriation of power as well.

17. See, in particular, the elegant statement of this argument in Joshua Cohen and Joel Rogers, *On Democracy* (Harmondsworth: Penguin, 1986).

the problem of economic power derived from class structures at the micro level of analysis is potentially of considerable importance.

Material Interests and Exploitation   In Marxist theory, these two kinds of material interest—interests in securing the conditions for material welfare and interests in enhancing economic power—are linked through the concept of *exploitation*: exploitation defines a set of mechanisms which help to explain both the distribution of economic welfare and the distribution of economic power. That is, by virtue of appropriating the surplus, exploiters are able both to obtain much higher levels of economic welfare (by consuming part of the surplus) and to have much higher levels of economic power (by retaining control over the social allocation of the surplus through investments). For the exploited, economic welfare is depressed by virtue of having surplus appropriated from them, and economic power drastically curtailed by being excluded from control over the allocation of the surplus.[18] Exploitation generates both deprivations and powerlessness, and material interests are structured around both of these. Within Marxism, therefore, to say that what members of a class hold in common is a common set of material interests is to argue that they have common interests with respect to the process of exploitation.[19]

Marxism is not the only theoretical tradition which sees the essential commonality of classes as rooted in common material interests. The Weberian concept of members of a class sharing common "life chances" based on their common market capacities, for example, is a specific way of grounding classes in common material interests. As in the Marxist

---

18. It should be noted that the arguments here do not depend upon the labor theory of value for its theoretical power. The value of the surplus product may or may not be determined by the amount of socially necessary abstract labor time embodied in it, and yet the control over that surplus can give people enhanced material welfare and social power.

19. It is worth noting that John Roemer's analysis of exploitation, which as many of the essays in this book have stressed has played an important role in my analyses of class structure in *Classes*, focuses exclusively on the first of these interests—interests in material welfare. He is not concerned with the way systems of exploitation constitute the basis for economic power, but simply for distributional outcomes. It is for this reason that, in the end, Roemer is able to argue that perhaps we should forget about exploitation as such and simply focus on the issue of the relationship between unjust distributions of resources and unjust distributions of welfare outcomes. (For this argument, see John Roemer, "Should Marxists Be Interested in Exploitation?," *Philosophy and Public Affairs*, vol. 14, pp. 30–65 (1985)). In his view nothing is really added to the analysis by identifying the causal mechanisms involved in this relationship as "exploitation," since the *moral* indictment revolves entirely around the issue of the unjustness of the initial distribution of assets. If, however, we see the problem of interests in economic power as central to class analysis, then it is hard to see how the concept of exploitation can be so marginalized since this economic power is based on the appropriation and control of the social surplus.

concept, it is not the common "life chances" (economic welfare) as such which defines common class membership, but a common relationship to the market capacities which generate such life chances. In the Weberian approach, there are as many classes in a society as there are types of market capacities that generate common life chances.

Where the Marxist and Weberian concepts of class sharply diverge is that Marxists, but generally not Weberians, analyze the linkage between class and material interests through the concept of *exploitation*.[20] Within the Marxist tradition, members of a class do not simply share a common attribute—common material interests—but those interests are relationally linked in a specific way to the interests of other classes through exploitation. Relationally defined classes, in these terms, do not simply have *different* material interests, as in the Weberian tradition: they have *opposed* material interests. While Weberians would certainly acknowledge that there are many circumstances in which class actors subjectively *perceive* their interests to be opposed to those of other actors, this perception cannot be traced back to any inherent antagonism of interests, but must be explained in terms of the particular construction of cultural meanings in the society.[21]

The objectively antagonistic character of the material interests of classes helps to explain, Marxists generally argue, why class structure should be associated with class conflict: if the material interests bound up with classes are inherently opposed to each other, then it would be expected that the divisions between structurally defined classes would have a tendency to be the basis for cleavages between conflicting groups. To be sure, this need not imply the inevitability and universality of class conflicts—a variety of social processes can block the translation of exploitation into collectively organized conflict. And it does not preclude the possibility of class *compromises*—stable institutional

---

20. Of course, there are theorists identified with the Weberian tradition who do talk about exploitation. Anthony Giddens and Michael Mann are notable examples. When they do so, I would argue, they are talking in a Marxian voice. This is particularly true for Giddens who has argued (personal communication) that in spite of the fact that everyone considers him a prime example of a neo-Weberian sociologist, he sees his work as at least as indebted to the Marxist tradition as to the Weberian. Giddens's views on exploitation and class are much more clearly laid out in his recent work, especially *A Contemporary Critique of Historical Materialism* (Berkeley: University of California Press, 1982) than in his earlier work directly on class theory, *The Class Structure of the Advanced Societies* (New York: Harper and Row, 1973). See also Michael Mann, *The Sources of Social Power* (Cambridge: Cambridge University Press, 1987).

21. The absence of a concept of exploitation and control over the surplus from the Weberian concept of class has also meant that most Weberians have treated the material interests linked to class structures exclusively in terms of the problem of the market-based acquisition of individual incomes. Characteristically, the problem of the linkage between class structures and social power has not been a systematic concern.

arrangements in which mutual concessions are made.[22] But it does provide a nonarbitrary theoretical grounding for the expectation that class structures shape class conflicts.[23]

Interests, Trade-offs, Strategies   The concept of interests, even when circumscribed as "material interests," is by no means unproblematic or uncontested. In recent years Marxists and others have become increasingly suspicious of claims concerning the "objective" interests of actors, interests which supposedly exist independently of the subjective understandings of those interests held by the actors themselves. To say that members of a class share common material interests, therefore, seems to imply that theorists know what is good for the people in a class—what is in their "true" interests—better than they do themselves.

This kind of criticism, however, really misses the theoretical point of the claim that common material interests constitute the critical commonality of class. To say that a group of actors share common material interests shaped by the social relations of production is to say that *they objectively face similar dilemmas and trade-offs in the pursuit of economic welfare and economic power.* Once again: it is not the distributional outcomes of welfare or power as such which define the critical commonality of class interests, but the common material conditions which shape the available choices and strategies with respect to those outcomes.

The expression "available choices and strategies" in this formulation can refer to choices faced by individuals in a class *as individuals* or to choices they face as potential members of organized collectivities. Thus, as an individual, to be a capitalist means that economic welfare depends upon extraction of surplus labor from workers, technical innovation, successful investment strategies, market competition with rival capi-

---

22. The view that the material interests of workers and capitalists are inherently antagonistic, however, does imply that a class compromise is a compromise; it does not obliterate the conflicts of interests, but contains those conflicts within bounds due to reciprocal (if asymmetrical) concessions.

23. Because Marxists regard the interests of classes as inherently antagonistic, they are committed to a much stronger set of predictions than are Weberians. For Marxists it is clear that if a society is characterized by class exploitation, then it would be surprising if no regular conflicts were observed between the allegedly antagonistic classes. The absence of systematic conflict, therefore, would imply the presence of some powerful mechanism which prevents the interest mechanisms from generating empirical conflicts. For a Weberian, on the other hand, since the interests specified by classes are merely different, not inherently conflictual, there are no particular general expectations one way or the other about the patterns of conflicts that will be associated with class divisions. In principle Weberians would be no more surprised by the presence of class conflict than by its absence in capitalism. As I will argue in section 4 below, the capacity to be surprised by one's observations is one of the strengths of Marxist class theory relative to its Weberian rivals.

talists; as an individual, to be a worker means that economic welfare depends upon successfully selling one's labor power to a capitalist and competing with other workers for better jobs. But both workers and capitalists also face distinctive structures of choices with respect to the collective pursuits of economic welfare. Workers, for example, face choices between various individualist market strategies (via training, promotions, geographical mobility, etc.) and various kinds of collective strategies (unionization, revolutionary politics, etc.). And, of course, they face the choice of participating in various kinds of ongoing collective strategies from which they might benefit or being a free-rider on the actions of others. To describe members of a class as sharing common material interests, therefore, suggests that they share common dilemmas with respect to collective action as well as individual pursuit of economic welfare and power.[24]

Now, in these terms to talk about the common material interests of workers is not to make a claim about which of the actual potential choices listed above are "best" for workers as individuals. No claim is being made, for example, that for any given worker it is objectively in their interests to pursue unionization strategies rather than geographical mobility strategies to advance their economic welfare. Rather, what is being claimed is that by virtue of being workers (that is, by occupying similar locations with respect to the relations of exploitation) they face broadly similar structures of trade-offs with respect to these kinds of choices.[25]

These kinds of choices and trade-offs rooted in the conditions for the pursuit of economic welfare can be defined both within the "game" of

---

24. To use the language of rational actor models, members of a class share common free-rider problems with respect to the collective pursuit of material interests. Thus, part of what capitalists have in common by virtue of being capitalists is an interest in increasing the free-rider problems for workers while decreasing them for capitalists, whereas part of what workers have in common by virtue of being workers is an interest in decreasing free rider problems for workers while increasing them for capitalists. It might be noted that this is essentially equivalent to what Nicos Poulantzas means when he says that the essential capitalist character of the capitalist state is constituted by the state's effects on organizing capitalists (overcoming their free-rider problems) and disorganizing workers (increasing their free-rider problems). See Nicos Poulantzas, *Political Power and Social Theory* (London: Verso, 1973).

25. The qualifying expression "broadly similar" obviously begs a number of difficult questions. How similar do the structure of choices have to be to be counted as "similar"? Workers in secondary labor markets or workers who are oppressed minorities may, for example, face different trade-offs and dilemmas (different structures of choices) from various other categories of workers. Does this mean that they are in a different *class*? It is essentially on the basis of such differences in material interests, for example, that some feminists have argued that female workers are in a different class from male workers. While such arguments are important and deserve serious consideration, I will not address them here.

capitalism and with respect to the choice between the game of capitalism and socialism. That is, to occupy a class location within capitalism is to face specific strategic alternatives within the capitalist game as well as to face strategic trade-offs with respect to struggles over the basic property relations of capitalism. In classical Marxism, where the class structure was conceptualized primarily at the abstract level of the mode of production as a game involving only two actors—workers and capitalists—there was a high level of congruence between the analysis of interests within the game of capitalism and the analysis of interests over which game was being played. The class forces lined up in the same way in both analyses. This was one of the central reasons why Marx and other classical Marxists felt that the intensification of class polarization and struggles within capitalism tended to enhance the possibility of class struggle over capitalism itself.

Once we move to more concrete and micro levels of analysis, however, and give specificity to the variations in class locations within capitalist class structures, the picture is no longer so simple. As we shall see, the terrain of material interests constituted by the class structures of concrete capitalist societies is not perfectly polarized, and there is not a simple relationship between the concrete matrix of material interests of actors constituted within the game of capitalism and the interests over what kind of game should be played.

2.2 Lived Experience

Some Marxists have questioned the adequacy of grounding the concept of class in material interests. Interests, it is argued, are causally efficacious only when they are embodied in the subjective understanding of actors. Theorists can define whatever they like to be the "material interests" of a class, but the people in a class will act on those interests only to the extent that they become actual, subjective preferences. Common material interests, therefore, only become part of the commonality of class membership if they generate a set of systematic experiences that actively shape subjective understanding.[26]

In these terms, common lived experience becomes the central, abstract content of the commonality of class membership. Instead of seeing class as an answer to the question "Who *gets* what and how?" it is seen as an answer to the question "Who *does* what and why?" The social

---

26. To use the idiom of rational actor models, the analysis of material interests focuses on the *feasible set* of alternatives facing actors (that is, the mechanisms which determine the trade-offs they face in pursuing material welfare and power), whereas the analysis of lived experiences focuses on the *preference ordering* of actors over this feasible set.

relations of production, in these terms, impose a set of practices on people within those relations. Those common practices systematically generate common experiences, which in turn are the basis for a common set of understandings about the world.

In the abstract model of the pure capitalist mode of production with a polarized relation between the bourgeoisie and the proletariat, there are three critical lived experiences which it can be argued constitute the commonality of the working class. First, and most obviously, there are experiences of being forced to sell one's labor power in order to survive. Showing up at the factory gate, being unable to reproduce oneself without entering the labor market, does not simply define a set of material interests of actors, but a set of experiences as well. Second, and perhaps more controversially, within production itself there is the experience of being dominated, bossed around, within work. Under a set of production conditions in which the critical task for employers is to extract surplus labor from their employees—to turn labor power into effective labor—experiences of domination will be an inherent aspect of the class relation itself.[27] Third, the inability of workers to control the allocation of the social surplus also generates a certain kind of lived experience— the experience of powerlessness in the face of social forces that shape one's destiny. In all of these cases, the critical issue is not the material interests as such which result from these practices, but the experiences, and associated subjectivities, which they generate.

In a way quite parallel to the linkage between material interests and exploitation, these aspects of lived experience are closely tied to the concept of *alienation* in the Marxist tradition. When Marx discusses

---

27. John Roemer has argued forcefully in several places that it is possible to construct a model of something like capitalism in which there is no coercion at the point of production, and thus, he argues, domination within production should not be seen as an inherent aspect of capitalist class relations. To make this argument, however, he has to assume that workers agree to perform a given amount of actual labor (effort) within work and that they do not "cheat" on this contract. Under this assumption, cheating is a deviation from the model that occurs at a lower level of abstraction (as is the case, for example, in cheating within exchange relations among capitalists). The counter-argument to Roemer's position, with which I agree, is that what Roemer is calling "cheating" by workers is inherent in the capital–labor relation by virtue of the antagonistic interests and asymmetries of that relation and is therefore not a problem that only enters at a lower level of abstraction. In the case of cheating among capitalists, because of the essential symmetries in the exchange relation, there is no reason to believe that the cheating is not also symmetrical (that is, each capitalist cheats from the other), and thus cheating need not enter the specification of the exchange relation itself. This is not the case for the performance of labor effort within the labor process. Being told what to do within the labor process and then being monitored sufficiently to see that you do it is therefore built into the capital–labor relation itself. For Roemer's views on these issues, see John Roemer, "New Directions in the Marxian Theory of Class and Exploitation," *Politics and Society*, vol. 11, no. 3 (1982).

alienation in the context of an analysis of what he calls human "species being," he argues how the loss of control over one's labor and over the product of one's labor generates a set of experiences that pervasively dominate one's life. Both exploitation and alienation are rooted in the same relational properties of production, but one is centered primarily around the material interests and the other the life experiences generated out of those practices.

An objection might be raised against this characterization of working-class lived experiences on the grounds that this is a largely *male* characterization. Feminists have correctly pointed out that the lived experience of women in the working class is in many respects distinctively different from that of men. In the present context, this issue is particularly striking for full-time working-class *housewives,* whose lived experience of class is clearly not adequately characterized by saying that they are "forced to sell their labor power in order to survive" or that they are "bossed around within production."[28] Only with respect to the broader experience of powerlessness with respect to the control of the surplus can men and women in the working class be said to share essentially the same "lived experiences," and even here there are probably significant gendered aspects to the experiences in question.[29] Because the lived experiences of women and men are so systematically different within the working class, it is not possible—the argument goes—to construct a meaningful "gender-blind" concept of class experiences.

This objection, I think, is not really to the characterization of the lived experiences linked to classes within the abstract capitalist mode of production as such, but rather to the theoretical legitimacy of that abstract concept itself. What is being questioned is the possibility of formulating an adequate abstract concept of class structure that identifies class mechanisms as such without simultaneously incorporating a gendered dimension in the conceptualization. The objection is thus to the very attempt at producing a gender-blind concept of class—that is, a concept that can be specified independently of any specification of gender mechanisms.

This set of claims, I believe, collapses the different levels of abstraction at which the problem of class structure and its effects can be analyzed: while it is legitimate to insist on the importance of gender for understanding and explaining the *concrete* lived experiences of people, it

---

28. This objection was raised by Barbara Laslett (personal communication).

29. A similar kind of argument could be constructed around the racial or ethnic dimensions of lived experience, or, for that matter, any dimension of lived experience that is linked in one way or another to class (for instance, age).

does not follow from this that gender must be incorporated in the *abstract concept* of class itself. To insist on this incorporation amounts to a denial of the very existence of distinct class and gender mechanisms. The implication is that we should abolish *both* of these concepts altogether and replace them with a single, fused concept, which perhaps could be called "clender" (class-gender). In such an approach people within clender categories may share common lived experiences, but these experiences cannot in any analytically coherent way be disaggregated into the effects of class mechanisms and gender mechanisms; they are the effects of clender mechanisms as such. *If* one believes that this is unlikely to be a useful way of conceptualizing the complex relationship between class and gender, then at this level of abstraction it becomes necessary to define class independently of gender and seek to understand their interactions rather than to merge them into a single, unitary concept.

Within a Marxist class structure concept, at the level of abstraction of the pure capitalist mode of production, there are no "housewives" of "male breadwinners" (but, equally, there are no *male* breadwinners as such). At this level of abstraction, therefore, it is impossible to specify the crucial differences in lived experiences of men and women in the working class that is generated by the concrete *intersection* of class relations and gender relations. In this specific sense, the concept of class is "gender blind" at the level of abstraction of modes of production. This does not mean, it must be stressed, that the concrete analysis of classes that deploys this concept need be gender blind. One can certainly study the ways in which concrete class structures are shaped by the forms of gender relations in the society, for example, or the ways that class and gender jointly shape forms of consciousness and collective action. But within this conceptual framework, gender relations, in general, should not be packed into the abstract concept of class itself.[30] I will thus, throughout this discussion, continue to assume that one can legitimately identify a set of lived experiences associated within abstractly defined common locations within class structures.

As in the case of interest-based concepts of the commonality of class, experience-based concepts are found in a variety of theoretical traditions besides Marxism. Most notably in contemporary social theory,

---

30. There could be special cases in which at the level of abstraction of mode of production gender relations might appropriately be considered a dimension of class structure. This could be the case, for example, in what is sometimes described as a "kinship mode of production" in which the essential social relations of production are constituted in part by gender. In such a situation it might not be possible to even describe the relations of production independently of the gender relations themselves.

Pierre Bourdieu's theory of class relies heavily on such an approach.[31]
Bourdieu attempts to elaborate a view of class around the dual concepts
of class *habitus* and *capital.* A class habitus is defined by a set of
common *conditions* in everyday life which produce common *conditionings* experienced by people and which, in turn, generate a common set
of internalized *dispositions* to act in particular ways. These dispositions
range from *tastes* (the central preoccupation of Bourdieu's book,
Distinction) to receptivities to particular ideological appeals and calls to
action. In Bourdieu's analysis, a class habitus is not simply constituted
within the workplace, but in community, schools, families and other
institutions as well. These institutional settings generate lived experiences (conditionings) over the life cycle which reinforce certain modes
of thought and action and undermine others. The decisive criteria which
distinguish classes are thus not reducible to differences in their material
interests (based on their control over different kinds of capital in
Bourdieu's analysis), but must include differences in their habituses as
well.

Anthony Giddens's analysis of class structure also puts considerable
emphasis on the role of lived experience in the constitution of classes.
For Giddens, classes are the outcome of a process through which economic *categories* (which he does not want to consider proper classes)
defined by market capacities are transformed into collectivities sharing
common lived experiences. He refers to this process as "class structuration." As in Weber's analysis, the location of people in the market—
whether they own property, skills, or mere labor power—determines a
set of material interests. These material interests, however, are insufficient to constitute "classes." In order for these economically determined categories to become classes, there must be some process by
which the lives of people with those interests become structured around
those interests. This can occur through a variety of mechanisms: restrictions on inter- and intragenerational mobility across economic categories provide a basis for the transmission and "reproduction of
common life experiences;"[32] the technical division of labor, especially
between manual and nonmanual labor, generates a set of distinctive
working conditions which define a common set of work experiences;
authority relations generate experiences of command and obedience;

---

31. See especially, Pierre Bourdieu, *Distinction* (Cambridge: Harvard University Press,
1984); "The Social Space and the Genesis of Groups," *Theory and Society*, vol. 14, no. 6
(1985), pp. 723–44; and "What Makes a Social Class?," *Berkeley Journal of Sociology*,
vol. 22 (1987), pp. 1–18.

32. Giddens, *The Class Structure of the Advanced Societies* (New York: Harper and
Row, 1973), p. 108.

and distributive outcomes create common experiences of community and living conditions. To the extent that these various processes of structuration overlap and correspond to the "objective" divisions of market capacities, then distinctive classes will be constituted in a class structure.[33]

One of the most explicit statements of this general approach in the Marxist tradition is found in E.P. Thompson's well-known discussion of class in *The Making of the English Working Class*:

> I do not see class as a "structure," nor even as a "category," but as something which in fact happens (and can be shown to have happened) in human relationships. . . . And class happens when some men, as a result of common experiences (inherited or shared), feel and articulate the identity of their interests as between themselves, and as against other men whose interests are different (and usually opposed) to theirs. The class experience is largely determined by the productive relations into which men are born—or enter voluntarily.[34]

While the category "interests" does enter into Thompson's statement, it is treated as a subjective category conceptually subordinated to the commonality of experiences rooted in common conditions of work and life. It is around these common experiences that the concept of class revolves.

2.3 Collective Capacity

Commonalities of interests and experiences are certainly the principal ways that Marxists ground the concept of class. But there is a third way

---

33. Similar kinds of arguments are made by other theorists commonly regarded as working in the Weberian tradition. David Lockwood, in *The Blackcoated Worker* (London: Routledge and Kegan Paul, 1958), builds a class structure concept around the dual dimensions of "market situation" and "work situation." The market situation dimension follows fairly closely the traditional Weberian account of market capacities based on different kinds of property (capital, skills, labor power). The theoretical status of the "work situation" dimension is somewhat less clear, but it seems that it is meant to tap the ways in which common working conditions are linked to common identities, presumably via the kinds of workplace experiences such conditions generate. It is at least partially on this basis that Lockwood argues that routinized white collar jobs are in a separate class from manual workers, even if under certain circumstances their material interests are essentially the same. Similar kinds of arguments are made by John Goldthorpe in his various analyses of the service class. See especially his essay, "On the Service Class: Its Formation and Future," in Anthony Giddens and Gavin McKenzie (eds), *Social Class and the Division of Labour* (Cambridge: Cambridge University Press, 1982), pp. 162–85.

34. E.P. Thompson, *The Making of the English Working Class* (Harmondsworth: Penguin, 1968), pp. 9–10.

which, while usually deployed in combination with one of the first two, is also important. The essential commonality of a class is sometimes seen as derived from its potential capacity for collective action. In particular, one of the central properties of the working class, it is often claimed, is that it has the potential capacity to organize collectively to overthrow capitalism and transform the social relations of production into socialism. In this view, the social relations of production do not merely distribute material interests or the pattern of lived experiences across classes; they also distribute a range of resources which underlie the potentials for collective action. For a category of agents to truly constitute a class they would have to at least have the potential capacity to organize society in their interests.

For Marx, the peasantry in mid-nineteenth-century France was not really a class precisely because it lacked any capacity for this kind of systemic collective action. In his view, while peasants may have shared common material interests and conditions of life (and thus, by implication, common experiences), they were so atomized and fragmented that they could not constitute a collectivity capable of transformative struggle. They were, in his words, like a sack of potatoes, remaining discrete individuals even when grouped together.[35] The working class, on the other hand, was seen by Marx to have this capacity for collective transformative struggle for two main reasons: first, workers were the direct producers of society's wealth and thus they collectively possessed the necessary knowledge to organize social production; and second, the concentration and centralization of capital generated by capitalism brought masses of workers into contact and interdependency with one another which generated the kind of solidarity and organizational capacity needed to challenge capitalist power.

Occasionally one does find this kind of argument outside of strictly Marxist approaches to class. Alvin Gouldner's analysis of the "New Class" in capitalist societies, and Ivan Szelenyi's and George Konrad's analysis of Eastern Europe intellectuals, both treat the *potential* for becoming a ruling class as an essential element in the claim that intel-

---

35. Marx, of course, may have been wrong in this judgment about the collective capacity of peasants. The point here is that he used the criterion of collective capacity as a way of distinguishing a full-fledged class from what might be called a proto-class. If we use the classical Marxist distinction between a class-in-itself (a class structurally defined) and a class-for-itself (a class collectively organized for struggle), then Marx is saying that a class-in-itself only exists even as a *class*-in-itself if it has the potential of becoming a class-for-itself.

RETHINKING THE CONCEPT OF CLASS STRUCTURE

lectuals should be treated as a class in the first place.[36] In more Marxist analyses, this same kind of argument is sometimes used to justify the claim that routinized office workers and unproductive laborers should not be considered to be working class: while they may share certain basic interests with workers, some theorists claim that they are not part of the collective capacity to transform and organize society, and thus they are not properly part of the working class as such.

2.4 Levels of Abstraction and the Commonality of Class Locations

At the highest level of abstraction of class analysis, all three of these effects of class relations are credible candidates for the essential criteria defining the commonality of class locations. At the level of abstraction of the capitalist mode of production, one can make plausible arguments that there is a certain kind of commonality of material interests, lived experiences, and capacities for collective action that are generated directly by the social relations of production as such. That is, the social relations of production in the capitalist mode of production directly determine certain critical aspects of interests, experiences, and capacities of actors defined by those relations. For the working class, for example, we can say that their location within capitalist social relations of production analyzed at the most abstract level directly determines:

1. a set of material interests opposed to those of capitalists by virtue of the relation of exploitation between them;

2. a set of common lived experiences bound up with selling labor power, being dominated within the labor process and being excluded from control over the social surplus;

3. a set of collective capacities for struggle rooted in the inter-dependencies among workers within the labor process and the centrality of workers to the overall process of social production.

If we were exclusively interested in analyzing capitalism abstractly as a mode of production, then we could probably treat the concept of class structure as built simultaneously around all three of these commonalities (although we might still want to give interests and experiences a logical

---

36. See George Konrad and Ivan Szelenyi, *Intellectuals on the Road to Class Power* (New York: Harcourt, Brace and Jovanovich, 1978), and Alvin Gouldner, *Intellectuals and the Rise of the New Class* (New York: Seabury Press, 1979).

priority over capacities within the concept of class structure).[37] The problem occurs when we try to move to lower levels of abstraction, particularly when we want to do so in a way that is analytically powerful at the micro level of analysis.

When class is analyzed at a relatively concrete, micro level of analysis there is no longer necessarily a simple coincidence of material interests, lived experience and collective capacity. As theorists who see lived experience as the pivotal issue in class analysis stress, the lived experiences of workers within the production process (let alone within the society at large) cannot be derived even in a complex way simply from their location within the abstractly defined relations of production as such. The same can be said for collective capacities. This means that when we specify the social relations of production at a relatively concrete, micro level of analysis, people occupying a common location within those relations will nevertheless have different lived experiences and collective capacities.[38]

---

37. Even at this abstract level of analysis, the capacity dimension of class analysis should be conceptually subordinated to the interests and experiences dimensions. Unless we have specified the interests of actors and their subjective understandings of the world, it makes little sense to describe their capacities to act as *class* capacities. Capacities to act are always relative to a set of interests and motivations, and these are derived from the first two dimensions. In order to even describe a class capacity as an instance of *working-class* capacity one must have a logically prior specification of the interests and/or experiences which define workers as workers. Interests and experiences thus have a logical priority over capacities.

38. In classical Marxism there was a general belief that at the concrete level of analysis these three conceptual foundations for class structure analysis had an historical tendency towards convergence for the working class in capitalist society: the category of agents sharing common material interests by virtue of capitalist exploitation progressively came to share increasingly profound common lived experiences by virtue of the progressive homogenization and proletarianization of working conditions, while at the same time their capacity for collective action was enhanced by the increasing concentration and centralization of capital. The structural boundaries of material interests, lived experience and collective capacity at the concrete and abstract levels of analysis thus had a tendency to increasingly coincide in the course of capitalist development.

Relatively few Marxists today accept this vision of the trajectory of capitalism and its implications for the analysis of class structure. Instead of becoming ever more polarized, the class structure appears to be becoming increasingly complex and differentiated, with an accompanying differentiation of material interests among employees. The lived experiences of employees both within production and outside of production have if anything become increasingly heterogeneous, rather than homogeneous. And the capacity for revolutionary transformation has become sufficiently problematic, at least in developed capitalist societies, that it seems hard to treat it as a decisive criterion of class structure analysis, even aside from the problem of the disjuncture between interests and experience. Whatever else one might want to say about the class structures of advanced capitalism, there does not seem to be a powerful tendency for simultaneous, overlapping polarization in terms of material interests, lived experiences and capacity for transformative struggle.

In light of this failure for interests, experiences and capacities to co-incide at the concrete level of analysis, class theorists face several choices. One possibility is to simply abandon the concept of an objectively given class structure altogether. This is essentially the position of Adam Przeworski, particularly in some of his more recent writings.[39] Classes are not structured prior to struggle; they are strictly the effects of the strategies of collectively organized actors, especially political parties. While those strategies may themselves be conditioned by the legacies of past struggles and by a host of structural properties of the society—political institutions, legal institutions, property relations—they are not conditioned by the distribution of people into an objectively given class structure as such. The "objectively" defined working class—whatever be the specific definition of that class—has no more "natural affinity" to support the socialist party than any other category of agents.[40]

Few class analysts have followed Przeworski's lead in categorically rejecting the concept of class structure. Most class theorists continue to believe that objectively constituted class relations are important for understanding material interests and/or lived experiences and/or collective capacities, and our theoretical task is to figure out appropriate ways of conceptualizing these relations.

A second general strategy for contending for the concrete non-coincidence of class interests, experiences and capacities would be to escalate the complexity of the concept of class structure at the concrete level of analysis by retaining all three aspects of the commonality of class location but allowing them to vary independently of each other. We

---

39. In Przeworski's earlier writings on the working class, he seemed to suggest that classes had a structural foundation that existed independently of the strategies of parties and other collective actors. Thus, for example, in his initial essay on social democratic voting, he defends the adoption of a narrow definition of the working class as manual industrial wage-earners, not simply because this was the view of socialist party activists, but also because this definition reflected a line of real division in the society: "But the specific definition also involves a bet on our part: a hypothesis that the line of sharpest divisions, of interest and values, lies between narrowly defined manual workers and other wage-earners" (*Capitalism and Social Democracy*, Cambridge: Cambridge University Press (1985), p. 105). In the final version of this argument, appearing in his coauthored book with John Sprague, *Paper Stones* (Chicago: University of Chicago Press, 1986), this claim to an objective status of the manual/nonmanual divide is dropped, and class definitions are viewed strictly as the outcome of the strategic choices of collective actors.

40. If one were to follow this line of thought in a completely consistent manner, then the *empirical* affinity of the working class for socialist and other progressive political orientations would be seen simply as the cumulative effect of the historical trajectory of ideologies, programs, and strategies of party elites. Since parties from the start mobilized "workers" on the basis of a discourse of class, parties today are to a greater or lesser extent constrained by the legacies of these past ideologically driven practices of mobilization.

could then define a kind of three-dimensional class structure space consisting of: class-interest structure, class-experience structure, and class-capacity structure. At the mode of production level of abstraction these three dimensions coincide: agents defined with respect to the class interest dimension of class structure also share common class experience and class capacity. At the lower levels of abstraction, the overlap of the three dimensions declines thus allowing for a much wider array of structural "locations" defined by the disjunctures between interests, experiences, and capacities.

This solution to the problem of the concrete noncoincidence of interests, experiences, and capacities adds such complexity to the concept of class structure that it risks adding more confusion than clarification. But there is an additional reason why I do not think it is a viable general strategy for dealing with these problems, at least at the current state of our theoretical knowledge: while there are a range of strategies for deriving concrete material interests from the abstract concept of class relations, I know of no parallel way of deriving concrete lived experiences and collective capacities.

As we shall see in section 3, on the basis of material interests, there are a number of specific analytical strategies for producing class structure concepts at lower levels of abstraction from the pure mode of production. For example, concrete class structures can be treated as specific combinations of different modes of production (or, equivalently for present purposes, types of production relations or types of exploitation). Within such a concrete class structure concept, different specific class locations and the material interests associated with them, are defined by the intersection of these multiple production relations in jobs filled by individuals.

I know of no comparable analytical strategy for producing a concrete concept of class structure built around collective capacities and lived experiences. One might try to construct such a strategy in a way analogous to the strategy based on interests just described. One could argue, for example, that there are distinctive forms of collective capacity or lived experience linked to each type of production relation, and thus the commonality of the class locations formed by the intersection of production relations is defined by a collective capacity or lived experience emerging out of the separate capacities/experiences associated with each relation taken separately. Such a strategy, however, seems implausible at best, and in any event, to my knowledge no one has even attempted constructing such a derivation of concrete experiences and capacities from abstract relational categories. For the moment, therefore, the only coherent way that I know of to generate systematically concrete concepts of class structure from the abstract concept of mode of production is via the category of material interests.[41]

This conclusion should not cause great dismay to theorists for whom the category of lived experience is seen as central to understanding social conflict and social change in class analysis. First of all, this conceptual strategy does not mean that lived experience has been banned from the concept of class structure altogether (let alone from class analysis in general). Lived experience is still an integral part of the *abstract* concept of class structure, and thus remains embodied in the concrete concepts as well (since they are all nested within the abstract concept). The point is that whereas the concrete, micro-level concepts of class structure attempt to embody a more complex and differentiated mapping of the material interests of actors than the abstract concept, they retain the relatively thin understanding of their lived experiences associated with the more abstract concept.[42]

Second, to reiterate a point already made, to say that concrete concepts of class structure can most systematically be built around exploitation and material interests does not in any way prejudge the *explanatory* importance of material interests relative to lived experience

---

41. It should be noted that this argument in favor of deriving concrete class structure concepts on the basis of material interests is somewhat different from the one I offered earlier in reply to Johanna Brenner's criticisms (see pp. 210–11). There I argued that since the lived experiences of workers were drastically different in different times and places, it seemed implausible to build a map of class structure on a logic of commonalities of such experiences, whereas it was possible to build such a map around material interests. It now seems to me that while my conclusion may have been justified, my arguments were not entirely on the mark. In the earlier argument against a concrete lived-experience based concept of class structure I was assuming a quite rich profile of lived experiences—one that included all of the diverse experiences generated by the practices of actors within production analyzed at a relatively low level of abstraction (since it is only at a concrete level that, for example, workers in Japan, South Africa, and the United States are distinguishable). The analysis I offered of material interests, in contrast, was based on arguments about mechanisms of exploitation analyzed at the highest levels of abstraction of class structure analysis. If the material interests of workers had been analyzed at the same level of abstraction as experiences, then they would also have been characterized by considerable contingency and heterogeneity (due to the specific circumstances of jobs, geographical location, industrial sector, not to mention things like race and gender). The real issue, then, is the extent to which we can construct a concrete concept of class structure based on material interests that is systematically derived from the more abstract concept, whereas we cannot do this for lived experiences, at least at the present stage of theoretical development.

42. That is, in the concrete micro-analysis of the working class, the lived experiences that we attribute to them directly by virtue of their *class* location are based on the abstract concept of class structure. No new complexity in the analysis of experiences is systematically added by moving to the more concrete and micro-analysis of class structure as such (although, of course, a rich array of new elements can enter the concrete analysis of lived experience by virtue of other principles besides class structure). In the case of material interests, by contrast, the concrete analysis embodies a much more complex picture of the matrix of these interests than is found in the abstract analysis.

or collective capacity. It could be the case, for example, that the most important cause of variations in the degree of militancy of working classes across countries is variations in their collective capacity for struggle or variations in the lived experiences within production, not their material interests as such. If anything, the identification of class *structure* with exploitation and material interests would facilitate discovering this conclusion (assuming, of course, that it is correct) since it acknowledges the independent explanatory potential of experience and capacity.[43]

Finally, in practice theorists who see lived experience as the pivotal category for class analysis generally do not narrowly tie lived experience to the relations *of* production. Thus, the kinds of lived experiences which they emphasize are not really candidates for inclusion in the concept of class structure as such anyway. For example, Michael Burawoy argues that the critical kinds of lived experiences that shape class consciousness of workers are determined by the social relations *in* production, rather than the social relations *of* production. In particular, they are generated by what he calls the political apparatuses of production which shape the forms of competition among workers and interactions with bosses on the shop floor.[44] Or, to take another example, Ira Katznelson places the ongoing lived experiences of workers at the core of his analysis of class formation. But for him the critical complex of experiences centers on the interrelationships between work and community, between the experiences workers have on and off the job. While the social life of working-class communities may be shaped in various ways by the social relations of production, they are not part of, or derivable from, those relations, and thus do not constitute part of class structure as such.[45] In terms of these kinds of analyses of lived experience, the decision to build the concrete, micro-level concepts of class structure around the problem of material interests does not in any way marginalize their central theoretical concerns.

I will therefore follow a general strategy of trying to elaborate the concept of class structure at a more micro and concrete level of analysis on the basis of the linkage between material interests and the social relations of production. I will try to do so in a way that is consistent with the more abstract concept of class structure as embodying lived experiences and collective capacities in addition to material interests, but these

---

43. It should be also noted that building the concrete concept of class structure around the dimension of material interests does not prejudge the relative explanatory importance of aspects of lived experience generated by mechanisms other than class (gender, race, nationality, etc.).

44. See Burawoy, *The Politics of Production*.

45. See Ira Katznelson, *City Trenches* (New York: Pantheon, 1981).

will not directly be the basis for the production of the more concrete micro concepts.

3 Attempts at Building an Adequate Map of the Class Structure

The decision to ground the production of concrete concepts of class structure in an account of relationally generated, antagonistic class interests is only a point of departure. A wide variety of specific strategies for actually elaborating the substantive content of such a class concept and developing an explicit set of criteria for class structural analysis are consistent with such a decision.

In my own work I have explored two different general approaches to this problem. These can be referred to as the *contradictory locations* approach and the *multidimensional exploitation* approach.[46] Both of these strategies are attempts at providing a positive theorization to the category "middle class" within an essentially interest-based framework. Each of these solutions, in my judgment, has attractive features to them, but—alas—each has serious problems as well. In what follows I will very briefly outline the central arguments of each approach and lay out their central weaknesses and strengths. I will then discuss the apparent attractiveness of neo-Weberian solutions and explain why I feel they do not offer a cogent alternative.

3.1 The First Solution: Contradictory Locations

Most class structure concepts are built on the unstated premiss that there is a one-to-one mapping between "locations" in a class structure (the places filled by human individuals) and "classes" themselves: every location is in one and only one class. In capitalist society this implies that everyone must be located in the working class, the capitalist class, the petty bourgeoisie or, perhaps, some entirely "new" class (appropriately called by some theorists, therefore, the "New Class"). The concept of contradictory locations within class relations was an attempt at breaking with this assumption: some locations in a class structure might be in two or more classes simultaneously. Managers, for example, could be understood as simultaneously in the working class and the capitalist class: they

---

46. In *Classes* I referred to both of these strategies as involving contradictory locations: "contradictory locations within *class* relations" for the first strategy, and "contradictory locations within *exploitation* relations" for the second. In the present context, the discussion will be facilitated by using the expression "multidimensional exploitation" for the second strategy.

were in the working class insofar as they had to sell their labor power in order to obtain their livelihood; they were in the capitalist class insofar as they dominated workers within production. And since the class interests of workers and capitalists were inherently antagonistic, a dual class location that combined these two classes was dubbed a "contradictory location within class relations."[47]

How can it be that a concrete location in a class structure can be simultaneously in two classes? Within a relational concept of class, class locations are positions-within-relations. In order for it to make sense to see a "location" as simultaneously in two (or more) "classes", therefore, it must be the case that class relations themselves are multidimensional or multifaceted.

In order to understand this claim, it is necessary to clarify briefly what I mean by the term "social relation." What is related within a social relation is not, strictly speaking, either a set of "positions" or a set of actual people as such, but rather a set of *practices*: social relations link practices to each other. The capital–labor relation defines a systematic relation between the practices of capitalists and workers within that relation. Conceptually, we cannot even define the practices of capitalists without reference to their connection to the practices of workers: capitalists *employ* workers who *sell* their labor power to capitalists. The verbs "employ" and "sell" designate relational practices in that they imply interacting practices of distinct agents. While for simplicity it is often useful to refer to social relations as binding together the people within the relation, this should be understood as a somewhat elliptical way of talking about the interactions among their practices.

To talk about the multidimensionality of a relation, therefore, is equivalent to talking about the multidimensionality of the practices structured within that relation. What we call the "capital–labor relation" should thus be viewed as a package of relational practices. In these terms, then, managers would occupy the bourgeois location within one aspect or dimension of these relational practices and the proletarian location within another.

That was the basic intuition underlying the conceptual strategy of contradictory locations. I elaborated this intuition in a variety of somewhat different ways.[48] These differences are not particularly important in the present context. The common thread was the view that the

---

47. At roughly the same time as I was elaborating the concept of contradictory class locations, G. Carchedi was working on essentially the same underlying insight in his functional definition of the new middle class as being constituted by the simultaneous presence of the "functions" of capital and of labor. See Carchedi, *The Economic Identification of Social Classes* (London: Routledge and Kegan Paul, 1977).

48. For a specific review of the development of the concept, see ch. 2 of *Classes*.

concept of "class relation" had two primary dimensions: property or ownership relations and possession or control relations. The former was linked to the concept of exploitation; the latter to the concept of domination. Managers occupied a capitalist location within control relations (that is, they dominated workers), but a working-class location within ownership relations (that is, they sold their labor power to capitalists).

This framework emerged as a specific solution to the problem of managers in the class structure. It was subsequently modified to try to accommodate the problem of professionals, experts, and credentialed specialists and technicians of various sorts. How should these kinds of jobs be located within a class structure? Unlike managers, they did not directly control workers, and thus could not easily be placed in the capitalist location on the domination dimension of class relations. By the logic of the concept of contradictory locations they thus did not seem to be simultaneously in the capitalist class and the working class. And yet, at least at an intuitive level, it did not seem appropriate to consider such jobs as simply an integral part of the working class.

The solution I came up with was to consider these class locations as simultaneously working class and *petty* bourgeoisie. This means that, rather than being a contradictory location *within* a given "mode" of production" (that is, within capitalist relations of production), they were a contradictory location that combined elements from two distinct kinds of production relations: capitalist relations and what is sometimes called petty commodity production relations. That is, expert/professional employees were petty bourgeois in so far as they had direct control over their *own* labor process (self-direction or autonomy within work), but were proletarian in so far as they had to sell their labor power to an employer in order to work. For want of a better expression, I called such positions "semiautonomous employees."

Finally, to complete the picture, small employers were characterized as a contradictory location that combined petty bourgeois and capitalist relations. Like the petty bourgeoisie they were direct producers working alongside their employees, but like capitalists they were exploiters of workers.

This first strategy of building a class structural concept capable of systematically handling the "middle class" has a number of attractive features. First, it is a strongly relational concept. The definitions of different class locations—both fundamental classes and contradictory locations—are all specified in relational terms. This is especially clear in the case of managers. But even for semiautonomous employees, the attempt was made to define the distinct social relations of petty commodity production and then incorporate this into the definition of their class location.

Secondly, while the concept of contradictory location was built around the interest-logic of class relations, it also suggested a particular set of experience-generating mechanisms linked to class. Domination and autonomy are aspects of work settings that are closely tied to daily experiences within production. The concept of contradictory locations thus managed to capture at a lower level of class structure analysis at least the thin notion of lived experience embodied in the more abstract concept. If we want the concept of class to provide a basis for linking material interests and lived experiences, then this particular strategy of analysis provides at least some foundations for this endeavor.

Finally, the idea of contradictory locations introduced into class analysis a desirable kind of explanatory indeterminacy. One of the purposes of trying to develop a more refined class structural concept was to facilitate analyses of the relationship between class structure and class formation, in which class formations were not seen as simply derivative of class structures. What was needed, then, was a class structural concept which systematically allowed for other causal factors to play a role in the translation of class structures into class formations. The concept of contradictory locations helps to open up this theoretical space. Since many locations in the class structure have dual (and even contradictory) class logics, this implies that their translation into class formations will be contingent upon social processes which mobilize action around one or another of these poles. This gives a theoretically specific, rather than just an ad hoc, role for political and ideological determinants of class formation.

Nevertheless, in spite of these strengths, the concept of contradictory locations quickly ran into difficulties. I will briefly mention only three of these here:

1. *Domination and exploitation* While in the rhetoric of the concept of contradictory locations, exploitation is treated as the basic interest-generating mechanism within class structures, nevertheless it does not actually enter into the specification of the class map in a very systematic manner. In practice the central novel categories of the analysis—managers and semiautonomous employees as contradictory locations within class relations—are both defined exclusively in terms of *domination* relations, not exploitation as such. This is not to deny that domination relations are an essential aspect of class structures in the Marxist tradition. But the analysis of domination should by systematically linked to exploitation, whereas in the development of the concept of contradictory class locations domination had effectively displaced exploitation.

2. *The state*   The concept did not offer a satisfactory way of dealing with the problem of the state in the analysis of capitalist class structures. This had two practical implications. First, the criteria used to define managers and semiautonomous employees within the capital–labor relation were simply applied to state employment with no modification or justification. Given that classes are supposed to be defined within distinctive types of social relations of production, it was at best a weakness of the framework that state employment was simply amalgamated to capitalist relations. Second, the lack of systematic elaboration of the problem of classes within the state also meant that the framework was unable to define the specificity of classes in post-capitalist, "state socialist" societies. Given that the concept of contradictory locations was meant to provide a general strategy for studying class structures in different kinds of societies, some way of dealing with the problem of class in such societies was needed.

3. *Operationalizations*   At a practical level, it was exceptionally difficult to operationalize for empirical research one of the contradictory locations that figured in the general conceptual framework: the category "semiautonomous employees". Autonomy within the labor process proved to be an extremely elusive concept; all attempts at operationalizing it had a suspiciously gradational (rather than relational) quality to them, and none of these attempts seemed reliable. Of course, operational difficulties need not invalidate an abstract concept, but they do tend to generate skepticism about the adequacy of the conceptualizations. At a minimum they undermine the usefulness of the conceptualization for the concrete investigation of class structure which was, after all, one of the central reasons for developing the new concepts in the first place.

3.2 The Second Solution: Multiple Exploitations

Given these conceptual problems, and a deepening sense that I could not effectively pursue my empirical research without resolving them, I attempted in various ways to elaborate an alternative general strategy. The steps in this initial rethinking the concept of class structure have been discussed thoroughly elsewhere, so I will not go into the details here. [49]

The basic idea of the new solution has been discussed a variety of times earlier in this book: different "modes of production" are based on

---

49. See *Classes*, ch. 3.

distinctive mechanisms of exploitation which can be differentiated on the basis of the kind of productive asset the unequal ownership (or control) of which enables the exploiting class to appropriate part of the socially produced surplus. Building on the work of Roemer, I distinguished four types of assets, the unequal ownership or control of which constituted the basis of distinct forms of exploitation: labor power assets (feudal exploitation), capital assets (capitalist exploitation), organization assets (statist exploitation), and skill or credential assets (socialist exploitation).[50] While pure modes of production can be identified with single forms of exploitation, actual societies always consist of different forms of combination of the different mechanisms of exploitation. This opens up the possibility that certain locations in the class structure are simultaneously exploited through one mechanism of exploitation but exploiters through another mechanism. Such positions, I argued, constitute the "middle class" of a given society. In capitalism the key instances of such locations are managers (who are capitalistically exploited but organization exploiters) and experts (who are capitalistically exploited but skill/credential exploiters).[51]

At the time I formalized this second strategy for solving the puzzle of the middle class, I felt that it had a number of theoretical advantages over the earlier concept of contradictory locations within class relations.

First, unlike in the earlier concept, exploitation-based interests occupy center stage. Claims about different mechanisms of exploitation are systematically deployed to define locations within a class structural matrix. While it was still the case that I never attempted to directly operationalize exploitation as such—the class map is built around relations to exploitation-generating *assets* rather than exploitation *per se*—nevertheless, exploitation was the organizing principle for the overall class structural analysis.

Second, the new formulation has a much stronger connection to the general Marxist theory of history, historical materialism, than did the earlier framework. The structural typology on which the class structure map was based had a clear standing within a general theory of the historical trajectory of social forms. The "sequence" feudalism–capitalism–statism–socialism could be characterized as a *logical* sequence of successive eliminations (or at least marginalization) of

---

50. For specific definitions of each of these forms of exploitation, see this volume, pp. 14–22.

51. Note that in the new framework, managers are not simultaneously in the bourgeois class and the working class, as in the original conceptual solution; rather, they are simultaneously in an organization-asset exploiting class and in the working class. They are not part of the bourgeoisie at all.

specific forms of exploitation.[52] This conceptual typology also gave the problem of the middle class a distinctive historical cast: the middle class of a society dominated by one mode of production was the principal contender for being the dominant class in the subsequent mode of production. The emergent bourgeoisie was the pivotal middle class of feudalism and the managerial-bureaucratic "class" is the central middle class of capitalism.

Third, it seemed that this new formulation also coped with the problem of the state more effectively than the original contradictory locations approach. At least it became possible to identify a specific form of exploitation (organization exploitation) and associated class relations with what is sometimes called a "statist mode of production."

Fourth, I initially thought that the shift from a domination-centered to an exploitation-centered concept of class structure avoided the messy operational problems that had been generated by the concept of "semi-autonomy." Rather than trying to situate professionals and experts in the class structure via the slippery concept of their self-direction within work, they were now situated with respect to their capacity to appropriate the surplus due to their monopoly of certain skills, particularly when this monopoly was legally certified through credentials.

Finally, as a kind of fringe benefit from this reconceptualization, the new class concept provided a particularly nuanced empirical map for studying the relationship between class structure and class formation. In the case of capitalist society, by introducing three distinct dimensions of the class structure—dimensions based on capital assets, organization assets and skill assets—the picture of class structure can become quite differentiated. The proliferation of concrete structural "locations" within this map allows for a much more subtle empirical investigation of the ways in which people within these locations become collectively organized into class formations.[53]

These seemed like substantial theoretical gains, and thus, while I recognized from the start that there were problems with the new

---

52. This is a logical sequence rather than an historical one, since there is no pre-supposition that actual societies must pass through these forms in a rigid, linear fashion. "Stages" can be skipped, and, perhaps, the actual order could be altered. If, for example, capitalism is restored in certain state socialist societies, one might interpret this as a reversal of two elements of the logical sequence.

53. Once it is no longer assumed that there is a one-to-one relationship between class structure and class formation—that is, that class structures impose limits on class for-mations but do not determine unique outcomes—then there is a considerable empirical pay-off for having a highly disaggregated picture of the class structure itself, since this allows for a more fine-grained description of the different ways in which these differ-entiated structural positions are actually formed into collectively organized coalitions.

concept, I enthusiastically reoriented my empirical work around it.[54] It now seems to me that these problems are more significant than I originally realized. In particular, I would stress the following issues, some of which have been brought up in certain of the essays in this book:

1. *Skill exploitation*   As I already indicated in my discussion of skill exploitation in Chapter 5 of this volume, there is a basic conceptual problem in treating surplus appropriation rooted in the ownership of skills or credentials as "exploitation" which does not exist for capitalist or feudal exploitation. An employee in a capitalist firm who has a high level of scarce skills (that is, skills which are scarce relative to their demand on the market), whether or not that scarcity is institutionalized through credentials, performs labor, and thus contributes to the social surplus. [55] When such an employee appropriates part of the social surplus through wages that are above the costs of reproducing labor power, the most natural way of describing the outcome is that this person has been able to appropriate part of the surplus which he or she produced. That is, instead of saying that this employee is an exploiter of unskilled labor power as is posited in the skill-exploitation concept, it would make more sense to say that they are simply *less* exploited by capitalists.

Of course, it could happen that certain credential holders are able to appropriate so much surplus that they become, in fact, net exploiters: they could retain all of the surplus which they produce and appropriate surplus from others. The problem is that since this appropriation remains entirely contingent upon the actual performance of labor by the credential holder, there is no simple way of distinguishing those credential holders who are real exploiters from those who are simply "privileged" by virtue of being less exploited than other employees.

This problem with skill exploitation is not simply the result of the fact that the "level" of skills varies more or less continuously (although this gradational quality to the distribution of the asset in question certainly adds to the problem). Imagine a world in which capital assets were normally distributed, with many employees owning nontrivial amounts of capital. While this would certainly affect the overall shape of the class

---

54. In *Classes* I wrote a section called "Once again, Unresolved Problems" in an effort to try to clarify the problematic aspects of the multiple-exploitations approach. At the time I treated these problems as unfinished tasks.

55. I am ignoring the problem of "unproductive" labor within the framework of the labor theory of value in this discussion, because it is not relevant to the analytical points being made. Even if one accepts the labor theory of value and the accompanying concept of unproductive labor, the issues raised here would still apply for credentialed *productive* labor.

structure, it would not pose the conceptual difficulties of skill assets since the income derived from the sheer ownership of capital inherently constitutes an exploitative transfer, that is, it involves the appropriation of surplus produced by others.[56] In this imaginery world, since many capital owners also perform labor and therefore contribute to the surplus as well, it may be difficult in some cases to ascertain whether or not a given capital owner is a *net* exploiter. It could happen, for example, that in some situations an owner of capital produces more surplus as a laborer than she or he appropriates as a capitalist. Nevertheless, even in such unusual and ambiguous situations, the capitalist in question is still unambiguously a *capitalist* exploiter by virtue of the transfers linked to capital ownership. It would therefore make sense to describe such a person as a capitalist exploiter by virtue of owning capital, and capitalistically exploited by virtue of selling labor power. In contrast, in the case of skill exploitation, one cannot distinguish the mechanism through which the individual appropriates their own surplus and the surplus of others.

Another way of stating this problem with skill exploitation is that the idea of credential or skill-based classes is less relational than the idea of capital-based classes. Knowing that a person owns capital intrinsically sets that person into a social relation with workers. That is, their practices as an owner of capital are inherently linked relationally to the practices of workers. This is true whether the capitalist in question is an actual employer (in which case the social relation in question is a quite direct linkage between employer and worker) or merely a rentier coupon-clipper owning stocks (in which case the relation between capitalist and worker is mediated through a series of other relations).

In the case of skill owners, there is not necessarily an inherent social relation that binds them to the unskilled in the required way. The possession of a skill or credential may help to constitute a distinctive kind of social relation with employers, reflected in the description that skill holders are "less exploited" than the unskilled, but this does not necessarily imply a social relation built around antagonistic material interests with the unskilled themselves. Such antagonisms *may* exist, of

---

56. This is not a completely watertight specification of exploitation, since it is possible to define certain specific conditions in which the appropriation of surplus via the ownership of capital might not be properly considered exploitation. Thus, for example, if workers' pensions are invested in shares in corporations, and if workers actually had ownership rights to those shares once they retired—suppose they could sell them and keep the "capital gains"—one might want to treat the flow of income to the workers derived from such ownership as a recuperation of past exploitation rather than exploitation in its own right. For present purposes, however, I do not think that such complications need to be introduced.

course, but they are not inherent in the relations that define owners of skills/credentials as such. Thus, credentials are a relatively ambiguous basis for defining a *class* relation, at least if we want the concept of class to be built around relations of exploitation.

2. *Capitalist managers and statism*   One of the implications of the multiple exploitations view of the middle class which has aroused the most skepticism concerns the alleged interests of managers within capitalism. If it is correct to claim that managers are simultaneously exploited by capitalists and yet organizational exploiters, then it follows that in principle they should have an objective material interest in the elimination of capitalist exploitation and the creation of a society within which organizational exploitation was the primary basis of class relations.[57] That is, it was claimed that there was an objective basis for managers to be anticapitalist and prostatist. What is more, this objective interest in statism should increase as one moves up managerial hierarchies, as the control over organizational assets becomes greater.

This characterization of managers flies in the face of most historical evidence. Undaunted, I argued that the obvious support of capitalism by managers in general, and by top managers and executives in particular, reflected the strength of capitalist "hegemony." Hegemony, in these terms is a situation in which one class is able to materially link the interests of other classes to its own. Above all, a hegemonic class attempts to tie the interests of potential rival classes to its interests as a way of neutralizing their latent opposition. In the case of managers this is accomplished through the organization of managerial careers and the

---

57. In a personal communication, Philippe Van Parijs points out that even if managers were properly described as organization exploiters, it does not necessarily follow that they should empirically be anticapitalist. He writes: "Roemer's exploitation criterion explicitly abstracts from the incentive effects of various types of production relations. Managers as a class may be capitalistically exploited (because of a below-average capital endowment) and yet lose out if capital assets were equally distributed if it turned out that the system would perform less efficiently (even after the transition period). The most powerful explanation of the managers' antisocialist alliance with capitalists, however, is probably that even if the total surplus were not to drop as a result of introducing [socialism], and even if, *as a class*, managers would (or might) then have a stronger hold on that surplus, there is a greater (or even greater) uncertainty as to whether, *as individuals*, their lot will be improved, because the demise of the people who granted them their organizational assets is likely to jeopardize their possession of these assets, and hence their sharing in whatever benefits the managerial class may gain from the change." While I think Van Parijs's comments are well taken, nevertheless since one of the main reasons for producing concrete class structure concepts was to facilitate the analysis of class formation, the staunchness of the opposition of managers, especially high-level corporate managers, to either statist or socialist organizations of production, does undermine the credibility of conceptualizing them as organizational-asset exploiters.

ability of managers to buy their way into the bourgeoisie (through investments, stock ownership, etc.). Such strategies, however, do not obliterate the latent conflicts of interest, but merely contain them within narrow limits. Under conditions of sustained capitalist crisis in which the material basis for this hegemonic integration of management declined, I argued, an anticapitalist statist politics of management could become an historical possibility.

This kind of argument sounds very much like special pleading. While it is not unthinkable that historical circumstances could arise in which managers in general would adopt a statist critique of capitalism, this possibility seems like a weak basis for understanding the essential class character of managers in capitalism itself.

In these terms, the original intuitions of the concept of contradictory class locations seem much sounder. In that framework it was quite natural that managers should have strong tendencies towards a pro-capitalist ideological orientation, and that these tendencies should increase as one moved toward the top of managerial hierarchies. Managers were theorized as simultaneously in the capitalist class and the working class, the balance between these two poles shifting towards the former as one moved up the hierarchy. Within this conceptual field, top managers and executives, therefore, would be expected to be resolutely procapitalist because they are fundamentally part of the bourgeoisie with only minor contradictory elements in their class location.

3. *Organizational assets and the state*   One of the appeals of the multiple exploitation approach was that it provided a more satisfactory way of incorporating state employment within a class structural analysis. In a "state mode of production," the state was seen as the site of the concentrated control over organization assets. The material basis of exploitation in a statist society, therefore, was conceived as the monopoly over organizational assets by the state bureaucratic class.

Whatever one thinks about this as a characterization of class and exploitation in state socialist societies, it does not in the end solve the problems of the analysis of state employment within capitalism generated by the concept of contradictory locations. As mentioned above, the original concept of contradictory locations essentially fused class locations in the state and private sectors. Above all, it treated "domination" (or authority) as a determinant of class location irrespective of the institutional site of that domination. The concept of organizational asset exploitation is guilty of precisely the same problem. In the map of class locations in capitalism, no account whatsoever is made of the institutional site of the organizational assets controlled by managers. Manager/bureaucrats in the state and in capitalist corporations are treated as situated in identical ways within the class structure because they bear a similar relation to their class-defining asset, organizational resources.

4. *Operationalizations* One of the reasons for shifting away from the concept of contradictory locations was the enduring problems of operationalizing the concept of "semi-autonomy." In the end, however, this problem has simply been displaced on to the categories of skills and credentials, which are, if anything, more difficult to operationalize in a consistent and theoretically meaningful way. There are two basic problems. First, as is often noted, it is very difficult to elaborate unambiguous criteria for the "level" of skill associated with different jobs. Should this be measured by the training time necessary to competently perform the job? By the cognitive complexity of the job? By the level of formal credentials required for the job?

Second, even if we solve the first problem, this would merely give us criteria for differentiating labor power in terms of the amount of skill embodied in it; it would not help us in specifying the actual productive *asset* capable of generating exploitation. Skills become the basis for exploitation only when they are monopolized sufficiently to allow the skill owner to appropriate surplus. (And even then, as pointed out above, much skill-based surplus appropriation should not be regarded as exploitation.) Without clear criteria for distinguishing the relevant levels of skill assets, it is quite ambiguous how these levels could be translated into class categories. Skill levels vary in a more or less continuous manner, and thus in the absence of a social relation linked to these assets, this introduces an inherent arbitrariness in using skill assets as such as a basis of defining class "locations."

It might seem that this operational problem in the use of skills as a basis of a dimension of the class structure would be reduced, or even eliminated, if we restrict the concept of skill assets to formally *credentialed* assets. Credentials certainly are more dichotomous than skills and they have more the character of a property right. And credentials also have a clear relational quality to them, since the institutions of credentialing have the effect of systematically excluding people from certain labor markets. Credentials thus do constitute the basis of a relation between the credentialed and uncredentialed.

Nevertheless, there are two serious problems with the use of credentials as the operational criterion for skill-based class relations. First, there are so many different kinds of credentials, and credentialing systems vary so significantly across countries, that the problem of arbitrariness in operationalization is not really solved by replacing skills with credentials. At the operational level, there is no clear criterion available to distinguish credentials that are constitutive of a class division from those which are not. Second, even if we could consistently compare credentials across labor markets and across countries, the basic problem of distinguishing the appropriation of one's own surplus from exploitation would remain. Credentials thus may be a useful way of defining certain kinds of labor market *privileges* (the privilege of being less exploited), but they do not solve the operational problems with skill exploitation in general.

Taken individually, responses to each of these problems are possible. Taken together, they seriously challenge the conceptual coherence of the proposal to analyze the class structure of capitalist societies as a multi-dimensional matrix rooted in capitalist, organizational, and skill exploitation.

4 The Weberian Temptation

Given these difficulties with the concepts of class structure built around contradictory class locations and around multiple exploitations, there are several broad choices about how to proceed. First, we could retain the abstract, simple polarized concept of class structure but abandon the project of trying to develop a repertoire of more concrete, micro-level Marxist class concepts derived from it. We could decide, for example, that the Marxist concept of class structure is analytically powerful for understanding the overall macro-dynamics of capitalist societies in general, but that we cannot systematically derive from this abstract concept a concrete concept of class structure capable of explaining variations in such things as state policies or individual consciousness.[58] Abandoning the goal of producing a micro-level, concrete concept of class structure, then, would open the door to a more eclectic choice of concepts for such micro-level problems. One could, for example, adopt

---

58. This position would be close to that argued for in Uwe Becker's essay in this book (see Chapter 4 in this volume). He argues that "the structural antagonism between labor and capital" is perhaps the most systematic and universal source of cleavage and struggle in capitalist societies, and thus clearly deserves to be given explanatory *importance* (although not, in his judgment, *primacy*) in the analysis of the universal dynamics of capitalism. But he rejects the claim that class *locations* have any particular explanatory force, or that variations in capitalist class structures have necessarily any particular theoretical importance in explaining variations in the histor*ies* of capitalist societies (as opposed to the universal, abstract dynamic tendencies of capitalism in general). This is equivalent to arguing for the importance of the abstract concept of class structure while rejecting the usefulness of corresponding concrete, micro-level class structure concepts.

Weberian class concepts for the analysis of variations in individual consciousness while retaining the abstract, polarized Marxist concept for understanding the structural dynamics of capitalism.

This response to the dilemmas of producing a satisfactory concrete, micro concept of class structure, might, in the end, be the best one can do; but it threatens to undermine the overall explanatory aspirations of Marxist theory. Even though I am critical of the attempt by methodological individualists to reduce all macro phenomena to micro explanations, nevertheless it seems to me that the explanatory force of the abstract, macro-level Marxist concept of class would be greatly compromised if it was unconnected to corresponding micro-level concepts, concepts that are closely tied to the lives and conditions of individuals. And it also seems to me that the explanatory potential of Marxist theory is undermined if its core concepts, in particular class, are only useful for understanding the long-term, epochal dynamics of social change, but not the variations across capitalist societies. If Marxist class analysis is to be theoretically powerful and politically useful, then it seems necessary to continue the attempt at forging concepts at the concrete, micro-level of analysis that are consistent with the more abstract concepts.

A second possible response to the conceptual problems we have been discussing is to retain both the abstract class structure concept and the concrete derivations from that concept, and decide simply to live with a certain level of conceptual incoherence. After all, all conceptual frameworks (in sociology at least) if pressed too hard reveal inconsistencies and weaknesses, and Marxist theories of class are no exception. If one wants to do empirical work on class, then at some point one has to suspend the preoccupation with the reconstruction of foundational concepts and get on with the business of studying the world, and this generally requires a tolerance for a certain degree of conceptual ambiguity and inconsistency. This does not mean abandoning altogether the project of eliminating such inconsistencies; one can still try to forge new conceptual solutions, either by way of a synthesis of previous ideas or through the introduction of new conceptual elements. But it does mean adopting a certain pragmatic attitude toward research and not waiting until all conceptual problems are resolved. This is essentially the response I have adopted to these enduring conceptual problems in my empirical projects.

There is, however, a third possible response. One can decide that these conceptual issues have been so persistent and apparently intractable that they probably reflect deeper problems in the larger theoretical framework of which they are a part. Rather than continue struggling with the problem of constructing an adequate Marxist concept of the middle class in capitalist societies, therefore, these problems might call into question the general Marxist theory of class itself. Before turning to a discussion of a range of new amendments to my previous conceptualizations in section 5, therefore, it is worth considering this more drastic remedy to the problems we have encountered, namely abandoning Marxist class analysis altogether.

Many of the conceptual difficulties bound up with the problem of the middle class within a Marxist framework appear to vanish within the Weberian tradition of class analysis. While of course there are still plenty of problems of operationalization within Weberian class structure analysis—the concepts of "market situation" and "work situation" which are used by Weberians such as John Goldthorpe both pose significant problems of operationalization and measurement—nevertheless, the category "middle class" does not pose the same kind of conceptual difficulties for Weberians that it does for Marxists.[59]

Why is this so? Weberians have an easier time than Marxists in forming a concept of the middle class because in the Weberian tradition the concept of class structure is relieved of three theoretical burdens which must be contended with in one way or another within a Marxist framework:

1. *Class, mode of production, and the theory of history* For Weberians, the concept of class structure does not have to be linked to an abstract concept of "mode of production." Classes within the Weberian tradition are viewed as categories of stratification specific to market societies, and thus there is no need to develop a general schema of class analysis that applies across different kinds of economic systems. And further, as a corollary of this, the concept does not have to figure in any general theory of history for Weberians as it generally does for Marxists. Even when, as often occurs today, Marxists reject the general Marxist theory of history—historical materialism—they nevertheless generally remain committed to a class-based *structural typology* of historical variations. Thus, even without the strong claims of historical materialism, the Marxist concept of class is under the theoretical constraint functioning within a typology of historical forms of variation

---

59. John Goldthorpe, in *Social Mobility in Modern Britain* (Oxford: Clarendon Press, 1980, pp. 39–42), for example, makes the following distinctions in developing his class structure concept: "high grade" versus "low grade" professionals; "higher-grade technicians" versus "lower-grade technicians"; managers in large versus small establishments; nonroutine versus routine nonmanual employees in administration and commerce. In each case there are difficult problems in defining nonarbitrary criteria for operationalizing these distinctions. Nevertheless, the conceptual status of these distinctions poses no difficulties within the overall class structure concept.

of class structures. The absence of this constraint for Weberians means that the specific problem of conceptualizing classes in capitalist society does not have to meet any criteria of coherence with the analysis of class structures of precapitalist or postcapitalist societies.

2. *Exploitation and antagonistic classes*   While the Weberian concept of class is relational (it is grounded in the problem of economic exchange relations), it is not based on an abstract model of polarized relations. In principle, then, Weberians can admit an indefinite number of additional classes besides workers and capitalists without having to postulate any underlying conflicts of material interest. All that is necessary is that a given class be characterized by a distinctive work situation and market situation, or, more broadly, by distinctive economically conditioned "life-changes" (to use a favorite Weberian expression). Marxists, on the other hand, have to produce concepts of specific class locations that are congruent with the underlying antagonistic logic of class relations based in exploitation. This does not mean that every distinction among class locations in a concrete, micro-level concept has to itself be polarized to some other distinction; but it has to somehow be systematically embedded in an analysis of such polarized, exploitative class relations.

3. *Ambitiousness of the theoretical ordering of concepts*   The Weberian concept of class, at least as it has been elaborated by contemporary neo-Weberians, does not attempt to specify and defend a systematic hierarchy of conceptual elements. There is no attempt, for example, to articulate a conceptual ordering of the problems of material interests, lived experiences, and capacities for collective action in the specification of class structures. This means that Weberians can deploy a variety of different kinds of criteria for defining aspects of class structures in a rather ad hoc manner without embarrassment. Weberians typically argue that class positions are defined by common work situations and market situations, but there is no attempt to construct a logical decomposition of these two concepts or to order them in a systematic way. Weberians are nearly always silent, for example, on the question of whether two jobs which share a common market situation but different work situations constitute divisions *within* a single class or *distinct* classes. The lower level of aspiration of conceptual and theoretical integration within the Weberian tradition compared to the Marxist tradition, therefore, facilitates taking a rather pragmatic, empirical attitude towards the introduction of specific distinctions in a class structure analysis without worrying too much about the implications for a larger theoretical structure.[60]

The absence of these three theoretical constraints makes it much easier to locate categories like professionals, technical employees, and managers in the class structure. It is sufficient, for example, to demonstrate that the marketable skills of these categories gives them distinctive economic advantages in the labor market. No conceptual difficulty is posed by the fact that ownership of skill assets does not correspond to any distinctive polarized social relation between skill owners and non-owners. All that is necessary is that skills (or, in principle, any other attribute) constitutes the basis for distinctively enhanced economic opportunities within exchange relations.

In a similar fashion, Goldthorpe argues that certain properties of work situations are the basis for the class structural differentiation of what he terms the "service class" from the working class.[61] He argues that such characteristics as exercising managerial authority or having a great deal of discretion, autonomy, and responsibility on the job means that the employer–employee relation must involve high levels of *trust*. This trust element, in turn, means that instead of a simple employment contract, the employment relation is constructed as a "service relation," the critical element of which is the centrality of *prospective rewards* rather than simply current remuneration. Primarily because these elements of the work situation systematically enhance economic opportunities (in the form of stable careers), they constitute the basis of a distinctive class, the "service class."[62]

---

60. Val Burris, in a personal communication, suggests that the relatively low level of aspiration for theoretical integration of the distinct elements of class theory in the Weberian tradition is due to certain general properties of Weberian theory: "(1) as a theory of social *action*, the Weberian theory is absolved of having to specify structural forms of causation; (2) because Weberian theory is unabashedly *multicausal* and rejects the primacy of class relations, it is not forced to pack so much into its concept of class; (3) because Weberian theory focuses on *exchange* relations, it deals with phenomena that are closer to the empirical level of lived relations as compared with the production relations that Marxists must reconstruct theoretically." For a further discussion of these themes, see Val Burris, "The Neo-Marxist Synthesis of Marx and Weber on Class," in *The Marx–Weber Debate*, edited by Norbert Wiley (London: Sage Publications, 1987), pp. 67–90.

61. Goldthorpe, "On the Service Class", *op. cit.* pp. 167–70.

62. There are places where Goldthorpe seems to suggest that it is the possession of power and responsibility as such, rather than the way in which such power-holding constitutes the basis for a distinct kind of employment relation, that provides the rationale for treating the service class as a distinct class (for example, Goldthorpe, *Social Mobility in Modern Britain*, pp. 39–40), but generally he seems to stress the ways in which work situations generate distinctive kinds of market situations (see especially "On the Service Class", pp. 170–71). Other writers (for instance, Lockwood, *The Blackcoated Worker*; Giddens, *The Class Structure of the Advanced Societies*) using a similar set of concepts suggest in various places that the workplace *experiences* of actors under these different work situations also differ systematically and constitute part of the justification for treating these differences in work situations as the basis for class structural differences.

The service class, defined in this way, is constituted around a distinctive kind of employment relation with superordinate employers (capitalists, corporate boards, the state). Within this definition, there is
nothing inherently antagonistic about this relation, and certainly there is
no implied *inherent* antagonism between the service class and nonservice class employees.[63] Of course, conflicts, perhaps even explosive
conflicts, may empirically occur among these classes, but the concept of
class itself is based simply on a notion of distinctive *differences* in
material interests and conditions among classes, not inherent cleavages.

Given the fact that the middle class is so much easier to contend with in
a Weberian framework, the question clearly arises: Why not simply
jump ship and adopt the Weberian approach? Frank Parkin, for one, has
argued that an impulse in this direction is implicit in the efforts of neo-
Marxists to grapple seriously with problems of class analysis:

> The fact that these normally alien concepts of authority relations, life-chances,
> and market rewards have now been comfortably absorbed by contemporary
> Marxist theory is a handsome, if unacknowledged, tribute to the virtues of
> bourgeois sociology. Inside every neo-Marxist there seems to be a Weberian
> struggling to get out.[64]

Once you adopt a fairly differentiated Marxist class concept of the sort I
have advocated, then in practice there is not actually all that much
difference in the nature of the empirical class structure "variables" that
are generated in neo-Marxist and neo-Weberian frameworks: after all,
both acknowledge in one way or another that differences in property,
skills/credentials/autonomy and authority are bases for differentiating
locations in the class structure. If you compare Goldthorpe's seven-
category class structure schema (or the more elaborate eleven-category
schema that contains a range of subclass divisions) with my analysis of
class structure in terms of multiple-exploitation mechanisms, for
example, you will find that in practical empirical terms the contrast is
not great.[65] Therefore, given that there is not all that much empirical
difference between many neo-Marxist and neo-Weberian class maps,
and given that the conceptual problems are greater within Marxist

---

63. Indeed, there is no inherent social relation of any sort between the service class as a
general category and nonservice class employees. Sometimes there exists an authority
relation linking these two, but not invariably. The relationship between the service class
and the working class is basically understood via the distinctive differences in their respective relations to their employers rather than a relation which directly binds them to each
other.

64. Frank Parkin, *Marxism and Class Theory: A Bourgeois Critique* (New York:
Columbia University Press, 1979), p. 25.

theory, why not, then, just opt for the Weberian approach?

If the *only* reasons for adopting a Marxist approach to the concept of class structure was the practical usefulness of the categories derived from the conceptual framework for micro-level empirical analyses of class, then there would be little reason to choose it over a range of neo-Weberian alternatives. The reason for adopting a Marxist strategy, then, has to rest on a commitment to the theoretical constraints that Marxist theory imposes on class analysis. More specifically, unless one sees the value of embedding the concept of class structure in an abstract model of modes of production in which classes are fundamentally polarized around processes of exploitation, then there would be no reason to accept the difficulties this abstract framework generates for the concrete analysis of classes.

My personal commitment to these constraints is grounded in three broad considerations: one political or normative, one theoretical and one methodological.

First, *politically*, the Marxist tradition broadly understood continues to provide, in my judgment, the most comprehensive and compelling theoretical framework within which to understand the possibilities for and obstacles to emancipatory social change. While a range of rival frameworks for radical social theory have emerged in recent years, none of these has yet achieved the level of analytical power for understanding

---

65. For an extended discussion of the differences between these two schemas, see Gordon Marshall, Howard Newby, David Rose, and Carolyn Vogler, *Classes in Modern Britain* (London: Hutchinson, 1988). One comment on this book is in order. It was written by members of the British research group in the Comparative Project of Class Structure and Class Consciousness. The heart of the book is an attempt at empirically comparing various properties of my class concepts and that of Goldthorpe. While there is a great deal that is of interest in this book, it suffers from a relative inattention to the difference between problems in the *operational choices* made by different theorists, and disagreements in the conceptual categories themselves. Thus, for example, they criticize my conceptual map of classes on the grounds that I have allocated certain people—such as a skilled machinist with a subordinate apprentice—into "managerial" class locations who should be properly classified as workers (as they are in Goldthorpe's framework). This may be a valid criticism, but it is simply a criticism of an operational criterion adopted in my reseach, not of the conceptual issues differentiating the two approaches. In terms of managerial authority, Goldthorpe and I share virtually the same conceptual criterion: in both cases the issue is real (not merely nominal) participation in the making of significant organizational policy decisions (the exercise of authority in Goldthorpe's case; the control over organization assets in my case). In my empirical work, because of my specific analytical objectives, I was particularly concerned with avoiding incorrectly describing a manager as a worker, and thus I deliberately adopted a "generous" set of operational criteria for defining managerial locations. This may have been a bad operational decision, but it does not reflect conceptual differences between my approach and Goldthorpe's. If one wants to compare two conceptual frameworks empirically, it is essential that the comparison rigorously distinguish such operational problems from the conceptual problems at issue.

large-scale processes of social change as that offered by the Marxist tradition.[66]

Second, *theoretically*, if one wants the concept of class structure simultaneously to figure centrally in analyses of both epochal social change *and* systematically structured social conflict within given types of society, then something very much like these conceptual constraints is necessary. To borrow a metaphor from rational choice theory, the ambition of Marxist theory is to link systematically an account of conflict within a given type of game to an account of the fundamental shifts from one kind of game to another. *If* class structure is to figure in such a theory, then it will need to be subjected to the kinds of conceptual constraints indicated above.

Finally, *methodologically*, I believe it is generally better to try to develop and reconstruct specific concepts within a clearly specified set of constraints than to do so in the absence of rigorously elaborated constraints. The Weberian tradition is generally characterized by quite ad hoc and diffuse conceptual specifications. While these may be grounded in certain abstract understandings of human action, they are not systematically derived from a general theory of society and its development. The choice between Marxist and Weberian concepts of class, therefore, is not strictly speaking a choice between concepts with equal theoretical standing. As Charles Camic has noted, the choice between Marxist and Weberian approaches is not really between two theories of society, but between a theory and nontheory.[67]

The implication of this methodological point about the status of class concepts within the Marxist and Weberian traditions is that the choice between these concepts cannot be reduced to a simple choice between their "explanatory power" in any given empirical setting. As a general metatheoretical proposition one would expect that in any given particular empirical context, it is easier to construct empirical categories that are highly correlated with what one is trying to explain when the

---

66. To avoid misunderstanding, two points of clarification are needed to this statement. First, the claim is about the Marxist *tradition*, defined in an ecumenical fashion, not about any particular theoretical position within that tradition. Second, the claim is not that this tradition provides the most fruitful framework for analyzing *every* question of relevance to radical projects of social change, but simply that it provides the best overall framework for the general problem of understanding the obstacles to and opportunities for emancipatory transformation. Thus, for example, the Marxist tradition probably does not—and perhaps can not—provide adequate tools for understanding many of the important issues bound up with gender oppression. As a result, for the study of gender some kind of linkage between Marxism and feminism is essential. Nevertheless, in my judgment Marxism remains the most comprehensive and productive general framework for developing macrostructural theory of large-scale emancipatory possibilities.

67. Personal communication.

theoretical constraints on such constructions are relatively weak than when they are strong. This is precisely what gives "empiricism" as a strategy of concept formation such appeal: the researcher is relatively free to modify definitions and to juggle concepts (the categories of observation and analysis) in response to the specific exigencies of any given empirical analysis without worrying about violating any theoretical constraints on concepts. In these terms, the Weberian tradition of class analysis is relatively more "empiricist" than the Marxist tradition.[68] The problem, of course, is that at the end of the day it may be much less clear what one has really *learned* cumulatively from such empiricist exercises beyond the predictions and observations of the specific analysis, since the categories deployed are not orchestrated within an elaborated, more abstract framework. If we want to gain knowledge not simply *about* a particular empirical problem, but *from* that problem, it is crucial that the concepts used in the analysis be as integrated into a general conceptual framework as possible.

These comments should not be interpreted as a devious way of getting a Marxist approach to class analysis "off the hook" of having to demonstrate its empirical power. *If* indeed it is the case that Weberian categories are consistently better predictors of micro-level empirical phenomena—for example, individual class consciousness, or variations in individual economic welfare, or propensities to participate in specific patterns of class formation—then this would be a challenge for a Marxist approach.[69] It would then be incumbent upon a defender of class analysis within a Marxist framework to try to explain these Weberian-generated results within the theoretical constraints of Marxism. One

---

68. I am treating empiricism in this context as a variable tendency: different analyses can be more or less empiricist—that is, operating under more or less strictly imposed theoretical constraints. The opposite pole of empiricism is thus theoreticism. I should also note that my comments here do not constitute a generalized critique of empiricism: there are contexts in which relatively empiricist analyses may be productive. In general in the practice of research I think it is desirable to cycle back and forth between relatively empiricist and relatively theoreticist modes of analysis.

69. I do *not* think that the case for the empirical superiority of Weberian categories for micro-level analysis has been proven. For reasons cited in footnote 62 above, in the one case where there has been a sustained, systematic empirical comparison of my own class structure concepts with that of a prominent neo-Weberian, John Goldthorpe, there are sufficient methodological problems in the empirical strategy that it is hard to draw any definitive conclusions. In any case, even in that comparison, the differences in the two approaches were not very striking empirically. Other less extensive cases of empirical comparisons between neo-Marxist and neo-Weberian class concepts have also not found dramatic differences in the brute "explanatory power." See, for example, W. Johnston and M. Ornstein, "Social Class and Political Ideology in Canada," *Canadian Review of Sociology and Anthropology*, vol. 22, (no. 3), pp. 369–95; David Livingstone, "What Class? What Consciousness?" (unpublished manuscript, Ontario Institute for Studies in Education, 1989).

hypothetical possibility, for example, might be something like the following:

> Let us introduce a distinction between the process of class formation under conditions of stable social reproduction in democratic capitalism and under conditions of systemic capitalist crisis. Under the first of these conditions, categories of economic actors become collectively organized on the basis of divisions of *immediate* material interests—divisions defined entirely within the "rules of the game" of capitalism; under the second set of conditions, social categories have a much higher probability of becoming organized around "fundamental interests," interests defined in terms of what game is to be played. Now, the kinds of distinctions in market situations embodied in Weberian class concepts do define divisions within immediate interests among sellers of labor power. Under conditions of stable reproduction, then, these are likely to become more salient as bases of social differentiation and collective organization. In short: Weberian class categories will have greater micro-level explanatory power under conditions of stable reproduction than under conditions of generalized economic crisis.

Other theoretical strategies for incorporating Weberian empirical results within a Marxist theoretical framework could also be entertained: these empirical findings could, perhaps, be treated as generated by the particular institutional organization of bargaining arrangements (as in the literature on corporatism), or as effects of the particular strategies of political parties (as in Przeworski's analyses of social democracy). In each of these possible lines of theoretical argument, the empirical observations generated within Weberian class analysis would be taken seriously rather than simply dismissed out of hand. The task of Marxist class analysis, then, would be to explain the "conditions of possibility" of the Weberian patterns.

A critique of empiricism is thus not equivalent to a critique of empirical research or of empirically grounded knowledge. The point is simply that the task of adjudicating between alternative general approaches to class analysis—alternative "paradigms," as they are sometimes called—is an arduous one, and cannot be reduced to the simple task of testing predictive power in a concrete empirical setting.

Weberian solutions, therefore, do represent a way of avoiding the conceptual knots generated by trying to conceptualize the middle classes within the Marxist tradition. But these solutions are purchased at the price of lowering the ambitiousness of one's theoretical aspirations and abandoning the attempt at consistency with the conceptual framework— Marxism broadly conceived—that remains the most coherent general approach to radical, emancipatory social theory. Sticking with that framework, however, creates headaches; since the conceptual knots won't disappear and cannot be indefinitely avoided by evasion, new efforts at untying them must be attempted. In what follows I will present some of the elements which may facilitate such an attempt.

5 New Complexities

Recall the basic task at hand: to produce a more differentiated repertoire of Marxist class structure concepts capable of being used effectively at concrete, micro levels of analysis. In this enterprise, the problem of the middle class has loomed large, both because of the conceptual difficulties it poses for attempts at rendering more concrete the abstract, mode of production concept of class and because of its salience in the micro-level processes that affect class formation.

Each of my previous strategies of constructing a comprehensive concept of class structure was built around a specific analytical principle: the notion that a given location in a class structure could be simultaneously in two or more classes (strategy 1) and the notion that a given location could be situated with respect to more than one mechanism of exploitation (strategy 2). In each case I tried to build a differentiated map of the class structure on the basis of a single principle. I cannot at this point offer a third general strategy of this sort which will dissolve the anomalies and difficulties of the previous two. Indeed, it is not obvious that the proper way to proceed is to search for a new, unitary principle for solving the puzzle of the middle class(es).

The structural problem of the middle class, however, is not the only important issue involved in elaborating a concrete, micro-level concept of class structure. In this section I want to explore a number of new complexities that bear not only on the problem of understanding the middle class, but on the problem linking class structures to individual lives in general. In section 6, then, we will return to the problem of the middle class and see how these new complexities may help to clarify its class character.

In the past, all of my work on class structure has treated class structures as sets of relationally defined "locations" filled by individuals, in which a location was basically equivalent to a "job." The class structure was thus essentially a relational map of the job structure. The underlying premiss of the analysis, as discussed in section 2 above, was that the nature of the material interests of *individuals* could be derived from an account of the social relations of production in which their *jobs* were embedded. The kind of complexity I introduced in order to generate a more differentiated map of class structures, therefore, was entirely preoccupied with the complexities of the relations in which jobs were embedded.

I now want to introduce a different sort of complexity. Without abandoning the centrality of work and production to the specification of class structures, I think the simple linkage of *individuals-in-jobs* to *classes* needs to be modified in several ways. First, some recognition needs to be taken both of the fact that individuals may occupy more than one formal job, and, furthermore, that class-based material interests may not be associated with "jobs" as such. Second, the description of class structure needs to include what I will call "mediated class locations," locations that are derived from various kinds of social networks rather than directly from individual participation in the relations of production. And third, an analysis of class structure must take account of what can be termed the *temporal dimension* of material interests, especially as these are tied to careers. As we shall see in section 6, each of these new complexities can help to understand the problem of the "middle class."

5.1 Multiple Locations

Virtually all discussions of class structure, including my own, assume that individuals occupy one and only one location in the class structure. While I have argued that some locations have a dual class character, I have nevertheless still assumed that individuals occupy unique locations.

There are two contexts in which this description is clearly inadequate. First, and most obviously, many people have more than one job. While in the United States, most people with second jobs are in jobs with the same class character as their "primary" job, this is certainly not the case in all times and places. In contemporary Hungary, for example, the large majority of second jobs are petty bourgeois (self-employed) whereas primary jobs are overwhelmingly employees of the state.[70]

The second context in which individuals can be thought of as occupying multiple locations is, I think, of more general importance for understanding the American class structure. Rather than having two proper jobs, many people are both owners of capitalist property (and accordingly receive some of their income as returns on capitalist investment) and are employees in a job. This situation is most notoriously the case for high level executives in large corporations, whose income comes both from direct salaries as employees of the corporation and from

---

70. According to Robert Manchin of the Institute of Sociology in Budapest while less than 5 percent of all Hungarians in the labor force are self-employed in their primary job, over 75 percent of all Hungarian households receive some income from self-employment. This is, needless to say, vastly higher than the corresponding figures in the United States.

stockholding in the corporation. But more generally, there is a fairly wide spectrum of people who are employees in jobs with sufficiently high pay that they are able to convert some of their employment earnings into capitalist property through investments and savings. In many cases, of course, such investments are trivial and only marginally shape the material interests of the individual. The United States is certainly far from the fantasy of a "People's Capitalism" in which share ownership is so widespread that the distinction between owners and workers begins to wither away. Nevertheless, for certain segments of the employee population, particularly managers and professionals, the ability to turn surplus income into capital can become a significant part of their class situation. These kinds of situations define a specific kind of complexity in the class structure, since certain people may occupy a different location in the class structure through their jobs and through their investments. Work and property ownership can be uncoupled.[71]

5.2 Mediated Class Locations

The second new complexity to the map of class structures concerns the various ways the class interests of people are conditioned by social relations other than their direct relation to the process of production (either through their jobs or their personal ownership of property). I will refer to this dimension of the class structure as "mediated" class locations in contrast to the "direct" class locations embodied in an individual's immediate job and personal ownership of productive assets. The most crucial example of these relations are those embedded in kinship networks and family structures, but in certain contexts the relation to the state can also constitute the basis for a mediated class location.

For certain categories of people in contemporary capitalism, location in the class structure is entirely constituted by mediated relations. This is most clearly the case for children. To say that children in a working class family are "in the working class" is to make a claim about the ways in which their class interests are shaped by their mediated relations (through their families) to the system of production, rather than by their direct location. Mediated class relations also loom large in understanding the class interests of housewives not in the paid labor force, the

---

71. Under certain circumstances, home ownership may also begin to function like a capitalist investment, if the rapid increase in housing prices gives the owners a substantial equity which they are able to use for investment purposes. Real estate speculation by workers is certainly not unheard of in the contemporary United States and, when it occurs, it should be treated as a specific kind of change in their class location.

unemployed, pensioners and students.[72] In each of these cases an adequate picture of their class interests cannot be derived simply from examining their direct participation in the relations of production.

A class structure at the concrete level of analysis, then, should be understood as consisting of the totality of direct and mediated class relations. This implies that two class structures with identical patterns of direct class relations but differing mediated relations should be considered structurally different. Consider the following rather extreme contrast for purposes of illustration:

Class Structure I   In 66 percent of all households, both husband and wife are employed in working-class jobs and in 33 per cent of households both husband and wife are co-owners of small businesses employing the workers from the other households.

Class Structure II   33 percent of the households are pure working-class households, 33 percent have a working-class husband and a small employer wife and 33 percent have a small employer husband and a working-class wife.

For a strict adherent of the view that class structures are constituted exclusively by the individual's direct relation to the means of production, these two class structures are the same: 66 percent working class, 33 percent small employers. If, however, class structures are defined in terms of the combination of direct and mediated class locations, then the two structures look quite different: in the first structure, two-thirds of the population is fully proletarianized (that is, both their direct and mediated class locations are working class); in the second structure, only one-third of the population is fully proletarianized.[73]

---

72. To say that mediated class relations are particularly salient in understanding the class location of full time housewives is not to prejudge the question of whether or not the gender relations between husbands and wives should be considered a form of "class relations." While I do not think that this is a useful way of understanding gender relations within families, even if one adopts this view, it would still be the case that mediated class relations would be salient for housewives. The class locations of a housewife married to a capitalist and a factory worker are not the same, even if their status as a "domestic worker" itself constitutes a gender-based class location. For a more extended discussion of the relevance of the concept of mediated class locations for understanding the class location of "housewives" and married women in the paid labor force, see my essay, "Women in the Class Structure," *Politics and Society* (March, 1989).

73. Examples like this are not entirely fanciful. It is quite conceivable that in a Third World country one could have two communities in which the same proportions of the labor force were engaged in proletarianized wage labor activities and in self-employed subsistence peasant agriculture, but in which these corresponded to entirely different patterns of household proletarianization.

The concept of mediated class relations is particularly relevant for the analysis of class and gender.[74] More specifically, it provides a way of approaching the problem of the interconnection of gender relations, family structure, and class. In conventional sociological discussions of social classes, as recently reaffirmed in a controversial paper by John Goldthorpe, the family, rather than the individual, is treated as the fundamental "unit" within class structures.[75] The class location of that family unit, in turn, is generally determined by the class location of the job of the "head of the household"—typically, the "male breadwinner." This has the effect of deriving the class locations of all family members, including both housewives and wives in the paid labor force, from the class locations of husbands.

The basic rationale for this conception of families and class structure involves two interconnected claims. (1) All members of a family share essentially the same material interests, since families constitute units of pooled income and consumption. Thus, even if different family members bring income into the family through different class-based mechanisms, these differences are homogenized via the pooled consumption of the family unit. (2) In the determination of the material interests of the family as a whole, the husband's market capacity has overwhelming importance, not simply because at any single point in time the income derived from that capacity is generally much higher than that derived from the market capacity of the wife, but also because over time the material welfare of the family will be maximized if it gives precedence of the husband's job class over that of the wife. An economically rational family, therefore, will generally act as if its class interests were identical to that of the male breadwinner.[76]

Both of these arguments have been subjected to considerable

---

74. The problem of the relationship between class structure and gender relations is not, by any means, simply a question of mediated class relations. At least four other theoretical issues are of considerable importance: (1) the role of gender mechanisms in sorting people into class relations; (2) the ways in which gender mechanisms can constitute the basis for systematic *divisions within* classes; (3) the problem of the causal effect of gender relations and gender conflicts on the form and development of class structures (and of class structure and conflict on gender relations); and (4) the conditions under which gender relations as such could be considered a specific type of class relation. Marxism traditionally has a much easier time contending with the first two of these issues than the last two. In any case, in the present context I will only directly address the problem of mediated class relations.

75. John Goldthorpe, "Women and Class Analysis: In Defense of the Conventional View," *Sociology*, vol. 17, no. 4 (1983), pp. 465–88.

76. Whatever criticisms one might want to bring against this view, it is important to note that it is *not* an inherently antifeminist view. One could argue, for example, that is is the institutions of male domination which generate the great disparities in market capacities of men and women and which, in turn, make it rational for men and women within individual families to give precedence to husbands' jobs over wives'.

criticism.[77] As a result, for a range of reasons which I will not review here, many people have objected to the simple identification of the class location of wives with that of their husbands. And yet, it also seems inappropriate to reduce the class of either husbands or wives in a family simply to their direct job class: should a school teacher married to a factory worker be seen as in the same class location as a fellow teacher married to a corporate manager or a capitalist? If the goal of the elaboration of a micro-level concept of class structure is to understand the impact of class structures on the material interests of individuals within that structure, and on this basis contribute to our understanding of their likely behavior, then some kind of differentiation between these two teachers is necessary.

The concept of mediated class locations provides one way of accomplishing this. The class location of husbands and wives should be treated as a function of both their direct class location and their mediated location. This means that in certain respects they can be viewed as sharing a common class location and in other respects as having—potentially—different class locations. The overall "class interests" of individuals, then, is formed out of some kind of weighted combination of these direct and mediated locations. This opens the door for a new sort of "contradictory location within class relations": contradictory combinations of direct and mediated locations.

Under different social conditions, the precise way in which direct and mediated class locations are linked in the lives of individuals will vary. For example, one might expect the mediated class location of married women to have greater weight than their direct class location in shaping their overall class interests when wives are particularly dependent economically on their husbands (because of larger gender-based labor market differentials and an absence of significant nonwage income support for women from the state) and when there is a low rate of divorce (and thus a high probability that the economic fate of wives is closely tied to that of their husbands). In contrast, lowered economic dependency and/or high rates of divorce should increase the relative weight of direct class locations on the overall material interests of

---

77. For critical commentaries on Goldthorpe's views, see A. Heath and N. Brittain, "Women's Jobs Do Make a Difference: A Reply to Goldthorpe," *Sociology*, vol. 18, no. 4 (1984), pp. 475–90 and M. Stanworth, 1984, "Women and Class Analysis: A Reply to John Goldthorpe," *Sociology*, vol. 18, no. 4 (1984), pp. 161–9. Goldthorpe responds to these attacks in "Women and Class Analysis: A Reply to the Replies," *Sociology*, vol. 18, no. 4 (1984), pp. 491–9. For a general assessment of the debate, see my essay, "Women in the Class Structure," *Politics and Society*, vol. 17, no. 1 (1989).

married women. In each case, however, the full specification of a person's micro-level location within a class structure requires an account of such mediated relations as well as the more conventional direct locations linked to jobs.

5.3 Temporal locations

One common objection to the kind of structural class analysis I have pursued is that it treats locations in an excessively static manner.[78] Imagine the following extreme case: a large corporation requires that all of its managers spend two years at various jobs on the shop floor doing the ordinary nonmanagerial work of the workers in the corporation. After two years they begin performing their proper managerial tasks. In such a case it would certainly be silly to say that during the initial two years these individuals were in the working class. Their performance of typically working-class tasks was simply part of the career structure of these managerial locations. Or, to state the matter more abstractly, there is a systematic temporal dimension to their class location.

The problem of this temporal dimension of class structures is particularly salient when one treats material interests as the central commonality of class locations. The concept of "interests" is inherently a forward-looking concept: to talk about interests is always to imply something about future states, not simply present configurations. Two individuals in identical working-class jobs in terms of statically defined relational characteristics would have very different material interests if one was certain to be promoted into a managerial position and one was certain to remain for life in a working-class position.[79]

Typically, analyses of the temporal dimension of class structures treat

---

78. This objection specifically to my approach was first raised by A. Stewart, K. Prandy, and R.M. Blackburn, *Social Stratification and Occupation* (London: Macmillan, 1980, pp. 271–2). They criticize my allocation of people into a working class and a managerial class on the basis of the authority relations of jobs, since a significant number of white collar workers so classified will eventually be promoted to management as a normal part of their careers.

79. Even if one regards lived experience as the critical commonality of class location, the temporal dimension of class remains important. One's subjective experience of the present is conditioned in part by one's anticipations of the future, and thus knowledge of career trajectories will not only affect material interests in the present but also lived experiences. To take a simple example, in certain large law offices it may be the case that in terms of the actual tasks being performed, the work of an experienced paralegal employee and a junior lawyer might not be that different. Nevertheless, they clearly face dramatically different career trajectories, and this will affect their immediate experience of what in other respects are similar duties.

this problem as one of *intra*generational "mobility."[80] The suggestion in such a characterization is that individuals "move" from one location to another, and thus the locations are definable independently of the movements. If, however, specific jobs are embedded in *careers*, and certain kinds of careers cross class lines, then it probably does not make sense to treat such movements as mobility at all. The managers in the prior example did not experience "mobility" from the working class into the managerial class; they participated in a managerial career in which they progressed from the early career stage to the mid-career stage in an orderly fashion. They were always in the "managerial class."

This line of discussion suggests that in analyzing the temporal dimension of class structures it is important to distinguish between class careers and mobility between careers. This is a distinction which is often made in sociological discussions of *occupational* careers but has generally been exceedingly difficult to operationalize empirically. This difficulty stems from the fact that many "careers" are not nearly as orderly or determinate as the example of managers cited above. Individuals in specific jobs face a given *probability* of promotion across class lines, but the probability may be far less than certainty. It is therefore often difficult empirically to differentiate a situation in which an individual simply progesses through the stages of a given career from a situation in which a person moves across careers. Or, to put the matter somewhat differently, there may be a certain degree of *temporal indeterminacy* in the class location of people.

The issue of the temporality of class locations applies to mediated class locations as well as direct class locations. In particular, it may be useful to understand the class location of married women as partially determined by what might be called their "shadow class", the class location they would occupy in the case of dissolution of their marriage, either through divorce or widowhood.[81] Since the shadow class for

---

80. To be somewhat more accurate, this kind of analysis by sociologists usually concerns intragenerational *occupational* mobility rather than *class* mobility as such. The issue under discussion, however, could just as easily apply to occupations: can an occupation be statically defined by a specific cluster of tasks and responsibilities within the technical division of labor or is it necessary, in some cases at least, to include a temporal ordering of tasks in the definition of an "occupation"? Such a temporally ordered occupation is often called a "career."

81. Johanna Brenner (in a personal communication) suggested that the concept of "shadow class" could be usefully deployed for certain categories of small employers and petty bourgeois. Because of the very high levels of bankruptcy in small businesses, many petty bourgeois and small employers may have a working-class "shadow class" and others a professional-employee "shadow class." The "location" of petty bourgeois in the class structure thus has a critical kind of temporal indeterminacy to it which should be important for their role in processes of class formation.

married women is frequently different from their current mediated class, this suggests that there is at least some temporal indeterminacy in the mediated class locations of many women, particularly given the relatively high rates of divorce. A fully elaborated account of class structure would need to take this kind of temporality into consideration.

For present purposes, the central point of all of this is that the class location of certain *jobs* cannot adequately be determined simply by looking at the relational properties of the job itself at one point in time. This is a particularly salient issue in establishing the class character of many professionals and credentialed experts, since it is frequently the case that the careers of such individuals normally take them on a trajectory of increasing responsibility and authority and increasing opportunity for actual capitalist property ownership (as discussed in 5.1 above).

It is, of course, an empirical question how much these temporal issues actually affect the overall character of the class structure in any given society. Most jobs are not part of well-ordered careers, and it seems likely that most careers are largely contained within a given class location. Nevertheless, for certain specific kinds of occupations, the temporal dimension of class may be essential for understanding their location in the class structure.

6 Back to the Middle Class

With these new conceptual elements in hand we can return to the problem of the "middle class." I will focus on the three categories that have provoked much of the discussion: professionals and experts; managers; and state employees.

6.1 Professionals and Experts

In many ways, experts and professionals of various sorts, particularly when they are not directly part of managerial hierarchies, constitute the category which has caused me (and others) the most persistent difficulty in formulating a coherent Marxist class structure concept. As indicated in section 3 above, neither of the solutions I have offered is entirely satisfactory. The skill exploitation approach is based on the problematic claim that the surplus appropriated by skill/credential owners necessarily constitutes exploitation of others, and this undermines the relational character of the class category built around skills. The semiautonomous employee solution does involve relations—since semiautonomy is only definable within a relation of domination—but these relations no longer seem bound up with questions of material interests and antagonism in the characteristically Marxist way.[82]

Lurking behind both of these solutions is the basic assumption that the *jobs* filled by experts or professionals (and perhaps other types of highly trained "mental labor") are not "really" in the working class. In some sense or other they are "middle class" and thus a conceptual justification for identifying their nonworking class location is needed. In a sense, the undertheorized intuition that credentialed experts were not in the working class provided the motivation for the attempt at "discovering" the conceptual criteria (semiautonomy and/or skill exploitation) that would validate this intuition.[83]

This is a powerful intuition and has certainly served as the backdrop for my efforts at solving the "problem of the middle class." Let us for a moment relax this assumption and resist the underlying intuition by examining the implications of an alternative view, namely that in and of themselves, *jobs* filled by credentialed professional or expert non-managerial employees are in working-class locations in the class structure. With this claim as a point of departure, what I will argue, then, is that the basis for considering nonmanagerial professionals and experts as potentially part of the middle class is not a relational property of their jobs as such, but rather certain properties of the temporal dimension of professional work.

Three considerations are particularly important in this regard. The first concerns the capacity of professionals and experts to capitalize their income. As I argued earlier in the discussion of skill exploitation, holders of scarce skills, especially when these are legally certified through credentials, can be viewed as generally able to appropriate a "rent" component in their wage. Since the major institutional mechanism for reproducing such rents are credentials, I will refer to these as "credential rents," to distinguish them from the more general concept of "employment rents."[84] Whether or not one wants to describe this rent as "exploitation," it does constitute a component of income above the costs of reproducing the labor power of the skill-holder. This is equivalent to saying that what I previously called "skill exploiters" command discretionary income.

---

82. The logic of the category semiautonomous employees thus closely resembles Goldthorpe's *service class* in which professionals/experts are pictured as having a distinctive kind of social relation with employers (autonomy, trust, service relation) quite different from the proletarianized capital–labor employment relation.

83. There are a variety of other ways of playing out this intuition. For example, Nicos Poulantzas, in *Classes in Contemporary Capitalism* (London: Verso, 1975), argued that mental labor was itself a form of domination of workers and thus placed professionals and experts outside of the working class.

In and of itself, such credential rents constitute a specific kind of labor market privilege and thus could be considered the basis for distinguishing among *strata* within the working class. This might in fact be an appropriate way in general of defining "strata" within a relational class theory: strata are differentiated by varying *degrees* of exploitation within a common location in the social relations of production. Strata within the bourgeoisie, accordingly, depend upon the amount of surplus they appropriate; strata in the working class, by the amount of discretionary income they earn through various kinds of credential rents.

When such rents are organized in careers in such a way that they are relatively large and increase over time, then they generate a significant capacity for individuals to convert these credential rents into capitalist property: income-producing real estate, stocks, bonds, etc. To the extent that the ownership of such capitalist property begins to constitute a significant source of future income, then the privileged "worker" in question begins to occupy a distinctive kind of contradictory location within class relations. Both in terms of interests in material welfare and in terms of interests in material power, professionals who accumulate significant savings and investments begin to share material interests with capitalists. In my initial class structure analysis, managers were characterized as "simultaneously capitalist and worker" because they occupied jobs in which they were dominated by capitalists while at the same time they dominated workers The new kind of contradictory location we are now examining can also be considered simultaneously in the capitalist class and in the working class, but in this case the duality of the class location comes from simultaneously owning capitalist property and selling labor power.

The second temporal issue in the class analysis of professionals and experts concerns career trajectories that move into managerial hierarchies. To the extent that it is a normal part of an orderly professional career that most professionals eventually become supervisors and

---

84. The concept of "employment rent" has been given a precise elaboration within a Marxist context in recent papers by Sam Bowles and Herbert Gintis. See especially Sam Bowles, "The Production Process in a Competitive Economy: Walrasian, Neo-Hobbesian and Marxian Models," *American Economic Review*, vol. 75, no. 1 (1985), pp. 16–36, and Sam Bowles and Herbert Gintis in "Contested Exchange" (*Politics and Society*, forthcoming). They demonstrate that *all* employed people, even under conditions of a pure competitive market equilibrium wage, receive at least some "employment rent" in their wages, where this is defined as a component of the wage above what Walrasians would call a "market clearing wage." The rents discussed here that are embodied in "skill exploitation" constitute a different kind of rent—a rent derived from the capacity of skill holders to restrict the supply of skilled labor power. It should in general be viewed as an additional form of rent above the employment rent described by Bowles and Gintis.

managers within the organizations in which they work, then it might be appropriate to consider those professionals and experts that are *outside* of the managerial hierarchy as nevertheless temporally inserted into the middle class. In the United States, roughly 70 percent of all experts are in fact either managers or supervisers. It therefore may be reasonable to treat most nonmanagerial professionals and experts as *pre*managerial. Thus, even if their current jobs are not in managerial contradictory locations, their careers typically are.

The third temporal issue which is bound up with professional careers concerns what might be termed the petty bourgeois shadow class of employees in many professional occupations. This is most clearly the case for the classic "free professions" such as doctors and lawyers, who in many capitalist countries have the relatively open option of self-employment.[85] In such a situation, the employee doctor is not "forced to sell" his or her labor power in the same sense as is the case for other working-class employees; they choose to sell their labor power over self-employment because it is their preference.[86] In recent years, the availability of self-employment options has increased considerably for employee-professionals through the expansion of a range of consulting practices. For example, many academics in the United States, and considerably more in certain other countries, earn a significant second income through self-employed consulting on the side. To the extent that such consulting opportunities expand and are regularly available, then, again, they affect the class location even of those employee professionals who do not take advantage of them, since the availability of such consulting opportunities affects the material interests of employee-professional locations in general (that is, it affects the trade-offs and dilemmas faced by people in such jobs).

---

85. This implies that in a capitalist country where self-employment is not generally a viable option for certain categories of professionals—for example, for doctors in Britain before the Thatcher government—the class location of these employee professionals is affected. Efforts by the Thatcher government to facilitate private practice in medicine potentially affects the class location of all doctors, whether or not they actually become self-employed.

86. There is, even for unambiguously proletarian class locations—unskilled manual workers in manufacturing—a certain ambiguity in the notion that they are "forced" to sell their labor power. As G.A. Cohen argues in his essay, "The Structure of Proletarian Unfreedom," in J. Roemer (ed.), *Analytical Marxism* (Cambridge: Cambridge University Press, 1986), this statement cannot be taken to mean literally that each and evey proletarian is individually forced to sell his or her labor power, since with sufficient sacrifices and luck, at least some in fact can, as individuals, escape the proletarian condition into self-employment. The point is that this option is not available to manual industrial workers as a class. In the case of some categories of professionals, on the other hand, it may be the case that the option of self-employment is available to as many as want to avail themselves of this alternative.

Given this way of analyzing the class character of professional employment, then even if we do not consider autonomy within work or the ownership of skills/credentials as such as appropriate criteria for differentiating locations within a class structure, nevertheless professionals and experts would generally be considered in "middle-class contradictory locations" by virtue of their capacity to capitalize their income and their career trajectories into managerial hierarchies and viable petty bourgeois options. This way of thinking through the issues, however, introduces a new kind of ambiguity into the analysis of class structures. How should we treat conceptually professionals who consume all of the credential rent in their income? Credential rents generate a *capacity* for acquiring capitalist property, but of course not all individuals who have that capacity will utilize it. Discretionary income can be translated into high standards of living rather than investments.[87] Similarly, not all professionals or experts in careers that normally involve movement into the managerial hierarchy actually ever become managers. How should we understand the character of their individual class location? Should it be defined by the *characteristic* career pattern of professionals or by the *actual* career trajectory of the individual in question? And, in a similar vein, how should we understand the class location of professionals who opt permanently to be employees?[88]

This may seem like a particularly scholastic issue reflecting the preoccupations of a professional pigeon-holer. But as in most problems of formal classification, these issues reflect real underlying conceptual problems.

To help clarify this issue it will be useful to recall the discussion of

---

87. Particularly in employment contexts in which there are very high levels of job security, there is no systematic inherent pressure of "skill exploiters" to capitalize their credential rents. Unlike in the case of entrepreneurial capitalists for whom the imperative to accumulate is inherent in their class location (since investment and accumulation is a necessary condition for their reproduction as capitalists), there is no comparable imperative for high paid employees to accumulate. Their reproduction is not contingent on the capitalization of their income.

88. It is worth noting that this problem of discrepancies between outcomes for individual professionals and the characteristic career structure of professional employment confronts any class theory that treats the category "professional" as having a particular class character. Thus, for example, John Goldthorpe argues that professionals belong in the "service class" by virtue of the responsibilities and authority they have on the job, the prospective rewards that are built into professional careers and the general "service contract" character of the employment relation. While such descriptions may be characteristic of professional employment, there are certainly many specific professional jobs that lack one or more of these properties. Although to my knowledge Goldthorpe never discusses this problem, he in effect attributes class locations to individuals on the basis of the characteristic patterns for their occupations rather than their actual, individual situation.

material interests in section 2 above. In explicating the idea that the commonality of class locations is defined by common relationally determined material interests, I argued that "material interests" should be understood as common material trade-offs and dilemmas in the choices people face concerning material welfare and power. In these terms, working in careers which generate credential rents sufficiently large to enable a person to capitalize their income defines a set of alternatives unavailable to someone whose wages are simply sufficient to cover the costs of reproducing labor power. In a sense, therefore, whether or not the capitalist investments are actually made is a secondary matter; the primary issue is being in a position which makes such investments possible.

Nevertheless, it remains the case that as a result of the actual choices made by individuals in these kinds of careers, their material interests in the future change. Two professionals in identical careers, one of whom has systematically invested discretionary income and one of whom has not, eventually have divergent class interests. Similarly, a professional or expert who fails to ever become a manager (through choice or happenstance) or who chooses never to engage in self-employment is likely to end up with different class interests from a professional who moves up managerial hierarchies or becomes self-employed. In all of these cases we face a problem of what could be termed a degree of *indeterminacy* or *objective ambiguity* in defining the location of individuals in the class structure. To a greater or lesser extent in these cases, class locations are partially indeterminate or ambiguous because they depend not simply upon observable properties of *current* jobs, but upon *future* states (capital ownership, managerial positions, self-employment) linked to those jobs, and these future states depend in part upon contingent choices and events. Thus, in addition to characterizing certain locations in the class structure as "contradictory locations within class relations," it now seems appropriate to characterize some as at least partially "objectively ambiguous locations."[89]

To recapitulate this argument about experts and professionals, one way of thinking about their concrete, micro-level class location is to focus on the temporal dimensions of class structures. In so far as pro-

---

89. Allowing a certain degree of indeterminancy in the location of professionals and experts in the class structure may help to explain why this category of social actors is frequently characterized by such high levels of internal ideological heterogeneity. Much more frequently than is the case for other segments of the "middle class", nonmanagerial professionals and experts can be found all over the ideological map. The objective temporal indeterminancy of their class location may allow for a variety of relatively contingent social processes that vary considerably among professionals and experts to have a relatively large impact on their ideological orientation.

fessionals and experts can systematically capitalize their surplus income (and thus become capitalist property owners), move into managerial positions in a routine career trajectory (and thus occupy a contradictory class location) and opt for self-employment (and thus become petty bourgeois), then their class location can be considered "middle class." Insofar as there is a certain degree of real temporal indeterminacy in each of these possibilities, then their class location has an objectively ambiguous status as well.

While these kinds of temporal arguments may go a long way towards understanding the nature of the material class *interests* linked to professional and expert employment, nevertheless I am not entirely satisfied that it adequately captures their overall location in the class structure. And, as noted at the beginning of this discussion of professionals, this treatment certainly goes against the intuitions of most Marxists (and, needless to say, non-Marxists as well) in which, quite apart from these temporal issues, the very character of professional employment is seen as nonproletarian.

I think the standard intuition comes from the *lived experience* dimension of class structure analysis, not their material interests as such. To recall the arguments of section 2 above, at the highest level of abstraction the working class is characterized by three fundamental aspects of lived experience derived from their location within the social relations of production: the experience of having to sell one's labor power to live; the experience of being bossed around within work (at least in the minimal sense of being told what to do), and the experiences of basic powerlessness with respect to the allocation of social resources. On each of these dimensions, the lived experience associated with professional employment is relatively nonproletarianized. First, by virtue of viable self-employment alternatives, the labor market has a less coercive aspect for professionals than for most other categories of employees. Second, within the employment relation professionals and experts exert much more control over their own work. And third, because of their career roles in corporations and bureaucracies, professionals are typically much more involved in decisions over the allocation and use of resources than are workers, even if they do not necessarily formally have the power to actually appropriate those resources. With respect to each of these aspects of lived experience, professionals and experts can be thought to be less alienated than fully proletarianized workers, and in this sense they are in the "middle class."

Although I did not define the issues in these terms, my initial characterization of professionals and experts as "semiautonomous employees" occupying a class location that was simultaneously in the working class and the petty bourgeoisie can be viewed as attempting to define the specificity of their class location in terms of the character of their lived experiences within work, not their interests. Because of the considerable difficulties I encountered in trying to use the concept of "semiautonomous employees" in empirical research I am hesitant to return to it as a basis for understanding the class character of professional/expert work, but it is important to recognize that it more closely corresponds to the underlying intuitions of many people about the class location of experts and professionals than does the argument based strictly on material interests.

6.2 Managers

There were two basic rationales for the shift in the treatment of managers as constituting a contradictory combination of capitalist and working-class locations (version 1) to the treatment of managers as organization asset exploiters (version 2). First, the general strategy of analysis of "contradictory locations within class relations" had been called into question because of conceptual problems with the category "semiautonomous employees." Since I was seeking a unitary conceptual strategy to solve the problem of the middle class, the difficulties with the category "semiautonomous employees" seemed to indict the concept of contradictory locations when applied to managers as well. If, however, we no longer try to discover a single strategy capable of simultaneously solving all of the various conceptual problems posed by different categories of "nonproletarianized employees," then it could well be the case that the concept of contradictory locations within class relations is an appropriate way for theorizing managers, while some other strategy is needed for other categories.

The second rationale for the shift away from the concept of contradictory locations for managers was that the introduction of the concept of organizational asset exploitation appeared to make it possible to link the analysis of managers within capitalism to the problem of classes in postcapitalist societies. Since one of the aspirations of Marxist class analysis is to see future forms of society as immanently present in earlier forms, treating the managerial middle class of capitalism as a latent dominant class in a future type of society based on control over organization assets was analytically attractive.[90] However, this conceptualization only made sense if it could be credibly argued that managers in capitalism, by virtue of their control over the organizational resources of production, had a material interest in a statist organization of production. Without contriving rather unlikely scenarios, this assertion seems implausible at best.

The two reasons I previously advanced for abandoning the treatment of managers as contradictory locations thus do not seem very compelling. Futhermore, the original conceptual strategy seems to capture much more effectively the distinctive dilemmas that managers face within a capitalist society. Seeing managers as a contradictory location within class relations combining capitalist and working-class practices immediately draws our attention to the ways in which managers are tied to capitalist interests and yet are not an integral part of the capitalist class. This concept also makes it clear why foremen and lower-level supervisors are much more likely to be drawn into coalitions with the working class in struggles, while higher-level managers and executives are much more likely to side consistently with the capitalist class.

While I think the class location of managers is best understood in terms of the original concept of contradictory locations, this does not mean that we should abandon the idea of organizational exploitation altogether. Organization exploitation, like skill "exploitation," generates employment-based rents in the earnings of managers. The rent reflected in organization exploitation, however, is generated by a different mechanism from that associated with skill exploitation. In skill exploitation the central mechanism is that a restriction on the supply of a particular kind of skilled labor power pushes up the equilibrium market wage above the costs of producing that kind of labor power. In the case of organization exploitation, the mechanism revolves around the effective power that managers have within production by virtue of their organizational responsibilities. Because of the difficulty in a purely repressive form of social control of managerial activity, for employers to insure loyalty and responsible exercise of authority, managerial careers have to be structured around systematic wage increases tied to promotion up hierarchies.[91] This hierarchically organized "incentive structure"

---

90. It should be added, I think, that this conceptualization was also aesthetically seductive. The treatment of the trajectory of history in terms of the progressive shedding of distinctive forms of exploitation in which the middle class of one form of society was the potential dominant class of the successor society had a high level of symmetry and elegance to it. It provided a way of retaining the essential intuitions of the classical vision of historical trajectory in historical materialism while allowing for a much more differentiated map of class structures and historical possibilities.

91. The difference in the mechanism through which managers and professionals appropriate part of the social surplus implies that they will adopt very different strategies in pursuing their class interests. For professionals the pivotal strategy is control over credentials, thus insuring their control over the supply of professional labor power. For managers, credentialism is clearly a secondary strategy. The protection of managerial prerogatives from direct interference by capitalist owners, particularly over the control of the managerial hierarchy itself, is the central way through which managerial surplus appropriation is reproduced. This strategy generally goes under the heading of "bureaucratization". Credentialization and bureaucratization thus constitute distinct stragegies, associated with distinct types of contradictory locations within class relations.

generates what can be called "loyalty rents" in wages of managers. As in the case of professionals and experts, this gives managers the capacity to capitalize their income, particularly when their careers involve movements into higher reaches of managerial hierarchies. Indeed, in the case of executives in large corporations, these loyalty rents may become so substantial that the managers in question are capable of becoming full-fledged capitalists through the acquisition of capitalist property. In such cases they really cease to occupy contradictory locations within class relations in spite of their normal status as an "employee" of the corporation.

6.3 The State

For Weberian sociologists, state employment in capitalist societies does not pose any particular problems for the analysis of class structures. If classes are fundamentally determined within market relations, and employees enter the state through basically the same kind of labor markets as they enter private employment, then the fact that some people are employed by capitalists and others by the state is largely irrelevant for specifying their class location.[92]

In contrast, state employment has always posed a serious problem for Marxist class structural analysis. If classes are defined by distinctive forms of social relations of *production,* how should employees within the state be treated in a class analysis? On the one hand, most employees in the state do not own any means of production and have to sell their labor power on a labor market in order to acquire their subsistence. On these grounds, as Weberians would argue, they would appear to be indistinguishable from employees in the "private sector." The problem, however, is that while they enter the labor market with the same kinds of resources as private sector employees, they leave the market for a very different kind of social relation: instead of entering a capital–labor relation, they enter a state–labor relation.

The issue here is not simply how we should understand the class character of the state as a *political* institution. Rather, the issue is how we should conceptualize in class terms the social relations of production within the state. Are there distinctive classes within the state in capitalist

92. It is for this reason that Goldthorpe explicitly rejects the relevance of the site of employment as a basis for divisions in class structures. See p. 170 in John Goldthorpe. "On the Service Class: Its Formation and Future," in Anthony Giddens and Gavin McKenzie (eds), *Social Class and the Division of Labour* (Cambridge: Cambridge University Press, 1982), pp. 162–85.

societies? Are the "locations" in the state outside of the class structure? Should the locations in the state simply be conceptually amalgamated with the corresponding classes of capitalism proper?

Most class analyses, whether of a Marxist or non-Marxist inspiration, simply ignore this issue altogether and apply the same criteria for defining class locations for employees in the state and in capitalist employment.[93] This is certainly how I have dealt with the issue in both of my class structural concepts: managers in capitalist corporations and state agencies were both treated as contradictory locations combining capitalist and working-class elements in the first concept, and were both treated as part of the middle class by virtue of organizational asset exploitation in the second concept.

When I developed the concept of organization asset exploitation, I hoped that this would provide a vehicle for dealing with the problem of the state and class structure. I argued that the monopolization of organizational assets defined the critical form of class relations in postcapitalist "statist" societies (societies within which the "state mode of production" was dominant). The state, in terms of the system of production, was thus viewed as the most superordinate site for the concentrated control of organizational resources. In capitalism, then, this meant that managers in capitalist corporations and managers in the state were both defined in class terms with respect to the same productive resource—organization assets—which in a postcapitalist society would become the basis for the state mode of production itself. Given this characterization of assets and exploitation, the state as such simply dropped out of the analysis of classes in capitalism.

This does not seem satisfactory. If a Marxist class theory is to respect the theoretical constraints discussed in section 3.3 above, then it is important that the concept of class structure be linked to the more abstract concept of mode of production, and this implies that some explicit conceptual account be taken of the problem of state employment.[94] One solution, of course, would be simply to argue that employees in the state are not in *any* class location; they are "outside" of the class structure. After all, as was argued in section 5.2 above, there

---

93. For example, Nicos Poulantzas attempts to define the class character of employees of the capitalist state in terms of the category "unproductive labor". All unproductive laborers, he argues, are part of the new petty bourgeoisie. However, since this argument applies equally well to unproductive laborers in capitalist employment (in banks, commerce, etc.), in the end there is no specificity for the class character of state employment as such in Poulantzas's analysis.

94. Employment in certain other sites—churches, nonprofit organizations, voluntary associations, unions, even political parties—pose similar problems. Here I will only discuss the issue of the state as such.

are many people in capitalist society who do not have a *direct* location in the class structure: children, pensioners, permanently disabled, students, perhaps housewives. State employees—and employees in a variety of other noncapitalist institutions—could be treated in a similar fashion. People within the state might still, of course, have *mediated* class locations through various kinds of social relations which tie them to capitalist production, but they would not be *directly* inserted into the class structure through their own jobs.

Such a treatment of state employees might possibly be appropriate for those people who work in what is narrowly the *political apparatuses* of the state—the taxing authority, the courts, the police, the administrative apparatuses of the executive, the legislature, etc. However, a great deal of what the state does in capitalist societies involves the production and distribution of use-values such as education, health, fire protection, sanitation, transportation, etc. These take place in what could be called the state service sector (or more generally, the state production sector since sometimes the products are actually things, not services). Typically these use-values are produced and distributed in distinctively *non*capitalist ways in so far as the products and services in question are generally not fully commodified as in capitalist production itself. But this does not make such state activities somehow outside of production.

Once it is recognized that the state is not simply a rule-making and rule-enforcing apparatus, but also a site of considerable social production, then it follows that the social relations within which such production takes place must be considered a variety of social relations of production. If these relations of production in the state involve processes of exploitation and domination, then they constitute the basis for a state-centered class structure.

This line of reasoning leads directly towards the concept of a "state mode of production" (or, at a minimum, state relations of production).[95] This is not a particularly attractive term, but it seems preferable to the alternative expressions that are sometimes deployed to capture the same idea (such as state socialism or bureaucratic collectivism). If we wish to provide a coherent account of classes constituted within the state, then, we must interrogate this illusive concept.

The concept of a state mode of production is notoriously under-theorized. In my previous work I tried to develop it in a more rigorous way through the analysis of organizational assets and organizational

---

95. The term "state relations of production" avoids a commitment to the thesis that such relations of production could become the dominant principle of organization of the society at large, whereas the concept "state mode of production" implies that this concept is quite parallel to the capitalist mode of production.

exploitation. That strategy, however, missed what is perhaps the essential feature of a state-centered system of production, namely the role of the state's coercive capacity to tax or in other ways appropriate the surplus. The state cannot reasonably be viewed simply as a giant corporation in which the material basis of the capacity of "state managers" to appropriate and allocate surplus is equivalent to that of corporate managers. I therefore do not think that the concept of organizational exploitation is a satisfactory way of approaching the problem of state production (even if it remains the case that organizational exploitation occurs within the state as within other complex organizations).

I cannot offer an alternative elaborated concept of the state mode of production. For the moment, therefore, let us operate with a rather simple set of undertheorized descriptions of the basic classes within these state-based relations of production: the dominant class would be defined as those agents in the state who politically direct the appropriation and allocation of the surplus acquired by the state; the subordinate class as those agents who directly produce use-values (goods and services) within the state; and, in a way analogous to contradictory locations in capitalism, contradictory locations inside of the state would be defined as state managers/bureaucrats who control the activity of state workers while being, at the same time, subordinated to the state dominant class.

If we restrict our analysis to class locations defined directly by *jobs*— that is, to "direct" class locations in the terms of section 5.2 above—then these various locations within the state would be viewed as distinct classes from those in the private, capitalist sector. We would have a state working class and a capitalist working class; state contradictory locations and capitalist contradictory locations; etc.

But, as I argued earlier, class structures should not be analyzed exclusively in terms of direct class locations; *mediated* class relations may be equally important in defining the contours of a class structure. I have already briefly noted the importance of mediated class relations for specifying the class location of one particular kind of actor: housewives. A housewife can be viewed as a direct producer within a particular form of production relations, sometimes referred to as "subsistence production" or "domestic production." In trying to understand a housewife's location in a class structure, it would, however, be unsatisfactory to simply look at her position within domestic production; her mediated class location via the way in which her household is inserted into capitalist class relations is equally—and perhaps even more—important. Thus, by virtue of mediated class relations, we describe the full-time housewife of a capitalist as in the capitalist class and the full-time housewife of a worker in the working class.

A similar kind of analysis is needed for the specification of the location of state employees in the class structure, although in this case the mediating relations are not generally grounded in family structures. In a capitalist society—that is, a society within which the capitalist mode of production is the dominant form of production relations—a worker in the state is not simply in a "state working class," but also through various kinds of mediating relations, linked to the capitalist working class. Above all, state workers occupy mediated locations within the capitalist working class via the commodified relations of labor markets. Similarly, the ruling "elite" in the state—the political directorate of state production—is not constituted in capitalist societies as an autonomous state dominant class; it is linked to the capitalist class through a variety of mediating social relations (career trajectories that move back and forth from public to private sectors; the ability of state elites to capitalize surplus income; etc.).

All of these mediated relations can exist with varying degrees of intensity. Different class locations in the state might have differing intensities of mediated links to classes in the private capitalist sector. It might be the case, for example, that in many capitalist societies contradictory locations within the state—middle level, career civil servants, and state officials—have the *weakest* mediated linkages to classes in the private sector. Unlike state workers, they are quite insulated from pressures of the capitalist labor market, and, unlike high level state elites, their careers are much more exclusively contained within the state. It might be expected, therefore, that people in these kinds of class locations within the state would be the most "statist" in their ideological orientation. On the other hand, it would generally be expected that top level state managers and elites in the capitalist state, should have the strongest mediated relations to the capitalist class structure. Without suggesting that the policies of the state can be viewed simply as the result of instrumental manipulations of the capitalist class itself, it would nevertheless in general be expected that the character of the class locations of the directorate of the capitalist state would be heavily shaped by mediated relations to the bourgeoisie.

The intensity of the mediated relations between classes in the state and capitalist sectors could also vary considerably across time and place. At one extreme one might imagine a capitalist society within which, on the one hand, state employment is highly insulated from the pressures of capitalist markets, where state employees have jobs for life in which the wages and working conditions are virtually unaffected by conditions in the capitalist labor market. In such a situation it might be appropriate to consider state workers and private sector workers as being in quite distinct classes. At another extreme, the state can significantly dissolve the division between state and private employment by imposing conditions of state employment by mimicking private capitalist employment relations within the state, particularly by tying wages of state employees to the capitalist labor market. In such situations, the mediated class location of state workers and private sector workers could be very powerful and largely negate any differences in their direct class locations.

The implication of this analysis of classes within the state is that so long as state employment occurs within a society in which the capitalist mode of production is dominant, one cannot define the class location of state employees exclusively in terms of their locations within state production relations.[96] To a greater or lesser extent, therefore, state employees occupy a kind of dualistic class location: direct locations within state classes and mediated locations within capitalist relations.[97]

This is, of course, not the only way to treat the problem of class relations within the capitalist state. Many theorists reject the concept of a state mode of production altogether. As a site of *production* in capitalist societies, state production can be treated simply as a peculiar form of capitalist production—one organized by public authority rather than private boards of directors. It is "capitalist" because it obtains its inputs from capitalist markets, it recruits its labor through capitalist markets, it is constrained in myriad ways by the process of private capital accumulation and, with some modification, its employment practices are largely shaped by capitalist practices of hierarchy and control. In this view, just as the household should not be viewed as a residual form of some precapitalist "domestic *mode* of production," but rather as the domestic sphere of capitalist production, so too state production in capitalism should not be treated as the forerunner of some postcapitalist mode of production, but rather is simply the "public sphere" of capitalist production. Rather than considering class locations within the state as in any way distinct from the class locations of capitalism proper, therefore, they should simply be fused to them.

This alternative view of state-based production relations in capitalist societies should certainly not be dismissed out of hand. Implicitly, at

---

96. This is essentially what it means to say that the capitalist mode of production is in fact "dominant": all other relations of production are, through one mechanism or another, integrated with capitalism in a subordinate manner. This does not imply that they have no effects of their own, but simply that their effects always occur within limits imposed by capitalist relations.

97. I refer to this situation as "dualistic class locations" rather than "contradictory locations" because there is no inherent reason why the interests generated by the direct and mediated relations contradict each other.

least, it is the approach which most theorists adopt in practice. Nevertheless, I feel that this view of state employment suffers from a kind of latent functionalism in its assessment of the relationship between state production and capitalist production.[98] To describe state production as *simply* the public sphere of capitalist production suggests that its logic of development and internal organization is not just *constrained by* capitalism, but is strictly *derived from* the logic of capitalism. That is, there is something called the "logic of capitalism" which is embodied in a number of interconnected spheres of production—domestic, capitalist proper, public/state. The articulation of such spheres, then, would be regulated by some kind of principle of functional integration. Without such a functional principle, it is hard to see how the public sphere of production could be treated as fundamentally capitalist in its character.

This kind of functional derivation of institutional logics has come under considerable criticism in recent years.[99] Instead of such a functional derivation, it seems to me more plausible to treat the degree to which state production in capitalism is effectively subsumed under a capitalist logic as a variable rather than a constant. Thus, the statist character of state production, and accordingly the noncapitalist character of the class relations constituted within state production, will also vary across time and place. In some instances—perhaps, for example, the United States—it might well be a reasonable first approximation simply to ignore the distinction between state and private employment in the analysis of class structures because state employment is so effectively tied to capitalism, whereas in other cases this might well not be appropriate.

7 Conclusion: Where Does This Leave Us?

I began this essay by arguing for the necessity of producing a repertoire of Marxist class structure concepts capable of effective deployment in concrete, micro-level analysis. The task was somehow to do this while

---

98. A similar point can be made about the treatment of domestic production as simply the domestic sphere of capitalist production. This characterization suggests that households follow an internal logic of organization of production that is strictly derivable from the logic of capitalism. While there are certainly effects of capitalist production on domestic production—particularly the progressive erosion of the scope of the latter—nevertheless domestic production does not seem reducible to simply a function of capitalism as such.

99. For a specific critique of Marxian versions of functionalism, see Jon Elster, *Making Sense of Marx* (Cambridge: Cambridge University Press, 1986), and "Marxism, Functionalism and Game Theory," in J. Roemer, (ed.), *Analytical Marxism* (Cambridge: Cambridge University Press, 1986).

remaining consistent with the abstract understanding of class relations in terms of interests, lived experience and collective capacity. The most effective way of doing this, I argued, was to try to generate more concrete, micro concepts of class structure on the basis of material interests and exploitation.

Let me try to summarize the various lessons that can be drawn from this attempt:

1. *Contradictory locations*   The "middle class" in capitalist society should primarily be understood in terms of the concept of contradictory locations within class relations. Above all, then, the middle class *within capitalism* is constituted by those locations which are simultaneously in the capitalist class and the working class.

2. *Secondary exploitations*   Skill exploitation and organization exploitation (or, equivalently, skill-generated scarcity rents and organization-generated loyalty rents) are probably best viewed as the basis for *strata* within classes rather than for class divisions as such. Such strata, however, can constitute the material basis for the emergence of distinct class trajectories as individuals turn the surplus appropriated through credential and loyalty rents into capitalist investment.

3. *Mediated locations and temporal trajectories*   In elaborating a micro-level concept of class structure—that is, a concept capable of understanding the ways in which individual lives are organized through class relations—class locations should not be understood simply in terms of the *direct* class relations within which *jobs* are immediately embedded. Class locations are also structured to a variable extent by mediated relations and temporal trajectories.

4. *Professionals and experts*   Temporal trajectories are particularly salient for understanding the class location of professionals, experts and other categories of credentialed labor power since the careers of such occupations frequently involve (1) movement into management, (2) the increasing capacity to capitalize employment rents, and (3) viable options of full-time or secondary self-employment. Such temporal trajectories, therefore, generally place professionals and experts into contradictory class locations (the "middle class") even if at a particular point in time they have not capitalized any of their income and are neither part of the managerial hierarchy itself nor self-employed. However, given the relatively underdetermined character of such trajectories for any given individual, professionals and experts may have, to a greater or lesser degree, what can be called objectively ambiguous class locations. In terms of the lived experience dimension of class

relations, professionals and experts generally experience work in a much less alienated way than workers, and this contributes to the general perception that they are "middle class."

5. *State employees*   Mediated relations are particularly salient for understanding the class location of state employees. While their direct class location can be seen as constituted within postcapitalist statist relations of production, to the extent that the conditions of production within the state are dominated by capitalist relations, their class location may be more fundamentally determined by their mediated locations than by their direct locations.

At the core of Marxist theory is an elegant and simple abstract picture of classes in capitalist societies: a fundamentally polarized class structure which constitutes the basis for the formation of two collectively organized classes engaged in struggle over the future of the class structure itself. We have now journeyed far from that simple core. Instead of only two, polarized classes, we have contradictory locations within class relations, mediated class locations, temporally structured class locations, objectively ambiguous class locations, dualistic class locations. Instead of a simple historical vision of the epochal confrontation of two class actors, there is a picture of multiple possible coalitions of greater or lesser likelihood, stability, and power contending over a variety of possible futures. The question, then, is whether this repertoire of new complexities actually enriches the theory or simply adds confusion.

This potential confusion can be reduced if these new complexities are seen as appropriate to different levels of abstraction in the analysis of classes. The appropriate level of abstraction depends upon the nature of the questions being asked. Thus, if one wishes to analyze the implications of epochal differences in class structures, the broad comparisons between feudal class structures and capitalist class structures might be appropriate. A simple two-class model of classes in capitalism—capitalists and workers—might provide the most powerful class map for such an investigation. If, however, one wished to embark on a more fine-grained analysis of the development of class structures within capitalist societies or the variations in such structures across capitalist societies, then invoking some of the complexities we have discussed would become necessary. And if one wanted to attempt a nuanced examination of the effects of location in a class structure on individual consciousness and action, then it would probably be desirable to introduce the full range of complexities that structure the class interests of individuals in time and place.

Index

abstraction, levels of 273–4, 295–6
"Address on the Anniversary of *The People's Paper*" (Marx) 141
adjudication, rival theories of class 55–6, 85–7, 103, 256
advertising, and production 172
alienation 208–9, 289–90
alternatives, hypothetically feasible 148–50
Althusser, Louis 79, 81, 129–31, 142, 145
American Journal of Sociology 75
Amin, Samir 89
analytical Marxism 53–4, 85–6, 99
assets 10–11, 250–1
  and class membership 17–22, 219
  exploitation 12, 14, 110–11
  jobs as 230–41
  organization 15ff., 146, 161, 162–3, 177, 178–80, 192, 199–201, 228–9, 250, 261–2, 306, 311–12, 339
  skill 14, 146, 149, 161, 163–4, 176–7, 178, 180, 192, 306, 308–10, 312
attitudes, class 32–3, 115
autonomy of worker 5, 28, 189, 304, 305

Balibar, Etienne 79
Beck, Bernard 171
Becker, Uwe 127–53, 313 n58
Belgium 235 n34
Berkeley, University of California at 47, 78, 79
Berkeley Journal of Sociology 78, 79

Bhaskar, Roy 58, 63, 81, 82, 101–2, 278 n12, 280
Blackburn, R.M. 259, 262, 329 n78
Bolsheviks 20 n39
Bourdieu, Pierre 170–1, 209–10, 292
bourgeoisie, 245
  contradictory class locations 24, 303
  and feudalism 203, 307
  rise of 138
  strata of 333
  temporal class locations 330 n81
Brenner, Johanna 184–90, 202, 206–8, 299 n41, 330 n81
Burawoy, Michael 47, 57, 75, 78–99, 100–4, 210–11, 300
bureaucracy, organization assets of 16–17
Burris, Val 157–67, 197, 201, 202, 317 n60

Camic, Charles 320
Capital (Marx) 141, 244
capital accumulation 202–3
capitalism
  class alliances 30–1
  conflict between capital and labor 128, 142–4
  contradictory class locations within 27
  exploitation 11, 14, 15, 18–20, 248, 250, 306
  in Marx's class theory 6, 139–40
  middle-class support for 202–3
  and skill assets 180

structural dynamics 137–8, 141–4
  without coercion 289 n27
*Capitalism, Class Conflict and the
  New Middle Class* (Carter)
  186–7
"Capitalism's Futures" (Wright)
  187–8
Carchedi, Guglielmo 105–25,
  159–60, 166, 177, 188
Cardoso, F.H. 89
careers
  structures 202
  temporal indeterminacy in class
    locations 330
Carter, Bob 186–7
centrality of class for Wright
  133–41
children, mediated class locations
  325, 342
class
  adjudication of theories 55–6, 85
  alliances 29–31, 37–40, 85
  analysis 117, 118, 121, 124,
    271–8, 314–23
  attitudes 32–3, 115
  conflict 181, 271
  contradictory locations 4–5, 7,
    24–8, 146–7, 158–61,
    173–83, 244–7, 252, 301–5,
    347
  definitions of 214–19, 222–3 n14
  domination versus exploitation
    4–6
  and exploitation 8–21, 41–3
  fractions 23
  habitus, 209–10, 292
  and identity 75, 205–11
  interests 202–5
  Marxist definitions of 13
  mobility effects 74–5
  objective interests 144–6, 150–2
  organization assets 23
  in postcapitalist societies 6–7
  real mechanisms 57–63, 81
  reductionism 129–31, 133, 145
  skills and 22–3
  theory 127–53
  Weberian definitions 13, 313ff.
  Wright's categories 113–14
  see also locations; middle classes;
    working class
Class, Crisis and the State (Wright)
  255

class consciousness 37–41, 271
  and class structure 114–16,
    118–24, 259
  competing models of
    consciousness-formation 62
  definition of 144, 259–60
  predictors 170–2
  surveys 64–7, 74–5, 181–3,
    257–8
  work relations and 184–90
class formation 144, 271
  and class location 181–2
  and class structure 28–9, 254–5
  definitions 246, 260–1
class structure 117–18
  attempts to build adequate map
    of 301–13
  in class analysis 271–8
  and class consciousness 114–15,
    118–24, 259
  and class formation 28–9, 254–5
  conceptual constraints 49–54,
    106
  definitions 246, 260–1, 278 and n
  essential characteristics of classes
    278–300
  exploitation and 191–201
  and class formation 28–9, 59–62
  logical structure 216–19
  mediated class locations 325–9,
    342, 343, 347
  micro/macro levels of analysis
    274–8, 283–4, 296
  multiple locations 324–5
  strata, intra-class 333, 347
  temporal locations 329–31, 347
  in Weberian analysis 315–16
  welfare-state capitalism 234–6
*Class Structure and Income
  Determination* (Wright) 84
classification, levels of abstraction
  273–4, 295–6
"clender" (class-gender) concept
  291
Cohen, G.A. 249, 334 n86
collective action, capacities for 280,
  293–5, 296
Colletti, Lucio 108
Collins, R. 160, 163
commitment 100–1
communism, and exploitation 21–2
The Communist Manifesto (Marx)
  141, 244, 245

Comparative Project of Class
    Structure and Class
    Consciousness 319 n65
Comte, Auguste 47
concept formation 272
conceptual constraints 49–54, 106
consciousness *see* class consciousness
consent, and production 95
contradictory class locations 4–5, 7,
    24–8, 146–7, 158–61, 173–83,
    244–7, 252, 301–5, 347
cottage industries 18
credential rents 332–3, 335–6
credentials 110–11, 164, 168, 176,
    192, 194, 201, 258, 261–2, 303,
    306, 309–10, 312–13
Critique of the Gotha Program
    (Marx) 12 n23

Dahrendorf, Ralph 7, 167
Democratic Party (USA) 40–1
democratic socialism 204–5
democratization, organization assets
    20, 21
"deskilling" 72
determination, structural 119–20
development, underdevelopment in
    Third World 89
dialectics 117–18, 119, 121
discourse, and "post-Marxism"
    133–4
discretionary income 203
discrimination, and exploitation 15
    n29, 225–6
Distinction (Bourdieu) 209, 292
distribution, and exploitation
    109–10, 113
dogmatic Marxism 53–4, 85–6, 101
domination, and exploitation 4–6, 7,
    13, 21, 149, 162, 247, 248, 304

economic development, education
    and 89–90
economic oppression 8
economic power 280, 282–4
economic welfare 280–2, 284–7
economics, neoclassical 283 n16
economism 129–31, 133, 145, 247
education 89–90, 168–71
Edwards, Richard 180
efficiency wage theory 231–3, 236
Elster, Jon 222–3 n14
emancipation 101–3

"embarrassment" of middle classes 3
empirical Marxism 54
empiricism 320–2
employment rents 332, 333 n84
Engels, Friedrich 79, 88, 127, 145
entrepreneurs 16, 228
epistemology 106–7
epochal change 138, 141
experience, lived 206–7, 280,
    288–91, 296, 298–300, 337
experts 258, 303, 306, 331–8, 347–8
    see also nonskilled; skilled
        employees
exploitation 4–6, 7, 107–13
    capitalist 11, 14, 15, 18–20, 248,
        250, 306
    and class 8–21, 41–3
    and class structure 191–201
    contradictory class locations and
        174–83, 247, 304
    definition of 217
    and distribution 109–10, 113
    education and 168–9
    feudal 11, 14–15, 16, 17–18,
        224, 227–8, 249–50, 306
    game theory 10–12, 15, 107–9,
        111–12, 113, 165–6, 216–17,
        247–9
    job assets 233–4
    in Marx's class theory 140
    and material interests 206, 284–6
    multiple 305–13
    noncapitalist forms 191
    organization assets and 110, 177,
        178–80, 192, 199–201,
        228–9, 339
    and production 14
    secondary 347
    skill-based 12, 14, 20–1, 110–11,
        180, 192, 193–9, 308–10
    socialist 11–12, 15, 248, 250, 306
    status 15–16, 224–6, 227, 248,
        250, 306
    in Weberian class analysis 316
    in Wright's model of class
        structure 146–50, 161–4
    see also discrimination;
        domination

Fabian socialism 169
families, mediated class locations
    327–8
fascism 138, 144

feminism 80–1, 290–1
    see also women
feudalism
    class alliances 30
    class struggle 138
    contradictory locations within 26
    exploitation 11, 14–15, 16,
        17–18, 224, 227–8, 248,
        249–50, 306
    merchant capitalists and 203
    organization of production 187
Feyerabend, Paul 48
Foucault, Michel 48
France 85, 96, 170, 294
Frank, André Gunder 89
Frankfurt School 129
"free professions" 334
French Communist Party (PCF) 98

game theory, analysis of exploitation
    10, 12, 15, 107–9, 111–12, 113,
    165, 216–17, 247–9
gender 63 n12
    gender-blind concepts of class
        290–1
    mediated class locations 326 n72,
        327–9
*General Theory of Exploitation and
    Class* (Roemer) 7, 216–17
Germany 138
Giddens, Anthony 160, 285 n20,
    292
Goldthorpe, John 261, 262, 263,
    293 n33, 315, 317, 318, 319 n65,
    327, 335 n88
Gouldner, Alvin 13 n24, 27 n47, 52,
    130, 294–5
Gramsci, Antonio 79, 86 n7, 129
Green parties 241
Grundrisse (Marx) 110

hegemony
    capitalism as 203, 205
    and class interests 310–11
Hegemony and Socialist Strategy
    (Laclau and Mouffe) 133–4
hierarchy, organization assets and 17
Hindess, Barry 131–2, 134, 143,
    144
Hirst, Paul 131–2, 134, 142, 143,
    144
historical materialism 102–3, 306,
    315

history, theory of 254
Hollingshead, August 169
home ownership 325 n71
housewives 290, 325–6, 342, 343
Hungarian Academy of Sciences
    95–6
Hungary 95–6, 98, 324

idealism 87, 102
identity, class and 75, 205–11
ideology 69–70, 122–3
imperialism 53, 88–9
"Inaugural Address to the IAA"
    (Marx) 141
income 32, 33, 34–6, 170, 192–5,
    199, 203, 218–19, 220–1,
    239–41
India 89–90
inequality
    and definition of class 219
    and exploitation 8, 12
insiders–outsiders approach, and
    unemployment 230–1, 236
Institute for African Studies 92
instrumental versus intrinsic interests
    281
intelligentsia, as contradictory
    location 27
interests
    intrinsic 281
    material 205–7 and n, 280–1,
        284–8, 329
    objective 5 n7, 144–6, 150–2,
        286
internal labor market 224–5
International Project on Class
    Structure and Class
    Consciousness 243
interviews 121–4
intrinsic versus instrumental interests
    281
Italy 138

János, Milos 95–6
Japan 299 n41
jobs, as assets 230–41

Kapitalistate 78
Katznelson, Ira 300
Kaunda, President of Zambia 96–7
Kautsky, Karl 112
Kieve, R.A. 166

knowledge
knowledge workers 189–90
positivist versus practical 87–90,
93
social and theoretical contexts
94–7, 98–9
Kolakowski, Leszek 87
Konrad, George 27 n46, 294–5
Kuhn, Thomas 47–8

Labor and Capital (Marx) 141
labor theory of value 112–13, 196,
249, 251, 284 n18
labor transfers 9–10
Laclau, Ernesto 131, 132–4, 142,
144, 145–6
Lakatos, Imre 47–8
Larson, M.S. 180
leisure 241
Lenin, V.I. 20 n39, 70, 79, 80, 86
n7, 88, 89
life chances 285, 316
lived experience 206–7, 280,
288–91, 296, 298–300, 337
locations
contradictory 4–5, 7, 24–8,
146–7, 158–61, 173–83,
244–7, 252, 301–5, 347
mediated 325–9, 342, 343, 347
multiple 324–5
temporal 329–31, 347
Lockwood, David 261, 293 n33
"loyalty rents" 340
Lukács, Georg 79, 145
Luxemburg, Rosa 79, 86 n7

macro levels, class structure 274–8,
283–4
*The Making of the English Working
Class* (Thompson) 293
managers 4, 5, 185–8
and anticapitalist movements
179–80
bimodal distribution of functions
95–6
class identity 208
class interests 202–5
class position 157–8
contradictory locations 27,
159–61, 245, 301
multiple exploitation 306, 310–11
organization assets 16–17,
199–201, 311–12

rationale for shift in treatment of
331, 338–40
temporal class locations 329–30
in Weberian class analysis 317
Mann, Michael 285 n20
Marshall, Gordon 243–65, 319 n65
Martin, Bill 178
Marx, Karl 47, 68, 79, 86 n7, 145
"Address on the Anniversary of
The People's Paper" 141
on alienation 289–90
analysis of inequality in socialism
12 n23
Capital 141, 244
on capitalist dynamics 141–2
class theory 127, 139–41
Communist Manifesto 141, 244,
245
Critique of the Gotha Program
12 n23
on French peasantry 294
Grundrisse 110
"Inaugural Address to the IAA"
141
Labor and Capital 141
The Poverty of Philosophy 141
on role of proletariat 185
survey research 70
Theories of Surplus Value 244
Theses on Feuerbach 88
*Marxist Inquiries: Studies of Labor,
Class and States* 75
Marxist structuralism 79
material interests 205–7 and n,
280–1, 284–8, 329
materialism, historical 102–3, 306,
315
mechanisms
nonclass 118, 121
real 57–63, 81, 83, 94
mediated class locations 325–9, 342,
343, 347
Meiksins, Peter F. 173–83, 197, 201,
202, 204, 205
methodology, conceptual constraints
49–54, 106
Michigan Survey 79
micro concepts, class structure
274–8, 283–4, 296
middle classes 270
and anticapitalist movements 202,
204
boundary with working class 256

capital accumulation 202–3
and capitalist dynamics 142
career structures 202
class interests 202–5
contradictory locations 24–8,
    146–7, 173, 303, 347
definitions 117, 207–9
"embarrassment" of 3
and exploitation 191–2
managers 338–40
multiple exploitation 307, 310
professionals and experts 331–8,
    347–8
state employees 340–6, 348
Weberian analysis 315
mining, Zambianization 90–2
mobility, temporal class locations
    329–30
monopoly rents 195
Mouffe, Chantal 133–4, 144, 145–6
multidimensionality, social relations
    302
multiple exploitations 305–13
multiple class locations 324–5
multiple oppressions 5–6

nationalization 20
neoclassical economics 283 n16
"New Class" 4, 13 n24, 294–5, 301
New Left 78
Newby, Howard 319 n65
nonclass mechanisms 118, 121
nonskilled 258
    see also experts; skilled
        employees
North, Colonel 171

objective class interests 5 n, 144–6,
    150–2, 286
OPCS 262–3
operationalizations
    contradictory class locations 305
    multiple exploitation 312–13
oppression, economic 8
organization assets 16–17, 20, 21,
    23, 110, 146, 161, 162–3, 177,
    178–80, 192, 199–201, 228–9,
    250, 261–2, 306, 311–12, 339
ownership
    capital assets 110
    investment 324–5
    of means of production 113

Panitch, Leo 118
Parkin, Frank 12 n22, 160, 163,
    167, 254, 318
peasantry, French 294
pensioners, mediated class locations
    326, 342
Perrone, Luca 73
Political Power and Social Class
    (Poulantzas) 129
politics 67–8, 90–4, 132
positivism 63–4
positivist knowledge 87–90, 93
The Possibility of Naturalism
    (Bhaskar) 82
post-capitalist society 6–7, 178
Poulantzas, Nicos 79, 83–4, 85, 98,
    192–31, 159, 188, 255, 287 n24,
    341 n93
poverty 8, 115–16
The Poverty of Philosophy (Marx)
    141
power 220–1
    economic 280, 282–4
practical knowledge 87–90, 93
Prandy, K. 259, 262, 329 n78
production
    and consent 95
    and domination 13
    and exploitation 14
    organization 16
    and ownership 113
productivity
    and income differentials 193–4
    organization assets 228–9
Professional Managerial Class 4
professionals 331–8, 347–8
    class identity 208
    class interests 202–5
    class position 157–8
    contradictory locations 159–61,
        303
    in Weberian class analysis 317
proletariat 254
    class consciousness 182
    in Marx's class theory 185
    proletarianization 190
property
    and definitions of class 13–14
    ownership 113
Przeworski, Adam 29, 131, 132–3;
    134, 142, 174–5, 202, 297,
    322
puzzle solving 85–7

quantitative research 71, 73–7
questionnaires 121–4

racial discrimination 15 n29, 225–6
rational choice Marxism 54 n4
Rattansi, A. 244, 245
real estate speculation 325 n71
real mechanisms 57–63, 81, 83, 94
realism
    realist ontology 103–4
    and science 82–4, 103
rentier capitalists 16
rents
    credential 332–3, 335–6
    employment 332, 333 n84
    'loyalty' 340
    monopoly 195
research
    interviews 121–4
    quantitative 71, 73–7
    survey data 68–73
revolution, science and 79–82, 88
revolutionary praxis 69–70, 97
Roan Selection Trust 90
Roemer, John 7–16, 17, 42, 107,
    110, 113, 146, 147–50, 161,
    165–6, 168–9, 173, 174, 197–8,
    216–17, 222–4, 247–51, 277
    n10, 284 n19, 289 n27
Rogers, Joel 282 n14
Rohatyn, Felix 179
Rose, David 243–65, 319 n65
Russian revolution 15, 20 n39, 138

Sartre, J.-P. 129
science
    and realism 82–4, 103
    and revolution 79–82, 88
scientific Marxism 47, 52–3, 81
secondary exploitations 347
self-employment 324, 334
semiautonomous employees 28, 74,
    303, 305, 307, 312, 331–2,
    337–8
service class 317–18, 342
sexual discrimination 15 n29, 225–6
Shapiro, Carl 232–3
share ownership 324–5
Shaw, George Bernard 169
skepticism 80, 100–1
skilled employees 258
    see also experts; nonskilled
skills

assets 22–3, 110–11, 146, 149,
    161, 163–4, 176–7, 178, 180,
    192, 193–9, 306, 308–10,
    312, 317
"deskilling" 72
exploitation 12, 14, 20–1
Skocpol, Theda 75
slavery 14 and n, 228
Smith, Adam 16
Social Democratic Party (Sweden)
    40
social relations, definition 302
socialism
    democratic 204–5
    socialist exploitation 11–12, 15,
        248, 250, 306
    see also state bureaucratic
        socialism
Socialist Review 98
Socialist Revolution 78
socioeconomic groups, OPCS
    definition 262–3
Sociological Association (University
    of Zambia) 96
South Africa 96, 299 n41
Soviet Union 16, 89, 211
Sraffian economists 9 n16
Stalinism 80, 138
state
    bureaucracy 248
    and contradictory class locations
        304–5
    employees 331, 340–6, 348
    multiple exploitation 307
    organizational assets and 311–12
state bureaucratic socialism
    class alliances 30–1
    contradictory locations 27
    organization assets 16–17, 20
state mode of production 342–6
statism 187–8, 250, 310–11
statistical analysis 68–73
status exploitation 15–16, 224–6,
    227, 248, 250, 306
Stewart, A. 259, 262, 329 n78
Stiglitz, Joseph E. 232–3
Stinchcombe, Arthur 168–72, 192
strata, within classes 333, 347
strategies, material interests 286–8
structural determination 119–20
structuralism 79, 117
students, mediated class locations
    326, 342

subjective class interests 75, 134
surplus product 282–3, 284 n18
  appropriation of 109
  skill exploitation 308–9
  surplus-transfer 198–9
surveys, 96–7
  class consciousness 37–41, 64–7
  data 68–73
Sweden 33, 34–41, 169, 170, 181–3,
  255, 259
Szelenyi, Ivan 27 n46, 294–5

tastes 292
technical employees, in Weberian
  class analysis 317
technocrats 170
temporal class locations 329–31, 347
tendency, as dialectical concept 119
texts, interpretation of 100
Thatcher government 334 n85
theology, Marxism as 100
theoretical practice 97–8
Theories of Surplus Value (Marx)
  244
theoristicist Marxism 54
theory construction 272
Theses on Feuerbach (Marx) 88
Third World, underdevelopment 53,
  88–9
Thompson, E.P. 129, 131, 293
trade-offs, material interests 286–8
trade unions 171, 185, 190
Trotsky, Leon 79, 80, 86 n7
truth 94, 99, 101–3, 104

underdevelopment, Third World 53,
  88–9
unemployment 8, 111–12, 213–14,
  230–41, 325–6
United States of America, 33,
  34–41, 82, 89, 169, 181–3, 255,
  256, 259, 299 n41, 324–5, 334
universal grant 239–41

value, labor theory of 112–13, 196,
  249, 251, 284 n18
Van Parijs, Philippe 213–41
Vogler, Carolyn 319 n65

wages, efficiency wage theory 231–3,
  236
Wallerstein, Immanuel 89
Warner, W. Lloyd 169
Wayne, John 171
wealth, and exploitation 8
Weber, Max 114, 257, 261–2
Weberian class analysis 13, 165,
  166–7, 173, 246, 249, 252–4,
  285, 314–23
welfare, economic 280–2, 284–7
welfare-state capitalism 232–3,
  234–6, 240
women
  in class structure 255, 287 n25
  feminism 80–1
  gender-blind concepts of class
    290–1
  housewives 290, 325–6, 342, 343
  lived experience of 290–1
  mediated class locations 325–6,
    327–9
  sexual discrimination 15 n29,
    225–6
  'shadow class' 330–1
  temporal class locations 330–1
work relations, and class
  consciousness 184–90
working class
  anticapitalism of 205
  boundary with middle classes 256
  capacity for collective action
    294–5
  class alliances 31
  class consciousness 181–3
  class location 295
  class structure and formation
    28–9
  lived experiences 289–90, 299
    n42, 337
  in Marx's class theory 6, 139–41
  position of women in 255
  strata 333
  temporal class locations 329–30

Zambia 96–7, 98
Zambia, University of 96–7
Zambian Copper Mines 90–2